Communications
in Computer and Information Science   2258

Series Editors

Gang Li , *School of Information Technology, Deakin University, Burwood, VIC, Australia*
Joaquim Filipe, *Polytechnic Institute of Setúbal, Setúbal, Portugal*
Zhiwei Xu, *Chinese Academy of Sciences, Beijing, China*

AF173158

Rationale

The CCIS series is devoted to the publication of proceedings of computer science conferences. Its aim is to efficiently disseminate original research results in informatics in printed and electronic form. While the focus is on publication of peer-reviewed full papers presenting mature work, inclusion of reviewed short papers reporting on work in progress is welcome, too. Besides globally relevant meetings with internationally representative program committees guaranteeing a strict peer-reviewing and paper selection process, conferences run by societies or of high regional or national relevance are also considered for publication.

Topics

The topical scope of CCIS spans the entire spectrum of informatics ranging from foundational topics in the theory of computing to information and communications science and technology and a broad variety of interdisciplinary application fields.

Information for Volume Editors and Authors

Publication in CCIS is free of charge. No royalties are paid, however, we offer registered conference participants temporary free access to the online version of the conference proceedings on SpringerLink (http://link.springer.com) by means of an http referrer from the conference website and/or a number of complimentary printed copies, as specified in the official acceptance email of the event.

CCIS proceedings can be published in time for distribution at conferences or as postproceedings, and delivered in the form of printed books and/or electronically as USBs and/or e-content licenses for accessing proceedings at SpringerLink. Furthermore, CCIS proceedings are included in the CCIS electronic book series hosted in the SpringerLink digital library at http://link.springer.com/bookseries/7899. Conferences publishing in CCIS are allowed to use Online Conference Service (OCS) for managing the whole proceedings lifecycle (from submission and reviewing to preparing for publication) free of charge.

Publication process

The language of publication is exclusively English. Authors publishing in CCIS have to sign the Springer CCIS copyright transfer form, however, they are free to use their material published in CCIS for substantially changed, more elaborate subsequent publications elsewhere. For the preparation of the camera-ready papers/files, authors have to strictly adhere to the Springer CCIS Authors' Instructions and are strongly encouraged to use the CCIS LaTeX style files or templates.

Abstracting/Indexing

CCIS is abstracted/indexed in DBLP, Google Scholar, EI-Compendex, Mathematical Reviews, SCImago, Scopus. CCIS volumes are also submitted for the inclusion in ISI Proceedings.

How to start

To start the evaluation of your proposal for inclusion in the CCIS series, please send an e-mail to ccis@springer.com.

Douglas D. Hodson · Michael R. Grimaila ·
Hamid R. Arabnia · Leonidas Deligiannidis ·
Torrey J. Wagner

Editors

Scientific Computing and Bioinformatics and Computational Biology

22nd International Conference, CSC 2024, and 25th International
Conference, BIOCOMP 2024, Held as Part of the World Congress in
Computer Science, Computer Engineering and Applied Computing,
CSCE 2024, Las Vegas, NV, USA, July 22–25, 2024, Revised Selected Papers

 Springer

Editors
Douglas D. Hodson
US Air Force Institute of Technology
Dayton, OH, USA

Michael R. Grimaila [iD]
US Air Force Institute of Technology
Dayton, OH, USA

Hamid R. Arabnia [iD]
University of Georgia
Athens, GA, USA

Leonidas Deligiannidis [iD]
Wentworth Institute of Technology
Boston, MA, USA

Torrey J. Wagner
US Air Force Institute of Technology
Wright Patterson AFB, OH, USA

ISSN 1865-0929   ISSN 1865-0937 (electronic)
Communications in Computer and Information Science
ISBN 978-3-031-85901-4   ISBN 978-3-031-85902-1 (eBook)
https://doi.org/10.1007/978-3-031-85902-1

This Springer imprint is published by the registered company Springer Nature Switzerland AG
The registered company address is: Gewerbestrasse 11, 6330 Cham, Switzerland

If disposing of this product, please recycle the paper.

Preface

It is our great pleasure to introduce this collection of selected papers presented at the 22nd International Conference on Scientific Computing (CSC 2024) and the 25th International Conference on Bioinformatics & Computational Biology (BIOCOMP 2024). Both conferences were held as part of the federated 2024 Congress on Computer Science, Computer Engineering, and Applied Computing (CSCE 2024), which took place from July 22 to July 25, 2024, in Las Vegas, Nevada, USA.

The CSCE 2024 Congress brought together papers from a diverse array of communities, including researchers from universities, corporations, and government agencies. Accepted papers are published by Springer Nature, and the proceedings showcase solutions to key challenges in various critical areas of Computer Science, Computer Engineering, and Applied Computing.

Computer Science (CS) is the study of computational systems, data processing, information management, and automation. Many applications in CS focus on solving problems that would be impossible or extremely difficult to address without the use of computers. It serves as a bridge between computational science and other scientific fields. The interdisciplinary nature of CS involves leveraging computers to understand and solve complex challenges, making it the science of using computers to advance scientific discovery. Computer Engineering (CE), on the other hand, integrates aspects of computer science, electronic engineering, and electrical engineering. It encompasses the design and production of computer hardware, such as chips, servers, supercomputers, embedded systems, and communication systems, among others.

Considering the above broad outline, the CSCE 2024 Congress was composed of the following focused conferences:

Applied Cognitive Computing (ACC); Bioinformatics & Computational Biology (BIOCOMP); Biomedical Engineering (BIOENG); Scientific Computing (CSC); e-Learning, e-Business, Enterprise Information Systems, & e-Government (EEE); Embedded Systems, Cyber-physical Systems, & Applications (ESCS); Foundations of Computer Science (FCS); Frontiers in Education (FECS); Grid, Cloud, & Cluster Computing (GCC); Health Informatics (HIMS); Artificial Intelligence (ICAI); Data Science (ICDATA); Emergent Quantum Technologies (ICEQT); Internet Computing & IoT (ICOMP); Wireless Networks (ICWN); Information & Knowledge Engineering (IKE); Image Processing, Computer Vision, & Pattern Recognition (IPCV); Modeling, Simulation & Visualization Methods (MSV); Parallel & Distributed Processing Techniques & Applications (PDPTA); Security & Management (SAM); and Software Engineering Research & Practice (SERP). The scope of each track can be found at: https://www.ame rican-cse.org/csce2024/conferences.

The primary objective of the CSCE Congress and its associated conferences is to foster opportunities for cross-fertilization between the fields of Computer Science (CS) and Computer Engineering (CE). The CSCE Congress is deeply committed to promoting diversity and eliminating discrimination, both in its role as a conference organizer and as a service provider. Our goal is to create an inclusive culture that respects and values differences, promotes dignity, equality, and diversity, and encourages individuals to reach their full potential. We are also dedicated, wherever possible, to organizing a conference that represents the global community. We sincerely hope that we have succeeded in achieving these important objectives.

The Steering Committee and the Program Committees would like to extend their gratitude to all the authors who submitted papers for consideration. This year's conferences received submissions from 46 countries, with approximately 42% of them coming from outside the USA. Each submitted paper underwent a rigorous peer-review process, with at least two experts (an average of 2.4 referees per paper) evaluating the submissions based on originality, significance, clarity, impact, and soundness. In cases where reviewers' recommendations were contradictory, a program committee member was tasked with making the final decision, often consulting additional referees for further guidance. The Congress followed the guidelines of COPE (Committee on Publication Ethics):

- Typical submissions underwent a single-blind peer review process, in which the authors remained unaware of the identities of the reviewers, while the reviewers were informed of the authors' identities.
- Papers authored by one or more members of the program committee, including co-chairs, were subjected to a double-blind peer review process, ensuring that neither the authors nor the reviewers were aware of each other's identities or affiliations.

The CSC 2024 Conference received 128 submissions, of which 25 papers were accepted, resulting in a paper acceptance rate of 19.5%. The BIOCOMP 2024 Conference received 27 submissions, of which 6 papers were accepted, resulting in a paper acceptance rate of 22.2%. This volume includes the 31 accepted papers from CSC 2024 and BIOCOMP 2024.

We are deeply grateful to the many colleagues who contributed their time and effort to organizing the Congress. In particular, we extend our thanks to the members of the Program Committees, the Steering Committee, the referees, and the Chairs and organizers of individual sessions and conferences. We would also like to express our appreciation to the primary sponsor of the conference, the American Council on Science & Education. The list of members of the Program Committee for each track can be found at: https://www.american-cse.org/csce2024/committees.

We extend our heartfelt gratitude to all the speakers and authors for their valuable contributions. We would also like to thank the following individuals and organizations for their support: the staff at the Luxor Hotel, the staff of Springer Nature, Soheyla Amirian (Pace University), Farzan Shenavarmasouleh (Medialab Inc., USA), and Farid Ghareh Mohammadi (Mayo Clinic, USA) for their assistance in various aspects of the event.

We are pleased to present a curated selection of papers from CSC 2024 and BIO-COMP 2024 conferences. These proceedings represent a collection of outstanding research contributions that reflect the diversity and depth of work in core areas of computer science and computer engineering.

Douglas D. Hodson
Michael R. Grimaila
Hamid R. Arabnia
Leonidas Deligiannidis
Torrey J. Wagner

Organization

Steering Committee – Co-chairs (CSCE 2024)

Hamid R. Arabnia	University of Georgia, USA
Leonidas Deligiannidis	Wentworth Institute of Technology, USA
Fernando G. Tinetti	Universidad Nacional de La Plata, Argentina
Quoc-Nam Tran	Southeastern Louisiana University, USA

Co-editors of CSC 2024 and BIOCOMP 2024 Proceedings – Publication Co-chairs

Douglas D. Hodson (Chair, CSC 2024 Sessions)	US Air Force Institute of Technology, USA
Michael R. Grimaila (Co-chair, CSC 2024 Sessions)	US Air Force Institute of Technology, USA
Hamid R. Arabnia (Co-chair, CSC 2024 & BIOCOMP 2024)	University of Georgia, USA
Leonidas Deligiannidis (Co-chair, CSC 2024 & BIOCOMP 2024)	Wentworth Institute of Technology, USA
Torrey J. Wagner (Co-chair, CSC 2024 Sessions)	US Air Force Institute of Technology, USA

Members of Steering Committee (CSCE 2024)

Babak Akhgar	Sheffield Hallam University, UK
Abbas M. Al-Bakry	University of IT & Communications, Iraq
Nizar Al-Holou	University of Detroit Mercy, USA
Hamid R. Arabnia	University of Georgia, USA
Rajab Challoo	Texas A&M University-Kingsville, USA
Chien-Fu Cheng	Tamkang University, Taiwan
Hyunseung Choo	Sungkyunkwan University, South Korea
Kevin Daimi	University of Detroit Mercy, USA
Leonidas Deligiannidis	Wentworth Institute of Technology, USA
Eman M. El-Sheikh	University of West Florida, USA
Mary Mehrnoosh Eshaghian-Wilner	University of California Los Angeles, USA

David L. Foster	Kettering University, USA
Henry Hexmoor	Southern Illinois University at Carbondale, USA
Ching-Hsien (Robert) Hsu	Chung Hua University, Taiwan; and Tianjin University of Technology, China
James J. (Jong Hyuk) Park	SeoulTech, South Korea
Mohammad S. Obaidat	University of Jordan, Jordan
Marwan Omar	Illinois Institute of Technology, USA
Shahram Rahimi	Mississippi State University, USA
Gerald Schaefer	Loughborough University, UK
Fernando G. Tinetti	Universidad Nacional de La Plata, Argentina
Quoc-Nam Tran	Southeastern Louisiana University, USA
Shiuh-Jeng Wang	Central Police University, Taiwan
Layne T. Watson	Virginia Polytechnic Institute & State University, USA
Chao-Tung Yang	Tunghai University, Taiwan
Mary Yang	University of Arkansas, USA

Research Tracks – Co-chairs (CSCE 2024)

Abeer Alsadoon (Co-chair, Health Informatics)	Charles Sturt University, Australia
Soheyla Amirian (Co-chair, Computer Vision & AI)	Pace University, USA
Hamid R. Arabnia (Co-chair, HPC)	University of Georgia, USA
Kevin Daimi (Co-chair, Security)	University of Detroit Mercy, USA
Leonidas Deligiannidis (Co-chair, Imaging Science, AI)	Wentworth Institute of Technology, USA
Richard Dill (Co-chair, Military and Defense Modeling)	US Air Force Institute of Technology, USA
Ken Ferens (Co-chair, Cognitive Computing & AI)	University of Manitoba, Canada
David de la Fuente (Co-chair, Information Management)	University of Oviedo, Spain
Farid Ghareh Mohammadi (Co-chair, Computer Vision & AI)	Mayo Clinic, USA
Michael R. Grimaila (Co-chair, Military and Defense Modeling)	US Air Force Institute of Technology, USA

Douglas D. Hodson (Co-chair, Military and Defense Modeling)	US Air Force Institute of Technology, USA
Masahito Ohue (Co-chair, Mathematical Modeling)	Tokyo Institute of Technology, Japan
Jose A. Olivas (Co-chair, Information Management)	University of CastillaLa Mancha, Spain
Javier Ordus (Co-chair, Quantum Computing & AI)	Baylor University, USA
Pablo Rivas (Chair, Quantum Computing & AI)	Baylor University, USA
Farzan Shenavarmasouleh (Co-chair, Computer Vision & AI)	MediaLab Inc, USA
Robert Stahlbock (Co-chair, Data Mining)	Universität Hamburg, Germany
Masami Takata (Co-chair, Mathematical Modeling)	Nara Women's University, Japan
Quoc-Nam Tran (Co-chair, Education & Bioinformatics)	Southeastern Louisiana University, USA
Nobuaki Yasuo (Co-chair, Mathematical Modeling)	Tokyo Institute of Technology, Japan

CSC 2024 Program Committee – Scientific Computing

Abbas M. Al-Bakry	University of IT and Communications, Iraq
Nizar Al-Holou	University of Detroit Mercy, USA
Hamid R. Arabnia	University of Georgia, USA
Azita Bahrami	IT Consult, USA
Juan-Vicente Capella-Hernandez	Universitat Politècnica de València, Spain
Kevin Daimi	University of Detroit Mercy, USA
Zhangisina Gulnur Davletzhanovna	Central Asian University, Kazakhstan; and International Academy of Informatization, Kazakhstan
Leonidas Deligiannidis	Wentworth Institute of Technology, USA
Richard Dill	US Air Force Institute of Technology, USA
Ryan D. Engle	US Air Force Institute of Technology, USA
George A. Gravvanis	Democritus University of Thrace, Greece
Michael R. Grimaila	US Air Force Institute of Technology, USA
Houcine Hassan	Universitat Politècnica de València, Spain
Douglas D. Hodson	US Air Force Institute of Technology, USA

George Jandieri	Georgian Technical University, Georgia; and Institute of Cybernetics, Georgian Academy of Science, Georgia
Abdeldjalil Khelassi	Abou Bekr Belkaid University of Tlemcen, Algeria
Byung-Gyu Kim	Sun Moon University, South Korea
Andrew Marsh	HoIP Telecom Ltd, UK
Ali Mostafaeipour	California State University, Fullerton, USA
Houssem Eddine Nouri	Institut Superieur de Gestion de Tunis, University of Tunis, Tunisia
Robert Ehimen Okonigene	Ambrose Alli University, Nigeria
James J. (Jong Hyuk) Park	SeoulTech, South Korea
Ashu M. G. Solo (Publicity)	Maverick Technologies America Inc., USA
Fernando G. Tinetti	Universidad Nacional de La Plata, Argentina
Hahanov Vladimir	Kharkiv National University of Radio Electronics, Ukraine
Shiuh-Jeng Wang	Central Police University, Taiwan
Layne T. Watson	Virginia Polytechnic Institute & State University, USA
Jane You	Hong Kong Polytechnic University, China
Masami Takata	Nara Women's University, Japan
Torrey J. Wagner	US Air Force Institute of Technology, USA
Yunlong Wang	IQVIA, USA
Heng (Fred) Wu	West Virginia State University, USA

BIOCOMP 2024 Program Committee – Bioinformatics and Computational Biology

Abbas M. Al-Bakry	University of IT and Communications, Iraq
Nizar Al-Holou	University of Detroit Mercy, USA
Hamid R. Arabnia	University of Georgia, USA
Hikmet Budak	Montana State University, USA
Kevin Daimi	University of Detroit Mercy, USA
Leonidas Deligiannidis	Wentworth Institute of Technology, USA
Youping Deng	University of Hawaii John A. Burns School of Medicine, USA
Mary Mehrnoosh Eshaghian-Wilner	University of Southern California, California, USAand University of California Los Angeles, USA
Ray Hashemi	Georgia Southern University, USA

George Jandieri   Georgian Technical University, Georgia; and
                                          Institute of Cybernetics, Georgian Academy of
                                          Science, Georgia
Abdeldjalil Khelassi   Abou Bekr Belkaid University of Tlemcen,
                                          Algeria
Byung-Gyu Kim   Sun Moon University, South Korea
Guoming Lai   Sun Yat-sen University, China
Ying Liu   St. John's University, USA
Prashanti Manda   University of North Carolina at Greensboro, USA
Muhammad Naufal Bin Mansor   Universiti Malaysia Perlis, Malaysia
Andrew Marsh   HoIP Telecom Ltd, UK
Robert Ehimen Okonigene   Ambrose Alli University, Nigeria
James J. (Jong Hyuk) Park   SeoulTech, South Korea
Ashu M. G. Solo (Publicity)   Maverick Technologies America Inc., USA
Tse Guan Tan   Universiti Malaysia Kelantan, Malaysia
Fernando G. Tinetti   Universidad Nacional de La Plata, Argentina
Quoc-Nam Tran   Southeastern Louisiana University, USA
Shiuh-Jeng Wang   Central Police University, Taiwan
Layne T. Watson   Virginia Polytechnic Institute & State University,
                                          USA
Mary Yang   University of Arkansas, USA
Jane You   Hong Kong Polytechnic University, China
Wen Zhang   Icahn School of Medicine at Mount Sinai, USA
Hao Zheng   Novo Vivo, USA

Contents

Section: Bioinformatics and Computational Biology (BIOCOMP)

Section: Military and Defense Modeling and Simulation

Performance Evaluation of Utilizing Rust for PCAP Analysis in Satellite Cybersecurity

Samual M. Asher and Douglas D. Hodson[✉]

Department of Electrical and Computer Engineering, U.S. Air Force Institute of
Technology, WPAFB, Dayton, OH 45433, USA
{samual.asher.1,douglas.hodson}@us.af.mil

Abstract. Previously, launched satellites were not designed with the
necessary resource capacity or safety protocols to integrate essential
Intrusion Detection Systems (IDS). This paper proposes the use of Rust
to develop a statistics-based IDS, leveraging the language's fast, efficient,
and memory-safe attributes. The paper begins by providing an overview
of cybersecurity threats to space infrastructure, introducing the fundamentals of intrusion detection, and outlining the architecture of space
systems as background knowledge. It then details the proposed methodology for using Rust to build a statistics-based IDS. By comparing this
approach with traditional methods, such as Python's pandas, the paper
aims to evaluate Rust's speed and efficiency, advocating for its adoption
in the development of more secure space systems.

Keywords: satellite cybersecurity · intrusion detection systems ·
rust · cyber-attack scenarios on satellites · rust for data analysis ·
python pandas

1 Introduction

Within moments of the invasion of Ukraine, the satellite communications
provider ViaSat experienced a massive outage, dealing a massive blow to
Ukrainian intelligence capabilities [1]. This incident underscores the need to
address these vulnerabilities in a robust, efficient, and safe manner. This paper
is organized as follows: Sect. 2 provides background information on space system
architecture. Section 3 discusses the utilization of PCAPs within Intrusion Detection Systems. Section 4 introduces the Rust programming language and underscores its potential advantages for cybersecurity applications. Section 5 describes
the experimental design and analyzes the results. Section 6 will look into future
steps. Finally, Sect. 7 offers concluding remarks and summarizes the paper's key
findings.

D. D. Hodson et al. (Eds.): CSCE 2024, CCIS 2258, pp. 3–8, 2025.
https://doi.org/10.1007/978-3-031-85902-1_1

2   Architecture

Space systems exhibit an architecture comprised of two primary components: a ground segment and a space segment [2]. The space segment consists of one or more satellites in orbit, whereas the ground segment includes the Command and Control Center (C2), ground stations for sending and receiving RF signals, and the terrestrial networks that facilitate this communication. Figure 1 illustrates the interconnectivity between the space segment, which includes the satellites, and the ground segment, encompassing the Command and Control Center, ground stations, and associated terrestrial networks. These signals carry telemetry data (health of the satellite and its subsystems) and network traffic used to issue commands to the spacecraft and its payload.

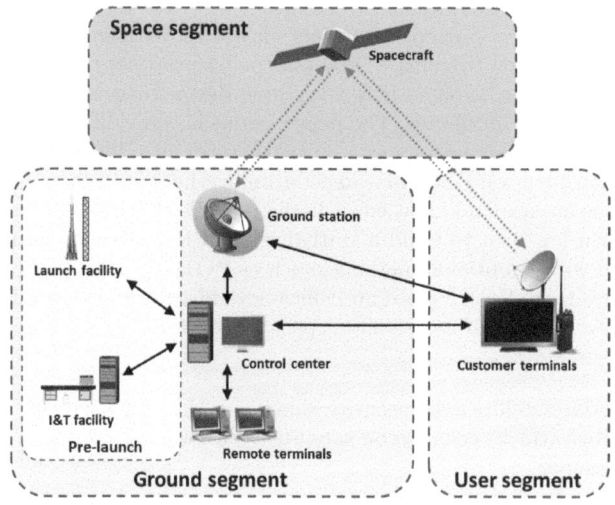

Fig. 1. Typical satellite architecture. Figure from [3]

3   Intrusion Detection Systems

Following the architecture review, it is crucial to address the security measures in place to protect these systems. One of the tools we have to combat attacks on space systems is an Intrusion Detection System (IDS). These tools are a type of Anomaly Detection System (ADS), that are engineered to detect and signal any irregular activities that may indicate a security breach. IDSs function by monitoring and analyzing data, such as network packet captures (PCAPs) in Network-based IDSs or host system logs in Host-based IDSs. Through a series of preprocessing and assessments, these systems evaluate whether observed behaviors are indicative of regular operation or suggest possible security incidents [4].

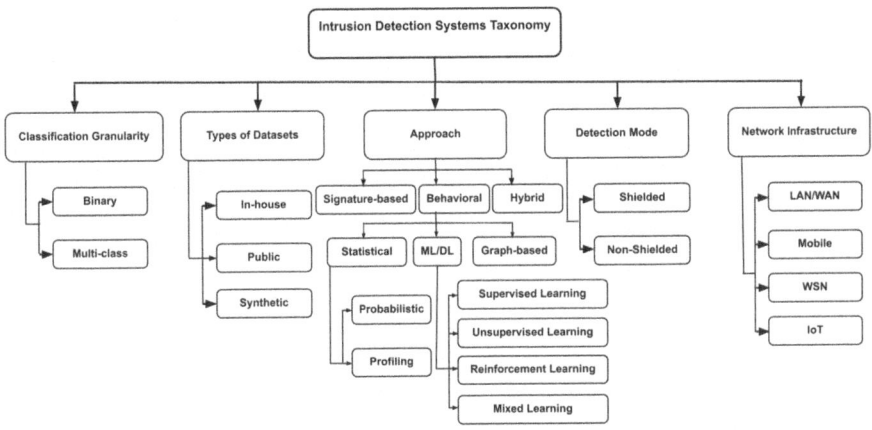

Fig. 2. Intrusion Detection Systems taxonomy. Figure from [4]

The array of IDS solutions available is diverse, as illustrated by the taxonomy chart in Fig. 2. This paper, however, will concentrate on detecting anomalies within PCAP data by employing a statistical T-Test, which is a fundamental method for identifying unusual patterns that may suggest security breaches.

4   Rust V. Python

Pandas, a widely used Python library for data analysis, gains additional performance benefits from its C and Cython backend [5]. However, this approach introduces security concerns due to the lack of memory safety in C and Cython, overshadowing Python's ease of use in a cybersecurity environment. The Office of the National Cyber Director (ONCD) recently published a report urging for software developers to adopt memory safe languages to limit cybersecurity risks [6]. In the report Rust is specifically called out as a memory safe language that meets multiple criteria including: allowing the code to be close to the kernel, supporting determinism, and not having, or the ability to override, the "garbage collector", but does emphasise that it has not been proven in space systems. Given the security and performance concerns highlighted by the ONCD, this paper intends to validate the theoretical advantages of Rust for data analysis in a cybersecurity context. Rust's memory safety and compiled nature, present a logical case for its use in critical environments, such as space systems.

5   Experimental Design and Results

We propose an experiment that will evaluate the performance of utilizing the Pandas Python library versus the Polars Rust library to perform a T-Test on potentially anomalous data. The experiment will consist of identifying anomalous traffic in the PCAP via abnormal packet length across common ports using two sets of data. The first dataset is normal traffic consisting of typical network traffic associated with day-to-day satellite operations. The second dataset is mixed traffic, consisting of normal traffic and traffic associated with the "attack". The data from each set is converted in to a dataframe with both Pandas in Python and Polars in Rust. This data is then graphed, shown on 3. From this graph we can see what looks like potential anomalous traffic. We then will run the T-Test on this subset of traffic to determine if there is a statistically significant difference, thus indicating anomalous traffic.

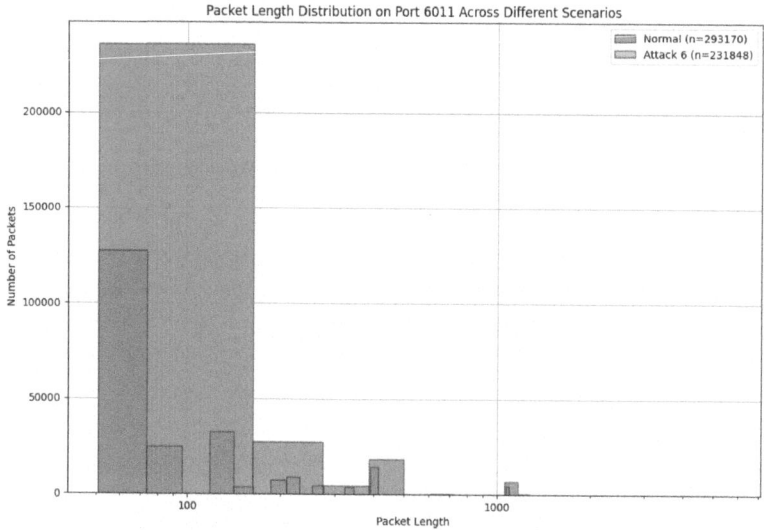

Fig. 3. Packet length distribution on port 6011

To assess the performance verses of the Polars Rust library as compared to the Pandas Python library, an experiment was setup as follows:

1. Extracted the destination port and packet length data from the dataset using the appropriate functions in Pandas and Polars.
2. Employed the SciPy library's ttest_ind function in Python to compute the T-Statistic and P-Value for the dataset.
3. Calculated the T-Statistic and P-Value in Rust by applying statistical functions available in the Polars library.
4. Conducted timed trials of the calculations across 1, 10, 100, and 1,000 iterations, repeating each for a total of 20 trials to ensure statistical significance.
5. Compiled the average computation time for each set of iterations and displayed the results in a graphical format, as depicted in Fig. 4.

When performing few calculations (1 and 10 iterations), we see the Rust approach demonstrating a notable performance advantage, performing the calculations 61% and 61.62% faster for 1 and 10 iterations, respectively. As the number

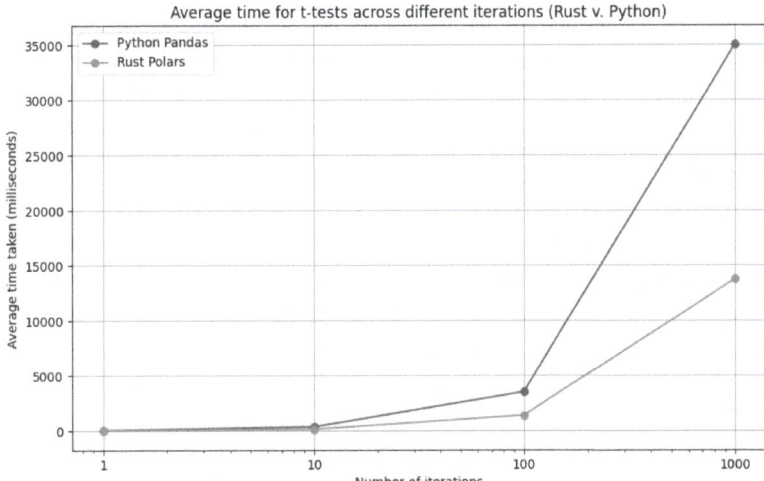

Fig. 4. Rust v. Python computation time

of calculations increases, we see that performance gap consistently observed. In the case of 100 iterations, we see the average time for Rust is 60.74% faster than Python. When we reach 1,000 iterations, the average time for Rust is 60.75% faster than Python. These results underscore Rust's superior efficiency in handling large-scale computations, likely attributable to its compiled nature and optimized memory management features.

6   Future Steps

For future considerations, we plan to dive deeper into the efficiency of Rust with computational resources during the experimental trials. Specifically, we plan to measure and analyze the memory and CPU usage across both Rust and Python implementations during each iteration of the trials. Additionally, we recommend to explore the application of more advanced machine learning techniques within the realm of Intrusion Detection Systems (IDS) for satellite cybersecurity. This exploration will involve evaluating various machine learning techniques and libraries in Rust and Python, assessing their performance and ease of use.

7   Conclusion

In conclusion, this paper has presented an analysis of the performance benefits of utilizing the Rust programming language, specifically through the Polars library, for conducting PCAP analysis in the context of satellite cybersecurity. Our experimental results have demonstrated that Rust offers significant speed advantages over Python, with performance improvements ranging from 60.74% to over 61%. Rust's compiled nature and efficient memory management makes it a superior choice for processing large datasets typical in space system communications.

Additionally, the implications of these findings extend beyond the immediate context of satellite cybersecurity. They suggest a broader applicability of Rust in fields requiring high-performance computing and real-time data analysis. The efficiency, safety, and speed of Rust, as evidenced in the recommendations from the Office of the National Cyber Director and our experiments, underscore its potential to enhance the development and implementation of Intrusion Detection Systems (IDS) and other critical cybersecurity measures.

Disclaimer. The views expressed in this paper are those of the authors and do not reflect the official policy or position of the United States Air Force, the Department of Defense, or the U.S. Government.

References

1. Boschetti, N., Gordon, N.G., Falco, G.: Space cybersecurity lessons learned from the viasat cyberattack. In: ASCEND 2022, p. 4380 (2022)
2. Manulis, M., Bridges, C.P., Harrison, R., Sekar, V., Davis, A.: Cyber security in new space: analysis of threats, key enabling technologies and challenges. Int. J. Inf. Secur. **20**, 287–311 (2021)
3. Swpb: Simplified diagram of segments of a satellite system. https://commons. wikimedia.org/wiki/File:Ground_segment.png
4. Alkasassbeh, M., Al-Haj Baddar, S.: Intrusion detection systems: a state-of-the- art taxonomy and survey. Arab. J. Sci. Eng. **48**(8), 10021–10064 (2023)
5. McKinney, W.: Python for Data Analysis: Data Wrangling with Pandas, NumPy, and IPython. O'Reilly Media, Inc. (2012)
6. Office of the National Cyber Director: Final ONCD Technical Report. The White House (2024). https://www.whitehouse.gov/wp-content/uploads/2024/02/ Final-ONCD-Technical-Report.pdf. Accessed 28 Feb 2024
7. Gulati, A.: Can rust finally replace C?: a qualitative and quantitative analysis. Amity J. Comput. Sci. **6**(2) (2022)

Austere Runway Simulated Identification

Luke H. Boyd IV, Scott L. Nykl, and Douglas D. Hodson$^{(\boxtimes)}$

Department of Electrical and Computer Engineering, U.S. Air Force Institute of
Technology, WPAFB, Dayton, OH 45433, USA
{luke.boyd.1,douglas.hodson}@us.af.mil, scott.nykl@au.af.edu

Abstract. The Air Force Institute of Technology (AFIT) is researching
airborne systems that can identify, characterize, and generate approach
paths to runways in austere environments. Such systems enable landings
in areas that are traditionally unserviceable. To begin work on a proof-
of-concept, we sought out to tackle the problem of identifying where the
aircraft should direct itself to find the runways via the use of April Tags
and Computer Vision.

Keywords: Computer Vision · April Tag

1 Introduction

Warfare requires mobility. Troops need to maneuver to contact. Mechanized
beasts of steel must traverse difficult terrain with perilous geography. Logisti-
cians need to coordinate transferal of large quantities of food, medicine, uniforms,
ammunition and weaponry. Naval vessels must brave the seas and oceans over
great distances. Aircraft have the luxury of flying at great heights and speeds
through the air, yet that luxury presents a problem: they have to land. Landing
an aircraft is by far the most difficult portion of flight. As a result, tremendous
sums of money have been poured into the construction of permanent runways
throughout the world. That presents a number of problems when it comes to
warfare, as control of these runways is critical to ensuring continued aerial operations.

At AFIT, we're exploring potential courses of actions to address these concerns. AFIT has begun research on automated systems that can identify and
land on runways in austere conditions. My goal through the work done over the
last few weeks is to begin construction of a proof-of-concept for initial identification from distance. When human pilots want to land on a runway, they first
must identify the runway at distance and begin their approach.

GPS and other Satellite Navigation technologies should not be relied upon as
they rely on consistent communication. Rather our methods should be harnessed
as they provide a degree of redundancy that satellites cannot. Via the use of high-
resolution cameras mounted to these smaller twin engine aircraft, and April Tags
printed onto a surface mounted near the runway, we can develop a system that
can recognize those April Tags and alter course to begin approach.

© The Author(s), under exclusive license to Springer Nature Switzerland AG 2025
D. D. Hodson et al. (Eds.): CSCE 2024, CCIS 2258, pp. 9–16, 2025.
https://doi.org/10.1007/978-3-031-85902-1_2

The rest of this paper is organized as follows: Sect. 2 will highlight background information, Sect. 3 will describe the experiment design and results, Sect. 4 will look into future steps, and Sect. 5 contains a conclusion.

2   Background Information

2.1   Problem Statement

In the rapidly evolving landscape of autonomous aviation, particularly within the realm of military and humanitarian operations, the ability to deploy unmanned aerial vehicles (UAVs) swiftly and safely in austere and remote environments is paramount. The challenge lies in ensuring precise landings in areas that lack conventional runway infrastructure, a scenario frequently encountered by Air Force personnel deployed in diverse global locations. Traditional navigation and landing systems, while effective in well-defined and equipped airstrips, fall short in rugged, undeveloped terrains where immediate and reliable UAV deployment is often most critical. This gap in capability presents a significant operational limitation, impacting the efficiency and scope of missions ranging from reconnaissance to critical supply deliveries in disaster-stricken or hostile regions.

The envisioned solution to this problem is the implementation of a system that utilizes April Tags, a sophisticated fiducial marker technology, to create identifiable landing zones for UAVs, including twin-engine Cessna drones, which are often employed for their versatility and payload capacity in various Air Force operations. By developing a portable, durable, and easily deployable AprilTag-marked tarp, the aim is to provide a "pop-up" landing infrastructure that drones can recognize and interact with autonomously. This system would enable Air Force personnel to establish instant runways anywhere in the world, under any conditions, with minimal setup time and without the need for existing landing strip infrastructure.

The primary challenge this initiative seeks to address is the development of a reliable and robust detection system that allows drones to accurately identify the AprilTag-marked tarps from varying altitudes and approach vectors, even in adverse weather conditions or low-light environments. This entails not only the refinement of the drone's onboard camera systems and image processing algorithms but also the design of the AprilTag itself to ensure maximum visibility and decode-ability from a distance. Furthermore, the system must be capable of guiding the UAV to a safe and precise landing, accounting for potential obstacles and surface irregularities within the designated landing zone. The successful implementation of this technology has the potential to revolutionarily enhance the Air Force's operational flexibility, allowing rapid, safe, and effective UAV deployment in the most remote or challenging environments, thereby significantly expanding the scope of humanitarian and tactical missions that can be supported.

2.2   April Tag

April Tags are a type of fiducial marker system that provides a robust and computationally lightweight solution for real-time three-dimensional positioning and orientation estimation, which is particularly valuable in the fields of robotics and augmented reality. Developed as part of a broader field of computer vision, April Tags consist of a square black-and-white pattern that allows for precise detection and decoding by a camera system. Each unique tag encodes an identifier, which can be used to distinguish between multiple tags within a single scene. This capability makes them an ideal tool for applications requiring high precision and reliability in object tracking and spatial orientation tasks.

The design of April Tags is optimized to be easily recognizable even under less than ideal conditions, such as low resolution, motion blur, and varying lighting conditions. The simplicity of the patterns ensures that they can be detected from a distance and at oblique angles, making them highly versatile for diverse applications (Fig. 1).

Fig. 1. A C-130 Hercules landing on a dirt runway during RED FLAG 22-2 Exercise (Color figure online)

2.3   Simulation Overview

This experiment was performed with the "Aftrburner" engine [1]. This engine is written in C and C++ and was created by Dr. Scott Nykl for use by AFIT students to perform experiments for Air Force efforts. The engine utilizes OpenGL

3 as well as relying on standardized libraries that attempt to ensure a degree of memory safety and performance optimization.

Inside of the engine we're running a simulated camera with a 56.0 degree field of view that, via pressing the space bar, allows us to take a photo and attempt to deduce the encoding and position of the April Tag in question. To simulate distance, the engine renders positions in terms of meters. All distance between coordinates in the world-space are measured in meters, providing a cohesive simulation environment. Meaning, if the camera was at position: 100.0, 20.0, 0.0. Then that camera was 100 m from the origin along the X axis, 20 m from origin along the Y axis, and had an altitude of 0 m (being on the ground). The sizing of the April Tag was also interpreted in this way, it being a square two dimensional object would mean that a size of 1 meant a Tag that was 1 m by 1 m.

Therefore, if the camera is positioned at 100.0, 100.0, 10.0. It was positioned 100 m from origin in both the X and Y axis and was 10.0 m off the ground. It would also stand to reason that by shrinking the April Tag we could assume a constant distance with a varying size of April Tag, or a varying distance with a constant size of April Tag.

For practical military application: large items are typically cumbersome and are at risk of being left behind by in a rush or lost. Additionally, since communication isn't something that should be assumed to be functional in an operational environment; the criteria by which this experiment was focused on is distance from the April Tag and the size of said tag (Fig. 2).

Fig. 2. An April Tag

3   Experimental Design and Results

In the pursuit of refining autonomous landing capabilities for UAVs in austere environments, a series of experiments were conducted within a state-of-the-art virtual engine, "Aftrburner," focusing on the interplay between high-resolution camera systems and AprilTag detection. Utilizing a simulated 4K camera setup, these experiments aimed to ascertain the maximum distance at which an April-Tag could be reliably detected and decoded, a critical factor in ensuring the operational viability of using such tags for drone landing zone identification. Remarkably, the results demonstrated that the AprilTag could be discerned from distances of up to 600 m, a promising outcome that underscores the potential of this technology in expanding the operational envelope of UAV deployments.

However, the emergence of a 600-meter detection threshold presents a multifaceted challenge, inviting scrutiny into whether this limit is an inherent characteristic of the AprilTag-camera interaction or a byproduct of the simulation's constraints. This distinction is crucial for several reasons. Firstly, the physical limitations of the 4K camera's sensor, including its resolution, pixel density, and light sensitivity, may inherently cap the detection range. These hardware characteristics, coupled with the optical properties of the camera's lens, delineate the boundaries of what is feasibly detectable at extended ranges.

Secondly, the simulation environment itself-though sophisticated-may not fully encapsulate the myriad of real-world variables that impact visual detection systems. Factors such as atmospheric conditions, lighting variability, and motion blur induced by drone dynamics can significantly influence detection efficacy in actual deployment scenarios. Moreover, the algorithmic treatment of the camera feed, including image stabilization, noise reduction, and tag decoding strategies, plays a pivotal role in the effective identification of AprilTags at distance.

Thus, while the 600-meter benchmark established in the "Aftrburner" simulations offers an encouraging testament to the feasibility of using AprilTags for UAV landing guidance, it also delineates a critical juncture for further investigation. Distinguishing between the physical and computational limitations encountered in these simulations will be essential for refining the system's design and deployment strategy. Advancements in camera technology, coupled with algorithmic optimizations, may hold the key to extending the detection range beyond the current threshold, thereby enhancing the versatility and reliability of UAV operations in remote or inaccessible locales.

4   Future Steps

As this research marks a significant step forward in the application of AprilTags for UAV landing in austere environments, it also illuminates the path for future investigations to enhance and validate the robustness of this technology. A critical area of focus for subsequent work will be to expand the simulation parameters within "Aftrburner" to encompass a broader spectrum of weather and lighting conditions. Such diversified simulations are essential for understanding the limits

Fig. 3. A screenshot from the Aftrburner engine

and capabilities of the AprilTag detection system under real-world operational scenarios (Fig. 3).

Firstly, incorporating varied lighting conditions, ranging from the low-light environments of dawn and dusk to the high-contrast scenarios of midday sun, will provide deeper insights into the optical challenges that might impact the camera's ability to detect AprilTags. Simulating the effects of direct sunlight, shadows, and reflections is crucial for developing adaptive image processing algorithms that can maintain tag detection reliability across the diurnal cycle.

Moreover, weather conditions significantly affect UAV operations, particularly the visual systems used for navigation and landing. Future simulations should include scenarios with rain, fog, and varying degrees of cloud cover to test the resilience of the AprilTag detection system against atmospheric interference. These conditions can reduce visibility, introduce noise, and degrade image quality, challenging the system's effectiveness.

Additionally, the impact of dynamic weather elements, such as wind and turbulence, on the UAV's stability and the consequent motion blur in captured images warrants exploration. Advanced simulations incorporating these factors will aid in the development of more sophisticated image stabilization and processing techniques, ensuring reliable AprilTag detection even under less than ideal flight conditions.

Exploring the integration of multispectral and infrared imaging could also provide avenues for overcoming the limitations posed by adverse weather and lighting. Such technologies may enable the detection of AprilTags beyond the visible spectrum, offering potential solutions for night-time operations or scenarios where visibility is severely compromised.

In pursuing these avenues of future work, the goal will be not only to solidify the foundational achievements of this research but also to expand the operational envelope of UAVs using AprilTag technology. By rigorously testing and adapting the system to withstand the diverse and unpredictable conditions encountered in real-world missions, we can move closer to a future where autonomous UAV landings in unstructured and challenging environments become a reliable and routine capability, vastly enhancing the scope and effectiveness of humanitarian, military, and exploratory endeavors.

5   Conclusion

In conclusion, this study has explored the innovative application of AprilTags in enhancing the autonomous landing capabilities of UAVs, particularly in scenarios demanding rapid deployment in austere and unstructured environments. Through a series of meticulously designed simulations using the "Aftrburner" virtual engine, we have demonstrated the potential of using high-resolution 4K cameras to detect AprilTags from distances up to 600 m, thereby establishing a viable method for identifying makeshift landing zones in diverse operational contexts.

While the 600-meter detection threshold represents a significant milestone in leveraging AprilTag technology for UAV landings, it also underscores the necessity for further research to dissect the nuances of this limitation. Is this threshold a fundamental limit imposed by the current state of camera and image processing technology, or is it an artifact of the simulation environment? Addressing this question is not merely an academic exercise but a crucial step towards realizing the full potential of UAVs in humanitarian, military, and exploratory missions.

The implications of this work extend far beyond the technical realm, offering a glimpse into a future where UAVs can be deployed with unprecedented flexibility and precision. By laying out an AprilTag tarp, personnel in any corner of the globe could create an instant, recognizable landing zone for drones, significantly enhancing mission capabilities and responsiveness in critical situations.

As we look to the future, the integration of advanced image processing algorithms, improvements in camera technology, and refinements in AprilTag design promise to push the boundaries of what is possible. This research not only contributes to the evolving field of UAV technology but also opens the door to a myriad of applications that can benefit from precise, autonomous navigation systems.

In harnessing the synergy between computer vision and UAV technology, we stand on the cusp of a new era in remote operations-a future where the skies are not just a frontier for exploration but a dynamic canvas for innovation and humanitarian aid.

Disclaimer. The views expressed in this paper are those of the authors and do not reflect the official policy or position of the United States Air Force, the Department of Defense, or the U.S. Government.

References

1. Nykl, S.: Aftrburner engine. https://www.youtube.com/@ScottNykl/playlistsc

Using Rhai to Create and Benchmark Bevy Entities

John H. Hardy and Douglas D. Hodson[✉]

Department of Electrical and Computer Engineering, U.S. Air Force Institute of
Technology, WPAFB, Dayton, OH 45433, USA
{john.hardy.22,douglas.hodson}@us.af.mil

Abstract. The paradigm shift within the industry towards multi-
threaded processing has engendered a novel approach to developing
highly performant and scalable computing applications. As the fundamental constraints of Object-Oriented programming languages become
increasingly apparent in such hardware environments, Data-Oriented
Design (DOD) endeavors to redirect developers' focus away from super-
fluous abstraction and towards the intricacies of efficiently manipulating
substantial volumes of data. While this methodology effectively harnesses
the capabilities of contemporary hardware, it also poses a barrier to
entry for novice developers and enthusiasts. The Rhai scripting language
presents a high-level Application Program Interface (API) that can seamlessly integrate into existing Rust projects, thereby fostering inclusivity
within this community. An investigation into the inherent performance
ramifications of adopting such an approach will be conducted within the
framework of DOD-centric data structures.

Keywords: Data Oriented Design · Rust · Bevy · Rhai

1 Introduction

Throughout the history of computer programming, conventional Object-
Oriented (OO) languages have traditionally relied upon Moore's law to counteract potential performance degradation associated with scaled computing. However, as silicon dies approach physical limits, the magnitude of performance
enhancements has diminished, prompting a shift towards multi-threaded solutions. OO designs, while convenient to model and understand systems, struggle
to accommodate these evolving constraints and are consequently facing obso-
lescence. In response to this challenge, the emerging field of Data-Oriented
Design (DOD) presents itself as a viable alternative to traditional Object-
Oriented methodologies. DOD capitalizes hardware designs by forcing the developer to consider cache utilization and the use of Single-Instruction-Multiple-Data
(SIMD) instructions available on modern hardware.

Scripting languages have served as a pivotal abstraction layer, enabling programmers to craft high-level code that "wraps", "connects" and orchestrates

D. D. Hodson et al. (Eds.): CSCE 2024, CCIS 2258, pp. 17–22, 2025.
https://doi.org/10.1007/978-3-031-85902-1_3

low-level system operations. This study endeavors to scrutinize the inherent performance ramifications associated with such environments within the framework of a DOD-based game engine. At its core, the research is driven by the fundamental inquiry into whether scripting languages natively diminish performance and if DOD can be leveraged to improve this.

The rest of this paper is organized as follows: Sect. 2 will highlight background information, Sect. 3 will describe the experiment design and results, Sect. 4 will look into future steps, and Sect. 5 contains a conclusion.

2   Background Information

2.1   Performance of Standard Rust Data Structures

The Rust programming language implements DOD by constraining or eliminating the use of OO design paradigms, thereby necessitating the employment of memory-safe and cache-aligned data structures. James McMurray [1] analyzes these systems by bench-marking the performance of various auto-vectorized Rust data structures.

McMurray conducts a series of three distinct experiments, employing a standard Rust vector to encapsulate a collection of data elements. The data elements used in the experiments are the standard template, dynamic template, and box template data types respectively. Each trial varies the numbers of elements in the list from one to five million. Figure 1 illustrates the outcomes of this investigation, with the horizontal axis denoting the quantity of elements within the respective list and the vertical axis representing the total execution time measured in milliseconds.

Evidently, the vector housing the standard template data type demonstrates markedly superior performance compared to the other data structures given sufficiently large numbers of elements. However, for vectors containing fewer than one hundred thousand elements, performance differences become inconsequential. McMurray posits that this trend can be explained by the inherent overheads associated with dynamic dispatch over complex data elements, stemming from the indirection of the primitive data. Conversely, monomorphization, the direct storage of primitive data, readily lends itself to vectorization by the Rust compiler, resulting in notable performance improvements. Consequently, it is advisable to circumvent indirection when handling extensive lists of data, aligning with one of the core tenets of Data-Oriented Design.

2.2   Benchmarking Bevy Data Types

The Bevy graphics engine provides a robust implementation of an Entity-Component System (ECS) that closely adheres to DOD principles. Analogous to the monomorphic vectors previously discussed, Bevy ECS's Table storage type is engineered for rapid query iteration, albeit at the expense of sluggish performance when adding or removing primitive data elements. In contrast, the Sparse Set storage type mirrors dynamically dispatched vectors, employing indirection

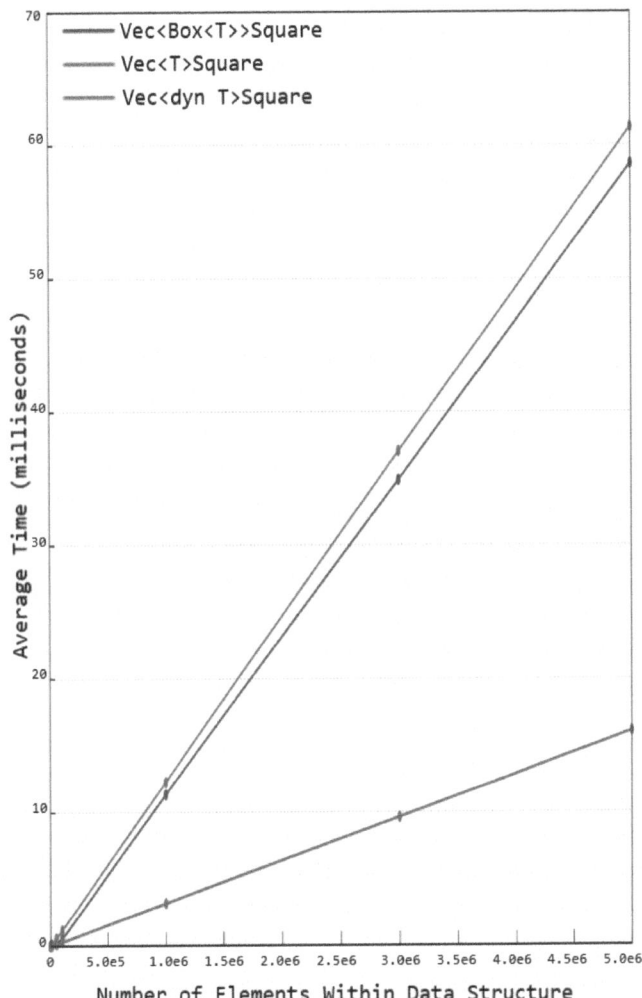

Fig. 1. Dynamic Trait Rust Data Structures Performance Comparison

for primitive data storage. While optimized for efficient data manipulation, this storage type compromises query speed. Within the Bevy framework, Tables serve as the standard for entities, with Sparse Sets recommended only when Table usage is infeasible. It is advised against mixing these storage types; however, the performance ramifications of such a strategy are also investigated.

2.3   Extending Benchmarks to Rhai

Expanding upon these endeavors, this study seeks to broaden the scope of assessment to encompass the Rhai scripting language. Rhai functions as a high-level interpreter that facilitates the execution of low-level Rust code. The objective is to determine whether the utilization of the Rhai interpreter in isolation leads to a notable decline in performance. Accordingly, the Rhai language is barely utilized for actual code composition and is employed solely for invoking predefined behaviors through function calls. In this way, the test suite utilized for benchmarking Bevy independently is transposed into the Rhai interpreter environment and executed.

3   Experimental Design and Results

The investigation follows a structured methodology comprising six experiments, each comprising ten trials. Initially, the first three experiments evaluate the cumulative time required for updating the positions of ten-thousand entities housed within Tables, Sparse Sets, and Mixed Table-Sparse-Set data structures, serving as the control group. Subsequently, the latter set of three experiments replicates the preceding trials, albeit with the positional update code transcribed into the Rhai-to-Rust interpreter and invoked from a Rhai script. The resultant execution times are depicted in the box and whisker plots illustrated in Fig. 2.

The data set exhibits significant variability in data points with no discernible trend, thereby suggesting the absence of any impact on performance attributable to the Rhai interpreter. Notably, both the Bevy-only and Bevy-over-Rhai Table data types manifest a noticeable improvement in performance relative to alternative data structures, a trend consistent with previous observations regarding monomorphic vectors. Of particular interest is the performance of the Mixed Sparse-Set-Table data type. In this configuration, ten-thousand entities, each characterized by position and velocity attributes, are stored in memory. Positions are represented within a Table, while velocities are managed through a Sparse Set. Subsequently, all entities undergo position updates based on their respective velocities. Intuitive conjecture suggests performance would fall between that of a pure Table and a pure Sparse Set approach, which indeed seems to be the case.

4   Future Steps

The findings derived from this experiment suggest that the Rhai interpreter, in isolation, does not impose inherent performance detriments upon the compiled binary of an application. However, this observation does not preclude the possibility of performance impacts arising from Rhai interpreter utilization under differing circumstances; rather, it implies that such impacts are not substantial when the interpreter is employed appropriately. Subsequent investigations necessitate a larger dataset to comprehensively assess the performance repercussions of diverse operations within Rhai. This could encompass examinations of variable assignment and manipulation, function declarations, addressing and changing values stored in memory, and the definition of novel data structures.

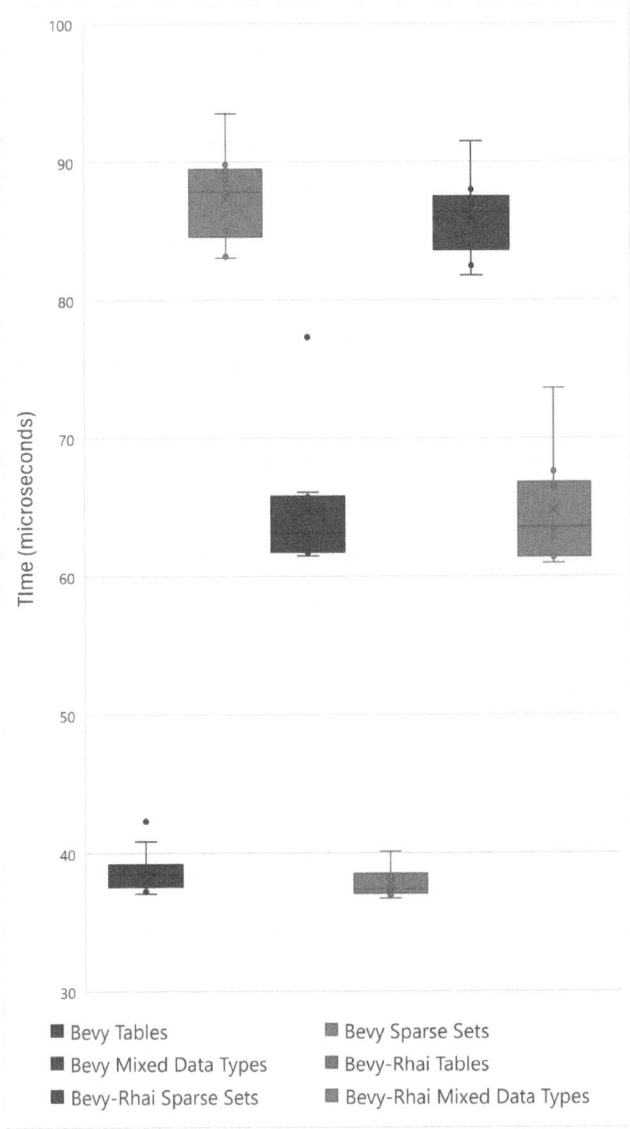

Fig. 2. Performance of Bevy Engine With and Without Rhai Interpreter

The task of adapting pre-existing data structures from Bevy to Rhai presents notable challenges, primarily due to the constraints imposed by the Rust borrow checker. In light of these constraints, a more feasible approach may involve creating these data structures independently and then directly integrating them into the Rhai interpreter.

5   Conclusion

Undoubtedly, it is evident that through the implementation of a Data-Oriented methodology coupled with regular benchmarking, the transformation of an established Rust project into a powerful Application Program Interface driven by Rhai scripting is feasible. Such an endeavor would facilitate accessibility for users or novice programmers, circumventing the necessity for comprehension of systems-level programming intricacies inherent in Rust.

A multitude of Rust programmers leveraging Bevy have recognized the need for integrated native scripting functionalities within the graphics engine. Such functionalities are deemed crucial owing to the intrinsic characteristics of the Bevy engine itself. Bevy, as a freely available and open-source game engine, is designed to counteract commercial endeavors aiming to dominate the independent game development domain. The overarching objective of this initiative is to empower novice game developers in crafting immersive and enjoyable environments, solely driven by their curiosity and dedication. Integration of the Rhai scripting language into this project promises to significantly enhance the accessibility of the engine, thereby broadening its appeal to a wider spectrum of potential developers.

Disclaimer. The views expressed in this paper are those of the authors and do not reflect the official policy or position of the United States Air Force, the Department of Defense, or the U.S. Government.

Reference

1. McMurray, J.: An introduction to data oriented design with rust. https:// jamesmcm.github.io/blog/intro-dod/

PyO3: Building Python Extension Modules in Native Rust with Performance and Safety in Mind

Price D. Johnson and Douglas D. Hodson[✉]

Department of Electrical and Computer Engineering, U.S. Air Force Institute of Technology, WPAFB, Dayton, OH 45433, USA
{price.johnson.1,douglas.hodson}@us.af.mil

Abstract. Python and Rust are both powerful programming languages, each offering unique benefits depending on individual use cases. Rust is a lower-level programming language built with speed and safety as integral features. Python, known for being more user-friendly, has an extensive library with over 350,000 publicly available packages [1]. Writing Rust software can be a daunting and meticulous task, as its syntax and strict compiler demand careful attention to detail. This meticulousness often pays off in the form of highly performant and safe code. Conversely, Python has a straightforward syntax that allows programmers a wide range of flexibility in writing code. However, Python's performance can be limiting, often requiring the use of native C or C++ libraries for computationally heavy tasks. This paper introduces the PyO3 crate, which enables programmers to seamlessly integrate native Python modules and Rust code within the same project, allowing for the development of high-performance Python extension modules using Rust. Additionally, it provides insights into interfacing between the two code bases using various PyO3 tools. This approach enables programmers to benefit from combining both languages while maintaining good coding standards by keeping them separate and interfacing between them. PyO3 opens the door for Rust to replace C and C++ in Python modules, offering a safer alternative while not compromising efficiency.

Keywords: PyO3 · python · rust · structures · interfaces · performance

1 Introduction

Now is the ideal time for programmers to transition away from developing native C and C++ libraries for computationally heavy tasks in Python, given the challenges these code bases present, such as security vulnerabilities and memory management issues. A recent report by The White House Office of the National Cyber Director (ONCD) highlights the Biden Administration's call to reduce memory safety vulnerabilities on a large scale by adopting memory-safe languages. This transition would help decrease the United States' cyber attack

D. D. Hodson et al. (Eds.): CSCE 2024, CCIS 2258, pp. 23–30, 2025.
https://doi.org/10.1007/978-3-031-85902-1_4

surface by preventing the exploitation of program memory vulnerabilities [2]. To make this transition, programmers should adopt Rust and its many memory-safe features. The way Rust differs from C and C++ is through the use of its ownership model and explicit borrowing rules. These core features, integral to the Rust model, prevent common memory-related issues during compile time, including buffer overflows, memory leaks, and null pointer references.

Since Rust is a newer programming language, and the longstanding C and C++ codebases have historically been the backbone for efficient Python modules, interfacing between Python and Rust has not been straightforward. Furthermore, moving away from native C and C++ is a grand and difficult task when so many python libraries are coupled with the lower level languages.

With the growing desire to shift away from memory-unsafe languages and the development of the PyO3 crate for Rust, past and future Python libraries should embrace PyO3's Rust bindings for Python. By replacing these native C and C++ libraries with Rust, code will have similar to if not better performance standards, protect against memory related vulnerabilities, and maintain code separation for readability, maintainability, and reusability. PyO3 is the solution for writing Python modules in Rust rather than C and C++.

The rest of this paper is organized as follows: Sect. 2 will provide background information and the motivation behind this paper, Sect. 3 will describe how the structuring of the Rust project works, Sect. 4 will demonstrate interfacing between the different code bases, Sect. 5 will highlight the performance benefits, Sect. 6 provides sample application code, and Sect. 7 contains a conclusion.

2   Background Information

Before the development of PyO3, the primary method of connecting Python and Rust code was through the use of the rust-cpython crate. The rust-cpython crate is another tool for connecting Rust and Python code by providing bindings to the Python C API. This way of connecting Rust and Python code meant programmers would have to manually handle memory management. Where the PyO3 crate differs from the older rust-cpython crate is its approach to memory management while abstracting away much of the complexity. With PyO3, all objects are owned by the library with all apis available with references [4]. The rust-cpython code owns its values, providing programmers with more flexibility in writing code but also incurring an overhead cost. PyO3's approach simplifies memory management for developers and reduces the risk of memory-related bugs. In contrast, with rust-cpython, the programmer owns Python objects [3]. This difference can potentially lead to memory-related vulnerabilities, as Python objects do not have explicit types like Rust does. It is advantageous to shield programmers from memory management concerns whenever possible.

Support for the rust-cpython crate has ceased due to the emergence of PyO3, which was inspired by rust-cpython's approach but offers a more streamlined way of writing Python extensions in pure Rust code [5]. PyO3 now leads the way in connecting Python and Rust code, offering a modern and efficient solution for developers.

2.1   Motivation

There is a growing momentum for developers to embrace memory-safe coding practices. This shift not only reduces the vulnerability of programs to cyber attacks but also ensures that code behaves as intended. Additionally, adhering to proper coding standards is facilitated by keeping code bases separate and interfacing between them. Rust is the lower-level programming language of the future and PyO3 will forever revolutionize writing performant code in Python.

3   Project Structuring

The PyO3 Rust crate allows for the clean separation of Rust and Python code within a project. This practice upholds good coding standards and promotes code readability, maintainability, and interoperability between the two languages. This separation of concerns allows developers to more easily understand different parts of the code base, allowing for clarity and reducing confusion. This separation is achieved through the use of PyO3 interfacing tools, which provide a single entry and exit point for any functions exposed to the other language. With clean code separation, developers can more easily understand the different parts of the code base. Mixing coding languages causes confusion, as code should be clear and concise. Similarly, PyO3 supports code maintainability by providing defined locations for separate Rust and Python code, ensuring that each part of the project is structured and organized properly. Moreover, PyO3 ensures code interoperability by allowing, through the use of interfacing tools, for clean integration of Rust and Python components in a single project.

PyO3 code is written within the 'src/lib.rs' file of your Rust project, where functions exposed to Python are defined. Since these are Rust defined functions, Rust's strong typing and memory safety features are preserved, ensuring a robust interface with Python. On the Python side, the code that utilizes the native Rust functionality is typically stored in separate files from the main project. These files are accessed by importing the library as if it were any other Python module. In conclusion, the PyO3 Rust crate offers a powerful solution for integrating Rust and Python, promoting best coding practices, improving code readability and maintainability, and allowing for efficient interoperability between the two languages.

4   Interfacing Between Rust and Python

There are mechanisms provided by PyO3 for interfacing between Rust and Python code, such as converting data types, calling functions, and handling errors. These mechanisms are what bind the different code bases, enabling smooth communication and interaction.

Luckily for programmers, PyO3 will automatically convert between Rust and Python types for you. This ensures proper type conversion while eliminating most of the work by the user. There is even the ability to define a 'Rust Struct'

Table 1. Python to Rust Type Mapping [3].

Python Type	Rust Type	Rust (Py-native) Type
object	–	`&PyAny`
str	String, Cow<str>, &str	`&PyUnicode`
bytes	Vec<u8>, &[u8]	`&PyBytes`
bool	bool	`&PyBool`
int	Any integer type (i32, u32, usize, etc.)	`&PyLong`
float	f32, f64	`&PyFloat`
complex	num_complex::Complex	`&PyComplex`
list[T]	Vec<T>	`&PyList`
dict[K, V]	HashMap<K,V>, BTreeMap<K,V>	`&PyDict`
tuple[T, U]	(T, U), Vec<T>	`&PyTuple`
set[T]	HashSet<T>, BTreeSet<T>	`&PySet`
frozenset[T]	HashSet<T>, BTreeSet<T>	`&PyFrozenSet`
bytearray	Vec<u8>	`&PyByteArray`
slice	–	`&PySlice`
type	–	`&PyType`
module	–	`&PyModule`
datetime.datetime	–	`&PyDateTime`
datetime.date	–	`&PyDate`
datetime.time	–	`&PyTime`
datetime.tzinfo	–	`&PyTzInfo`
datetime.timedelta	–	`&PyDelta`
typing.Optional[T]	Option<T>	–
typing.Sequence[T]	Vec<T>	`&PySequence`
typing.Iterator[Any]	–	`&PyIterator`

in Python using the '#[pyclass]' attribute. Table 1 shows the mapping of Python types to Rust types

Defining Python functions within Rust is straightforward. The '#[pyfunction]' attribute separates a Python function from Rust functions. Once the attribute is attached to a Python function and the function is properly defined, the function needs to be added to a module using the 'wrap_pyfunction!' macro [3]. A programmer may utilize options to further customize their Python function. One example of an option is the '#[pyo3(name = "custom_name")]' option that exposes a custom name to Python. There are even options that can be assigned to functions which work with arguments. In conclusion, defining Python functions within Rust is a straightforward process, made possible by PyO3's attributes and macros.

Error handling in Rust differs from that in Python. While Python uses the familiar try-catch block to raise specific errors when a block of code encounters an issue, Rust employs a 'Result' wrapper to manage errors [7]. That means there needs to be a way for PyO3 to handle errors across the two languages. In PyO3, the 'create_exception' macro is what allows programmers to take their uniquely defined exceptions and be thrown to Python [8]. Listing 1.1 demonstrates what that error handling would look like.

Listing 1.1. Error handling demonstration.

```
create_exception!
(mymodule, MyError, pyo3::exceptions::PyException);
```

Now errors are handled in Rust code and raise exceptions that can be caught and handled in Python code. In summary, error handling in Rust differs from Python's approach, with Rust using the Result wrapper to manage errors. PyO3 provides the 'create_exception' macro to bridge this gap.

5   Performance Considerations

Using Rust for performance-critical modules can enhance a project's overall performance compared to using Python alone. Rust is a lower-level compiled language while Python is only an interpreted language, meaning Rust code can be executed directly by the computer's processor while Python code must be interpreted. Rust does an excellent job at optimizing code, resulting in faster execution speeds and lower resource consumption compared to Python. Rust's memory management system also eliminates the need for a garbage collector, reducing overhead and improving performance in applications that require a sizable piece of memory. Compared to C and C++, Rust can be optimized enough to have the same performance as these lower level languages [10]. Rust's combination of being a compiled, lower-level language with strong optimization capabilities and efficient memory management makes the language stand out over Python and a competitive option against C and C++.

The research conducted in this project presents a benchmarking analysis comparing the performance of data structures implemented in PyO3 Rust extensions against native Python implementations. The benchmarked data structures include Structure of Arrays (SoA), Array of Structures (AoS), linked lists, and vectors. Rust and Python implementations of each structure were compared, using PyO3's wrapping functionality. Benchmarks assessed data access and manipulation, running for 100 iterations across varying element sizes. Results revealed that Rust data structures outperformed native Python implementations. The research proves Rust's memory management system and data-oriented design results in superior performance compared to pure Python.

5.1   Parallelism

Building native Python modules in Rust allows programmers to take advantage of parallelism, or multi-thread processing. Python cannot execute CPU-bound tasks in parallel due to the Global Interpreter Lock (GIL), which restricts concurrent execution of Python bytecode on multiple CPU cores within the same process [6].

CPython also has to deal with the infamous Global Interpreter Lock. This makes threading in CPython a bad fit for CPU-bound tasks and often forces developers to accept the overhead of multiprocessing because only one thread can execute Python bytecode at a time. In PyO3, parallelism can be easily achieved since PyO3 needs to hold the GIL by default when called from Python [3]. True parallelism can exponentially decrease the execution time of CPU-bound tasks compared to using threads in CPython, which are constrained by the GIL. This allows developers to fully utilize multi-core processors for applications where performance is desired.

6   Example Application

Ensure PyO3 is added as a dependency within your 'Cargo.toml' file. The extention-module feature is enabled to make this a Python extension rather than a binary crate [8]. Also, ensure to include Maturin. Maturin streamlines the development and distribution of Python packages that incorporate Rust. Since Maturin is only being used during development, it can just be added as a dependency.

Listing 1.2. Cargo.toml file.

```
[ dependencies ]
pyo3 = "0.20.3"
features = ["extension-module"]

[dev-dependencies]
maturin = "0.9"
```

Below is sample code demonstrating how to generate native Python modules. The function multiplies all numbers within an array and returns the result as a string [3]. The '#[pyfunction]' attribute is used to define a Python function. The '#[pymodule]' attribute is used to define a Python module that contains the function, making it accessible from Python as a module even though it has been written in Rust code. Within '#[pymodule]', there is the 'add_wrapped' method of 'PyModule' which does the actual wrapping of the Rust function to be used within a Python module.

Listing 1.3. src/lib.rs.

```
use pyo3::prelude::*;
use pyo3::wrap_pyfunction;

#[pyfunction]
// Product of all numbers in array as string.
fn string_product(numbers: Vec<usize>)
-> PyResult<String> {
let product: usize = numbers.iter().product();
Ok(product.to_string())
}

#[pymodule]
// A Python module implemented in Rust.
fn array_product(py: Python, m: &PyModule)
-> PyResult<()> {
m.add_wrapped(wrap_pyfunction!(string_product))?;

Ok(())
}
```

This example demonstrates how to generate native Python modules with Rust, enabling developers to efficiently perform calculations, such as multiplying all numbers in an array, which can be computationally intensive. The last step would be to build the project using Maturin.

Install Maturin:

Listing 1.4. src/lib.rs.

```
pip install maturin
```

Run Maturin to build your project:

Listing 1.5. src/lib.rs.

```
maturin develop
```

7 Conclusion

The PyO3 crate provides a solution for creating native Python modules with Rust. By embracing the PyO3 crate, programmers can leverage the strengths of both Python and Rust while maintaining good coding practices. PyO3 simplifies the process of connecting Rust and Python code, alleviating much of the associated stress. This approach not only enhances the overall performance of projects but also aligns with the growing momentum for memory-safe coding practices, making Rust a better replacement for C and C++ in performance-critical Python modules.

Disclaimer. The views expressed in this paper are those of the authors and do not reflect the official policy or position of the United States Air Force, the Department of Defense, or the U.S. Government.

References

1. Dang, A.: Project description: all packages. PyPI (2022)
2. Back to the Building Blocks: A path toward secure and measurable software. The White House (2024)
3. Pyo3 user guide. v0.6.0-alpha.2 (2019)
4. Singh, K.: Speeding up python with rust, what works and what doesn't! Collection of musing and ramblings (2021)
5. Apodaca, R.L.: Python extensions in pure rust with rust-cpython (2022)
6. Wei, S., Song, G., Zhu, S., Ruan, R., Zhu, S., Cai, Y.: Discovering parallelisms in python programs. In: ESEC/FSE 2023: Proceedings of the 31st ACM Joint European Software Engineering Conference and Symposium on the Foundations of Software Engineering (2023)
7. Flitton, M.: Speed Up Your Python with Rust: Optimize Python Performance by Creating Python Pip Modules in Rust with PyO3. Packt Publishing (2022)
8. Khandaker, M.A.: Propagating user defined error from rust to python. Medium (2023)
9. Klundert, S.: Calling rust from python using pyo3. Said van de Klundert Website (2021)
10. Costanzo, M., Rucci, E., Naiouf, M., Giusti, A.D.: Performance vs programming effort between rust and C on multicore architectures: case study in n-body. In: 2021 XLVII Latin American Computing Conference (CLEI) (2021)
11. PyO3 - Github. https://github.com/PyO3
12. Yegulalp, S.: How rust can replace C, with python's help. InfoWorld (2017)
13. Maturin user guide. https://www.maturin.rs/

Leveraging Python Interpreters
for Concurrency in SeQUeNCe

Brett M. Martin[1], Douglas D. Hodson[1(✉)], and Michael R. Grimaila[2]

[1] Department of Electrical and Computer Engineering, U.S. Air Force Institute of
Technology, WPAFB, Dayton, OH 45433, USA
{brett.martin.4,douglas.hodson}@us.af.mil
[2] Department of Systems Engineering, U.S. Air Force Institute of Technology,
WPAFB, Dayton, OH 45433, USA
michael.grimaila@us.af.mil

Abstract. With the advent of the Navy Research Laboratory's
announcement of the establishment of the Washington D.C. Metropolitan Quantum Research Consortium (DC-QNet), there has been much
interest in the modeling and simulation of the quantum communication network testbed. To that end, we explore in this research the basic
functionality of the Simulator of QUantum Network Communication
(SeQUeNCe), the developmental Python/C API Interpreters module,
and their viability as technologies to be used for high-performance simulation of quantum networks. In this paper, we outline the integration of
sub-interpreters with a parallel SeQUeNCe experiment to demonstrate
true multi-threading concurrency in quantum network simulations.

Keywords: Quantum Communication Networks · Discrete Event
Simulation

1 Introduction

In the area of research and development, the United States Department of
Defense has always valued the modeling and simulation of developing technologies as part of the standard acquisitions process [1]. The ability to produce digital prototypes of real-world technologies helps to reduce cost and overall time
spent in the acquisitions cycle. With the introduction of the Navy Research Laboratory's (NRL) Washington D.C. Metropolitan Quantum Network Research
Consortium (DC-QNet), there is a growing interest in developing cutting-edge
simulation methodologies for such quantum communication networks [2].

This research explores the developmental Interpreters module, a bleeding-
edge Python feature for true multi-threading concurrency, and it's potential
usefulness as a tool to improve on the performance of the Simulator of QUantum Network Communication (SeQUeNCe), a discrete-event simulator for quantum networks. Section 2 provides a brief background on the technologies used

D. D. Hodson et al. (Eds.): CSCE 2024, CCIS 2258, pp. 31–41, 2025.
https://doi.org/10.1007/978-3-031-85902-1_5

throughout this research. Section 3 covers an analysis of the parallel implementation of a SeQUeNCe example along with the design methodology of a multi-threaded implementation using the Interpreters module. In Sect. 4, the performance analysis of the threaded implementation is evaluated against the parallel implementation. Finally, our conclusion is laid out in Sect. 5.

2   Background

We first present a brief introduction to the technologies used in this research, including a foundational understanding of discrete event simulation of quantum communication networks in SeQUeNCe and of the developmental Interpreters module from the version 3.12 release of the Python/C API.

2.1   SeQUeNCe Quantum Network Simulator

SeQUeNCe is an open-source software package for the modeling and simulation of quantum communication networks, available on Github [3,4]. Built with Python for ease-of-use, SeQUeNCe provides a user-friendly interface for the rapid-prototyping of simple quantum network simulations.

The simulator consists of five modules to include hardware, application, and entanglement, resource, and network management [5]. A SeQUeNCe simulation typically consists of one or more node objects, each with their own set of hardware component objects whose behavior are governed by customizable protocol classes, that belong to one–or more in the case of a parallel simulation–timeline object. The overall application module contains simulation-specific details such as hardware, logic, and the timeline class, which handles the scheduling and execution of events for all assigned entities based on an internal simulation clock.

Hardware components are objects that represent physical components of a real-world classical or quantum network, such as a photon emitter, memory module, or single photon detector (SPD). Hardware components on a node all inherit from an entity superclass, which provides the framework for all hardware connections on a node. The entity's *get* method is used to receive photons from any hardware component in the entity's *receiver* list.

Optical and classical channels are used to simulate physical fiber-optic connections between nodes and include a set of parameters that can be used to adjust various physical properties such as distance and attenuation.

Entanglement management refers to an object class that is used in the control and manipulation of states within the various hardware components in a network. It manages qubit fidelity, entangles memory modules across nodes, and is responsible for modifying entanglement distances. In the case of a simple Bell State Measurement (BSM) node, an entanglement generation protocol handles the entanglement that occurs from spontaneous parametric down-conversion.

Resource manager modules control and direct the flow of data between the hardware elements for any given node. A memory manager, for instance, manages the quantum memory state, while the rule manager uses pre-defined logic to direct protocols within the node. Similarly, the network management module coordinates and directs protocols of nodes within an overall network. A reservation queue determines if an inbound request can be fulfilled, and if it can, a routing queue forwards the request to the appropriate nodes.

2.2 Python Interpreters Module

Python Enhancement Proposal (PEP) 554 proposed a standard library module that would allow for the instantiation of multiple interpreters in a single process [6]. While the ability to have more than one interpreter–called subinterpreters–is not necessarily a new feature, it was traditionally difficult to use without experiencing errors and race conditions because of Python's global interpreter lock (GIL).

Because Python is an interpreted language, the bytecode created at runtime is handled by a single interpreter that executes instructions sequentially. Even in cases where more than one interpreter exists in a running program, the GIL acts as a mutex to prevent more than one interpreter from operating at a time. This is why the Multithreading library does not provide truly concurrent threads; instead, it creates the illusion of concurrency by repeatedly handing off ownership of the GIL. However, with the acceptance of PEP 684, the concept of a per-interpreter GIL was introduced that would allow for real threading concurrency [7].

At the time of writing, the Interpreters module is exclusively accessible within the Python/C API for version 3.12, with Python API support expected in the version 3.13 release, per PEP 719 [8]. Because this developmental module lacks a Python API interface, it is, for now, intended for a limited user base, serving only a specific subset. Nevertheless, there are resources available that showcase straightforward applications of the module, derived from test cases within the code base [9].

PEP 554 also briefly mentions the intent to introduce *channel* data structures as a means of cross-interpreter data communication [6]. While interpreter channels do exist in the current Interpreters module, they exist only to demonstrate communication within the same interpreter. According to the source code, cross-interpreter channels are not functional [10].

3 Experiment Methodology

The SeQUeNCe software package includes several examples that showcase the ability of the simulator to perform basic functions of real-world quantum networks, like quantum key distribution (QKD) and multiple-node entanglement distribution. Similarly, there are a number of parallel SeQUeNCe examples that showcase several parallel implementations of quantum network simulations using the message-passing interface (MPI). In this paper, we examine the Phold (or parallel hold) example, because of its simplicity and non-reliance on a quantum management server, as the candidate simulation model for redesign with Interpreters support.

3.1   Parallel Hold Model

Although not directly referenced in the SeQUeNCe documentation, parallel hold (Phold) is a widely-used simulation model for evaluating parallel performance benchmarks [11]. The Phold example included as part of the parallel SeQUeNCe package effectively simulates a system of nodes that generate a prescribed quantity of events and uses a conservative synchronization algorithm to ensure that each event is sent to and scheduled on the appropriate node. As the most basic of the included parallel examples, Phold does not include any SeQUeNCe functionality that involves quantum states and, as a result, does not require the quantum manager server that would otherwise be required if quantum states were to be maintained between nodes.

The Phold test script makes use of multiple parallel timeline objects–one per process–to handle event management. Prior to initializing and running the simulation, all of the nodes are distributed across the number of available processes. Each node then produces a number of events and schedules them. If an event belongs to another node, it's added to the timeline's event buffer; otherwise, its scheduled to run on the current timeline. Each timeline is then prompted to begin the simulation.

At the start of the simulation, each timeline communicates the contents of its event buffer to the other timeline objects using a call to the MPI *all-to-all* method. The timeline stores these lists of collected events and clears the event buffer before passing each event to the timeline's *schedule* method. The scheduler pushes the event to the list of events to be executed if it belongs to the current timeline, but adds it back to the event buffer otherwise. After event scheduling, if the event list for the current timeline is not empty, the entire list is iterated over and the processes attached to each event are executed if and only if the event's scheduled time does not lie outside the synchronization window.

3.2   Functionality Milestones

The primary distinction between a typical SeQUeNCe simulation and the Phold example is the utilization of two object classes that leverage MPI features to achieve parallelism: *ParallelTimeline* and *PholdNode*. In order to reproduce the functionality of the Phold simulation with sub-interpreters, the MPI-driven features of these classes must be replaced with those from the Interpreters module. Our solution was the creation of a derivative Python package based on parallel SeQUeNCe that replaced all multi-processing functionality with truly concurrent multi-threading with Interpreters.

As we have already mentioned, an independent package capable of running the Phold model on separate sub-interpreters would require modified versions of the *ParallelTimeline* and *PholdNode* classes because of their heavy use of MPI for simultaneous execution of code and inter-process communication. An Interpreters-based Phold model–which we have tentatively called threaded hold (Thold)–would therefore require the ability to run multiple instances of the same script on multiple sub-interpreters and support for communication between interpreters. To achieve this functionality, we established multiple milestones to demonstrate the capabilities of the constituent elements within our Interpreters-based framework.

Basic Functionality. To set up a basic test of sub-interpreter functionality, we utilize a number of test cases located in the test module of the Python/C API source code as our initial reference [10]. These serve as milestones towards fully integrating the Interpreters module into SeQUeNCe simulations.

The first test involves instantiating a sub-interpreter inside of a thread using Python's threading module, as seen in Listing 1.1. This code segment highlights how Interpreters execute code: a Python program is passed into the sub-interpreter's *run* method. Beforehand, the *dedent* method from the textwrap library ensures proper whitespace alignment within the embedded script. Consequently, everything within this string is executed on the sub-interpreter as an independent script.

Listing 1.1. Spawning and running code on a Python sub-interpreter.

```python
from test.support import interpreters
from threading import Thread
from textwrap import dedent

print(interpreters.get_main())
sub = interpreters.create()

code = dedent("""
    from test.support import interpreters
    print(interpreters.get_current())
    """)

t = Thread(target=sub.run, args=(code,))
t.start()
```

The next test involves structuring our script to resemble a conventional MPI program, running more than one instance of the same script simultaneously. However, in the test shown in Listing 1.2, the script executes on multiple interpreters rather than distinct processes. By leveraging the ability of any interpreter to reference it's own unique identifier, we can restrict certain sections of code to specific interpreters. The design pattern we created in this listing achieves this by checking the current interpreter ID against the main interpreter ID. If these IDs match, the subsequent code segment, which is reserved exclusively for the main interpreter, will spawn a sub-interpreter. If the IDs do not match, then the block of code following the *else* statement will be executed by the sub-interpreter. Everything following the *if-else* statements will be executed on both interpreters.

Additional code restrictions, such as main interpreter's responsibility for managing the cleanup of sub-interpreters following program execution, can be implemented in a similar fashion. That is, by comparing the current interpreter ID with the *get_current* method with either the main or sub-interpreter IDs.

Listing 1.2. Running the same Python script on the main and sub-interpreters.

```python
from test.support import interpreters
from threading import Thread
from textwrap import dedent
import os

main = interpreters.get_main()
cur = interpreters.get_current()

if main.id == cur.id:
    # Run main interpreter-specific code here:
    sub = interpreters.create()
    file_path = os.path.join(os.getcwd(),
        'current_file.py')
    with open(file_path, 'r') as file:
        file_contents = file.read()
    code = dedent(file_contents)

    t = Thread(target=sub.run, args=(code,))
    t.start()

else:
    # Run sub-interpreter code here:
    pass

# Run code on both interpreters here
```

In order to fulfil our aforementioned requirement of cross-interpreter communication, we borrow example code from the *TestSendRecv* test class located in the Interpreters test module. A modified version of the test case that demonstrates sending data over a channel on the main interpreter is shown in Listing 1.3.

Listing 1.3. Passing encoded data over an interpreter channel in the main interpreter.

```python
from test.support import interpreters

recv, send = interpreters.create_channel()
orig = b'spam'
send.send_nowait(orig)
```

```
obj = recv.recv()

print(f"{orig}_==_{obj}")
```

Despite the existence of a number of test cases in the Interpreters test module, comments in the code base indicate that the communications unit tests for reading and writing with different interpreters are broken [10]. However, when we observe the methods used to manage interpreter channels in the support module, along with the attributes and methods contained within the *RecvChannel* and *SendChannel* classes, we see that all of the required functionality for cross-interpreter communication is available regardless of unit test functionality.

In Listing 1.4, we demonstrate simple cross-interpreter communication using interpreter channels. When a channel is created using the *create_channel* method, a tuple containing the receiver and sender channels is returned. Although these channel object variables cannot be directly referenced by or passed as an argument to another interpreter, the *list_all_channels* method from the support module can return a list containing all open interpreter channels. Using this method, determining which channel ends are responsible for the read and write operations on a given interpreter is trivial.

Additionally, the *recv* method of the *RecvChannel* class accepts a float value for delay that is, by default, set to 10 milliseconds. The delay is used to wait for a short period of time after attempting to read from a channel before performing another read operation. For the sake of improving simulation performance, we set this value to zero.

Listing 1.4. Passing encoded data over a channel from the main interpreter to a sub-interpreter.

```
from test.support import interpreters
from threading import Thread
from textwrap import dedent

recv, send = interpreters.create_channel()

code = dedent("""
    from test.support import interpreters
    (recv, send) =
        interpreters.list_all_channels()[0]
    obj = recv.recv(_delay=0)
    print(data)
    """)

orig = b'spam'
send.send_nowait(orig)
```

3.3 Threaded Hold Model

By using Listings 1.1–1.4 as the foundational building blocks, we developed a distinct Python package, which we have tentatively named *thread_timeline*, that we created in support of our Thold test model [12]. Due to a number of limitations with the Interpreters model–which we will discuss more in Sect. 4– this new package required modified versions of several files from SeQUeNCe's code base. The *ParallelTimeline*, and *PholdNode* classes, in particular, required completely new files to replace MPI functionality with the above Interpreters design patterns.

Changes from Parallel to Threads. To replace the MPI features in the Phold test with Interpreters, we look primarily at the *ParallelTimeline* and *PholdNode* classes and the overall Phold test application. Because the Phold test is intended to be executed with MPI, we know that the same Phold test application is run on all processes at once. In order to facilitate this functionality in the Thold test application, we use the Listing 1.2 design pattern as the starting point. In the section of the script we reserved for main interpreter-specific code, we add to our initial design pattern by spawning two sets of send/receive channels–one set per interpreter. In the sub-interpreter code block, we iterate over the groups of interpreter channels generated from the *list_all_channels* method and assign the sub-interpreters send and receive channels to those with IDs matching the sub-interpreter ID. The remainder of the code is executed in much the same way Phold runs, except that the *ParallelTimeline* and *PholdNode* classes are replaced with the *ThreadedTimeline* and *TholdNode* classes, respectively.

The *ThreadedTimeline* class accepts the appropriate send and receive channel objects as constructor arguments and–because the Thold model does not manage quantum states–removes all quantum manager functionality. In addition, the MPI all-to-all communication that occurs in the timeline's *run* method is replaced with simple, synchronized write and read operations from each timeline's event buffer over the proper interpreter channels. The *timeline* super-class is also modified to remove references to the quantum manager and NumPy.

The *TholdNode* class represents a single node that exists simply to generate events and coordinate, schedule, and run them across the entire network of nodes on all timelines. The Interpreters module is not currently supported by NumPy, so the pseudo random number generation (PRNG) functionality that NumPy provides for the *PholdNode* class is replaced in *TholdNode* with methods from Python's standard library. In particular, the *exponential* method from NumPy's random module is replaced with the *expovariate* method, which behaves similarly to *exponential* except that it accepts the reciprocal of the *rate* argument in order to produce similar results, as shown in Fig. 1.

Lastly, the *Entity* class is modified from it's original implementation to remove the reference to a *Photon* object in its *get* method. The PRNG features are also omitted because including generator support would demand more effort than what is necessary within the scope of this research.

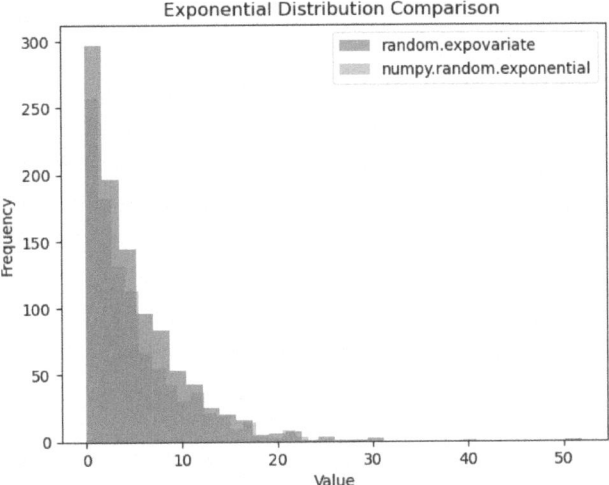

Fig. 1. Comparison of results from the Python standard library's *expovariate* method against NumPy's random exponential distribution.

4   Results and Challenges

In this research, we leveraged the bleeding-edge Python/C API Interpreters module in effort to recreate the parallel SeQUeNCe Phold example with support for true concurrency using threads. Using the Phold model as a benchmark, we evaluated our new Thold model for execution time under various workloads with one node per timeline per interpreter. The results, which are shown in Fig. 2 and Table 1, show the clear improvement of the Thold example over Phold.

Table 1. Simulation execution times (in seconds) for Phold and Thold tests.

init work	Phold execution (sec)	Thold execution (sec)
10	0.204	0.282
100	1.376	0.922
500	5.393	3.426
1,000	11.334	6.974

While the Thold model clearly demonstrates superior performance over the Phold model, numerous issues with the Interpreters module currently hinder its seamless integration with the SeQUeNCe package. For one, the module is still in development. According to PEP 734, multiple interpreters are not expected to become a part of the standard library until the release of Python version 3.13, which according to the Python 3.13 release schedule won't occur until October

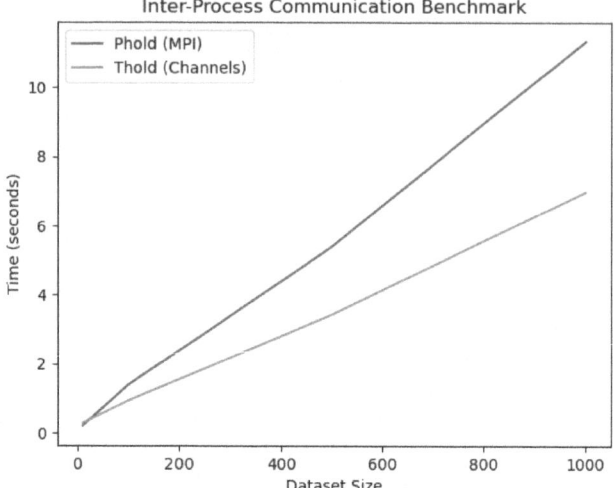

Fig. 2. Execution time benchmark results for Thold test against the parallel SeQUeNCe Phold test.

2024 for the full release [8,13]. In addition, some packages, like NumPy, do not currently support sub-interpreters. Ordinary SeQUeNCe simulations perform massive amounts of mathematical computations through NumPy and extensively employ NumPy for quantum information processing in conjunction with the Quantum Toolbox in Python (QuTiP). Attempting to import NumPy, or any library that references NumPy, inside of a sub-interpreter will immediately throw an import error.

Cross-interpreter communication is also currently still in development. While we were able to implement a workaround for synchronous cross-interpreter data transmission in our Thold model, a means of passing channel objects into sub-interpreter code using string formatting, as outlined in PEP 554, does not work [6].

The SeQUeNCe simulator, despite its release in 2021, suffers from incomplete documentation. Code comments are virtually nonexistent, making the prospect of interpreting component functionality a time-consuming task. Similarly, the official documentation does not adequately cover enough of the core simulator concepts to provide a clear picture of how certain aspects of the environment function. This is especially true of the section of the documentation written for parallel simulation. The SeQUeNCe GitHub repository suffers the same disorganization. Some example files require the user to checkout an entirely separate branch in order for it to work as intended, making it difficult to locate working use-cases. Some files, such as the JSON files for loading network-specific parameters for parallel simulations, are outright missing.

5   Conclusion

In our Thold example, we demonstrated how the discrete-event simulation components of SeQUeNCe could leverage sub-interpreters to improve simulation performance. However, the fledgling nature of these technologies, coupled with the lack of support from third-party packages like NumPy, make the inclusion of the quantum component impossible with the tools available. The Python/C API Interpreters module and the SeQUeNCe simulator are novel technologies that, albeit useful to some extent, are still in development. Further time and refinement are required before they can be meaningfully used in conjunction for the purpose of quantum network simulations.

Disclaimer. The views expressed in this paper are those of the authors and do not reflect the official policy or position of the United States Air Force, the Department of Defense, or the U.S. Government.

References

1. Money, A.: Modeling and simulation in support of the air force acquisition process. SAF/AQ. (1997). https://apps.dtic.mil/sti/tr/pdf/ADA345593.pdf
2. Cage, P.: NRL announces the Washington metropolitan quantum network research consortium (DC-QNET). U.S. Naval Research Laboratory (2022). https://www.nrl.navy.mil/Media/News/Article/3060477
3. Wu, X., Kolar, A., Chung, J., Jin, D., Zhong, T., Kettimuthu, R., Suchara, M.: Sequence: a customizable discrete-event simulator of quantum networks. Quantum Sci. Technol. **6**(4), 045027 (2021). https://doi.org/10.1088/2058-9565/ac22f6
4. Wu, X., et al.: SeQUeNCe: simulator of quantum network communication (2023). https://github.com/sequence-toolbox/SeQUeNCe
5. Welcome to the SeQUeNCe documentation page - SeQUeNCe 0.5.2 documentation. https://sequence-toolbox.github.io/index.html
6. Snow, E.: PEP 554 – Multiple interpreters in the Stdlib. Python.org (2023). https://peps.python.org/pep-0554/
7. Snow, E.: PEP 684 – A per-interpreter GIL. Python.org (2022). https://peps.python.org/pep-0684/
8. Wouters, T.: PEP 719 – Python 3.13 release schedule. Python.org (2023). https://peps.python.org/pep-0719/
9. Heinz, M · Real multithreading is coming to Python   Learn how you can use it now (2023). https://martinheinz.dev/blog/97
10. Python/cpython at 3.12 (2023). https://github.com/python/cpython/tree/3.12
11. Cardoen, B., Manhaeve, S., Tendeloo, Y., Broeckhove, J.: A PDEVS simulator supporting multiple synchronization protocols: implementation and performance analysis. Simulation **94**. (2017). https://doi.org/10.1177/0037549717690826
12. Martin, B.: Brettmartin4/sequence-interpreters: leveraging python interpreters module for use in sequence quantum network simulator (2023). https://github.com/brettmartin4/sequence-interpreters
13. Snow, E.: PEP 734 – Multiple interpreters in the Stdlib. Python.org (2023). https://peps.python.org/pep-0734/

Benchmark Performance of a Rust-Based Python Extension

Ethan J. Schofield and Douglas D. Hodson[✉]

Department of Electrical and Computer Engineering, U.S. Air Force Institute of Technology, WPAFB, Dayton, OH 45433, USA
{ethan.schofield.1,douglas.hodson}@us.af.mil

Abstract. This paper presents a benchmarking analysis comparing the performance of data structures implemented in PyO3 Rust plugins against native Python implementations. The benchmarked data structures include Structure of Arrays (SoA), Array of Structures (AoS), linked lists, and vectors. Rust and Python implementations of each structure were compared, facilitated by PyO3's wrapping functionality. Benchmarks assessed data access and manipulation, running for 100 iterations across varying element sizes. Results revealed the Rust data structures outperformed the native python implementations with the exception of the Rust AoS plugin.

Keywords: Python · Rust · Data-Oriented Design · Benchmark · Performance

1 Introduction

The trade-off between ease of development and runtime performance is a characteristic challenge in Python, where the language's dynamic nature and interpreted execution can lead to increased time complexity for certain operations. As a result, understanding these aspects is crucial when comparing the performance of Python with a statically-typed language like Rust, where memory management decisions are made at compile time and a strong emphasis is placed on achieving high performance. This paper explores these trade-offs by benchmarking data structures implemented in both PyO3 Rust plugins and native Python, shedding light on the comparative efficiency of data access and manipulation across the two languages.

The rest of this paper is organized as follows: Sect. 2 will highlight background information, Sect. 3 will describe the experiment design and results, Sect. 4 will look into future steps, and Sect. 5 contains a conclusion.

2 Background Information

2.1 Python

Python is a dynamically-typed, high-level programming language renowned for its simplicity and readability. Its flexibility allows for rapid development and

D. D. Hodson et al. (Eds.): CSCE 2024, CCIS 2258, pp. 42–49, 2025.
https://doi.org/10.1007/978-3-031-85902-1_6

easy integration of diverse programming paradigms, making it a popular choice for a wide range of applications. One of the key features contributing to Python's appeal is its dynamic typing system, which allows developers to write code without explicitly specifying variable types. While this flexibility promotes ease of use, it comes at the cost of potential runtime overhead, as type checking and conversions occur during program execution.

Python's automatic memory management is facilitated by a garbage collector, which handles the allocation and deallocation of memory, easing the burden on developers. However, the garbage collector's activity introduces inefficiencies in program execution, impacting the overall runtime performance. Additionally, Python's interpreted nature means that certain optimizations and memory management decisions are deferred until runtime, potentially affecting the efficiency of data manipulation tasks.

2.2 Rust

Rust is a statically-typed systems level programming language. It has gained prominence for its emphasis on performance, memory safety, and zero-cost abstractions. At the core of Rust's design philosophy is a focus on empowering developers with fine-grained control over memory management while eliminating common pitfalls such as null references and data races. Unlike interpreted languages like Python, Rust's memory management decisions are made at compile time, allowing for efficient utilization of resources and predictable runtime behavior.

One of Rust's distinctive features is its ownership system, which ensures memory safety without the need for a garbage collector. The ownership system is based on concepts such as ownership, borrowing, and lifetimes, enabling developers to write concurrent and memory-efficient code without sacrificing safety. The absence of a garbage collector means that Rust programs experience minimal runtime overhead related to automatic memory management, resulting in more predictable and consistent performance.

Rust's approach to memory management also extends to its support for low-level control over data layout, cache locality, and alignment. This level of control is particularly evident when utilizing data structures like Structure of Arrays (SoA), where the developer can carefully organize data in memory to optimize cache access patterns. This feature is crucial for achieving high performance in scenarios where memory access speed is a critical factor, such as in scientific computing or high-performance computing applications.

Additionally, Rust's ownership model encourages developers to manage memory efficiently, preventing common issues like memory leaks and dangling pointers. The language also provides abstractions like lifetimes to ensure safe and precise control over memory references. This paper explores how Rust's design choices, including its compile-time memory management and ownership system, influence the performance of various data structures when compared to native Python implementations, shedding light on the advantages and trade-offs associated with Rust's approach to system-level programming.

2.3 PyO3

PyO3 serves as a bridge between the Python and Rust programming languages, allowing developers to seamlessly integrate Rust functionality into Python applications through the creation of Rust plugins. This capability is analogous to the use of C or C++ modules in Python, providing an avenue for leveraging the performance advantages and memory efficiency inherent in Rust while still benefiting from Python's high-level features.

PyO3 enables the implementation of Rust plugins for Python, opening the door to a hybrid development approach that combines the strengths of both languages. Leveraging Rust's memory safety features, such as its ownership system and absence of a garbage collector, PyO3 allows developers to create plugins that not only deliver high performance but also maintain a strong focus on memory safety. This is particularly crucial for scenarios where both speed and reliability are paramount.

Through PyO3, developers can harness Rust's compile-time memory management to ensure efficient resource utilization, while the ownership system helps prevent common memory-related pitfalls, such as data races and memory leaks. This amalgamation of Rust's system-level capabilities with Python's ease of use allows for the development of plugins that exhibit the speed and memory efficiency associated with low-level languages like Rust, without compromising on the safety and expressiveness provided by Python.

In the context of benchmarking data structures, the utilization of PyO3 enables a direct comparison between native Python implementations and their Rust counterparts. This paper explores the performance implications of implementing data structures using PyO3, shedding light on how the integration of Rust into the Python ecosystem influences the efficiency and safety of data manipulation tasks in a mixed-language environment.

3 Experimental Design and Results

The experimental setup was conducted on a system featuring a B650 Tomahawk Wifi motherboard, 32GB DDR5 RAM, and an AMD Ryzen 7 7700X CPU. The operating system utilized was Windows 11 Pro Build 22621.3155. The PyO3 environment was configured through the command line using Maturin 1.4.0, with Python version 3.12.2. The project was initiated using the command *maturin new -bindings pyo3 -mixed projectname*. Subsequently, the project was opened in Visual Studio Code, and a Python virtual environment (version 3.12.2) was established using *python -m venv .venv*. Following virtual environment activation, Maturin installed NumPy and Matplotlib for result plotting. Rust version 1.76.0 was employed, with dependencies outlined in the Cargo.toml file, including PyO3 version 0.20.2 and Rand 0.8.

3.1 Data Structures

This study's benchmarked data structures included SoA, Arrays of Structures (AoS), linked lists, and vectors. A comparative analysis was conducted, juxtaposing SoA with AoS and evaluating linked lists against vectors. Each data structure was meticulously implemented in Rust and subsequently wrapped using PyO3 to enable seamless interaction within Python environments. For each Rust data structure, a Python equivalent was developed, facilitating a direct comparison aimed at assessing performance variances.

The distinction between AoS and SoA is crucial for understanding data organization and its impact on computational efficiency. In Rust, as in C++, AoS encapsulates data as an array of structures, where each structure contains the data for an entity, such as a player in a game. Conversely, SoA organizes data as a structure of arrays, where each array holds one type of data for all entities. This fundamental difference influences memory layout and access patterns, potentially affecting performance.

Listing 1.1. Additional Type Conversion Function Required for AoS.

```
// Implementing FromPyObject for Player
impl<'a> FromPyObject<'a> for Player {
    fn extract(ob: &'a PyAny) -> PyResult<Self> {
        // Extracting attributes from Python object
        let name: String =
            ob.getattr("name")?.extract()?;
        let health: f64 =
            ob.getattr("health")?.extract()?;
        let location: (f64, f64) =
            ob.getattr("loc")?.extract()?;
        let velocity: (f64, f64) =
            ob.getattr("vel")?.extract()?;
        let acceleration: (f64, f64) =
            ob.getattr("acc")?.extract()?;

        Ok(Player { name, health, loc, vel, acc })
    }
}
```

For the AoS implementation, compatibility with Python necessitated an additional layer of wrapper functions to handle type conversions for player attributes which can be seen in Listing 1.1. This requirement stems from the necessity to declare the type of each vector within the Python-calling structure explicitly. In contrast, the SoA implementation did not require special wrapper functions, as its structure naturally facilitated more straightforward type declarations for Python interaction.

Rust's standard LinkedList collection was utilized alongside PyO3 to facilitate its integration into Python. This integration was achieved by encapsulating the LinkedList functionalities within a simple PyO3 wrapper. The wrapper, denoted as PyLinkedList, exposed the LinkedList's operations through methods within a class of the same name. Correspondingly, a Python class named LinkedList was developed to mirror the functionalities of Rust's LinkedList, ensuring a direct comparison of analogous data structures. Additionally, the comparison extended to vectors, with Rust's native Vec¡T¿ being juxtaposed against Python's built-in list type to evaluate performance across different data structures.

3.2   Benchmarking Methodology

Benchmarks encompassed data access and manipulation for each data structure and conducted 100 iterations at each of the following element sizes: [100, 1000, 2000, 5000, 10000, 50000, 100000, 1000000, 3000000, 5000000]. Operations included player position updates based on player velocity for AoS and SoA and integer data access and squaring for linked lists and vectors.

3.3   Procedure

Benchmarking utilized the time.perf counter() function. Each iteration involved generating a new clean structure, initiating a timer, running the structure-testing function, stopping the timer, and calculating the total time and average iteration time for each element size.

Table 1. Benchmark performance of data structures at 5,000,000 elements.

Data Type	Total Time	Average Time per Iteration
Rust SoA	0.737313	0.007373
Rust Linked List	3.303458	0.033035
Rust Vector	7.896567	0.078966
Python AoS	71.201438	0.712014
Python SoA	73.182115	0.731821
Python Linked List	19.054834	0.190548
Python Vector	20.201626	0.202016
Rust AoS	436.129552	4.361296

3.4   Results

In Python, both AoS and SoA performed similarly, as Python's memory management is handled by a garbage collector and does not emphasize data-oriented design. Consequently, structuring the data in SoA in Python does not yield a significant performance increase, unlike in languages that exploit memory storage in relation to the CPU. Rust, with its focus on data-oriented design, demonstrates this capability with the Rust SoA implementation exhibiting the best

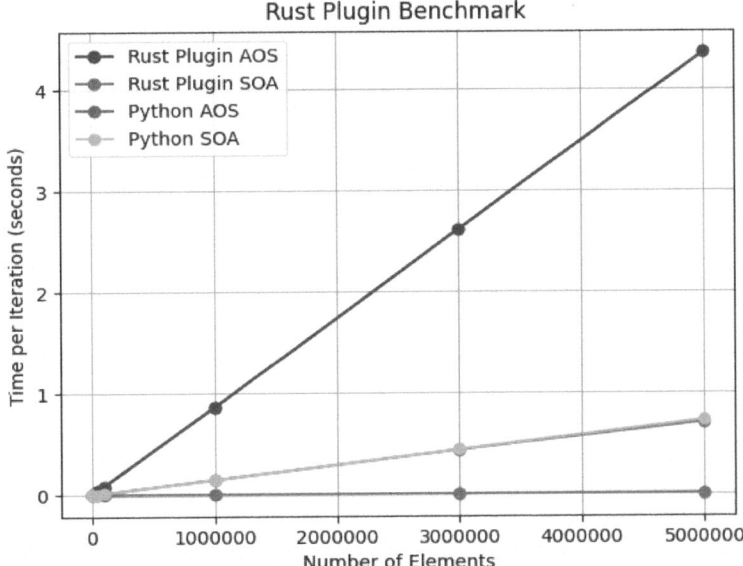

Fig. 1. Rust and Python SoA vs AoS Benchmarks

performance. TIn Rust, rapid memory access is achieved through its ownership and borrowing system, which allows for precise control over memory allocation and deallocation. This system enables Rust to minimize runtime overhead by eliminating the need for a garbage collector. The ownership model ensures that only one part of the code can have mutable access to data at a time, reducing contention and improving memory access efficiency. As a result, the Rust SoA implementation in the context of the benchmark outperforms other approaches, showcasing the language's prowess in optimizing data-oriented designs for superior performance. Additionally, PyO3 seamlessly converts between Rust's vector data type and Python's list data type. Consequently, for this implementation, the overhead of transitioning from Python to Rust is minimized, given that the Rust implementation utilizes vectors to store player data (Figs. 1 and 2).

Figure 3 displays results for linked lists and vectors. Notably, the Rust Linked List plugin outperformed the Python Linked List, while the Rust Vector plugin similarly surpassed its Python counterpart. The simplicity of the Rust Vector's wrapper, compared to the AoS plugin, likely contributed to its superior performance. In Table 1 it shows the Rust linked list outperformed the Python linked list by 0.1575 s per iteration and the Rust vector outperformed the Python vector by about 0.12305 s per iteration.

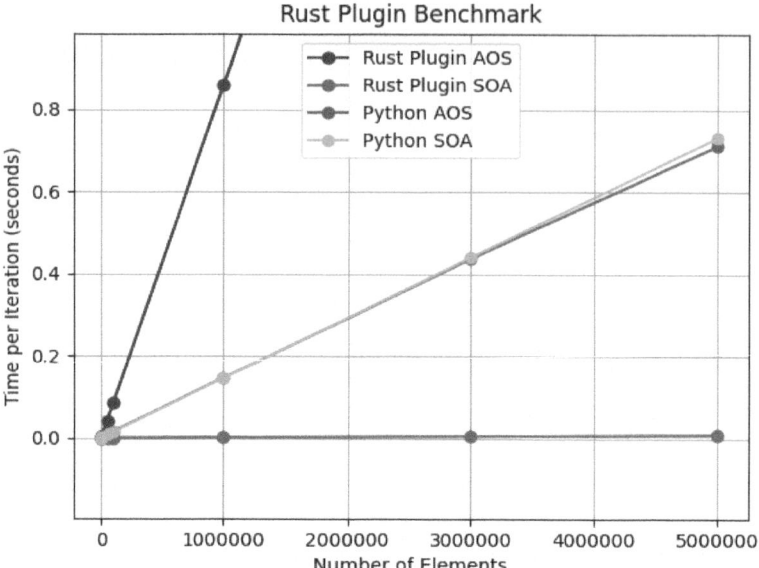

Fig. 2. Rust and Python SoA vs AoS Benchmarks Zoomed

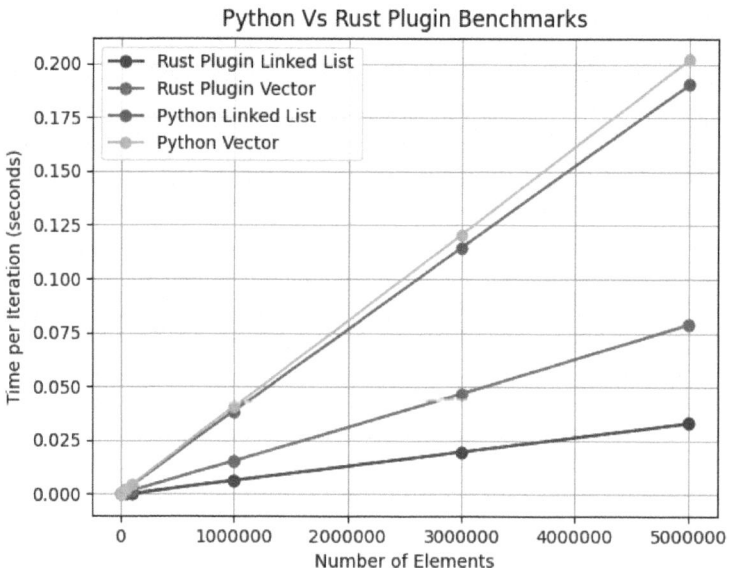

Fig. 3. Rust and Python Linked List and Vector Benchmarks

4   Future Steps

Investigating further into benchmarking performance of other data structures like trees and graphs may be a next step. Additionally, further testing of using a plugin like this in a Python project should be tested. Python is primarily built around ease of use, so if the Rust plugin through PyO3 is not easy to use in some circumstances then it may make sense to use pure Python. Furthermore, if performance is a serious concern then using Rust or another low level programming language may be the solution instead of trying to implement better performance into Python.

5   Conclusion

In conclusion, PyO3 offers a powerful tool for implementing Rust built plugins for Python. This can dramatically increase the time taken to process data and run programs in Python. This tool offers sizeable performance increases when all the data manipulation and processing can be done in Rust. However, if there is a need to alter the data in both Rust and Python then using PyO3 may be a sub optimal choice as moving the data structure to and from PyO3 introduces overhead with each conversion between the languages. This paper showed that implementing SoA in Rust provided significant performance improvements over both Python AoS and SoA implementations. This paper also showed that both Rust linked lists and vectors outperformed their Python counterparts.

Disclaimer. The views expressed in this paper are those of the authors and do not reflect the official policy or position of the United States Air Force, the Department of Defense, or the U.S. Government.

References

1. Klabnik, S., Nichols, C.: The rust programming language. https://doc.rust-lang.org/beta/book/index.html
2. McMurray, J.: An introduction to data oriented design with rust (2020). https://jamesmcm.github.io/blog/intro-dod/
3. PyO3 user guide. https://pyo3.rs/v0.20.3/
4. Rossum, G. V.: Glue it all together with python. https://www.python.org/doc/essays/omg-darpa-mcc-position/
5. Comparing python to other languages. https://www.python.org/doc/essays/comparisons/

Quantum Error Correction in Repetition Codes

James A. Williams, Douglas D. Hodson$^{(\boxtimes)}$, and Laurence D. Merkle

Department of Electrical and Computer Engineering, U.S. Air Force Institute of
Technology, WPAFB, OH 45433, USA
{james.williams.252,douglas.hodson,laurence.merkle}@us.af.mil

Abstract. This paper explores the extension of classical error correction
techniques to quantum codes, elucidating the opportunities and challenges therein. By using a Repetition code, the author shows how the
formalism of encoding, error propagation, error recovery via a MWPM
decoder, and decoding work in the regime of quantum circuits. Some
pitfalls are mentioned, and the work concludes with potential future
research avenues for partial completion of a masters degree in computer
science at AFIT.

Keywords: Quantum repetition code · stabilizer generator error
syndrome and the syndrome graph · error chains · decoders

1 Introduction

1.1 Motivation

Quantum states are described as "probability waves" through vectors in Hilbert
space, an infinite dimensional vector space that admits time-dependant, oscil-
lating complex amplitudes - which need to be summed before they are squared
(resulting in a unique take on probability theory). The most fundamental quantum system is a Two-Level System (TLS), which can be written as a superposition of the ground and excited states of an atom, for example, where
$|\psi\rangle = c_g|g\rangle + c_e|e\rangle$ such that $\sum |c_i|^2 = 1$.

Quantum Algorithms rely on properties of superposition to enable their
computational speedup. Simple examples include the Deutsche-Joza algorithm,
where the oracle only needs to be polled once to determine balanced inputs [3].
In order to perform any quantum algorithm, we need to maintain the quantum
superposition that is so powerful in the "amplitude engineering" that generally
guides, with high probability, quantum algorithms to acceptable solution(s). We
can loosely think of a quantum algorithm as a set of quantum states that prop-
agate through a maze of logic gates, emerging at the end to an eigenstate that
has eigenvalues (probability amplitudes) that interfere to form a bitstring that
corresponds to our answer.

Quantum states themselves are sensitive to both bit- and phase-flip errors
that can destroy superposition (if a bit-flip error occurs on a superposition state,

D. D. Hodson et al. (Eds.): CSCE 2024, CCIS 2258, pp. 50–61, 2025.
https://doi.org/10.1007/978-3-031-85902-1_7

we could alter the desired interference effects $|\psi\rangle \xrightarrow{X} b|0\rangle + a|1\rangle)$. Furthermore, measurement of a superposition state collapses the quantum information therein. For example: If $|\psi\rangle = a|0\rangle + b|1\rangle$ is measured in the standard $|0\rangle$ basis, one obtains, by the Born Rule: $|\langle 0|\psi\rangle|^2 = |a|^2$, and the act of measurement will project the wavefunction into the post-measurement state $|0\rangle$.

1.2   Precis of Quantum Error Correction

Quantum Error Correction is a field of study that generally uses "Entanglement to Fight Entanglement" [4]. If we can design a circuit that is redundant, in that our quantum information is now encoded into a higher dimensional subspace (called a "logical qubit") that is itself composed of many quantum TLS acting in tandem (aka, "physical qubits"), we can introduce new lines called ancilla qubits, and perform entangling operations between the ancilla and the data qubits (using CNOT gates). Then, when we measure the ancilla, we can find from the correlations (entanglements) what the data qubits are doing, even though we did not disturb them by a direct projective measurement (e.g. the post-measurement state is an invariant of the input state). This paper will discuss the means by which we build this circuit, use the ancilla measurement to determine the location of errors, and apply appropriate logical operations to correct our information. To be sure, we will not decode the qubits until the entirety of the computation is complete.

Noise arises in qubits due to several sources: not all two-level systems are perfect, and they can be perturbed by interactions with the environment, by neighboring qubits, and by noise in the measurement and logic gates themselves. If some particles from the environment are entangled with our system of interest, and atoms in the bulk are entangled with those, we have a coupled noise source, akin to environmental measurement errors that generally manifests in our system as amplitude damping and phase noise. Such fluctuations can cause our quantum information to scatter into the environment, and make any quantum computation hopelessly useless. This can be visualized well on the Bloch Sphere: If the density matrix of the information tends towards one-half of the identity, we say that the quantum state is purely mixed, and all information has collapsed into the classical realm.

We wish to protect quantum information against the effects of noise and decoherence, and do so through a group of logical gates known as a stabilizer code. A Stabilizer code uses XYZ Pauli operators with a joint eigenvalue of $+1$. This will be explored in Sect. 2.2.

This paper uses a CSS stabilizer code, short for the inventors: Calderbank, Shor, and Steane. [13]. A CSS stabilizer is a set of generators that satisfy the union of I, X and Z errors. Selecting a handful of operations from the family of **stabilizers**, we can produce a **generator** (also known as "check operators"). This generator is sequence of logical gates that encodes our quantum information into a protected subspace. If we measure the results of a generator code on our system, we obtain a value known as the error syndrome. If the error syndrome is zero, the generators commute with the error. If the error syndrome is one, the generators anticommute with the error [5]. These operations will be described in Sect. 3.2.

Once we have the error syndrome, we need to use a decoder (like the MWPM algorithm) to find the appropriate recovery operations. Section 2, will describe how the Minimum Weight Perfect Matching (MWPM) algorithm can be used to determine the appropriate error syndrome, shown more directly in Sect. 3. Finally, Sect. 4 will look into how this can be extended to MS thesis work, summarizing in the Sect. 5.

2   Background Information

2.1   Discretization of Quantum Errors

Even though the time-evolution of a quantum system is continuous (as represented by continuous rotations on the Bloch sphere), we can discretize or digitalize errors via the Pauli operators. Once the errors are discretized, we can map by analogy to classical error correction, our quantum codes. In particular, any 2×2 matrix A can be represented by 4-dimensional vector of Pauli matrices, such that any single-qubit gate can be decomposed into an arbitrary linear superposition of the Pauli operators:

$$A = \vec{\xi} \cdot \vec{\sigma} = a\mathbb{I} + bX + cY + dZ$$

This means any error can be expanded into a linear combination of X, Y, and Z errors (or no error, as represented by the identity matrix).

2.2   The Eigenspace of the Pauli Operators

In order to understand this more fully, we need to explore the algebra of Pauli operators. In this section, we will look at the eigenspace of these matrices, and extend them to higher-dimensions required of repetition codes.

Pauli matrices are defined by a cyclic permutation rule as follows: $XZ = iY$. From this relation, we see that $ZX = -iY$, quickly showing that X and Z operators commute with each other. Furthermore, the Pauli operators are SU(2), Special: determinant ± 1, Unitary: their inverse is their complex conjugate transpose, and is equal to itself, and (2) for 2-dimensional. If you exclude the identity matrix, the Pauli operators are also traceless. Unitarity implies $\sigma_i^2 = \mathbb{I}$. Through this relation, we see that Pauli matrices commute with themselves.

It also behooves us to calculate the eigenspaces of each Pauli matrix. The eigenvalue of the identity matrix $\mathbb{I}_2$ is 1 with multiplicity 2, yielding any orthonormal basis, as summarized by the completeness relation: $\mathbb{I} = \sum_i |i\rangle\langle i|$.

The eigenvalues of X are ± 1 and correspond to the Hadamard basis $|+\rangle = \frac{1}{\sqrt{2}} \begin{pmatrix} 1 \\ 1 \end{pmatrix}$ for the $+1$ eigenvalue, and $|-\rangle = \frac{1}{\sqrt{2}} \begin{pmatrix} 1 \\ -1 \end{pmatrix}$ for the -1 eigenvalue.

The eigenvalues for Z are ± 1, and correspond to the Computational basis $|0\rangle$ for the positive eigenvalue and $|1\rangle$ for the negative eigenvalue.

The Y operator has eigenvalues ± 1, corresponding to eigenvectors $|y_+\rangle = \frac{1}{\sqrt{2}}\begin{pmatrix} i \\ -1 \end{pmatrix}$ and $|y_-\rangle = \frac{1}{\sqrt{2}}\begin{pmatrix} i \\ 1 \end{pmatrix}$.

We can therefore expand the Pauli operators into their respective eigenbases to obtain:

$$X = 1|+\rangle\langle+| - 1|-\rangle\langle-|$$

$$Z = 1|0\rangle\langle0| - 1|1\rangle\langle1|$$

In order to find the Pauli-Y, we can apply the cyclic permutation rule and transform the formula to match the aforementioned eigenvalues, thereby finding an eigenstate composed of a mixture of $+$ and $-$ Hadamard bases vectors:

$$Y = \frac{i}{\sqrt{2}}\left(|0\rangle\langle1| + |1\rangle\langle0|\right) \rightarrow i\left(|+\rangle\langle-| - |-\rangle\langle+|\right)$$

Just as an X operation on the standard basis is a bit flip, and the Z operation is a phase flip; when we change to the Hadamard basis, the X operation introduces a -1 phase, and the Z operation flips the basis states from $|+\rangle$ to $|-\rangle$. In order to understand the error syndrome, we also need to understand the controlled-not gate in both the standard basis and the Hadamard basis representations.

2.3   The Controlled-NOT (Quantum) Gate

We will stipulate that the CNOT gate is the gate that, when operating on a set of two qubits (control and the target), will perform a bit flip (a not gate) on the target qubit if and only if the control qubit is 1. This operation is a combination of projectors leading to the identity operation on the first qubit and the bit flip operation on the second qubit. This can be written in Dirac notation as follows: $C|00\rangle = |00\rangle$; $C|01\rangle = |01\rangle$; $C|10\rangle = |11\rangle$; $C|11\rangle = |10\rangle$

Reconstructing the matrix C gives:

$$C = \begin{pmatrix} 1 & 0 & 0 & 0 \\ 0 & 1 & 0 & 0 \\ 0 & 0 & 0 & 1 \\ 0 & 0 & 1 & 0 \end{pmatrix}$$

Let's look at what the two-qubit states look like in the Hadamard basis. By writing the tensor products of every permutation of $\{|+\rangle, |-\rangle\}$ like the example below, we can write our CNOT gate in the Hadamard basis representation.

$$|++\rangle = \tfrac{1}{2}(|00\rangle + |01\rangle + |10\rangle + |11\rangle) = \tfrac{1}{2}\begin{pmatrix} 1 \\ 1 \\ 1 \\ 1 \end{pmatrix}.$$

Ultimately, we reconstruct our CNOT as: $C|++\rangle = |++\rangle$; $C|+-\rangle = |--\rangle$; $C|-+\rangle = |-+\rangle$; $C|--\rangle = |+-\rangle$

This makes the CNOT in the Hadamard Basis:

$$\frac{1}{2} \begin{pmatrix} 1 & 1 & 1 & 1 \\ 1 & -1 & 1 & -1 \\ 1 & 1 & -1 & -1 \\ 1 & -1 & -1 & 1 \end{pmatrix}$$

2.4   Encoding: The 3-Qubit Repetition Code

The basic scheme of error correction is to protect information (0,1) through a redundant encoding. In quantum systems, an unknown state cannot be copied: a result known as the no-cloning theorem. We therefore need to build our redundancy in another way.

For a 3-qubit repetition code, we find that the following encoding protects against single qubit X errors [8]:

$$|0\rangle_{\text{code}} = |\overline{0}\rangle = |000\rangle$$

$$|1\rangle_{\text{code}} = |\overline{1}\rangle = |111\rangle$$

We can also transform each 0 and 1 to the Hadamard basis to correct against single-qubit Z errors:

$$|+\rangle_{\text{code}} = |\overline{+}\rangle = |+++\rangle$$

$$|-\rangle_{\text{code}} = |\overline{-}\rangle = |---\rangle$$

We note that this repetition code is different from cloning the quantum state, as $|\psi\psi\psi\rangle = (a|0\rangle + b|1\rangle)^{\otimes 3}$, which is an entangled state.

2.5   The Recovery Operation

These codes can then be concatenated to ensure we can correct against both X and Z errors on single-qubits in the chain, and we thereby obtain a 9 qubit code. Below, we show a simple 3 qubit version, augmented with 2 ancilla qubit lines. Once we have encoded the state, it will undergo errors. We need to find a way to perform a recovery procedure to correct for these errors. Supposing our codeword is $|\psi\rangle$, and our recovery operation is R, and some state $|\phi\rangle$ where the errors have moved away from the data qubits, we find that for some error string $E = \alpha\mathbb{I} + \beta X + \gamma Y + \delta Z$ that occurs on the jth qubit:

$$R(E|\psi\rangle) = |\psi\rangle \otimes (\alpha|\phi_{X_j}\rangle + \beta|\phi_{Y_j}\rangle + \gamma|\phi_{Z_j}\rangle + \delta|\phi_{\mathbb{I}_j}\rangle)$$

3   Experimental Design and Results

3.1   Brief Description of the MWPM Algorithm

The Minimum Weight Perfect Matching (MWPM) Algorithm was first published by Jack Edmonds in 1965 [1,2]. Edmonds won the 1985 John von Neumann

Theory Prize [12] for his contributions to the theory of efficient combinatorial algorithms. Even though the MWPM algorithm contains two subroutines: (1) Blossom Algorithm (2) "path finding algorithms". [5] the MWPM algorithm is frequently refered to as the "Blossom Algorithm", and is used to find the path of minimum weight within a graph.

A decoder takes in the error syndrome and attempts to find the recovery operation. The MWPM algorithm can solve for X and Z errors in a quantum circuit efficiently. Here we will explore the MWPM for a repetition code (Later, we will apply it to a surface code; see citation 6 in PyMatching paper). In our incarnation, the vertices of the graph correspond to "endpoints of error chains in a quantum computer" [6], whereas the edges are weighted by the number of errors required to link them. The number of vertices increases as the circuit is running and the errors continue to accrue [6].

The steps of a MWPM decoder is to [5]:

1. Check that a single qubit Z anticommutes with two XX stabilizers.
2. Generate the matching graph, where each node is an X check operator, and each edge is a single-qubit Z error
3. Find the Errors
4. Calculate the Syndrome Graph
5. Determine the MWPM (the minimum weight error consistent with the syndrome)
6. Perform the corrections

Before we can understand the MWPM algorithm, we need to understand how to extract an error syndrome from an encoded quantum state. Let's initialize the below circuit such that the input qubits are $|\psi\rangle = \alpha|\overline{0}\rangle + \beta|\overline{1}\rangle$, with the ancilla initialized to $|00\rangle$ (Fig. 1).

Note that the measurement of the ancilla (the last two qubits in the chain) gives us the error syndrome. The first measurement asks: are the first two qubits the same or different? The second measurement asks: are the second and third qubits the same or different?

Let's suppose an X error occurred on the second qubit in our quantum register. If we divide the circuit into pieces and calculate the wavefunction at each step, we obtain the following:

$$\alpha|010\rangle|00\rangle + \beta|101\rangle|00\rangle$$

$$\alpha|010\rangle|00\rangle + \beta|101\rangle|10\rangle$$

$$\alpha|010\rangle|10\rangle + \beta|101\rangle|10\rangle$$

$$\alpha|010\rangle|11\rangle + \beta|101\rangle|10\rangle$$

$$\alpha|010\rangle|11\rangle + \beta|101\rangle|11\rangle$$

Finally, upon measurement, we obtain the error syndrome $|11\rangle$ in both cases, which shows us that the first and second qubit are different, and the second and third qubits are different. Furthermore, the act of measurement on this

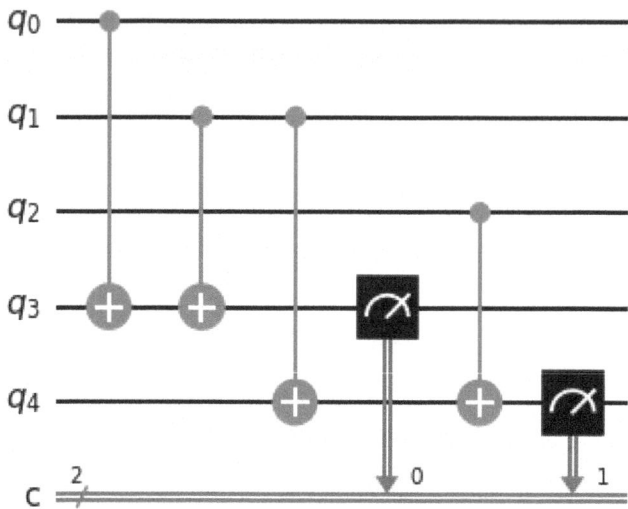

Fig. 1. Calculating the Error Syndrome for a Quantum Repetition Code

state did not affect our data qubits. This is because our post measurement state collapses back to the original input wavefunction (albeit, with errors). The recovery operation for this circuit would therefore be to place an X operator on each of the second qubits. Knowing that we input a repetition code, measuring the parity in this way allows us to pinpoint that the second qubit has an X error (for if the second qubit had a Z error, the encoded zero would remain unchanged, and the encoded 1 would accrue a -1 phase). This procedure uses the MWPM algorithm in the following way: a single X operator represents the minimum number of errors that could have occurred (1 X operator), rather than any other odd number of Xs and even number of Zs.

3.2 Stabilizer Algebra

Now we want to build a bit of intuition about the stabilizer algebra. If our encoded state is $|\psi\rangle = \alpha|000\rangle + \beta|111\rangle$, then the Z operator will check the parity of the two qubits as follows: If we separate these by parity, we find the even parity:

$$Z \otimes Z \otimes \mathbb{I}|000\rangle = +1|000\rangle$$

$$Z \otimes Z \otimes \mathbb{I}|001\rangle = +1|001\rangle$$

$$Z \otimes Z \otimes \mathbb{I}|100\rangle = +1|110\rangle$$

$$Z \otimes Z \otimes \mathbb{I}|111\rangle = +1|111\rangle$$

and the odd parity:

$$Z \otimes Z \otimes \mathbb{I}|010\rangle = -1|010\rangle$$

$$Z \otimes Z \otimes \mathbb{I}|010\rangle = -1|011\rangle$$

$$Z \otimes Z \otimes \mathbb{I}|100\rangle = -1|100\rangle$$

$$Z \otimes Z \otimes \mathbb{I}|100\rangle = -1|101\rangle$$

This shows us that our three-qubit repetition code is stabilized by $Z \otimes Z \otimes \mathbb{I}$ and $\mathbb{I} \otimes Z \otimes Z$. Of course, X will measure the parity in the Hadamard basis.

3.3   The Bell Basis

We can generate the Bell Pairs by initializing a qubit in either 0 or 1, tacking on another qubit in 0 or 1, applying the Hadamard to the first qubit, and applying the CNOT to the pair. To apply the Hadamard only to the first qubit but not the second, we would have $H \otimes \mathbb{I}$. To apply the Hadamard only to the second qubit, but not the first, we would have $\mathbb{I} \otimes H$. To apply the Hadamard to both qubits, we would have $H \otimes H$ This sequence of operations generates the following Bell Pairs $|\psi^\pm\rangle, |\phi^\pm\rangle$:

$$|\psi^+\rangle = \frac{1}{\sqrt{2}}(|0\rangle_A|0\rangle_B + |1\rangle_A|1\rangle_B)$$

$$|\phi^+\rangle = \frac{1}{\sqrt{2}}(|0\rangle_A|1\rangle_B + |1\rangle_A|0\rangle_B)$$

$$|\psi^-\rangle = \frac{1}{\sqrt{2}}(|0\rangle_A|0\rangle_B - |1\rangle_A|1\rangle_B)$$

$$|\phi^+\rangle = \frac{1}{\sqrt{2}}(|0\rangle_A|1\rangle_B - |1\rangle_A|0\rangle_B)$$

We note that the $|\psi^\pm\rangle$ states have a correlation: qubit A always equals Qubit B, but it can carry the phase information. etc. For $|\phi^\pm\rangle$ states, we have an anti-correlation: qubit A is always opposite of Qubit B, subject to some phase information.

3.4   What Do These Bell States Look Like in the Hadamard Basis?

You could write the original Hadamard in the +-basis, and then you would just need to know what the CNOT looks like. After some algebraic manipulation, we obtain the same Bell states:

$$\frac{1}{\sqrt{2}}(|++\rangle_{AB} + |--\rangle_{AB})$$

$$\frac{1}{\sqrt{2}}(|++\rangle_{AB} - |+-\rangle_{AB})$$

$$\frac{1}{\sqrt{2}}(|-+\rangle_{AB} + |--\rangle_{AB})$$

$$\frac{1}{\sqrt{2}}(|-+\rangle_{AB} - |+-\rangle_{AB})$$

3.5   Writing the Stabilizers in the Bell Basis

If we wish to extend this to two qubits, we leverage the tensor-product operations and obtain the following 16 operators [cite YouTube]:

$$I \otimes I, I \otimes X, I \otimes Y, I \otimes Z$$

$$X \otimes I, X \otimes X, X \otimes Y, X \otimes Z$$

$$Y \otimes I, Y \otimes X, Y \otimes Y, Y \otimes Z$$

$$Z \otimes I, Z \otimes X, Z \otimes Y, Z \otimes Z$$

We can use a property of the tensor product to quickly find the eigenvalues and eigenvectors of such superoperators.

By looking specifically at $|\psi^+\rangle = \begin{pmatrix} 1 \\ 0 \\ 0 \\ 1 \end{pmatrix}$ and $|\psi^-\rangle = \begin{pmatrix} 1 \\ 0 \\ 0 \\ -1 \end{pmatrix}$, we see that

$$|\psi^+\rangle\langle\psi^+| = \begin{pmatrix} 1 & 0 & 0 & 1 \\ 0 & 0 & 0 & 0 \\ 0 & 0 & 0 & 0 \\ 1 & 0 & 0 & 1 \end{pmatrix}, \text{ and } |\psi^-\rangle\langle\psi^-| = \begin{pmatrix} 1 & 0 & 0 & -1 \\ 0 & 0 & 0 & 0 \\ 0 & 0 & 0 & 0 \\ -1 & 0 & 0 & 1 \end{pmatrix}$$

We also see the state $|\phi^+\rangle\langle\phi^+| = \begin{pmatrix} 0 \\ 1 \\ 1 \\ 0 \end{pmatrix} \langle\phi^+| = \begin{pmatrix} 0 & 0 & 0 & 0 \\ 0 & 1 & 1 & 0 \\ 0 & 1 & 1 & 0 \\ 0 & 0 & 0 & 0 \end{pmatrix}$, with $|\phi^-\rangle\langle\phi^-| =$

$$\begin{pmatrix} 0 \\ 1 \\ -1 \\ 0 \end{pmatrix} \langle\phi^-| = \begin{pmatrix} 0 & 0 & 0 & 0 \\ 0 & 1 & -1 & 0 \\ 0 & -1 & 1 & 0 \\ 0 & 0 & 0 & 0 \end{pmatrix}$$

Finally, we can perform the operations for the mixtures of Bell states,

$$|\psi^+\rangle\langle\phi^+| = \begin{pmatrix} 0 & 1 & 1 & 0 \\ 0 & 0 & 0 & 0 \\ 0 & 0 & 0 & 0 \\ 0 & 1 & 1 & 0 \end{pmatrix} \text{ and } |\psi^-\rangle\langle\phi^-| = \begin{pmatrix} 0 & 1 & -1 & 0 \\ 0 & 0 & 0 & 0 \\ 0 & 0 & 0 & 0 \\ 0 & -1 & 1 & 0 \end{pmatrix}$$

we see that we can write the X stabilizer in terms of this basis: First we calculate

$$X \otimes X = \begin{pmatrix} 0X & 1X \\ 1X & 0X \end{pmatrix} = \begin{pmatrix} 0 & 0 & 0 & 1 \\ 0 & 0 & 1 & 0 \\ 0 & 1 & 0 & 0 \\ 1 & 0 & 0 & 0 \end{pmatrix}$$

$$= \frac{1}{2} \left(|\phi^+\rangle\langle\phi^+| + |\psi^+\rangle\langle\psi^+| - |\phi^-\rangle\langle\phi^-| - |\psi^-\rangle\langle\psi^-| \right)$$

Notice that for the X stabilizer, the Bell states will + configuration have eigenvalue +1, and the Bell states with - configuration have eigenvalue −1. Similarly, for the Z stabilizer:

$$Z \otimes Z = \begin{pmatrix} 1Z & 0Z \\ 0Z & -1Z \end{pmatrix} = \begin{pmatrix} 1 & 0 & 0 & 0 \\ 0 & -1 & 0 & 0 \\ 0 & 0 & -1 & 0 \\ 0 & 0 & 0 & 1 \end{pmatrix}$$

$$= \frac{1}{2} \left(|\psi^+\rangle\langle\psi^+| + |\psi^-\rangle\langle\psi^-| - |\phi^-\rangle\langle\phi^-| - |\phi^+\rangle\langle\phi^+| \right)$$

Notice that the Z stabilizer has positive eigenvalues for the psi states, and negative eigenvalues for the phi states. Furthermore, because each set of stabilizers is written in the Bell basis, the set of eigenstates are the same for each stabilizer.

How can we calculate the commutation relations required for applying the MWPM algorithm? (Recall item 1: Check that a single qubit Z anticommutes with two XX stabilizers.)

$$Z \otimes X \otimes X + X \otimes X \otimes Z$$

$$= \begin{pmatrix} 1 & 0 \\ 0 & -1 \end{pmatrix} \otimes \begin{pmatrix} 0 & 0 & 0 & 1 \\ 0 & 0 & 1 & 0 \\ 0 & 1 & 0 & 0 \\ 1 & 0 & 0 & 0 \end{pmatrix} + \begin{pmatrix} 0 & 0 & 0 & 1 \\ 0 & 0 & 1 & 0 \\ 0 & 1 & 0 & 0 \\ 1 & 0 & 0 & 0 \end{pmatrix} \otimes \begin{pmatrix} 1 & 0 \\ 0 & -1 \end{pmatrix}$$

We see that $Z \otimes X \otimes X$ is:

$$= \begin{pmatrix} 0 & 0 & 0 & 1 & 0 & 0 & 0 & 0 \\ 0 & 0 & 1 & 0 & 0 & 0 & 0 & 0 \\ 0 & 1 & 0 & 0 & 0 & 0 & 0 & 0 \\ 1 & 0 & 0 & 0 & 0 & 0 & 0 & 0 \\ 0 & 0 & 0 & 0 & 0 & 0 & 0 & -1 \\ 0 & 0 & 0 & 0 & 0 & 0 & -1 & 0 \\ 0 & 0 & 0 & 0 & 0 & -1 & 0 & 0 \\ 0 & 0 & 0 & 0 & -1 & 0 & 0 & 0 \end{pmatrix}$$

and $X \otimes X \otimes Z$ is:

$$\begin{pmatrix} 0 & 0 & 0 & 0 & 0 & 0 & 1 & 0 \\ 0 & 0 & 0 & 0 & 0 & 0 & 0 & -1 \\ 0 & 0 & 0 & 0 & 1 & 0 & 0 & 0 \\ 0 & 0 & 0 & 0 & 0 & -1 & 0 & 0 \\ 0 & 0 & 1 & 0 & 0 & 0 & 0 & 0 \\ 0 & 0 & 0 & -1 & 0 & 0 & 0 & 0 \\ 1 & 0 & 0 & 0 & 0 & 0 & 0 & 0 \\ 0 & -1 & 0 & 0 & 0 & 0 & 0 & 0 \end{pmatrix}$$

Clearly, these matrices do not commute.

4   Future Steps

In the author's opinion, this work was used as a mental exercise to begin thinking about the tools and techniques used in QECC. Glaring ommisions include, but are not limited to discussion of Hamming distance and Hamming weight, as well as the Hamming Parity Check Matrix. More exploration into the theory of generators and the decoding operation needs to be performed. One should also extend these techniques to a classical Shannon communication channel. The depolarizing noise model, a common selection for simple quantum circuits was not discussed. Furthermore, Monte Carlo trials to estimate logical error rates. Numerous libraries such as PyMatching, Autotune and QECSIM can be applied to this process.

Future work will apply the MWPM algorithm to surface codes: a type of toric code that is more robust than the simple repetition code. These surface codes transform a quantum circuit with four qubits into a two-dimensional grid composed of plaquette and vertex operators. Each of these have their own quantum observables, and the error correction is performed by analyzing paths throughout this lattice. Certain topological tricks, such as the introduction of exchange statistics via anyons, are then applied to this code. There is also little discussion of Fault Tolerance and the gate fidelities required to reach it. Another research question is: which of the following leading technologies is most likely to reach fault tolerant quantum computing first: crystalline lattice Ion traps, superconducting Josephson Junction qubits in the transmon regime, neutral systems such as Rydberg atoms or Bose Einstein Condensate, or semiconducting systems such as quantum dots?

5   Conclusion

This paper showed how to apply the MWPM algorithm to a quantum repetition code: extracting the error syndrome from a stabilizer, extending the stabilizer algebra to the uniquely quantum Bell states, and showed how this code could be extended, paving the way for future work and simulations in quantum error correction

Disclaimer. The views expressed in this paper are those of the authors and do not reflect the official policy or position of the United States Air Force, the Department of Defense, or the U.S. Government.

References

1. Edmonds, J.: Paths, trees, and flowers. Can. J. Math. **17**, 449–467 (1965)
2. Edmonds, J.: Maximum matching and a polyhedron with 0,1-vertices. J. Res. Natl. Bureau Standards-B Math. Math. Phys. 69B Nos. 1 and 2 (1965)
3. Jordan, S.: Quantum algorithm zoo (2022)

4. Preskill, J.: Reliable quantum computers. Ser. A Math. Phys. Eng. Sci. **454**(1969), 385–410 (1998). https://doi.org/10.1098/rspa.1998.0167

5. Higgott, O.: PyMatching: a python package for decoding quantum codes with minimum-weight perfect matching (2021). arXiv:2105.13082 [quant-ph]

6. Fowler, A.G.: Minimum weight perfect matching of fault-tolerant topological quantum error correction in average o(1) parallel time (2014). arXiv:1307.1740 [quant-ph]

7. Houck, A.: Surface Codes and Quantum Error Correction (2017). https://www.youtube.com/watch?v=BgmqtLQz27A

8. Shor, P.: Quantum error correcting codes and fault tolerance (2021). https://www.youtube.com/watch?v=buIbd_aXAHw

9. Reichart, B.: Mini Crash Course: Quantum Error Correction (2014). https://www.youtube.com/watch?v=hV5FTsyKE8A

10. Gottesman, D.: Quantum Error Correction and Fault Tolerance (Part 1) (2012). https://www.youtube.com/watch?v=ltJ1jXQeDl8

11. Gottesman, D.: Quantum Error Correction and Fault Tolerance (Part 2) (2012). https://www.youtube.com/watch?v=cUqys29d0YA

12. Awardee(s), I.E.F.: John von Neumann Theory Prize: Winner(s) (1985). https://www.informs.org/Recognizing-Excellence/Award-Recipients/Jack-Edmonds

13. Calderbank, A.R., Shor, P.W.: Good quantum error-correcting codes exist. Phys. Rev. A **54**(2), 1098–1105 (1996). http://dx.doi.org/10.1103/PhysRevA.54.1098

Investigating Selective Reliability
with the Laminar Networking Package

Ryan D. Winz and Douglas D. Hodson[✉]

Department of Electrical and Computer Engineering, U.S. Air Force Institute of
Technology, WPAFB, OH 45433, USA
{ryan.winz.1,douglas.hodson}@us.af.mil

Abstract. The guaranteed delivery of *all* messages in the order sent,
is the backbone for the Internet and other networking applications. In
time-critical applications, however, this form of reliability hinders performance. In some instances, being able to select different forms of reliability
defined by a mix of data delivery attributes is more optimal. To achieve
this objective, we will look at the ideals behind the Laminar networking
package, which allows a more selective mix of reliability and ordering
to be associated with the data. To accomplish this, it defines multiple
"channels" between two networked applications.

Keywords: Networking · TCP · UDP · reliability · packet loss ·
distributed systems

1 Introduction

Sending messages between two devices on a vanilla Internet Protocol-based (IP-
based) network is inherently unreliable. Depending on the location of the sender
and receiver, a packet of information may travel through a long, winding path
of cables, routers, and switches before finally arriving at its destination. There's
plenty of room for the packet to get dropped, resulting in a gap of information.

To alleviate this, the Transmission Control Protocol (TCP) is used to ensure
packet delivery and correct ordering [1]. It does this through redundant sending and reordering of packets until the proper stream of information has been
received. This is in contrast with the User Datagram Protocol (UDP), where
messages are sent without any guarantee of delivery (i.e., "best effort").

Selection of which protocol to use (either TCP or UDP), is typically an all
or nothing decision. In cases where all information is essential, like viewing a
webpage, full reliability and ordering of messages is ideal. For multiplayer games
played with a centralized server, only the most recent data (e.g., enemy position)
is useful, and therefore a less "reliable" protocol is desired.

In specific use cases, a form of "selective reliability" is often needed. This
paper aims to analyze a middle ground between fully guaranteed delivery/order-
ing and best effort delivery through the use of the Laminar networking package.

D. D. Hodson et al. (Eds.): CSCE 2024, CCIS 2258, pp. 62–71, 2025.
https://doi.org/10.1007/978-3-031-85902-1_8

2   Background Information

2.1   Rust Programming Language

Before analyzing the principles of Laminar, it's important to understand the foundations of the programming language its coded in.

Ranked as the most admired programming language by developers in 2023 [2], Rust has recently garnered a lot of attention from the coding community. Rust is a systems-level programming language in which the compiler considers memory safety. While it takes practice to learn, Rust provides speed that rivals the C programming language, but with the memory safety of a garbage collected language. A wide array of third party libraries, such as Laminar, are published in a public repository and called crates. Further in depth information about Rust is out of the scope of this paper.

2.2   Networked Multiplayer Gaming

A use case for where the selective reliability of data is desirable is online multiplayer video games. It's a challenging problem to have asynchronous (i.e., independent) applications with synchronized virtual simulations connected via messages passed through thousands of miles of cables.

The Laminar networking package was built to be used within a game engine and, therefore, its primary use cases line up with that of a multiplayer networked game. Still, the basic principles are applicable to a wide variety of software development areas.

2.3   Distributed Interactive Simulation

Distributed Interactive Simulation (DIS) is a standardized protocol that enables asynchronously executing virtual simulations to communicate and participate in a larger distributed simulation [3]. Each application (i.e., "simulation") connects to the network, and sends messages (known as Protocol Data Units, or PDUs) to all other participants, while receiving and interpreting PDUs from others. This strategy is similar to that of game networking, as each application (i.e., simulation or game) is executing asynchronously. Often the application (i.e., simulation) is written by different people, but as long as they exchange messages (i.e., PDUs) in the DIS standardized format, the larger distributed simulation system will function correctly. DIS does not define (but suggests) how data is to be sent through various protocols (UDP or TCP); despite this, UDP is often used.

A analogous comparison to the gaming world would be a Forza racing game networked with a Mario Kart racing game to compete against each other. While they may have different underlying code and physics, they execute independently of each other and send positional updates using a defined standard. Each simulation would have to account for the differences in physics and game features (i.e. what would a Forza car do when hit by the dreaded blue shell), but this gives a quick look into the interoperability requirements built into the DIS protocol.

Messages passed between simulations need to contain a robust amount of information. The most important message passed is that of entity state, containing basic information such as position and velocity. Other messages include simulation management (i.e. start, stop, entity creation, etc.) and detonate (i.e. a simulation has determined that an entity has been destroyed). When associating messages (i.e., "data") to selective reliability, it becomes apparent that some messages necessitate a higher guarantee of delivery than others. If an entity state packet is dropped, the inconsistency lasts until the next state packet is delivered. In other words, newer state messages nullify the old state messages and only the most recent state is important. For a simulation management or detonation packet, however, only one instance is sent per event occurrence. If one of those is dropped, inconsistencies among connected simulations will grow. For example, some participants may believe an entity that has been detonated is still active. Selectively reliable communication becomes valuable.

3   Reliability and Ordering

As mentioned before, most internet traffic utilizes TCP. The pillar of TCP is the reliable delivery of *all* messages, in the order sent. The delivery of messages and the order to be delivered are not necessarily dependent on each other and can be implemented as two separate mechanisms.

3.1   Reliability

Reliability involves guaranteeing the delivery of a packet even under congested network conditions where packet loss occurs. While the internet is generally reliable, with packet delivery upwards of 99%, delivery failure is still a possibility. If all data is essential, a dropped message can render a web page, file, or video useless.

In order to combat this, messaging protocols typically use an acknowledge, or ack, system. Every message is sent with a unique incremental identification number and, upon receipt, an acknowledgement message with that id number is sent back to the original sender. Therefore, the sender knows that the specific packet was delivered successfully. If a packet spends a specified amount of time unacknowledged, the sender will resend an identical copy. It may be the case that the acknowledgement itself was dropped, but when 100% delivery is paramount, the redundancy is acceptable.

Figure 1 shows example message flows between two hosts connected through a reliable networking protocol. The top instance shows the case where no messages are dropped (which is most common in a modern network). Host 1 sends a message and host 2 follows with an acknowledgement. The second case depicts where the message is dropped on the way to host 2. Since no acknowledgment is received by host 1, after a certain time interval (represented by the vertical green dashed line), an identical message is sent. The message is received and an acknowledgement is returned. The final case represents where the message is received by host 2, but the resulting acknowledgement is dropped. Host 1 cannot be certain the message was received, so it sends a redundant packet after the time interval. Host 2 receives this packet and determines that it has already processed the message and ignores it, but still sends an acknowledgement to tell host 1 the message has been received.

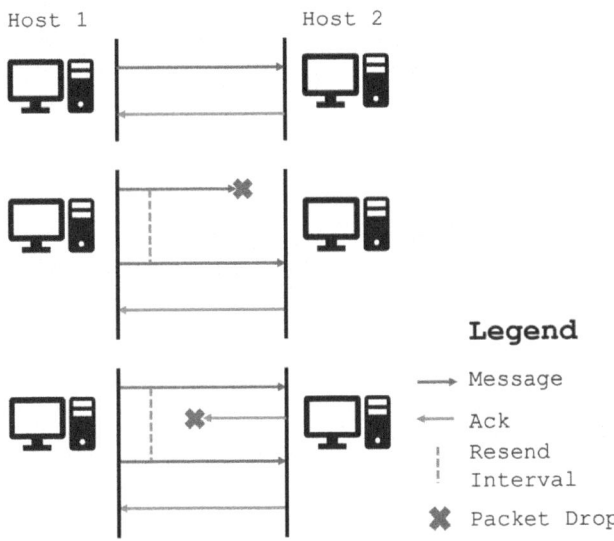

Fig. 1. The different cases for message acknowledgements with dropped packets

There are many ways to implement a clever ack system as opposed to the simple 1:1 message and acknowledge workflow described above. Glen Fielder, a game designer with decades of multiplayer networking experience, describes a robust method to mitigate the dropping of acknowledge packets [4]. Since identification numbers are sequential, a 32 bit field can be included with each bit representing the acknowledgement of the current and previous 31 packets. Therefore, each packet will be acknowledged up to 32 times, greatly reducing the likelihood of re-sending an already delivered message. Figure 2 shows a visual example of how a four bit field can acknowledge previous consecutive packets. In the top case, the current sequence number is 16. A bit field of 1101 represents that 3 of the previous 4 packets have been acknowledged (13, 14, and 16). At the bottom, the next packet is received and the sequence is updated to 17. A bit field of 1011 shows that packet 15 is still unacknowledged, but 14, 16, and 17 are.

The other component of implementing a functioning reliability system is the data structures used to store which id numbered packets have been acknowledged. Glen Fielder describes a buffer array that loops around to efficiently look up, store, and remove entries. Entries that are sufficiently old are overridden

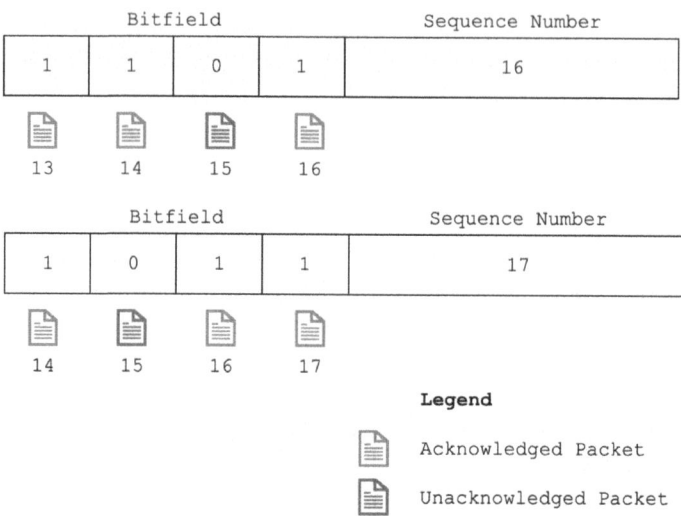

Fig. 2. An example representation of how a four bit field can acknowledge four packets at once

due to the looping nature of the data structure. Finally, a sender must also store packets that have not been acknowledged in the case of re-sending them. Upon acknowledgement, messages can be removed from memory or stored in a log of some sorts.

3.2   Ordering

Ordering messages is a natural extension of the previously mentioned reliability mechanism. Since packets are sequentially numbered, a receiving entity will easily be able to decipher which messages are in which order. For example, if one receives messages 1, 3, 4, and 5, it knows that there is a missing message somewhere, whether due to delay or drop. The additional overhead to implement an ordering system is simply the receiver storing future packets in a data structure until it's the next sequentially. In the previous example, messages 3, 4, and 5 would have to be stored in a buffer until 2 arrived. Once that happens, the buffer would process the other three messages in order and be emptied. The performance implications for requiring message ordering can be costly. Even though messages 3, 4, and 5 had been received, they couldn't be processed until message 2 arrived. This creates a blocking phenomenon that hinders real-time systems and is one of the reasons TCP isn't always desirable.

A related tactic to ordering is sequencing [5]. In sequencing, only the newest data matters and old data is discarded. Say packets arrive in the order of "1, 3, 2, 5, 4", only packets 1, 3, and 5 will be processed, while 2 and 4 will be thrown away. This is even more lightweight than the full ordering described above as messages do not have to be stored in a buffer. Upon receiving a packet, the payload is either processed immediately or thrown away. A typical use case for this is entity position information in a simulation or video game. A client doesn't care about where an entity was three packets ago, only the most recent position. This effectively removes the blocking that occurs in fully ordered messaging.

Figure 3 depicts a visual representation of ordering schemes on the same packet arrival sequence of "1, 3, 5, 2, 4". Each line represents a message queue upon the receipt of a new packet (depicted by the bold square). A solid box line represents the packet has been processed, while a dotted line box represents the message is stored in a data structure waiting for earlier packets to arrive in order to be processed. An 'X' over the box represents the packet is out of date and is ignored.

The unordered case is the most basic, where each message that is received is processed instantly. The sequenced case is similar, except the last two packets, 2 and 4, are entirely ignored. The ordered case is the most complicated, since packets 3 and 5 are stored in a data structure and remain unprocessed when they first arrive. When packet 2 arrives, both 2 and 3 are processed, and when packet 4 arrives, 4 and 5 are processed.

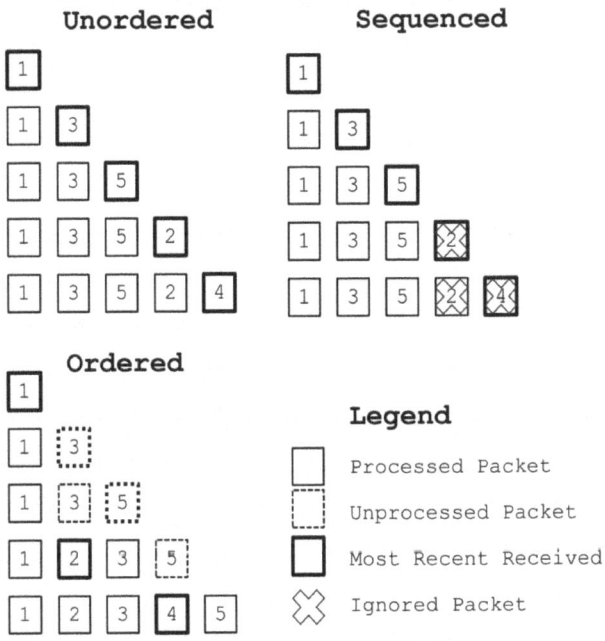

Fig. 3. The different ordering methods with a packet delivery order of 1, 3, 5, 2, 4

4   Laminar

Laminar is a lightweight, application-level transport protocol built on top of UDP that provides configuration for customized reliability and ordering. Laminar is written in the Rust programming language and can be found on the crates.io package registry [6]. The specific use case for this package is exactly what the past few sections have touched on: when only some level of reliability and ordering is necessary and message timeliness is paramount. Specifically, a highly networked system, where packets are sent at high rates, such as a multiplayer video game, is where Laminar's properties shine.

4.1   Five Types of Delivery

Now that we've extensively discussed the different properties and delivery guarantees of a networking protocol, it's time to dive into what ways a programmer can select to send messages in Laminar. There are 5 different ways a message can be sent, depicted in Fig. 4.

Reliability Type	Packet Drop	Packet Duplication	Packet Order	Packet Delivery
Unreliable Unordered	Any	Yes	No	No
Unreliable Sequenced	Any + old	No	Sequenced	No
Reliable Unordered	No	No	No	Yes
Reliable Ordered	No	No	Ordered	Yes
Reliable Sequenced	Only old	No	Sequenced	Only newest

Fig. 4. The five packet delivery methods offered by Laminar [5]

Unreliable Unordered: same principle as UDP; deliver message without any ordering or any guarantee

Unreliable Sequenced: the message may or may not get there, but the receiver will only process it if it's newer than all previous message; can be used for entity state (position, orientation, etc.)

Reliable Unordered: all messages will be received, but they may be processed out of order (i.e. messages processed as soon as receipt, instead of waiting for missing ones)

Reliable Ordered: same principle as TCP; ensure all messages are delivered and process them in order

Reliable Sequenced: resend messages that have not been acknowledged and are newer than the last sequence number acknowledged by the receiver

4.2   Packet Headers

To better understand the difference between the various delivery methods, we'll uncover what's going on under the hood. More specifically, we'll look at the information stored within a packet header before being sent. It's important to note that the decision to choose which delivery method is made upon packet creation. Laminar creates the packet with the payload and any additional overhead to achieve the desired reliability and ordering. This overhead is in the form of packet headers. Figure 5 depicts the different headers, the fields included in each, and the size, in bytes.

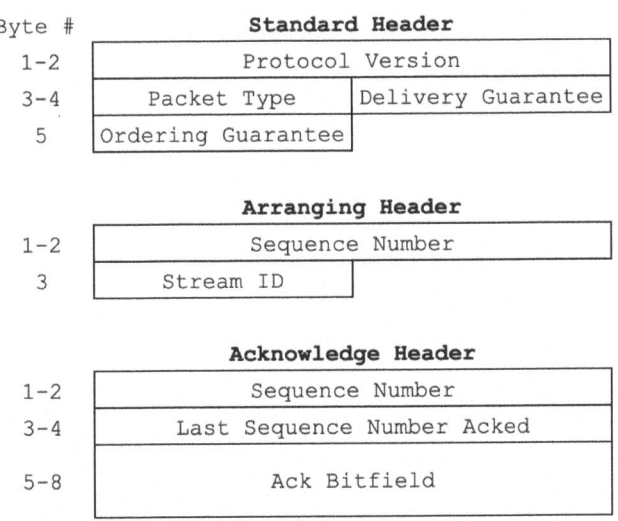

Fig. 5. The different headers appended to the beginning of Laminar packets

The standard header is appended to every laminar packet and contains the protocol version, packet type, delivery guarantee, and ordering guarantee. The protocol version allows sender and receiver to ensure they are running the same version of Laminar. The next three are fields are enumerations. Packet type can be a regular packet, fragment, or heartbeat. Fragmented messages and heartbeats are features of Laminar that are not covered in this paper, but add additional functionality. The fact that packet type is a byte long provides capability to add even more types in future updates. Delivery guarantee and ordering guarantee are exactly what we have discussed throughout: reliable & unreliable and unordered, sequenced, & ordered, respectively. Upon reading the standard header, the receiver knows which other headers are present before the data payload based on these two guarantee flags. Figure 6 shows which headers are present for each delivery method.

				Total Bytes
Unreliable Unordered	Standard Header			5
Unreliable Sequenced	Standard Header	Arranging Header		8
Reliable Unordered	Standard Header	Acknowledge Header		13
Reliable Ordered	Standard Header	Acknowledge Header	Arranging Header	16
Reliable Sequenced	Standard Header	Acknowledge Header	Arranging Header	16

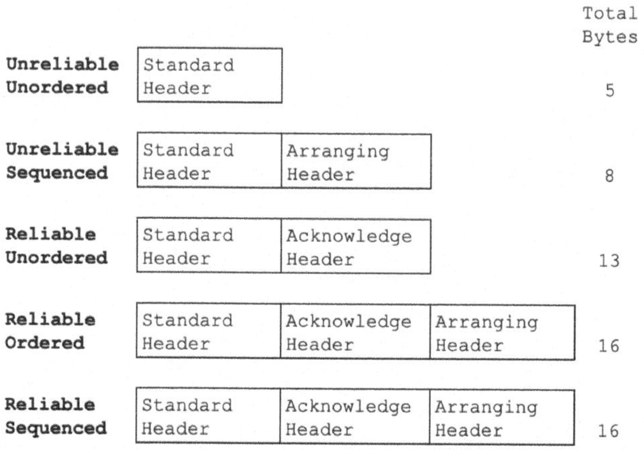

Fig. 6. The different packet headers used for each delivery method

The arranging header contains a sequence number and a stream ID. The stream ID allows the programmer to determine which packets need to be ordered together. Instead of ordering every single message that comes through together, there can be distinct "channels" to send an ordered packet through. Unrelated things like a chat message and player movement do not need to be sequenced in conjunction. It's inefficient to not process a chat message when we are waiting on an earlier player movement. Instead, both these messages will be sent with a different stream ID. With this field being a byte in size, Laminar allows for 256 different arranging streams. The sequence number is a two byte field that contains an incremented value pertaining to the specific stream. Therefore, the first packet sent on the example chat and player movement streams will both be 0.

Finally, the acknowledge header contains three additional fields at 8 bytes long. First is the sequence number, similar to the arranging header sequence, but not attached to a specified stream. Therefore, a reliable ordered packet can have a different sequence number in the arranging header and acknowledge header. This field gives the receiver an idea of what messages have been received and which ones haven't due to its incremental nature. Gaps in-between sequence numbers received shows dropped packets. The last sequence number acked field tells the receiver what the last acknowledgement was actually received by the sender. The receiver uses this in the ack bitfield to send potentially redundant acknowledgements of 32 consecutive packets as described earlier in the paper with the Gaffer on Games technique.

5   Conclusion and Future Steps

Laminar provides an attractive offering to networked application developers who want a little more control over how data is sent compared to the pillar networking protocols of UDP and TCP. Still, it's not without its shortfalls. Being an application-level protocol, it requires all applications on the network to have this package to be able to talk to each other. To further complicate things, Laminar is only coded in Rust, which while we've discussed the advantages of, still greatly limits the amount of applications it can interact with. Software engineers with code bases in other languages would have to adopt at least a networking portion of code in Rust to interoperate. Additionally, UDP and TCP have been heavily optimized and ingrained into networking. While Laminar has taken ideas from some of the best in the multiplayer gaming industry, there is still some inefficiencies in areas like the packet header, where a boolean flag (i.e., delivery guarantee) is represented by a whole byte. While this is a small effect that only reduces the allowed payload size, it is indicative of the optimization improvements that could be made.

Future steps in this research include utilizing and testing Laminar in different use cases, specifically tied to Distributed Interactive Simulation. By incorporating a network emulation tool, we can easily build up a test bed to experiment with Laminar code. Specifically, the performance can be compared to that of UDP and TCP.

Disclaimer. The views expressed in this paper are those of the authors and do not reflect the official policy or position of the United States Air Force, the Department of Defense, or the U.S. Government.

References

1. Dordal, P.: An Introduction to Computer Networks (2022)
2. Stack Overflow: 2023 Developer Survey. https://survey.stackoverflow.co/2023/
3. IEEE STD 1278.1: IEEE Standard for Distributed Interactive Simulation - Application Protocol
4. Fielder, G.: Reliable Ordered Messages. https://gafferongames.com/post/reliable_ordered_messages/
5. Post, T.: Laminar Book. https://timonpost.github.io/laminar/intro.html
6. Laminar Crate. https://crates.io/crates/laminar

An Entanglement Swapping Throughput Analysis for Quantum Networks Using Linear Quantum Optics

Kurt T. Spranger, Michael R. Grimaila$^{(\boxtimes)}$, and Douglas D. Hodson

Air Force Institute of Technology, Wright-Patterson AFB, Dayton, OH, USA
`michael.grimaila@us.af.mil`

Abstract. Decomposing complex systems into smaller abstract functional blocks and developing mathematical models to represent their behavior is an important activity towards developing comprehensive system understanding. In this paper, we extract an essential functional block known as Bell State Measurement from a notional quantum network system implemented using linear quantum optics. Bell State Measurement is required for the geographic distribution of unknown quantum states via quantum teleportation and entanglement swapping. A statistical model is developed to estimate the probability of successfully sending an unknown quantum state across a quantum network segment using entanglement swapping. The abstract model greatly simplifies the performance analysis of a quantum network in terms of its throughput. This paper is introductory in nature and is intended to help those who are relatively new to modeling, simulating, and analyzing ideal quantum networks.

Keywords: Bell State Generation (BSG) · Bell State Measurement (BSM) · Einstein Podolsky Rosen (EPR) pairs · entanglement · entanglement swapping · quantum teleportation

1 Introduction

In classical communications analysis the concept of signal-to-noise ratio (SNR), often expressed in decibels, is used to determine the performance of a communication line or network. A basic equation for SNR can be expressed as:

$$\frac{P_r}{N_t} = \frac{P_t G_t G_r}{k T_0 B_n F_{ns} L_{atm} L_{fs} L_{rs}} \tag{1}$$

where [1]:

P_r is the power (or signal) received, N_t is the noise of the system, P_t is the power transmitted, G_t is the gain of the transmitter/antenna, G_r is the gain of the receiver antenna, k is Boltzmann's constant, T_0 is the standard temperature, B_n is the noise bandwidth, F_{ns} is the system noise figure, $L_{atm}, L_{fs}, and L_{rs}$ are the losses due to the atmosphere, free-space, and the receiver respectfully.

Quantum networks are inherently different than classical networks and introduce several new concepts and variables that must be accounted for when evaluating quantum network performance [2]. For example, when implementing a quantum network using linear quantum optics, the rate that you can reliably generate entangled photons, send them over fiber, and conduct Bell state measurements is of paramount importance. A quantum network throughput model requires model parameters including the probability of generating an entangled photon pair, that capture the rate entangled photons can be generated, the probability photons will successfully make it through the fiber, and the probability that a successful Bell state measurement will occur. In our abstract model, we identify the functional block responsible for generating entangled photon pairs as the Bell State Generator (BSG) block. Similarly, we identify the functional block responsible for conducting Bell state measurements as the Bell State Measurement (BSM) block.

The requirement to successfully conduct a Bell state measurement (BSM) in a terrestrial quantum network necessitates the use of a high precision timing distribution protocol such as the White Rabbit (WR) protocol, to assure sub-nanosecond timing precision agreement among the nodes in the quantum network [3, 4]. The WR protocol uses two classical light sources to provide bidirectional communication between two nodes and provides distributed sub-nanosecond timing resolution over a fiber segment. The high precision timing enables the participating WR nodes to estimate the length of the fiber, and the propagation delay, between nodes which changes over time as a function of environmental conditions such as temperature, stress, and vibration. The ability to track the propagation delay between nodes at some level of precision is critical to ensure activities in a quantum network can be precisely temporally coordinated. In this case, the two classical WR light sources must coexist with the quantum signal on the same fiber segment. This classical-quantum coexistence in a quantum optical network requires the combination of bidirectional conventional "bright" light sources as required by the WR protocol and a unidirectional "weak" single photon level source used to carry the quantum states between the nodes. Unfortunately, the conventional "bright" light sources induce stimulated Raman scattering (SRS) energy across the spectrum, seen as noise in the quantum optical signal band and negatively impacts the success of quantum network operations.

In a quantum network using the WR protocol, as quantum entangled photons travel through fiber, they experience all of the impairments a classical signal encounters (e.g., attenuation, signal absorption, dispersion), but there are other impairments (e.g., Brillion scatter, Raman scattering, Mie scattering) which must be considered that can be detrimental to the quantum network performance [5, 6, 7].

Figure 1 shows an abstracted view of a portion of a typical quantum network using polarization-based encoding and the WR protocol conducting Entanglement Swapping (ES) to extend the range of a quantum network. In this case, Alice and Bob each generate their own EPR entangled photon pair using the BSG block and send one-half of their pair to Charlie where a Bell state measurement occurs in the BSM block [8]. Charlie reports the result of the BSM to Alice and Bob over the classical WR channel enabling them to complete the entanglement swapping protocol which entangles Alice's and Bob's EPR pair together. For this use case, Alice and Charlie (and Bob and Charlie) are connected by a single-mode classical-quantum coexistence fiber segment (solid line) found in a typical quantum network.

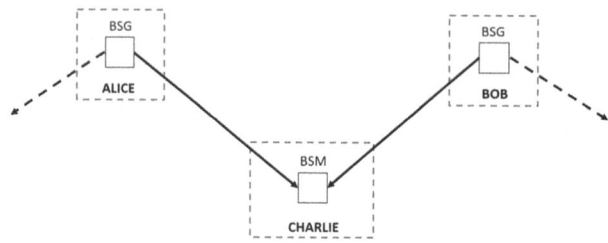

Fig. 1. Abstracted Entanglement Swapping Use Case

2 Bell State Generation

Ideally, a Bell State Generation (BSG) block will randomly generate one of the four possible maximally entangled Bell states when triggered as shown in Table 1.

Table 1. Four Maximally Entangled Bell States

Generalized Quantum State $|\psi\rangle_{AB}$	Polarization Encoded Quantum State $|\psi\rangle_{AB}$
$|\Phi^+\rangle_{AB} = \frac{1}{\sqrt{2}}(|00\rangle_{AB} + |11\rangle_{AB})$	$|\Phi^+\rangle_{AB} = \frac{1}{\sqrt{2}}(|HH\rangle_{AB} + |VV\rangle_{AB})$
$|\Psi^+\rangle_{AB} = \frac{1}{\sqrt{2}}(|01\rangle_{AB} + |10\rangle_{AB})$	$|\Psi^+\rangle_{AB} = \frac{1}{\sqrt{2}}(|HV\rangle_{AB} + |VH\rangle_{AB})$
$|\Phi^-\rangle_{AB} = \frac{1}{\sqrt{2}}(|00\rangle_{AB} - |11\rangle_{AB})$	$|\Phi^-\rangle_{AB} = \frac{1}{\sqrt{2}}(|HH\rangle_{AB} - |VV\rangle_{AB})$
$|\Psi^-\rangle_{AB} = \frac{1}{\sqrt{2}}(|01\rangle_{AB} - |10\rangle_{AB})$	$|\Psi^-\rangle_{AB} = \frac{1}{\sqrt{2}}(|HV\rangle_{AB} - |VH\rangle_{AB})$

However, when using linear quantum optics, entangled photon pairs are created through a process known as Spontaneous Parametric Down-Conversion (SPDC). A Type I SPDC generates entangled photon pairs with the same polarization (e.g., $|\Phi^+\rangle_{AB}$ or $|\Phi^-\rangle_{AB}$) while a Type II SPDC generate entangled photon pairs with orthogonal polarizations ($|\Psi^+\rangle_{AB}$ or $|\Psi^-\rangle_{AB}$). For this reason, when using linear quantum optics only two of the four possible maximally entangled Bell states can be generated. As we will see, when using linear quantum optics, we will use Type II SPDC to generate entangled photon pairs with orthogonal polarizations ($|\Psi^+\rangle_{AB}$ or $|\Psi^-\rangle_{AB}$). We can also characterize a BSG by the rate at which the photon pairs can be generated and the probability of a single pair (as opposed to no pairs or two or more pairs) being generated.

3   Bell State Measurement

Ideally, a Bell State Measurement (BSM) block can distinguish all four of the maximally entangled Bell states. However, when implementing a BSM block using linear quantum optics, only two of the four maximally entangled Bell states with orthogonal polarization can be detected ($|\Psi^+\rangle_{AB}$ or $|\Psi^-\rangle_{AB}$). The linear quantum optics BSM apparatus is composed of four Single-Photon Detectors (SPD), two Polarizing Beam Splitters (PBS), and a Beam Splitter (BS), as depicted in Fig. 2. Ideally, the two photon pulses must enter the BSM at the same time to obtain a successful measurement. However, typical photon pulses widths are measured in the hundreds of picoseconds, so coordinating the arrival of the pulses requires the use of the WR precision timing protocol. If the pulses do not overlapping by at least 90%, the probability of a successful Bell state measurement drops significantly.

When the photon pulses arrive at the BS, they will advance through the based on the phase of the input Bell state. For $|\Phi^+\rangle_{AB}$ and $|\Psi^+\rangle_{AB}$, the photon pulses will exit the same BS port. For $|\Phi^-\rangle_{AB}$ and $|\Psi^-\rangle_{AB}$, the photon pulses will exit the opposite BS ports. The photon pulse then pass through the PBS based on their polarization and the orientation of the PBS and hit a SPD (ideally) causing the detector to click.

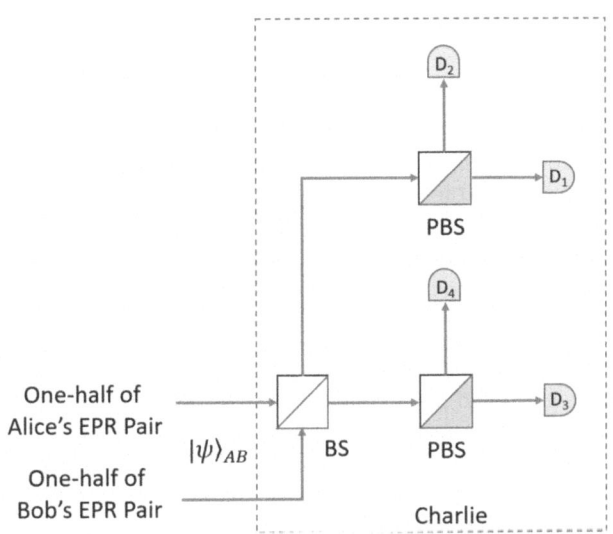

Fig. 2. Abstract Bell State Measurement (BSM) Apparatus

Depending on which of SPDs click, the Bell state can be determined. Table 2 enumerates the input Bell state and which detectors should click. If no detector clicks, one detector clicks, or three or more detectors click; then the Bell state measurement is deemed to have failed. Since SPD measure one or more photons, even if multiple photons hit a detector it only clicks once. This is why the $|\Phi^+\rangle_{AB}$ state cannot be determined. The $|\Phi^-\rangle_{AB}$ state cannot be determined because of the Hong-Ou-Mondel (HOM) effect which states two identical photons entering a BS will exit the BS out the same port [8].

Table 2. Bell State Measurement (BSM) of Polarization Encoded Bell States

Input State $|\psi\rangle_{AB}$	Coincidences
$|\Phi^+\rangle_{AB} = \frac{1}{\sqrt{2}}(|HH\rangle_{AB} + |VV\rangle_{AB})$	None - Cannot Determine
$|\Psi^+\rangle_{AB} = \frac{1}{\sqrt{2}}(|HV\rangle_{AB} + |VH\rangle_{AB})$	D_1 and D_2 click OR D_3 and D_4 click
$|\Phi^-\rangle_{AB} = \frac{1}{\sqrt{2}}(|HH\rangle_{AB} - |VV\rangle_{AB})$	None - Cannot Determine
$|\Psi^-\rangle_{AB} = \frac{1}{\sqrt{2}}(|HV\rangle_{AB} - |VH\rangle_{AB})$	D_1 and D_4 click OR D_2 and D_3 click

The measurement of entangled pairs using linear quantum optics impose a 50% loss in throughput unless it is assumed that the arriving photon pairs are only in the $|\Psi^+\rangle_{AB}$ and $|\Psi^-\rangle_{AB}$ states which is the case when using a BSG using Type II SPDC.

4 A Statistical Model to Evaluate Entanglement Swapping Throughput

The purpose of this paper is to introduce a simple abstract statistical model to evaluate the expected throughput of entanglement swapping when using linear quantum optics. The parametric model contains nineteen distinct parameters which can be adjusted. Seven of the parameters are related to the Alice subsystem and the fiber link from Alice to Charlie, seven of the parameters are related to the Bob subsystem and the fiber link from Bob to Charlie, and the remaining five are Charlie subsystem specific parameters. The seven parameters used to characterize the Alice/Bob subsystem and their fiber link to Charlie are:

- Total BSG Rate ($Total_{BSG_{Rate}}$) [pulses/second] represents the rate that entangled photon pairs can be generated per second. The rate is chosen to be the same for Alice and Bob and is limited by the hardware implementing the BSGs.
- BSG Single Photon Pair Generation Probability ($BSG_{SinglePair_{Prob}}$) [probability] is the probability the BSG successfully produces a single entangled photon pair, in contrast to zero pairs or two or more pairs. If the BSG produces zero or two or more entangled photon pairs, then the BSG is deemed to have failed. Higher values increase the probability of successful entanglement, contributing to the success of subsequent quantum operations.
- Fiber Path Loss ($Fiber_{PathLoss}$) [dB/km] accounts for attenuation of the signal in the fiber per km. Since this is a loss, the value is in units of negative dB.
- Fiber Length ($Fiber_{Length}$) [km] characterizes the length of the fiber between nodes.
- Fiber Noise Rate ($Fiber\_Noise_{Rate}$) [photons/sec] characterizes the number of noise photons present in the fiber link rate per second. In the use cases, the noise is assumed to result from Stimulated Raman Scattering (SRS) due to the use of the White Rabbit protocol.

- Polarization Correction Error (PCE) Mean Average (PCE_{mean}) [deg] represents the mean average of a normal/gaussian distributed PCE which is the fiber's ability to maintain the polarization of the quantum signal when traveling through the fiber. Higher values mean the quantum signal which arrives at the BSM is not in the expected polarization orientation and will induce error in Bell state measurement.
- Polarization Correction Error Standard Deviation (PCE_{StdDev}) [deg] represents the standard deviation of the PCE Mean Average and indicates it's variance.

Each of the preceding seven parameters are related to the Alice-Charlie path and the Bob-Charlie path, for a total of fourteen parameters.

The five parameters used to characterize the Charlie subsystem are:

- BSM Pulse Overlap Percentage ($BSM_{PulseOverlap_{Percentage}}$) [percentage] represents the amount of overlap in the photon pulses sent by Alice and by Bob when they arrive at Charlie. The photon pulses from Alice and Bob must significantly overlap when arriving at Charlie for the Bell state measurement to be successful. This value indexes into a look up table to determine the success probability ($BSM_{OverlapSuccess_{Probability}}$) [probability]. For example, Table 3 shows the success probability given the percentage the pulses overlap. If the pulses overlap more than 90%, the Bell state measurement success probability is 100%. If the overlap is between 70% and 90%, the Bell state measurement success probability is only 80%. If the overlap is less than 70%, the Bell state measurement success probability is 0% and has deemed to have failed.

Table 3. BSM Pulse Overlap Percentage and BSM Overlap Success Probability Look Up Table

$BSM_{PulseOverlap_{Percentage}}$	$BSM_{OverlapSuccess_{Probability}}$
90 – 100 %	100 %
70 – 90 %	80 %
<70 %	0 %

- BSM State Detection Percentage probability ($BSM_{StateDetection_{Percentage}}$) [probability] reflects the ratio of the number of maximally entangled Bell states generated by the BSG that are received that can be successfully measured using the BSM. When using linear quantum optics, this is set to 100% since the BSG will generate only $|\Psi^+\rangle_{AB}$ and $|\Psi^-\rangle_{AB}$ states and the BSM can only measure $|\Psi^+\rangle_{AB}$ and $|\Psi^-\rangle_{AB}$ states.
- Single Photon Detector (SPD) Detector Efficiency ($SPD_{Detector_{Eff}}$) [probability] represents the probability of an SPD clicking when one or more photons arrives at the detector. Higher detection efficiency improves the likelihood of a successful Bell state measurement.
- Single Photon Detector (SPD) Dark Count Rate ($SPD\_DarkCount_{Rate}$) [counts/sec] describes the rate at which the SPD will erroneously "clicks" in the absence of incoming photons. Higher dark count rates reduce the likelihood of a successful Bell state measurement.

- Single Photon Detector (SPD) After Pulse Probability ($SPD_{AfterPulse_{Prob}}$) [unitless] represents the probability of the SPD retriggering due to delayed responses after a detection event. Higher after pulse rates introduce errors and reduce the likelihood of a successful Bell state measurement.

Together, the nineteen model parameters are combined to calculate the number of successful entanglement swaps per second. The model for calculating this rate is shown in Eq. 2:

$$\frac{Successful_{BSM}}{second} = \frac{Total_{BSG_{Rate}}}{second} * AliceToCharlie_{success_{probability}} * BobToCharlie_{success_{probability}}$$
$$* Charlie_{success_{probability}} \tag{2}$$

where:

$$scenario_{success_{probability}} = \left(BSG_{SinglePair_{Prob}}\right) * \left(1 - Fiber_{PathLoss_{Prob}}\right) * \left(1 - Fiber_{Noise_{Prob}}\right)$$
$$* \left(1 - Fiber_{PCE_{Prob}}\right) * \left(\frac{BSM_{Overlap_{Percentage}}}{100}\right) * \left(\frac{BSM_{StateDetection_{Percentage}}}{100}\right)$$
$$* \left(\frac{SPD_{Detector_{Eff}}}{100}\right) * \left(1 - SPD_{DarkCount_{Prob}}\right) * \left(1 - SPD_{AfterPulse_{Prob}}\right) \tag{3}$$

$$Fiber_{PathLoss_{Prob}} = 1 - 10^{\frac{-Fiber_{PathLoss} * Fiber_{Length}}{10}} \tag{4}$$

$$Fiber_{Noise_{Prob}} = \frac{Fiber\_Noise_{Rate}}{Total_{BSG_{Rate}} * BSG_{SinglePair_{Prob}}} \tag{5}$$

$$Fiber_{PCE_{Prob}} = 1 - (\cos(PCE_{mean} + PCE_{StdDev}))^2 \tag{6}$$

$$SPD_{DarkCount_{Prob}} = \frac{SPD\_DarkCount_{Rate}}{Total_{BSG_{Rate}} * FiberToBSM\_Success_{Rate}} \tag{7}$$

To show the contribution of each parameter, eleven use cases (A through K) were created with A representing an ideal/perfect case, then each following case varying one parameter to see how it affects the overall model. The final use case (K) varies several parameters to expected values to give a more realistic result. The values of the parameters and results are captured in Table 4, a blank cell means the value is what is listed in use case A for the same parameter.

As evident in Table 4, the probability or ability to produce a single entangled EPR pair and the path loss of the fiber greatly affect the final BSM success rate. Additionally, the overlap of the photons from Alice and Bob at Charlie's BSM as well as the ability of Charlie's BSM to distinguish between the EPR states used are the third and fourth largest contributors to the overall BSM success rate. On the other side, polarization correction error and dark count rate both appear to not make a significant impact on the overall BSM success rate.

Table 5 shows two more scenarios (L & M) where multiple parameters were degraded from ideal conditions. Both these scenarios produced significantly lower successful BSM rates and demonstrate how the probability of the BSG producing a single photon pair, and the path loss in the fiber greatly affect the overall BSM success rate.

Table 4. Results of 11 Use Cases for Entanglement Swapping Parametric Model

Parameter/Use Case	A	B	C	D	E	F	G	H	I	J	K
BSG											
BSG_Single_Pair_Prob_A	1	0.0001									0.001
Fiber											
Fiber_PathLoss_AC [dB/km]	0		0.4								0.2
Fiber_Length_AC [km]	25		25								25
Fiber_Noise_Rate_AC [photons/sec]	0			7000							7000
PCE_mean_AC [deg]	0				0						0
PCE_StdDev_AC [deg]	0				10						10
BSM											
BSM_Overlap_Percentage [%]	100					80					100
BSM_StateDetection_Percentage [%]	100						50				100
SPD											
SPD_Detector_Eff [%]	1							75			80
SPD_DarkCount_Rate [count/sec]	0								7000		200
SPD_AfterPulse_Prob	0									0.2	0
Successful_BSM rate	100000000	10000	10000000	99993000	96984631	60000000	50000000	75000000	99993000	80000000	22657.90951
Difference from Ideal Conditions [%]	0.00%	99.990%	90.00%	7.00E-05	3.02%	40.00%	50.00%	25.00%	7.00E-05	20.00%	99.977%

Table 5. Results of 2 Uses Cases for ES Parametric Model

Parameter/Use Case	L	M
BSG		
BSG_Single_Pair_Prob_A	0.001	0.0001
Fiber		
Fiber_PathLoss_AC [dB/km]	0.2	0.2
Fiber_Length_AC [km]	5	25
Fiber_Noise_Rate_AC [photons/sec]	7000	7000
PCE_mean_AC [deg]	0	0
PCE_StdDev_AC [deg]	5	10
BSM		
BSM_Overlap_Percentage [%]	100	100
BSM_StateDetection_Percentage [%]	100	100
SPD		
SPD_Detector_Eff [%]	80	80
SPD_DarkCount_Rate [count/sec]	200	200
SPD_AfterPulse_Prob	0	0
Successful_BSM_rate	58489.105	576.0615971
Difference from Ideal Conditions [%]	99.942%	99.999%

5   Conclusions and Future Work

In this paper, we presented a model of a quantum teleportation network and how decomposing a complex system into a series of smaller abstract mathematical expressions can be very helpful in analyzing a quantum communications link. Specifically, we identified and enumerated the basic quantum circuit blocks found in the ideal Quantum Teleportation protocol quantum circuit; BSG and BSM. When one conducts analysis of a quantum teleportation network, one will understand how to effectively measure the probable performance of the network.

Our hope is that this paper enables the reader to develop a better understanding of how to analyze quantum teleportation networks. While this information is introductory in nature, it can provide value to those who are new to modeling, simulating, and analyzing ideal quantum networks.

Disclaimer. The views expressed in this paper are those of the authors and do not reflect the official policy or position of the U.S. Air Force, the Department of Defense, or the U.S. Government.

References

1. Middlestead, R.W.: Communication range equation and link analysis. In: Digital Communications with Emphasis on Data Modems: Theory, Analysis, Design, Simulation, Testing, and Applications, pp. 557–601. John Wiley & Sons Inc. (2017)
2. Van Meter, R.: Quantum Networking, Hoboken. John Wiley & Sons Inc., NJ (2014)
3. IEEE Standard for a Precision Clock Synchronization Protocol for Networked Measurement and Control Systems, IEEE Std 1588-2019 (Revision of IEEE Std 1588-2008), pp. 1-499, 16 June 2020
4. Lipinski, M., Wlostowski, T., Serrano, J., Alvarez, P.: White rabbit: a PTP application for robust sub-nanosecond synchronization. In: 2011 IEEE International Symposium on Precision Clock Synchronization for Measurement, Control and Communication, Munich, Germany (2011)
5. Marcuse, D.: Dispersion in Fibers. In: Light Transmission Optics, pp. 480–516. Van Nostrand Reinhold Company Inc, New York (1982)
6. Long, D.A.: The Raman Effect. John Wiley & Sons Ltd. (2002)
7. Agrawal, G.P.: Nonlinear Fiber Optics. Elsevier Inc., London (2019)
8. Hong, C., Ou, Z., Mandel, L.: Measurement of subpicosecond time intervals between two photons by interference. Phys. Rev. Lett. **59**(18), 2044–2046 (1987)
9. Bennett, C.H., Brassard, G.: Quantum cryptography: Public key distribution and coin tossing. Theoretical Comput. Sci. **560**, 7–11 (2014)
10. Einstein, A., Podolsky, B., Rosen, N.: Can quantum-mechanical description of physical reality be considered complete? Phys. Rev., 777–780, 15 May 1935.
11. Ekert, A.K.: Quantum cryptography based on bell's theorem. Phys. Rev. Lett. **67**(6), 661–663 (1991)
12. Fiber Optical Networking: The WDM System, Fiber Optical Networking, 23 April 2015. https://www.fiber-optical-networking.com/the-wdm-system.html. Accessed 1 Jan 2024
13. Keiser, G.: Fiber Optic Communications. Springer, Singapore (2021)

Section: Scientific Computing and Applications

Notes on Symmetric Generalized Tent Map: Route to Chaos

Peter Chtcheprov[1]([✉]) and Andrei Chtcheprov[2]

[1] University of North Carolina, Chapel Hill, NC 27599, USA
pchtch@unc.edu
[2] Independent Researcher, Chapel Hill, NC 27516, USA
and_ch@yahoo.com

Abstract. Many known non-linear dynamic maps follow similar behavioral patterns such as periods of double cascading and islands of stability before reaching the fully developed chaotic regimes. The paper introduces a novel family of parametric generalized tent maps that do not follow the above route to chaos. Instead of forming well defined and observable cascading patterns, all cyclic structures become dynamically unstable with bifurcation branches scattered inside narrow subdomains that can overlap. The method of Lyapunov Exponent is applied to characterize transitions to chaotic regimes. The paper demonstrates the ergodic property of the dynamic process by computing invariant distributions of the map. A closed-form distribution for the developed chaos is derived. A zone of instability exists where ergodic property fails.

Keywords: Dynamic Chaos · Numerical Methods · Distributions

1 Introduction

Parametrized logistic maps and their generalizations have been intensively studied both theoretically and computationally for the last few decades [1–6]. Among many interesting properties discovered in such dynamic maps, the central focus is on studying transitions from non-chaotic patterns observed for smaller values of a map parameter to chaotic regimes that occur when a map parameter increases. For smaller values of the map parameter dynamic iterations usually converge to a single point called a fixed point. When the map parameter increases the fixed point becomes unstable, so the dynamic pattern changes and gives rise to the so-called period of double cascading [1–6]. The double cascading behavior is characterized by a formation of stable and observable P-cycles with P = 2, 4, 8, …, when after some initial iterations the dynamic map only goes through a discrete set of values. Analysis shows that each P-cycle exists in a certain range of map parameter values. As the number of cycles P increases the corresponding map parameter intervals where P-cycle exist become smaller. Destructions of stable cyclic patterns and their transformations to the next level P-cycles occur when cycles become unstable. The double cascading property is observed in many known dynamic maps and often viewed as an intrinsic feature of non-linear dynamic processes. For larger values of the map parameter the above double-cascading behavior dramatically changes.

© The Author(s), under exclusive license to Springer Nature Switzerland AG 2025
D. D. Hodson et al. (Eds.): CSCE 2024, CCIS 2258, pp. 83–95, 2025.
https://doi.org/10.1007/978-3-031-85902-1_10

The maps exhibit irregular dynamic patterns with a presence of the so-called islands of stability. Despite the above-described route to chaos is typical for many non-linear maps, not all of them (e.g., the tent map [5, 7]) follow it. Since the class of dynamic processes that do not exhibit the double-cascading and islands of stability behavioral patterns is not very wide, it is of interest to expand that class and explore generalizations of the tent map. The main objective of the paper is to introduce a novel family of generalized tent maps denoted GTM (p, q, a) and study in detail properties of a dynamic process GTM $(1/2, 1/2, 1)$. The paper shows that for GTM $(1/2, 1/2, 1)$ the route to chaos does not follow the traditional double cascading and islands of stability patterns due to dynamic instability of all cyclic structures.

The next important research question is the existence of dynamic behaviors that show a dependence on the initial conditions provided the map parameter remains fixed. The paper finds such a zone of instability when GTM $(1/2, 1/2, 1)$ generates different patterns for the same map parameter but different starting points. Such behavior is rather unique and not typical for most known dynamic maps.

Another central point of interest for complex non-linear dynamic processes is the notion of dynamic chaos. Many definitions of chaos exist in the literature [1, 2, 5, 6, 8, 9]. They reflect criteria and conditions that characterize dynamic and topological properties of chaotic regimes. Such a large variety of chaos definitions illustrates not only a significant interest in exploring the chaotic behavior of non-linear dynamic systems but also the tremendous complexity of the subject. Some of postulated properties of the chaos, e.g., density of periodic orbits and topological transitivity, are not easy to check in practice, so Lyapunov Exponent [2–4, 10] has become one of the major computational tools in practical applications. The paper explores applications of the Lyapunov Exponent method to study transitions to chaotic regimes of GTM $(1/2, 1/2, 1)$ and the above-mentioned zone of instability.

The fourth important aspect of chaotic maps is the ergodic property [2, 7]. From a modeling point of view, ergodicity means that after many iterations distributions of generated data points will converge to the limiting distributions (attractors). As was shown in [2, 4], dynamic maps can mathematically be represented as stochastic processes with invariant distributions. The existence of such invariant distributions that are equal to the limiting distributions is a manifestation of ergodicity. In fact, as is hypothesized in [2, 4] based on outcomes of multiple numerical experiments, a distribution of a chaotic process is a limit of corresponding (unstable) P-cycle distributions, i.e., the set of P-cycle distributions is dense in the space of all distributions. The above hypothesis not only illustrates why dynamic chaos is internally structured in terms of density of periodic orbits as was initially formulated in [1] but also explains the ergodic behavior. Indeed, since each P-cycle distribution, by definition, is a characteristic of an ergodic process, the limit of P-cycle distributions, i.e., the attractor, should also represent the ergodic process.

The paper is structured as follows. First, a novel class of parametrized dynamic processes called a generalized tent map GTM (p, q, a) is introduced, and a detail analysis of a process GTM $(1/2, 1/2, 1)$ is conducted. The paper also outlines the importance of the Lyapunov Exponent method to characterize transitions to chaotic regimes. Next, the dynamic system is re-formulated in terms of a sequence of random variables, and the conditions under which transformations of random variables become invariant are determined. The paper also describes an efficient numerical procedure that is used for fast computations of invariant distributions and explorations of dynamic and ergodic properties of the map. It is shown that ergodicity fails in the zone of instability. Finally, the paper derives a closed-form distribution of the developed dynamic chaos. This is a very important result because closed-form distributions are known only for a limited set of logistic maps. R coding language is used for all computations and graph plotting.

2 Properties of Generalized Trent Map

A family of Generalized Tent Maps $GTM(p, q, a)$ is defined by the equations (1a) – (1b)

$$x_{k+1} = g(x_k; \mu; p, q, a), k = 0, 1, 2, \ldots \tag{1a}$$

$$g(x; \mu; p, q, a) = a\mu x^p \theta\left(\frac{1}{2} - x\right) + \mu(1 - x)^q \theta\left(x - \frac{1}{2}\right) \tag{1b}$$

In (1a) - (1b), $\mu \geq 0$ is a map parameter, $p \geq 0$ and $q \geq 0$ are exponents, $a > 0$ is an adjustable constant that controls a map discontinuity at $x = 1/2$, and $\theta(x)$ is a Heaviside function. For example, function $g(x; \mu; 1, 1, 1)$ corresponds to a classical tent map $GTM(1, 1, 1)$ [5, 7]. Below input parameters p, q, a of the function $g(x; \mu; p, q, a)$ may be omitted for a description convenience. The process (1a) – (1b) requires an initial value x_0 from [0, 1]. A spectrum of admissible values of parameter μ should guarantee that the sequence $\{x_k\}_{k=0}^{\infty}$ will remain on interval [0, 1]. The case $\mu = 0$ is trivial. Below a detail analysis for $\{p, q, a\} = \{1/2, 1/2, 1\}$ is conducted. This iteration process is described by the function

$$g(x; \mu; 1/2, 1/2, 1) = \mu\sqrt{x}\theta(1/2 - x) + \mu\sqrt{1 - x}\theta(x - 1/2) \tag{2}$$

Function (2) is continuous at $x = 1/2$ but not differentiable. It is symmetric with respect to $x = 1/2$ and attains its maximum at this point. Sequence $\{x_k\}_{k=0}^{\infty}$ remains on [0, 1] if $\max_x g(x; \mu) \leq 1$, i.e., $0 \leq \mu \leq \mu_{max}$, where $\mu_{max} = \sqrt{2}$. . Below some properties of the iteration process (1a, b) – (2) are studied.

Fixed points of (1a, b) – (2) are solutions to the equation $x = g(x; \mu)$. The first point is trivial $x_*^{(1)} = 0$. Let $\mu_*^{(2)} = 1/\sqrt{2}$. The other two fixed points that belong to interval [0, 1] are $x_*^{(2)}(\mu) = \mu^2$ if $0 \leq \mu \leq \mu_*^{(2)}$, and $x_*^{(3)}(\mu) = \left(-\mu^2 + \sqrt{\mu^4 + 4\mu^2}\right)/2$ if $\mu_*^{(2)} \leq \mu \leq \mu_{max}$. Points $x_*^{(2)}(\mu)$ and $x_*^{(3)}(\mu)$ that are formally functions of μ agree when $\mu = \mu_*^{(2)}$. To analyze stability of the above fixed points, the derivative of $g(x; \mu)$ with respect to x is studied

$$\frac{\partial g(x; \mu)}{\partial x} = \frac{\mu}{2\sqrt{x}}\theta(1/2 - x) - \frac{\mu}{2\sqrt{1 - x}}\theta(x - 1/2) \tag{3}$$

Derivative (3) does not exist at $x = 1/2$. In practice, stability of the fixed points means a convergence of the dynamic process (1a) – (2a) to these points. The fixed point stability

condition is $|\partial g(x; \mu)/\partial x| < 1$. Obviously, $x_*^{(1)}$ is not stable. Since $\left|\partial g\left(x_*^{(2)}; \mu\right)/\partial x\right| <$
1, $x_*^{(2)}(\mu)$ is stable and the convergence of the dynamic process (2) to $x_*^{(2)}$ is expected
for $0 \leq \mu \leq \mu_*^{(2)}$. Let $\mu_*^{(3)} = 2/\sqrt{3}$. To study a stability of the fixed point $x_*^{(3)}(\mu)$,
inequality $\left|0.5\mu/\sqrt{1 - x_*^{(3)}}\right| < 1$ should be solved for μ. Its solution is $0 \leq \mu < \mu_*^{(3)}$.
Since $x_*^{(3)}(\mu)$ belongs to interval $[1/2, 1]$, the fixed point is stable when $\mu_*^{(2)} \leq \mu < \mu_*^{(3)}$.

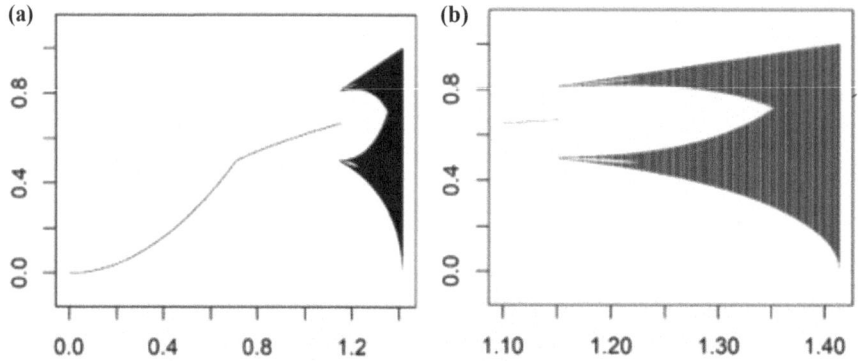

Fig. 1. a. Bifurcation Diagram, $0 \leq \mu \leq \mu_{max}$. b. Bifurcation Diagram, $1.1 \leq \mu \leq \mu_{max}$.

A convenient tool to explore dynamic processes is a bifurcation diagram that shows
locations of iteration points at different values of parameter μ. To plot the diagram,
300,000 iterations (1) - (2) are run starting form a randomly drawn initial x_0. The last
15,000 points are plotted. Figure 1a shows the bifurcation diagram for $0 \leq \mu \leq \mu_{max}$.
The horizontal axis corresponds to parameter μ and the vertical axis displays values x. As
is observed, if $0 \leq \mu < \mu_*^{(2)}$ the iterations (2) converge to the fixed point $x_*^{(2)}(\mu) = \mu^2$,
and such behavior agrees with the above theoretical calculations. When $\mu = \mu_*^{(2)}$, the
fixed point $x_*^{(2)} = 1/2$ is "transformed" to $x_*^{(3)}$ and the convergence to the fixed point
$x_*^{(3)}(\mu)$ is observed for larger values of μ. When $\mu = \mu_*^{(3)} \approx 1.155$, the fixed point $x_*^{(3)}$
becomes unstable. Both curves $x_*^{(2)} = x_*^{(2)}(\mu)$ and $x_*^{(3)} = x_*^{(3)}(\mu)$ look smooth except
for the transition point $\left(\mu = \mu_*^{(2)}, x = 1/2\right)$. Figure 1b shows a more detailed plot in
the range $1.1 \leq \mu \leq \mu_{max}$. The double cascading behavior is not observed. Such pattern
is not different from the behavior of classical tent map GTM (1, 1, 1).

For an integer P, let an iteration function $g^{(P)}(x; \mu)$ represent a P-composition of
$g(x; \mu)$ maps. For example, if P = 2, $g^{(2)}(x; \mu) = g(g(x; \mu); \mu)$. A P-cycle (also called
a P-orbit) is defined as a set of distinct points x such that $g^{(P)}(x; \mu) = x$. In practice,
numerical and graphical procedures are used to find the solution to the above equation.
A case P = 2 is discussed below. Let $(\xi_1(\mu), \xi_2(\mu))$, $\xi_1(\mu) \neq \xi_2(\mu)$ be a 2-cycle, i.e.
$g^{(2)}(\xi_i; \mu) = \xi_i$, $i = 1, 2$. The case $\xi_1(\mu) = \xi_2(\mu)$ is called a degenerate 2-cycle. Three
scenarios are possible.

Scenario 1: $\xi_1(\mu) < 1/2$ and $\xi_2(\mu) < 1/2$. In this case, $\xi_2 = \mu\sqrt{\xi_1}$ and $\xi_1 = \mu\sqrt{\xi_2}$. Direct calculations show that the only solution is $(\xi_1(\mu), \xi_2(\mu)) = (0, 0)$ or

$(\xi_1(\mu), \xi_2(\mu)) = \left(x_*^{(2)}, x_*^{(2)}\right)$. Since $\xi_1(\mu) = \xi_2(\mu)$ both cases represent degenerate 2-cycles.

Scenario 2: $\xi_1(\mu) \geq 1/2$ and $\xi_2(\mu) \geq 1/2$. In this case, $\xi_2 = \mu\sqrt{1 - \xi_1}$ and $\xi_1 = \mu\sqrt{1 - \xi_2}$. This results in a quartic equation for $\xi_1 : \xi_1^4 - 2\mu^2\xi_1^2 + \mu^6\xi_1 + \mu^4 - \mu^6 = 0$ and a similar equation for ξ_2. The real solutions should belong to $[1/2, 1]$. The obvious solution is a degenerate 2-cycle $(\xi_1(\mu), \xi_2(\mu)) = \left(x_*^{(3)}, x_*^{(3)}\right)$.

Scenario 3: $\xi_1(\mu) < 1/2$ and $\xi_2(\mu) \geq 1/2$. In this case, $\xi_2 = \mu\sqrt{\xi_1}$ and $\xi_1 = \mu\sqrt{1 - \xi_2}$. This results in quartic equations: $h_1(\xi_1) = \xi_1^4 - 2\mu^2\xi_1^2 - \mu^6\xi_1 + \mu^4 = 0$ and $h_2(\xi_2) = \xi_2^4 + \mu^6\xi_2 - \mu^6 = 0$. By direct calculations, $h_1(0) > 0$ and $h_1(1/2) = 1 - 2\mu^2(\mu^2 - 1)^2 < 0$ if $\mu > \mu_*^{(3)}$, the real solution ξ_1 exists. Similarly, since $h_1(1/2) = 1/16 - \mu^6/2 < 0$ if $\mu > \mu_*^{(3)}$ and $h_2(1) > 0$, the real solution ξ_2 exists.

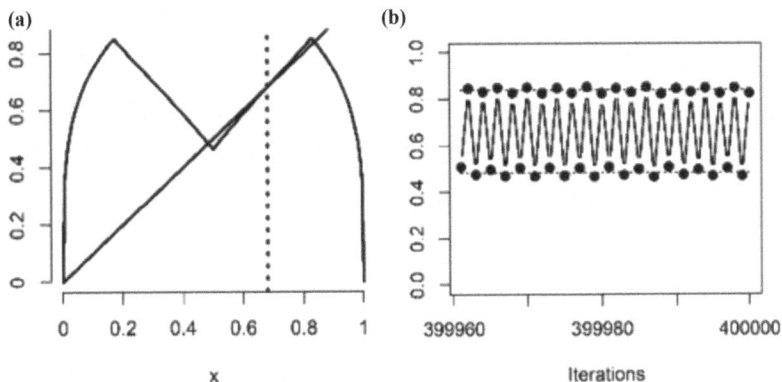

Fig. 2. a. Plots: $y = x, y = g^{(2)}\left(x; \mu_*^{(3)} + 0.05\right)$. b. Plot of $\{x_k\}$, $\mu = \mu_*^{(3)} + 0.05$.

The above arguments show the existence of (possibly degenerate) 2-cycles. According to the bifurcation diagrams of Figs. 1a and b, non-degenerate 2-cycles are not observed in numerical experiments, so they must be unstable. To study such behavior, Fig. 2a reports plots $y = g^{(2)}\left(x; \mu_*^{(3)} + 0.05\right)$ and $y = x$, for $\mu = \mu_*^{(3)} + 0.05$, i.e., slightly above the value at which the fixed point $x_*^{(3)}$ becomes unstable. The intersections of two plots are the solutions to the equation $x = g^{(2)}(x; \mu)$. The vertical dotted line corresponds to the fixed point $x_*^{(3)}(\mu)$. There are three intersection points that correspond to 2-cycles. The first 2-cycle $(0, 0)$ is degenerate and unstable. The second 2-cycle corresponds to $\left(x_*^{(3)}, x_*^{(3)}\right)$. It is also degenerate and unstable. To find the value of the third point located between 0.4 and 0.5, a numerical R procedure, called *uniroot*, is employed to calculate the 2-cycle: (~0.4843117, ~0.838813). Its existence corresponds to Scenario 3. Derivatives $\partial g(x; \mu)/\partial x$ at the above 2-cycle points are approximately equal to 0.8655 and -1.498316 and the absolute value of their product is greater than 1. Hence, the cycle is not stable and, thus, not observed.

To analyze the behavior of the sequence $\{x_k\}$, Fig. 2b reports last 40 values of 400,000 iterations (1) - (2). Values $\{x_k\}$ are shown as circles with consecutive points connected by lines. Two horizontal dotted lines correspond to the 2-cycle (~0.4843117, ~0.838813). If the cycle were stable, the sequence $\{x_k\}$ would "converge" to the 2-cycle. Instead, the sequence $\{x_k\}$ is concentrated above and below the 2-cycle points (~0.4843117, ~0.838813) forming two pairs of "narrow" regions as if each 2-cycle branch became "scattered" in a small domain. Two regions are separated from each other by a large gap, and this is also seen in Figs. 1a and b. Statistical analysis is conduced to compute mean and standard deviations of $\{x_k\}$ samples inside each domain. To form samples the last 50,000 data points are collected. The points with values below 0.6 are assigned to the first sample and the remaining points are in the second sample. The corresponding sample mean values are ~0.4863223 and ~0.8368396 that almost coincide with the above 2-cycle points. The sample standard deviations are ~0.017 and ~0.011. The behavior shown in Figs. 2b is called an almost period pattern.

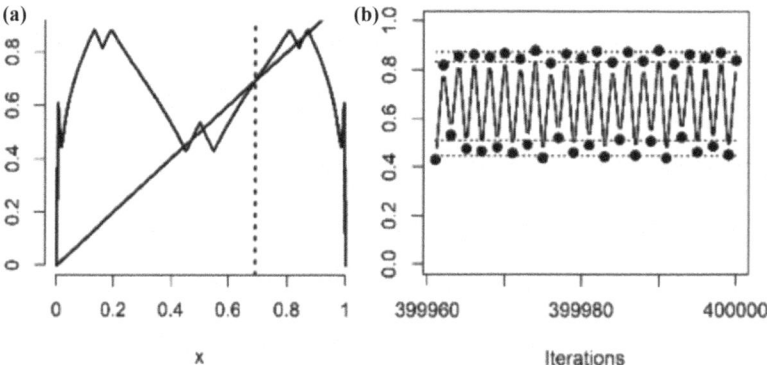

Fig. 3. a. Plots: $y = x, y = g^{(4)}(x; 1.25)$. b. Plot of $\{x_k\}$, $\mu = 1.25$.

Based on the above results it is hypothesized that each branch of a P-cycle is unstable and gets scattered into narrow subdomains. To further illustrate the hypothesis, Fig. 3a shows plots $y = g^{(4)}(x; 1.25)$ and $y = x$. Implementation of *uniroot* allows one to find an unstable 4-cycle: (~0.511962, ~0.8739313, ~0.4438269, ~0.8327542). Figure 3b reports connected last 40 points of 400,000 iterations (1)–(2). Four horizontal dotted lines correspond to the above 4-cycle. As is observed, each branch of the 4-cycle is scattered and form subdomains. Two bottom subdomains and two upper subdomains overlap, so no internal gaps exist, but there is a large gap between the upper and bottom regions (see the bifurcation diagrams 1a and 1b).

The patterns become more complex if the number of cycles P increases. Figures 4a and b show $g^{(P)}(x; \mu)$ plots for P = 8 and 16, $\mu = 1.3$ and 1.33 correspondingly. An unusual behavior of (1)–(2) is observed near $\mu_*^{(3)}$. It is discussed in the next section where the Lyapunov Exponent method is described. It will be shown that the convergence in this range depends on initial value x_0.

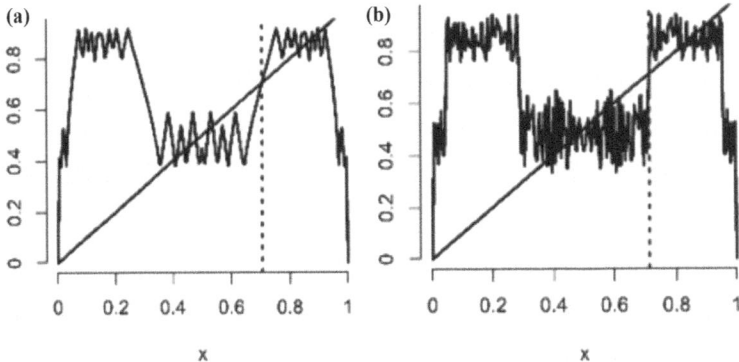

Fig. 4. a. Plots: $y = x$, $y = g^{(8)}(x; 1.3)$. b. Plots: $y = x$ and $y = g^{(16)}(x; 1.33)$.

3 Lyapunov Exponent, Chaos and Zone of Instability

Lyapunov Exponent is a very convenient computational tool widely used by researchers in practical experiments to characterize dynamic chaos. Lyapunov Exponent is a quantitative way to express non-predictability of chaotic regimes due to its sensitivity of dynamic processes to initial conditions. The paper adopts the ideas from [2–4, 10]. First, $M_1 = 5,000$ iterations (2) are run from the initial condition drawn as a random number from interval [0, 1]. The last value is used as the initial condition to run additional $M_2 = 5,000$ iterations. These M_2 values $\{x_k\}$ are substituted to the formula to compute Lyapunov Exponent $\lambda(\mu)$

$$\lambda(\mu) = \frac{1}{M_2} \sum_{k=1}^{M_2} \log \left| \frac{\partial g(x_k; \mu)}{\partial x} \right| \tag{4}$$

The solid line in Fig. 5a shows Lyapunov Exponent (4) for all values of μ. The dotted horizontal line corresponds to zero. Since in the range $0 \leq \mu \leq \mu_*^{(2)}$ iterations (1) – (2) converge to the fixed point $x_*^{(2)}(\mu) = \mu^2$, it is verified by direct calculations that $\lambda(\mu)$ has a constant value. If $\mu_*^{(2)} \leq \mu \leq \mu_*^{(3)}$, iterations (1) – (2) converge to $x_*^{(3)}(\mu)$, so $\lambda(\mu) = \log \left| 0.5\mu \left(1 - x_*^{(3)}(\mu) \right)^{1/2} \right|$. The $\lambda(\mu)$ curve shown in Fig. 5a has a small vertical "jump" from negative to positive values near $\mu_*^{(3)}$. To explore that domain in detail, Figs. 5b reports $\lambda(\mu)$ in the range of μ between 1.14 and 1.16. The Lyapunov Exponent curve has a zig-zag behavior and alters its sign.

For further analysis several numerical experiments are run with $\mu = 1.1508$ and different initial values x_0. In the first set of experiments $x_0 = 0.1$, and iterations are run multiple times starting from the same initial value. Each time a converge to $x_*^{(3)}$ is observed. In the second set of simulations, $x_0 = 0.2$ and multiple runs show a pattern like the one shown in Fig. 2b, i.e., almost periodic behavior. In the third set of numerical experiments, x_0 is randomly drawn from the uniform distribution. Two types of outcomes are observed, iterations either converge to $x_*^{(3)}$ or show almost periodic behavior. The above concludes that the behavioral pattern is dependent on the initial value. To verify

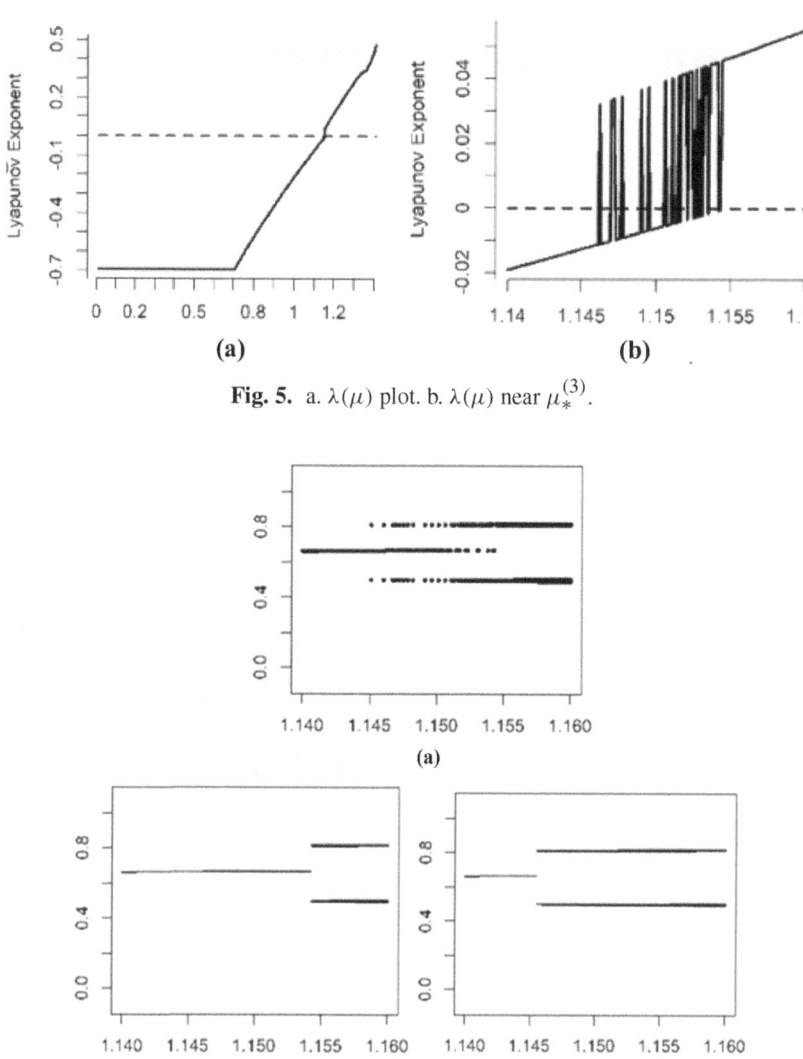

Fig. 5. a. $\lambda(\mu)$ plot. b. $\lambda(\mu)$ near $\mu_*^{(3)}$.

Fig. 6. a. Bifurcation plot: random selection of x_0. b. Bifurcation plot: $x_0 = 0.1$. c. Bifurcation plot: $x_0 = 0.2$.

this hypothesis, Fig. 6a reports the bifurcation diagram near $\mu_*^{(3)}$. The dots in the center of Figs. 6a correspond to $x_*^{(3)}(\mu)$. Along with a convergence to the single point, the almost period behavior is also observed for some values of μ. These results are linked to different initial values x_0 that are randomly drawn for each iteration sequence. Figures 6b and c show the bifurcation diagrams when all iterations start from $x_0 = 0.1$ or $x_0 = 0.2$ correspondingly. The above results show the existence of the zone of instability with strong dependency on the initial conditions. Obviously, the ergodicity property fails in this zone. Experiments with some other initial values demonstrate that almost periodic patterns exist for many starting points. Sample means and standard deviations calculated for almost periodic sequences and used as comparison metrics show that almost periodic orbits have equal statistical values. This concludes that in the zone of instability all sequences will converge either to the fixed point or almost periodic orbits with equal statistical characteristics.

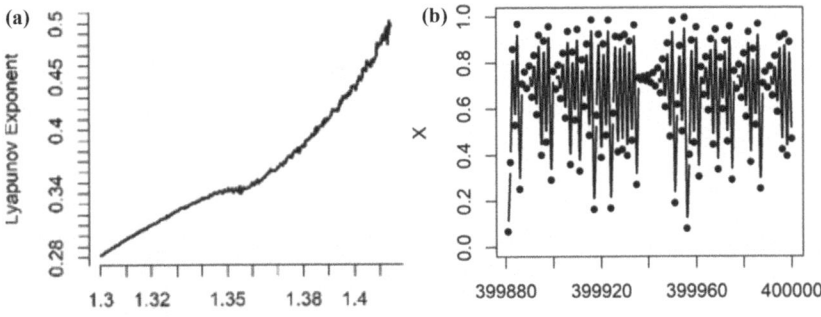

Fig. 7. a. $\lambda(\mu)$ near $\mu = \sqrt{2}$.. b. Plot of sample sequence $\{x_k\}$, $\mu = \sqrt{2}$.

The domain $\lambda(\mu) < 0$ is non-chaotic while the domain $\lambda(\mu) > 0$ (i.e., $\mu > \mu_*^{(3)}$) is considered as chaos. Another well-defined feature of chaos is topological transitivity [1, 2, 9]. The bifurcation diagrams of Figs. 1a and b show that if $\mu_*^{(3)} < \mu <\sim 1.35$ the interval of iteration points $\{x_k\}$ is divided into two subdomains. The existence of internal gaps in the bifurcation diagram indicates that topological transitivity condition is not met. Thus, accounting for both positiveness of Lyapunov Exponent and topological transitivity requirements, only region $\mu >\sim 1.35$ can be viewed as chaos. Figure 7a shows a plot of $\lambda(\mu)$ in this domain. In Fig. 7b connected dots illustrate the behavior of generated sequence (1) (in the range 399,880 – 400,000 iterations) for the developed chaos that corresponds to $\mu = \sqrt{2}$.

4 Invariant Distributions

The process (1) – (2) can be viewed from two different perspectives. The first one, which has been considered so far, is to treat the dynamic sequence (1a) as a deterministic process generated from the equation (2). One important question in the theory of non-linear dynamics is if the process possesses ergodic properties [5, 7]. One practical way to verify ergodicity is to calculate the distribution of the process. Let $F_{(N)}(x; \mu)$ be an empirical cumulative distribution function that describes the distribution of the sequence points $\{x_k\}_{i=0}^N$ for large values of N. If the ergodic property holds then there exists the limiting distribution $F_{attr}(x; \mu)$, called the attractor distribution, such that $\lim_{N \to \infty} F_{(N)}(x; \mu) = F_{attr}(x; \mu)$ regardless of the initial value x_0 from interval $[0, 1]$ (with possible exception of sets of zero measure). For numerical computations the interval $[0, 1]$ is divided into M subintervals that form a grid $G_M = \{x_{(i)}\}_{i=0}^M$. Functions $F_{(N)}(x; \mu)$ are defined in the nodes of the grid (same notation $F_{(N)}(x; \mu)$ will be used for these "grid" functions).

To generate empirical distributions $F_{(N)}(x; \mu)$, number of iteration points is counted in each subinterval of the grid G_M (like in histogram calculations). Then these numbers are normalized by N to get the corresponding interval frequencies. Finally, values of $F_{(N)}(x; \mu)$ are defined at the nodes of G_M as cumulative frequencies. In numerical experiments reported below, $300{,}000 - 600{,}000$ iterations (2) are run first. The attractor distribution $F_{attr}(x; \mu)$ is evaluated by computing cumulative frequencies for the last $100{,}000$ iteration points.

The second point of view on the dynamic process (1a) is to treat it as a stochastic process. Follow [2, 4, 7], let $(\Omega, \mathcal{F}, \mathbb{P})$ be a probability space (measure space), where $\Omega = \{\omega\}$ is a space of elementary events, $\mathcal{F}$ is a σ-algebra and $\mathbb{P}$ is a probability measure. It is assumed [12] that $\Omega = \Omega$ and $\omega = x_0$. The stochastic process is defined as a sequence of random variables $\{X_k(\omega; \mu)\}$ on $(\Omega \times [0, 1, 2, \ldots], \mathcal{F}, \mathbb{P})$:

$$X_{k+1}(\omega; \mu) = g(X_k(\omega; \mu); \mu), k = 0, 1, 2, \ldots \tag{5}$$

Given ω, the original sequence (1a) is a realization (or trajectory) of the stochastic process (5). The latter is, in fact, deterministic and its stochasticity is due to the randomness of $X_0(\omega; \mu)$ only [7]. One of the manifestations of the ergodicity is invariance of the corresponding distributions of random variables $\{X_k(\omega; \mu)\}$. Let $F_k(x; \mu) = \mathbb{P}(\omega : X_k(\omega; \mu) < x)$ be the cumulative distribution function (CDF) of random variable $X_k(\omega; \mu)$ The distribution invariance condition means that all distributions $F_k(x; \mu)$ are identical for any index k, i.e. there exists the cumulative distribution function $F(x; \mu) = F_k(x; \mu), k = 0, 1, 2, \ldots$ that solves the equation:

$$\mathbb{P}(\omega : X_{k+1}(\omega; \mu) < x) = \mathbb{P}(\omega : g(X_k(\omega; \mu), \omega) < x)$$

$$= \mathbb{P}\left(\omega : \mu\sqrt{X_k(\omega; \mu)} < x | X_k(\omega; \mu) < 1/2\right)$$

$$+\mathbb{P}\left(\omega : \mu\sqrt{1 - X_k(\omega; \mu)} > x | X_k(\omega; \mu) \geq 1/2\right) \tag{6a}$$

$$F(x; \mu) = F(\alpha(x; \mu)) - F(\beta(x; \mu)) + 1 \tag{6b}$$

$$\alpha(x; \mu) = x^2/\mu^2, \beta(x; \mu) = 1 - x^2/\mu^2 \tag{6c}$$

The above system of equations has a closed form solution if $\mu = \mu_{max}$:

$$F\left(x; \sqrt{2}\right) = x^2 \tag{7}$$

that is verified by direct calculations.

The system of equations (6a) – (6c) is solved by a numerical procedure introduced in [2]. Function $F(x; \mu)$ is defined in the nodes of the grid G_M. To avoid multiple notations, such "grid" functions will also be denoted by $F(x; \mu)$. In general, values $0 \leq \alpha(x; \mu) \leq 1$ and $0 \leq \beta(x; \mu) \leq 1$ in (6c) do not coincide with the grid nodes. In this case, the corresponding functional values are computed based on a linear interpolation between closets points of G_M. Such interpolated values will be denoted by $\widehat{F}^{(n)}\left(\alpha\left(x_{(i)}; \mu\right)\right)$

and $\widehat{F}^{(n)}\left(\beta\left(x_{(i)};\mu\right)\right)$. Given $F^{(0)}\left(x_{(i)};\mu\right)$, equations (6a)–(6c) are solved by numerical iterations:

$$F^{(n+1)}\left(x_{(i)};\mu\right) =$$

$$\gamma\left[\widehat{F}^{(n)}\left(\alpha\left(x_{(i)};\mu\right)\right) - \widehat{F}^{(n)}\left(\beta\left(x_{(i)};\mu\right)\right) + 1\right]$$

$$+(1-\gamma)F^{(n)}\left(x_{(i)};\mu\right), n = 0, 1, 2, \dots \qquad (8)$$

In (8), γ is a weight parameter. Computations are run over all points $\{x_{(i)}\}$ of G_M. The iteration process stops if $\max_{G_M}\left|F^{(n+1)}\left(x_{(i)};\mu\right) - F^{(n)}\left(x_{(i)};\mu\right)\right| < \epsilon$ for a small value ϵ. A convergence of iterations (8) would mean the existence of the invariant distribution $F(x;\mu) = \lim_{n\to\infty} F^{(n)}(x;\mu)$. The existence of such invariant distribution also implies $F_{attr}(x;\mu) = F(x;\mu)$, i.e., ergodicity.

To demonstrate that $GTM(1/2, 1/2, 1)$ possesses the ergodic property several numerical experiments are run with the following parameters: number of grid nodes $M = 1000$, accuracy $\epsilon = 10^{-3}$, and weight parameter $\gamma = 0.9$. To avoid "infinite" iteration loops due to potential divergence of (8) the maximum number of iterations is limited by 2000. Initial function is taken $F^{(0)}\left(x_{(i)};\mu\right) = x_{(i)}$. In the first experiment, $\mu = \sqrt{2}$ and numerical results (8) are compared to the closed-form solution (7). In Fig. 8a the solid line represents the function (7), the dot-dashed line, dashed line and dotted line are results after 1, 2 and 3 iterations (8). The dotted line coincides with the solid line and is almost invisible. Figure 8a demonstrates a fast convergence of the developed iteration procedure. In the second experiment, $\mu = 1.38$ that corresponds to the chaotic region. Results are shown in Fig. 8b. In this experiment the same computation grid $G_M = \{x_{(i)}\}_{i=0}^{M}$ with $M = 1000$ is used; 300,000 iterations (1a) are run, and the attractor distribution is based on the last 100,000 points. The solid line represents the attractor distribution, the dot-dashed line, dashed line and dotted line are results after 1, 2 and 5 iterations (8). In the third experiment reported in Fig. 8c $\mu = 1.3$ and this is outside of the chaotic range. The solid line represents the attractor distribution, the dot-dashed line, dashed line and dotted line are results after 5, 10 and 20 iterations (8). The convergence of (8) is slower compared to the previous example. As was reported in [2], a slow convergence is due to the non-smoothness of distribution functions.

5   Discussion and Conclusions

The paper introduces a novel generalized tent map called $GTM(1/2, 1/2, 1)$ and studies its properties. It is shown that for values of the map parameter μ belonging to interval $(0, 1/\sqrt{2})$, the iteration process (1)–(2) is convergent to the single fixed point $x_*^{(2)} = \mu^2$. If $1/\sqrt{2} < \mu < 2/\sqrt{3}$, iterations (2) converge to the fixed point $x_*^{(3)} = \left(-\mu^2 + \sqrt{\mu^4 + 4\mu^2}\right)/2$. When $\mu = 2/\sqrt{3}$, the fixed point $x_*^{(3)}$ becomes unstable. The bifurcation diagrams plotted in Figs. 1a and b show that in contrast to many known non-linear maps for which a route to chaos is characterized by periods of double

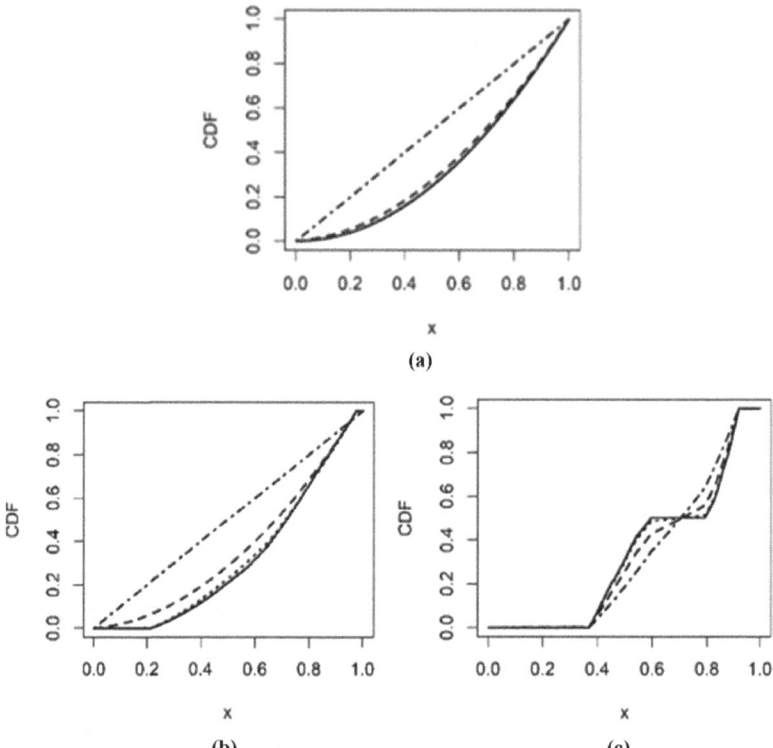

Fig. 8. a. Convergence of iterations (8) to $F\left(x; \sqrt{2}\right)$. b. Iteration convergence, $\mu = 1.38$. c. Iteration convergence, $\mu = 1.3$.

cascading and islands of stability, no such behavior is observed for GTM (1/2, 1/2, 1). It is demonstrated that P-cycles, as solutions to the equations $y = g^{(P)}(x; \mu)$ and $y = x$, exist but are not dynamically stable. These results are reported in Figs. 2, 3 and 4. The graphs show that at intersection points the tangent lines to $g^{(P)}(x; \mu)$ plots always have absolute values of slopes greater than 1.

To explain such non-typical behavior of GTM (1/2, 1/2, 1), a detailed analysis is conducted. As is shown, when the fixed point $x_*^{(3)}$ becomes unstable, its bifurcation branch becomes scattered around two branches of unstable 2-cycle forming two narrow domains separated by a gap (Fig. 2b). A similar behavior is also observed for larger values of μ. For example, Fig. 4b shows an iteration plot for $\mu = 1.25$. Iteration points are scattered around branches of the unstable 4-cycle forming subdomains that overlap.

Analysis of the Lyapunov Exponent plot shown in Figures 5 demonstrates that a chaotic pattern is observed for larger values of μ. If conditions of chaos include both positiveness of Lyapunov Exponent and topological transitivity, only domain $\mu >\sim 1.35$ exhibits the chaotic behavior. The paper also demonstrates the existence of the zone of instability for values of the map parameter near $\mu_*^{(3)}$ as is shown in Figs. 5a and 6a – 6c. Given a fixed map parameter but different starting points, iterations (1) – (2) will either converge to the fixed point or show almost periodic behavior. Such behavior, which is not typical for most known dynamic maps, can be considered as an intrinsic feature of GTM (1/2, 1/2, 1).

The paper also addresses a very important question of ergodicity of non-linear dynamic processes. The standard way to illustrate ergodicity is to compute attractors by running multiple iterations (1a). Along with the above approach the paper presents the second method that is based on a representation of the iteration sequence (1) - (2) by the stochastic process (5). It is assumed that the random process has the invariant distribution. To calculate the distribution, a very efficient algorithm (8) is applied. Plots of Figures 8a – 8c confirm the ergodic property of GTM (1/2, 1/2, 1) by comparing invariant distributions and attractors. The paper also reports the closed-form distribution $F\left(x; \sqrt{2}\right) = x^2$. Not many closed-form distributions are derived for known logistic maps, so this result is very important for a theoretical study of chaos. The ergodic property fails in the zone of instability where the strong dependency on initial conditions is observed.

Acknowledgments. The authors thank William P. Rice for reviewing the project and providing valuable feedback.

Disclosure of Interests. This work was funded by and is the responsibility of the authors. No support or incentives were provided by any funding agency, grant or contract.

References

1. Devaney, R.L.: An Introduction to Chaotic Dynamical Systems, 3rd edn. CRC Press, Boca Raton (2021)
2. Chtcheprov, A., Rice, W.P., Chtcheprov, A.: Overview of empirical distribution function computational framework to explore chaotic dynamic systems. In: Proceedings of the 2023 International Conference on Scientific Computing, pp. 623-627. IEEE Computer Society, Las Vegas (2023)
3. Chtcheprov, A., Chtcheprov, A., Rice, W.P.: The LM(1/2,1/2,1) – A special case of generalized logistic maps, ResearchGate (2019)
4. Chtcheprov, A., Rice, W.P., Chtcheprov, A.: Cumulative distribution function analysis of logistic map, ResearchGate (2021)
5. Elaydi, S.N.: Discrete Chaos with Applications in Science and Engineering, 2nd edn. Chapman & Hall/CRC, New York (2007)
6. Effah-Poku, S., Obeng-Denteh, W., Dontwi, I.K.: A Study of chaos in dynamic systems. Hindawi J. Math. (2018)
7. Shiryaev, A.N.: Essentials of Stochastic Finance: Facts, Models, Theory, 1st edn. World Scientific, Singapore, River Edge (1999)
8. Banks, J., Brooks, J., Cairns, G., Davis, G., Stacey, P.: On Devaney's definition of chaos. Am. Math. Mon. **90**(4), 332–334 (1992)
9. Vellekoop, M., Berglund, R.: On intervals: transitivity = chaos. Am. Math. Mon. **101**(4), 353–355 (1994)
10. Pikovsky, A., Politi, A.: Lyapunov Exponents: A Tool to Explore Complex Dynamics. Cambridge University Press, Cambridge (2016)
11. Chan, K., Tong, H.: Chaos: A Statistical Perspective, 1st edn. Springer, New York (2001)
12. Shiryaev, A.N.: Probability, 2nd edn. Springer, New York (1995)

Scalable Service Model and Scheduler for Delay-Sensitive Services

Csaba Lukovszki$^{(\boxtimes)}$ [ID] and József Bíró [ID]

Department of Telecommunications and Artificial Intelligence, Budapest University of
Technology and Economics, Műegyetem rkp. 3., Budapest 1111, Hungary
`{lukovszki,biro}@tmit.bme.hu`

Abstract. Efficient resource management is crucial in modern networks
due to the stringent requirements of emerging services. As networks
become more complex with technologies such as 5G, edge computing,
service-defined networking, scalable packet scheduling becomes essential.
In parallel, there is a growing revolution in latency-sensitive applications,
with different latency requirements of 5G and beyond services. To promote delay-sensitive traffic in a scalable manner, this paper presents
a general delay-oriented analysis of multi-queue systems. Based on this
model, we present a scheduling rule and scheduler implementation for
delay proportional and fair services that can serve delay-sensitive traffic
more efficiently and in scalable way than previous solutions.

Keywords: 5G and beyond services · scheduling · scalability ·
fairness · delay differentiation · analysis

1 Introduction

Efficient resource management is crucial in modern networks due to the strict
demands of emerging services like virtual and augmented reality, internet-of-
things related applications, and support of autonomous vehicles, which require
low latency and high reliability. As networks become more complex with the
introduction of technologies like 5G, edge computing, and service defined networking, scalable packet scheduling becomes essential for ensuring that delay-
sensitive data packets are delivered predictably. Meeting with increased expectations for high-quality services requires efficient resource allocation, and service
mechanisms to ensure the desired quality while maintaining efficiency and scalability.

The research leading to these results is funded by the EU Chips-JU organization
under grant agreement 101112089, within the project AIMS5.0 and from the part-
ners' national programs and funding authorities. Part of this work is created within
the Arrowhead fPVN project, supported by the Chips-JU and its members, as well
as by national funding authorities from involved countries under grant agreement no.
101111977.

Effective resource management is vital in the radio access network (RAN) of both 5G and beyond networks, particularly for tasks that require minimal latency. The RAN plays a pivotal role in coordinating communication between user equipment (UE) and aggregation network, comprising base stations responsible for wireless connectivity and efficient packet service.

There is an ever growing revolution of delay-sensitive application with different latency requirements [24, 26]. While high-speed mobile streaming, massive machine-type communication (mMTC) [22], and ultra-reliable low latency communications (URLLC) of 5G networks and integrated sensing and communication (ISAC), extended reality (XR) of 6G networks require low-latency network services, emerging new application, such as tactile internet (TI) and application of digital twin (DT) technologies claim real-time underlying packet transferring services. Therefore, in the RAN, efficient allocation of radio resources and scheduling of packet transmissions are essential to minimize latency and meet the quality of service (QoS) requirements of these applications.

As new applications and technologies emerge, the demand for communication services grows. According to [8, 25] 5G and beyond communication systems will address this massive rise in services and applications requiring more efficient networks with higher data rates, reduced latencies, greater spectrum efficiencies, increased energy efficiency, and expanded network capacity.

To promote delay-sensitive traffic, this paper presents a general delay-oriented modeling of multi-queue schedulers. Through this model, we present a scheduler implementing a proportional delay service that can serve delay-sensitive traffic more efficiently and scalably than previous solutions.

To accomplish the goal of the paper, Sect. 2 reviews related research on delay-sensitive services and schedulers. Following the summary of the initial queuing model and the notations enumerated in Sect. 3 analytical model is presented in Sect. 4 to depict the delay induced by scheduling decisions. Utilizing this model, Sect. 5 derives the scheduling decision rule for implementing proportional delay packet service, while the scheduler implementation is detailed in Sect. 6. Finally, conclusions are drawn in Sect. 7.

2 Related Work

Over the last decade, advanced scheduling algorithms and techniques have been employed in the RAN to prioritize and allocate resources based on factors such as channel conditions, traffic load, QoS requirements, and user mobility. This ensures that delay-sensitive traffic receives the necessary resources and is transmitted with controlled delay. In terms of continuous improvement, [20] provides a comprehensive overview of flexible multi-user scheduling features and summarizes 5G design standards and enhanced QoS architectures.

Various aspects of QoS have been investigated, including effective resource allocation and management in the RAN [6], efficient downlink [2, 18] and uplink scheduling [16], and how scheduling schemes address spectrum, interference efficiency and energy-efficient allocation issues to meet the QoS performance requirements of 5G RAN systems [19].

Essentially, the literature distinguishes between channel-independent (CIS) and channel-dependent scheduling (CDS). CIS strategies, also referred to as classical strategies, allocate resources equally among users without considering their traffic type or channel conditions [15]. In contrast, dynamic CDS focuses on optimally allocating resources based on transmission conditions and user expectations [17]. In real-world mobile communication systems, various factors must be addressed in resource management. These factors include channel quality indicators, achievable average data rates, queue status, and desired QoS [14].

To detail QoS requirements, a variety of performance metrics can be used, such as delay, throughput, goodput, fairness [9], spectral efficiency over radio links [23], packet loss ratio [10], that are handled with different scheduling schemes. [14] offers a comprehensive classification of scheduling schemes based on these capabilities.

In addition to conventional approaches, contemporary schedulers can benefit from machine learning algorithms for multi-metric optimization. Researchers are exploring various machine learning methodologies to enhance resource allocations and meet the QoS requirements of upcoming 5G and beyond 5G wireless networks [1]. However, such multi-metric solutions may encounter scalability challenges, particularly at the customer level in RAN. Trade-off must be hold between scalability and multi-modal optimization. While multi-model optimization addresses most of the requirement in packet level, scalable solutions can concentrate on intricate resource allocation and management schemes at the control plane level, while maintaining a simple packet service.

Concerning scalability objectives, relative service differentiation offers a promising solution. For delay-oriented services, proportional delay differentiation offers delay performance metrics for each service class proportional to a specific constant $\frac{d_i}{d_j} = \frac{c_i}{c_j}$ [3]. By the introducing the parameter t, the target delay ratio for a multi-class system can be formulated using the following equation.

$$d_i = c_i t \tag{1}$$

The class of proportional delay schedulers and associated allocation schemes has been extensively explored in the literature [11–13], encompassing proportional fair schedulers, that dynamically allocate resources in real-time, such that is done in proportional delay services [7].

The majority of proportional delay schedulers bases on the concept of waiting time priority scheduler (WTP) [3–5,11,13], which registers the arrival time of each packet in the queuing system and the packet priorities are calculated on the actual waiting time. However, implementing proportional delay services with this approach raises scalability concerns, as it scales with the number of packets in the system.

The delay model proposed in this paper is suitable for implementing a scheduler that surpasses the performance of the standard WTP scheduler, even under light-load conditions, as demonstrated for two classes in [21]. Moreover, it exhibits no scalability issues, since scaling with the number of classes rather than the packets in the system.

3   Queuing System Model and Notations

In the queuing system, depicted in Fig. 1 variable-sized packets from multiple classes can be stored, managed, and scheduled for transmission on the outgoing link, according to a predefined scheduling rule. The link capacity is assumed to be constant, and the queuing system incorporates infinite, first-in-first-out queues to store packages for each class. Moreover, the scheduler follows non-preemptive and work-conserving paradigms.

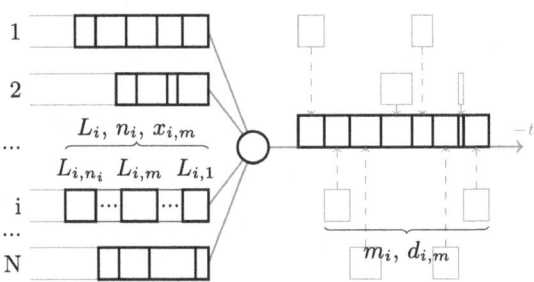

Fig. 1. Queuing system model

As illustrated in Fig. 1 the system consists of N queues, where each class-i queue contains n_i packets at a given time instant, where $i \in [1...N]$. Every packet in class-i has a specific length denoted as $L_{i,m}$, representing the time required for transmission on the outgoing link, while m identifies the position of the packet in the queue, so $m \in [1...n_i]$. Consequently, the total length of a class-i queue is $L_i = \sum_{m=1}^{n_i} L_{i,m}$, and the total work in the queuing system is $L = \sum_{i=1}^{n} L_i$. Up to the current time instant, each packet in the queues has suffered a delay of $x_{i,m}$, defined as the difference between the current time and the time of arrival.

Following the work-conserving principle, scheduling occurs immediately after the completion of the preceding transmission. At this moment, the scheduler selects the next class to serve based on the current system state. The first packet from the selected queue is then forwarded without preemption.

In the model, transmitted packet service delays are continuously recorded. At each scheduling instant, it is assumed that m_i class-i packets are served experiencing a delay of $d_{i,k}$ from arrival to the end of transmission.

In the following, we assume local optimality, meaning that at the moment scheduling decision is made, only information about packets that have already arrived or been served is available, that means the system is closed. Under this assumption, the aggregated delay of class-i packets is determined by the following five factors.

Transmitted Packets Delay (D_i): The aggregated delay of packets that have been already transmitted.

$$D_i = \sum_{m=1}^{m_i} d_{i,m} \tag{2}$$

Queuing Time (X_i): The total delay experienced by packets in the queue until the given time instant.

$$X_i = \sum_{m=1}^{n_i} x_{i,m} \tag{3}$$

Queuing Delay (J_i): The time that class-i packets must spend in the queue, due to service of preceding packets in the same queue.

$$J_i = \sum_{m=1}^{n_i} (n_i - m) L_{i,m} = n_i L_i + \sum_{m=1}^{n_i} m L_{i,m} \tag{4}$$

Scheduling Delay (S_i): The additional delay caused by the service of packets from other classes. This delay is governed by the specific scheduling rule in place.

Transmission Delay (T_i): The total time needed to transmit class-i packets.

$$T_i = \sum_{m=1}^{n_i} L_{i,m} = L_i \tag{5}$$

Based on the aforementioned notation, the calculation for the average delay of class-i packets can be expressed as follows.

$$d_i = \frac{1}{m_i + n_i} \left(\overbrace{D_i + X_i}^{W_i} + \overbrace{J_i + S_i}^{I_i} + T_i \right) \tag{6}$$

In the following the sum of queuing delay and scheduling delay is referred as *upcoming delay* and marked with $I_i = J_i + S_i$ for class-i, while $W_i = D_i + X_i$.

The scheduler has impact only on the scheduling delay, so the following analysis will concentrate on that delay factor.

4   Scheduling Delay

The scheduler aims to make optimal decisions regarding packet service based on specified constraints, and the current state of the queuing system. Throughout our analysis, we adopt the concept of local optimality, assuming that at the time of scheduling decisions no additional packet will arrive to the system.

From the perspective of class-i scheduling delay, any scheduler can operate between two boundaries, $S_i^{min} \leq S_i \leq S_i^{max}$. The first boundary is set when class-i have absolute priority over other classes. Packets of class-i must then await the service of preceding packets from the same class-i exclusively, encapsulated in the variable J_i. This way minimum scheduling delay of class-i packets is zero.

$$S_i^{min} = 0 \tag{7}$$

The opposite boundary is set when the service of all non class-i packets has priority over the class-i packets. The additional delay beyond the queuing delay J_i is the time that class-i packets have to wait for the service of all other packets.

$$S_i^{max} = n_i \sum_{j \neq i} L_j = n_i(L - L_i) \tag{8}$$

With respect to the achieved scheduling delay, a scheduler can operate within the aforementioned boundaries. The delay is influenced by scheduling decisions at each packet transmission, which subsequently alters the state of the queues.

Figure 2 illustrates the states for a system with three queues, where each dimension represents the number of packets in the class-i queue. The queue state after the s-th step is a three-dimensional coordinate $\boldsymbol{k}(s) = (k_1, k_2, k_3)$, with the initial queue state at the time of the first decision being $\boldsymbol{k}(0) = (n_1, n_2, n_3)$. When a class-$i$ packet is served, the queue state in the relevant dimension decreases by 1, so $k_{i,(s+1)} = k_{i,(s)} - 1$. In the example, during the first step ($s = 1$), the packet served is the first from class-2, $(j, m) = (2, 1)$. Generally, under local optimal condition, the scheduler aims to move from the starting point $\boldsymbol{k}(0) = (n_1, n_2, n_3)$ to the origin $\boldsymbol{k}(M) = (0, 0, 0)$ by taking M unit steps along the dimensions. This process involves steps equal to the total number of packets in the system at the starting point, $M = \sum_{i=1}^{N} n_i$, which is 8 in this example.

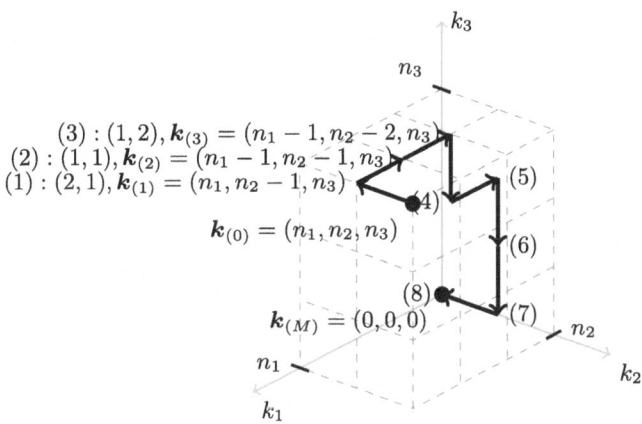

Fig. 2. Queue state and its changes during packet service

The delay of class-i packets is dependent on the number of packets previously served from non class-i queues. To describe the service order, series of $\boldsymbol{k}$ is introduced, which is defined to describe the queue state after each packet service.

Definition 1 (Queue state after service) *The number of $k_{i,(j,m)}$ represents the number of class-i packets, that are served after the m-th class-j packet.*

The definition describes packet scheduling order, since after service of m-th class-j packet $k_{i,(j,m)}$ packets will remain in the class-i queue, clearly describing the packet service and the resulted queue state order.

The value $k_{i,(j,m)}$ represents the number of packets in the class-i queue that must wait for the service of the m-th class-j packet with a size of $L_{j,m}$. As a result, it increases the total scheduling delay for class-i packets by $k_{i,(j,m)}L_{j,m}$. By summing this for each packet in each queue, the total aggregated scheduling delay can be calculated using the following expression.

$$S_i = \sum_{\substack{j=1 \\ j \neq i}}^{N} \sum_{m=1}^{n_j} k_{i,(j,m)} L_{j,m} \tag{9}$$

Here we can see, that scheduling delay of class-i in Eq. (9) does not count packet service from the same class, since it is involved in queuing delay already. Consequently, the upcoming delay can be described as $I_i = \sum_{j=1}^{N} \sum_{m=1}^{n_j} k_{i,(j,m)} L_{j,m}$. Also we must note that k values for service is the same class is independent from the scheduling decision, such as $k_{i,(i,m)} = (n_i - m)$, as it is obvious from Eq. (4).

4.1   Basic Attributes

Before proceeding with further evaluation, attributes of **k** should be specified.

Proposition 1 (Conservation law). *For any non-preemptive work-conserving scheduler,*

$$K = \sum_{i=1}^{N} \sum_{\substack{j=1 \\ j \neq i}}^{N} \sum_{m=1}^{n_j} k_{i,(j,m)} = \sum_{i=1}^{N} \sum_{j=1}^{i-1} n_i n_j \tag{10}$$

Proof. As a first step complete the summation with k values, when $j = i$.

$$\sum_{i=1}^{N} \sum_{j=1}^{N} \sum_{m=1}^{n_j} k_{i,(j,m)} = \sum_{i=1}^{N} \sum_{j=1}^{i-1} n_i n_j + \overbrace{\frac{1}{2} \sum_{i=1}^{N} n_i^2 - \frac{1}{2} \sum_{i=1}^{N} n_i}^{\sum_{i=1}^{N} \sum_{m=1}^{n_i} k_{i,(i,m)}} \tag{11}$$

The left size shows the summation of k values until the system becomes empty. By employing the notation applied in the queue state space representation and recalling $M = \sum_{i=1}^{N} n_i$, we can express the following.

$$\sum_{i=1}^{N} \sum_{j=1}^{N} \sum_{m=1}^{n_j} k_{i,(j,m)} = \sum_{s=1}^{M} \sum_{i=1}^{N} k_{i,(s)} = ... \tag{12}$$

At each step of the service $\sum_{i=1}^{N} k_{i,(s)}$ denotes the summation of $\mathbf{k}_{(s)}$, equivalent to the total number of packets in the system after the service of s-th packet.

Since during the service sequence this summation starts at M, in each step decreases by one and finally achieves 0, continuing from Eq. (12), we can write the following.

$$\ldots = \sum_{s=1}^{M}(M - s) = \frac{1}{2}MM - \frac{1}{2}M = \ldots \tag{13}$$

Substitution of M and employment identity of $\sum_{i=1}^{N}\sum_{j=1}^{i} n_i n_j = \frac{1}{2}\sum_{i=1}^{N} n_i \sum_{j=1}^{N} n_j + \frac{1}{2}\sum_{i=1}^{N} n_i^2$ yields the following result for Eq. (13).

$$\ldots = \frac{1}{2}\sum_{i=1}^{N} n_i \sum_{j=1}^{N} n_j - \frac{1}{2}\sum_{i=1}^{N} n_i = \sum_{i=1}^{N}\sum_{j=1}^{i} n_i n_j - \frac{1}{2}\sum_{i=1}^{N} n_i^2 - \frac{1}{2}\sum_{i=1}^{N} n_i \tag{14}$$

The final step is to substract element added in the first step in Eq. (11).

$$K = \sum_{i=1}^{N}\sum_{j=1}^{i} n_i n_j - \sum_{i=1}^{N} n_i^2 = \sum_{i=1}^{N}\sum_{j=1}^{i-1} n_i n_j \tag{15}$$

Equation (15) proofs the proposition statement. □

4.2 Fixed Size Packets

Throughout the subsequent analysis, consider a hypothetical system, where each queue contains packets of identical size, denoted as $l_i = L_{i,m}$ for all $m \in [1..n_i]$. First define $e_{i,j}$ values according to the following equation, where $i, j \in [1..N]$.

$$e_{i,j} = \begin{cases} \sum_{m=1}^{n_j} k_{i,(j,m)} & \text{if } j \neq j \\ 0 & \text{if } j = i \end{cases} \tag{16}$$

Based on local optimal criteria, and the introduction of l_i and $e_{i,j}$, the scheduling delay in Eq. (9) is transformed into the following formula.

$$S_i = \sum_{j=1}^{N} l_j \sum_{m=1}^{n_j} k_{i,(j,m)} = \sum_{j=1}^{N} l_j e_{i,j} \tag{17}$$

In the equation above, $e_{i,j}$ aggregates the occurrences when a class-i packet must wait for the service of a packet from class-j, and the summation of $e_{i,j}$ values still uphold to the conservation law defined in Eq. (10), namely $K = \sum_{i=1}^{N}\sum_{j=1}^{N} e_{i,j} = \sum_{i=1}^{N}\sum_{i=1}^{i-1} n_i n_j$.

By forming vectors s and l using S_i and l_i values, respectively, and a matrix E from $e_{i,j}$ values the Eq. (17) can be expressed in a more concise manner.

$$s = E \cdot l \tag{18}$$

In Eq. (18) vector l enumerates the packet sizes of classes, while the matrix E determines sequence of packet service. The resulting vector s encapsulates the scheduling delay of different classes, which defines a point in the N-dimensional hyperspace of $\{S_i\}$. Subsequently, the focus is put on the examination of the point cloud defined by potential service sequences.

Consider two scheduling sequences, defined by matrices $\mathbf{E}_1$ and $\mathbf{E}_2$, where $\mathbf{E}_1 \neq \mathbf{E}_2$. Now, suppose we make an elementary modification in service order, such that a class-i packet is scheduled earlier than a class-j packet. It is evident that $\mathbf{E}_1$ can be transformed into $\mathbf{E}_2$ by applying a series of these elementary modifications. Thus, to examine the point cloud defined by all individual service sequences, it suffices to focus on this elementary step, only. Formally, this elementary step modifies $e_{i,j}$ and $e_{j,i}$ in matrix $\mathbf{E}$. Since one class-i packet no longer has to wait for a class-j packet service, $e_{i,j}$ is decreased, while, due to the same reason and the conservation law of Eq. (10), $e_{j,i}$ is increased by 1.

$$e'_{i,j} \Leftarrow e_{i,j} + 1 \qquad e'_{j,i} \Leftarrow e_{j,i} - 1 \tag{19}$$

The elementary modification in the service order leads to a different scheduling delay, which can be represented as a step in the space of $\{S_i\}$. Given that the matrix $\mathbf{E}$ is changed only in the positions (i, j) and (j, i) according to the Eq. (19), the change in scheduling delay results the following.

$$\Delta s = s' - s = (\mathbf{E}' - \mathbf{E})\, l = [\overset{1}{0} \dots \overset{i}{-l_j} \, \overset{j}{\dots l_i} \overset{N}{\dots 0}]$$

This step results in a movement with a slope of $[-l_j, l_i]$ and normal vector of $[l_i, l_j]$. As this statement is independent of the other dimensions and the actual value of $\mathbf{E}$ each point represented by s vector lies on a hyperplane with the following normal vector.

$$n = [l_1, .., l_i, ..l_N] \tag{20}$$

As shown on Fig. 3 the hyperplane representing scheduling delays is truncated into a polygon by boundary delays, see Eqs. (7) and (8). The vertices of the polygon are determined by the extreme delay values $s^{(i,j,k)}$, which correspond to the strict priority order of classes (i, j, k).

To determine equation defining the hyperplane, an arbitrary point must be chosen. In the further analysis, we opt for the centroid of the polygon representing the scheduler capabilities.

Since the coordinates of the centroid of a polygon are the average of the corresponding coordinates of its vertices, the vertices must first be determined. In the queuing system, each vertex corresponds to a specific strict priority order. With N classes, there are $N!$ permutations, resulting in the polygon having $N!$ vertices.

The scheduling delay of class-i packets for a particular priority order (p) can be calculated by the following equation.

$$S_i^{(p)} = n_i \sum_{j:p_j < p_i} L_j \tag{21}$$

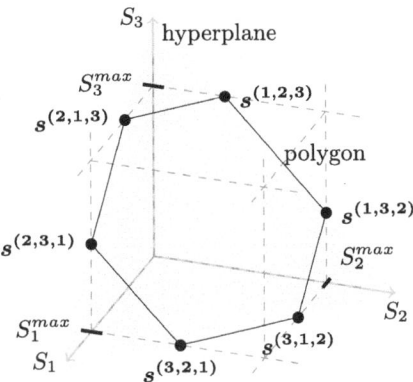

Fig. 3. Scheduling delay hyperplane and polygon in three-dimensional space

The average of $S_i^{(p)}$ counts all permutations of strict priority orders where class-j has lower priority than class-i, thus transmitted earlier. While this occurs in half of the permutations, average can be simplified as follows.

$$\bar{S}_i = \frac{1}{N!} \sum_{(p)} S_i^{(p)} = \frac{1}{N!} \sum_{(p)} n_i \sum_{j:p_j < p_i} L_j = \frac{1}{2} n_i \sum_{j \neq i} L_j \tag{22}$$

As the result we can derive the coordinates of the polygon centroid.

$$\bar{s} = \left[\bar{I}_i\right], \quad \bar{S}_i = \frac{1}{2} n_i (L - L_i) \tag{23}$$

Referring back to the normal vector from Eq. (20) and the centroid coordinates from Eq. (23) the Cartesian equation of the scheduling hyperplane is derived as follows.

$$\sum_{i=1}^{N} l_i (S_i - \bar{S}_i) = \sum_{i=1}^{N} l_i \left(S_i - \frac{1}{2} n_i (L - L_i)\right) = 0 \tag{24}$$

Furthermore, boundaries defined by Eqs. (7) and (8) form the scheduling polygon over the scheduling hyperplane.

4.3 Feasible Region of Scheduling Delay

The scheduling delay (S_i) is ultimately determined by decisions made by the scheduling algorithm. The range of S_i is restricted by the current state of the system, including factors such as queue sizes, packet order, and packet lengths. These limitations define a region of feasible S_i values achievable during scheduling, known as the feasible region.

Proposition 2 (Feasible region). *Let* $l_i^{max} = \max_m(L_{i,m})$ *the maximum and* $l_i^{min} = \min_m(L_{i,m})$ *the minimum of the packet sizes for each class-i. Besides* $L_i^{max} = n_i l_i^{max}$, $L_i^{min} = n_i l_i^{min}$ *and* $L^{max} = \sum_{j=1}^N L_j^{max}$, $L^{min} = \sum_{j=1}^N L_j^{min}$. *Then* S_i *must meet the following boundary conditions, if* $i \in [1..N]$.

$$\sum_{i=1}^N l_i^{max}\left(S_i - \frac{1}{2}n_i(L^{max} - \frac{1}{2}L_i^{max})\right) \leq 0 \tag{25}$$

$$\sum_{i=1}^N l_i^{min}\left(S_i - \frac{1}{2}n_i(L^{min} - \frac{1}{2}L_i^{min})\right) \geq 0 \tag{26}$$

$$S_i \geq S_i^{min} = 0 \tag{27}$$

$$S_i \leq S_i^{max} = n_i(L - L_i) \tag{28}$$

Proof. Beginning with Eq. (9), and replacing the packet sizes with their maximum values while recalling the notation $e_{i,j}$ from Eq. (16), we derive the following expression for the upper bound of S_i.

$$S_i \leq \sum_{j=1}^N l_j^{max} \sum_{m=1}^{n_j} k_{i,(j,m)} = \sum_{j=1}^N l_j^{max} e_{i,j} \tag{29}$$

Equation (29) forms the similar relationship as Eq. (17), with the exception that packet size changes from l_i to l_i^{max}. Therefore, the equation defines a plane, and all the arguments and conclusions made in Sect. 4.2 remain valid with the substitutions $l_i = l_i^{max}$ and $L_i = n_i l_i^{max}$, thereby confirming the validity of Eq. (25), and with the substitutions $l_i = l_i^{min}$ and $L_i = n_i l_i^{min}$, validity of Eq.(26).

Additionally, Eqs. (27) and (28) define the minimum and maximum scheduling delays, which are exactly aligned with Eqs. (7) and (8), respectively.   □

5 Derivation of Delay Sensitive Scheduling Rule

Assume a queuing system with fixed-size packets for each class (see Sect. 4.2) and the parametric formulation of target delay among classes in Eq. (1). Under the local optimal condition, the delay achievable by each class until the system becomes empty can be determined as the intersection point of curve defined by target delay and the plane describing the delays achievable by the scheduling algorithm (see Eq. (24)). If the intersection is within the feasible region, the scheduler can achieve the target delay for each class.

To find the intersection, Eq. (24) must be transformed from the $\{S_i\}$ space to the $\{d_i\}$ space. Using the relationship between d_i and S_i given in Eq. (6), the hyperplane can be determined by the following equation.

$$\sum_{i=1}^N l_i\left((n_i + m_i)d_i - \left(W_i + J_i + T_i + \frac{1}{2}n_i(L - L_i)\right)\right) = 0 \tag{30}$$

Due to the linear properties of transformation in Eq. (6), the plane in the space of $\{d_i\}$ retains all the properties of hyperplane in the space of $\{S_i\}$. The normal vector is transformed to $\boldsymbol{n} = [\{l_i(m_i + n_i)\}]$, while the centroid is converted and described by the following equation.

$$\bar{\boldsymbol{d}} = [\bar{d}_i], \ \bar{d}_i = \frac{1}{n_i + m_i}\left(W_i + J_i + T_i + \frac{1}{2}n_i(L - L_i)\right) \tag{31}$$

By substituting the parametric equation of the proportional delay differentiation service from Eq. (1) into the Cartesian equation of the hyperplane from Eq. (30) and solving the resulting equation for the parameter t, the intersection in the space of $\{d_i\}$ is given by the following equation.

$$\boldsymbol{d}^* = [d_i^*], \ d_i^* = c_i \frac{\sum_{k=1}^{N} l_k \left(W_k + J_k + T_k + \frac{1}{2}n_k(L - L_k)\right)}{\sum_{k=1}^{N} c_k l_k (n_k + m_k)} \tag{32}$$

Deriving the scheduling based on the above evaluations, it is important to consider that scheduling will be performed at each packet transmission rather than for all packets in the queue. Hence, when a class-j packet of size $L_{j,1}$ is assumed to be transmitted, the queuing state is considered to change, which is represented by the conditional hyperplane, centroid $(\bar{\boldsymbol{d}}^{|j})$, and the intersection of hyperplane and target delay curve $(\boldsymbol{d}^{*|j})$. These parameters are derived by modifying Eqs. (30), (31), and (32) by using the following substitutions.

$$\begin{aligned}
L_j &\leftarrow L_j - L_{j,1} \\
J_j &\leftarrow J_j - (n_j - 1)L_{j,1} \\
(n_j, m_j) &\leftarrow (n_j - 1, m_j + 1) \\
W_k &\leftarrow W_k + (n_k - 1)L_{k,1} \ \forall k \in [1..N]
\end{aligned} \tag{33}$$

Regarding the polygon in the hyperspace referring the conditional transmission of class-j packet, if the intersection is close to the boundary, the scheduling options will be limited. It is crucial to ensure the achieved delays align with the target.

Consequently, the proposed scheduler selects the class of packet for transmission whose conditional intersection is closest to the centroid of the conditional scheduling polygon. The Euclidean distance is calculated in the space of $\{d_i\}$ for each class-j packet conditional scheduling. The squared distance for class-j packet conditional scheduling is given by the following equation.

$$dist_j^2 = d^2\left(\bar{\boldsymbol{d}}^{|j}, \boldsymbol{d}^{*|j}\right) = \sum_{i=1}^{N}\left(\bar{d}_i^{|j} - d_i^{*|j}\right)^2 \tag{34}$$

Figure 4 illustrates a scenario where a class-1 packet is considered for transmission. In this example, the system state changes, resulting in increased minimum delay bounds for class-2 and class-3, and a reduced maximum delay bound for class-1, along with a modified normal vector of the plane. The resulting changes in the polygon and the movement of the centroid are highlighted in the figure. Additionally, the target delay line intersects with the conditional scheduling hyperplane at a point denoted by "X" in the figure, which measures a certain distance from the centroid.

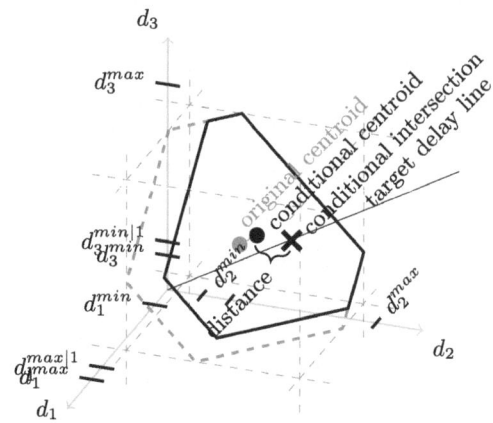

Fig. 4. The scheduling polygon and its modification when transmission of a class-1 packet is assumed

6   Proportional Delay Differentiation Scheduler

In this section, we present the scheduler that implements the proportional delay differentiation packet service, building on the model and analysis discussed earlier. Below, we enumerate all the events related to scheduling process and provide detailed explanations of the parameter updates and decisions involved. In the following, the actual time is denoted by t, the last event time is denoted by t', and for simplicity X_i and D_i are combined into $W_i = X_i + D_i$.

Initialization: The initialization event is triggered at system startup. As a result, all system state parameters are reset to their default values.

$$(t, t') \leftarrow (0, 0) \tag{35}$$

$$(J_i, L_i, n_j, m_j, W_j) \leftarrow (0, 0, 0, 0, 0) \quad \forall j \in [1..N] \tag{36}$$

Packet Arrival: Upon the arrival of a class-i packet with a length of L_{i,n_i+1} to the system, relevant system parameters should be updated. Additionally, if a packet arrives when the system is empty, a scheduling event should be triggered.

$$L_i \leftarrow L_i + L_{i,n_i+1}$$
$$J_i \leftarrow J_i + L_i$$
$$n_i \leftarrow n_i + 1$$
$$W_j \leftarrow W_j + n_j(t - t') \quad \forall j \in [1..N] \tag{37}$$
$$t' \leftarrow t \tag{38}$$

Scheduling: At the scheduling time instant first all W_j values should be updated according to Eqs. (37) and (38) then the distance between the intersection point and centroid of the scheduling polygon needs to be calculated for each non-empty class using Eq. (34) based on the conditional updated parameters described in Eq. (33). The packet from the class with the lowest distance will be selected for transmission.

End of Transmission: After the completion of class-i packet with length of $L_{i,1}$ the system does the following steps:

– *Parameter update*: System parameters are updated according to the following equations.

$$J_i \leftarrow J_i - (n_i - 1)L_{i,1}$$
$$L_i \leftarrow L_i - L_{i,1}$$
$$(n_i, m_i) \leftarrow (n_i - 1, m_i + 1)$$

– *Queue status check*: Following the successful transmission of a packet from class-i, a check is made on the queue size. If the queue is found to be empty, a reset operation is performed exclusively for class-i, restoring its parameters to their default values as prescribed by Eq. (36). In the case when all queues become empty Eq. (35) is also called and the system enters into a hold state, awaiting the next packet arrival event.
– *Trigger scheduling event*: If the system is not in a hold state, as the last step new scheduling event is triggered.

6.1   Busy Period Management Policies

In practical scenarios with light traffic loads, the duration of the busy period may be too short to attain the target delay ratio outlined in Eq. (1). However, the desired performance could still be achieved by concatenating multiple busy periods. For this reason, parameter reset should not be triggered as mentioned in the "Queue status check" section until the system reaches a predetermined busy period threshold, such as when $min_i(m_i) > 10$ or $\sum_i m_i > 10$.

6.2 Scalability

In many cases, scalability poses a significant challenge when implementing low-level processing solutions like packet scheduling. This challenge is particularly evident in telecommunications networks where resources are often limited near the user, or near central servers handling a vast number of classes or packets. When investigating scalability, two key issues come to light.

Concerning resource efficiency, the proposed scheduling method scales up with the number of classes, while remains independent of the number of packets. This stands in contrast to other solutions found in the literature. [3, 4, 11–13] For each class, only five values need to be stored, namely W_i, L_i, J_i, m_i, and n_i.

In terms of computational complexity, the proposed solution relies solely on strict and predefined basic arithmetic operations. As such, it imposes minimal computational load, even on low-end processors available nowadays.

7 Conclusions

Meeting the demands of delay-sensitive traffic remains a significant challenge in modern telecommunications networks. The multi-modality of services introduces numerous parameters that must be carefully considered during packet service. Many existing approaches offer efficient, but complex solutions, while our work addresses this challenge with a straightforward, manageable, and scalable solution by presenting an analytical model focusing on packet service delays.

Our study investigates a multi-queue system to analyze the achievable average class delays comprehensively. As a result of our research, we developed an analytical model that encapsulates the complexities of the system in a lightweight way. The scheduling algorithm derived from this model offers superior scalability and performance compared to industry-standard schedulers, as demonstrated in this paper and referenced work [21].

References

1. Ahmed, K.I., Tabassum, H., Hossain, E.: Deep learning for radio resource allocation in multi-cell networks. IEEE Netw. **33**(6), 188–195 (2019)
2. Capozzi, F., Piro, G., Grieco, L., Boggia, G., Camarda, P.: Downlink packet scheduling in LTE cellular networks: Key design issues and a survey. IEEE Commun. Surv. Tutor. **15**(2), 678–700 (2013)
3. Dovrolis, C., Ramanathan, P.: A case for relative differentiated services and the proportional differentiation model. IEEE Netw. **13**(5), 26–34 (1999)
4. Dovrolis, C., Stiliadis, D., Ramanathan, P.: Proportional differentiated services: delay differentiation and packet scheduling. SIGCOMM Comput. Commun. Rev. **29**(4), 109–120 (1999)
5. Dovrolis, C., Stiliadis, D.: Relative differentiated services in the internet: issues and mechanisms. In: Proceedings of the 1999 ACM SIGMETRICS International Conference on Measurement and Modeling of Computer Systems, SIGMETRICS 1999, pp. 204–205. Association for Computing Machinery, New York (1999)

6. Ejaz, W., Sharma, S.K., Saadat, S., Naeem, M., Anpalagan, A., Chughtai, N.: A comprehensive survey on resource allocation for CRAN in 5G and beyond networks. J. Netw. Comput. Appl. **160**, 102638 (2020). https://doi.org/10.1016/j.jnca.2020.102638

7. Han, A.X., Lu, I.T.: Optimizing beyond the carrier by carrier proportional fair scheduler. In: 34th IEEE Sarnoff Symposium, pp. 1–5 (2011)

8. Hossain, E., Hasan, M.: 5G cellular: key enabling technologies and research challenges. IEEE Instrum. Meas. Mag. **18**(3), 11–21 (2015)

9. Jain, R., Chiu, D., Hawe, W.: A quantitative measure of fairness and discrimination for resource allocation in shared computer systems (1998)

10. Khan, N., Martini, M.G., Bharucha, Z., Auer, G.: Opportunistic packet loss fair scheduling for delay-sensitive applications over LTE systems. In: 2012 IEEE Wireless Communications and Networking Conference (WCNC), pp. 1456–1461 (2012)

11. Lai, Y.C.: Packet schedulers to provide proportional delay differentiation and reduce packet queueing delay simultaneously. In: 2004 IEEE International Conference on Communications (IEEE Cat. No.04CH37577), vol. 4, pp. 1968–1972 (2004)

12. Lai, Y.C., Chang, A.: A non-work-conserving scheduler to provide proportional delay differentiated services. In: IEEE Global Telecommunications Conference, 2004, GLOBECOM 2004, vol. 3, pp. 1723–1727 (2004)

13. Lai, Y.C., Li, W.H.: A novel scheduler for proportional delay differentiation by considering packet transmission time. IEEE Commun. Lett. **7**(4), 189–191 (2003)

14. Mamane, A., Fattah, M., Ghazi, M.E., Bekkali, M.E., Balboul, Y., Mazer, S.: Scheduling algorithms for 5g networks and beyond: classification and survey. IEEE Access **10**, 51643–51661 (2022)

15. Mansouri, W., Ali, K.B., Zarai, F., Obaidat, M.S.: Chapter 27 - radio resource management for heterogeneous wireless networks: Schemes and simulation analysis. In: Obaidat, M.S., Nicopolitidis, P., Zarai, F. (eds.) Modeling and Simulation of Computer Networks and Systems, pp. 767–792. Morgan Kaufmann, Boston (2015)

16. Mehaseb, M.A., Gadallah, Y., Elhamy, A., Elhennawy, H.: Classification of LTE uplink scheduling techniques: an M2M perspective. IEEE Commun. Surv. Tutor. **18**(2), 1310–1335 (2016)

17. Myung, H.G., Oh, K., Lim, J., Goodman, D.J.: Channel-dependent scheduling of an uplink SC-FDMA system with imperfect channel information. In: 2008 IEEE Wireless Communications and Networking Conference, pp. 1860–1864 (2008)

18. Nasralla, M.M., Khan, N., Martini, M.G.: Content-aware downlink scheduling for LTE wireless systems: a survey and performance comparison of key approaches. Comput. Commun. **130**, 78–100 (2018)

19. Olwal, T.O., Djouani, K., Kurien, A.M.: A survey of resource management toward 5g radio access networks. IEEE Commun. Surv. Tutor. **18**(3), 1656–1686 (2016)

20. Pedersen, K., Pocovi, G., Steiner, J., Maeder, A.: Agile 5G scheduler for improved E2E performance and flexibility for different network implementations. IEEE Commun. Mag. **56**(3), 210–217 (2018)

21. Saito, H., Lukovszki, C., Moldován, I.: Local optimal proportional differentiation scheduler for relative differentiated services. In: Proceedings of ICCCN 2000 - IEEE International Conference on Computer Communication and Networks, Las Vegas, Nevada, US, pp. 540–546. IEEE, October 2000

22. Sharma, S.K., Wang, X.: Toward massive machine type communications in ultra-dense cellular IoT networks: current issues and machine learning-assisted solutions. IEEE Commun. Surv. Tutor. **22**(1), 426–471 (2020)

23. Tomazic, S.: Encyclopedia of Wireless and Mobile Communications, chap. Spectral Efficiency. CRC Press, Boca Raton (2008)
24. Wang, C.X., et al.: On the road to 6g: visions, requirements, key technologies, and testbeds. IEEE Commun. Surv. Tutor. **25**(2), 905–974 (2023)
25. Wong, V., Schober, R., Ng, D., Wang, L.: Key Technologies for 5G Wireless Systems. Cambridge University Press, Cambridge (2017)
26. Zhang, L., Liang, Y.C., Niyato, D.: 6G visions: mobile ultra-broadband, super internet-of-things, and artificial intelligence. China Commun. **16**(8), 1–14 (2019)

Regret-Minimization Heuristics for Identifying Monotone Boolean Functions

Michael Laszlo$^{(\boxtimes)}$ and Sumitra Mukherjee

Nova Southeastern University, Fort Lauderdale, FL, USA
{mjl,sumitra}@nova.edu

Abstract. In many applications that involve identification of an unknown monotone Boolean function (MBF), the cost of inferring the value of a vector using monotonicity is negligible compared to the cost of querying its value. Accordingly, heuristics to identify MBFs seek to minimize the number of vectors queried. The order in which queried vectors are selected determines the number of queries needed. This paper presents a method for MBF identification that iteratively selects vectors to be queried based on a regret-minimization criterion. We observe that the best extant heuristic may be considered a special case of our approach and present alternate regret functions that perform no worse than this heuristic.

Keywords: Boolean lattices · chain decomposition · monotone Boolean functions · automated inferencing

1 Introduction

A pair of n-dimensional binary vectors v and w are comparable if one precedes the other. Vector $v = (v_1, v_2, ..., v_n)$ precedes vector $w = (w_1, w_2, ..., w_n)$ if $v_i \leq w_i$ for $i = 1, 2, ..., n$. We use $v \preccurlyeq w$ to denote this relationship and say that v is a predecessor of w, and w a successor of v, and refer to the relation as proper if, in addition, $w \neq v$. A Boolean function $f : \{0,1\}^n \to \{0,1\}$ is said to be monotone if $f(v) \leq f(w)$ for all pairs of comparable vectors $v \preccurlyeq w$. If the value $f(v)$ of a vector v in a monotone Boolean function (MBF) f is known, the values of all its predecessors may be inferred as 0 if $f(v) = 0$, and the values of all its successors may be inferred as 1 if $f(v) = 1$.

Each MBF has a set of *border* vectors whose values cannot be inferred. Vector v belongs to the *0-border* if and only if (iff) $f(v) = 0$ and $f(w) = 1$ for all its proper successors $w \succ v$; v belongs to the *1-border* iff $f(v) = 1$ and $f(w) = 0$ for all its proper predecessors $w \prec v$. Each MBF has a unique 0-border and a corresponding unique 1-border. We call a vector *classified* if its value is known. To classify a vector whose value cannot be inferred from the values of previously classified vectors, we *query* an oracle. Since the value of border vectors cannot be inferred, the size of the border is a lower bound on the number of vectors whose values must be queried to classify all 2^n vectors in an MBF of n variables.

M. Laszlo and S. Mukherjee—Contributed equally to this work.

© The Author(s), under exclusive license to Springer Nature Switzerland AG 2025
D. D. Hodson et al. (Eds.): CSCE 2024, CCIS 2258, pp. 113–122, 2025.
https://doi.org/10.1007/978-3-031-85902-1_12

The number of distinct MBFs of n variables is given by the Dedekind numbers $D(n)$, which has been computed for $n \leq 9$ (https://oeis.org/A000372) as shown in Table 1.

Observing that the cost of classifying a vector via inference is negligible compared to the cost of querying its value in many applications that involve MBF identification, [13] presents a heuristic that, on average, requires fewer queries than alternative approaches presented in [2, 6, 10, 12]. Their heuristic iteratively selects vectors to be queried using the following procedure: The difference between the numbers of predecessors and successors of each unclassified vector is computed, and a vector with minimum absolute difference is queried. They rank heuristics based on the mean number of queries needed, with means computed on all $D(n)$ MBFs for $n \leq 5$, and on subsets of MBFs for $6 \leq n \leq 11$.

The order in which vectors are queried determines the number of queries needed to identify an MBF. We present a regret-minimization framework for iteratively selecting vectors to be queried. We show that the heuristic presented in [13] falls under this framework, and we present alternative regret functions that perform no worse than their heuristic. We evaluate heuristics on all MBFs for $n \leq 6$, and on subsets of MBFs for $7 \leq n \leq 11$.

The rest of this paper is organized as follows: Section 2 summarizes key articles that we build on. Section 3 explains our regret-minimization approach and presents alternate regret functions for selecting vectors to be queried. Section 4 compares these regret functions on all $D(n)$ MBFs for $n \leq 6$. Section 5 presents results on subsets of MBFs of more than six variables. Section 6 identifies directions for future work.

Table 1. Number of monotone Boolean functions for $n \leq 8$.

n	$D(n)$	Reference
1	3	[4]
2	6	
3	20	
4	168	
5	7,581	[3]
6	7,828,354	[14]
7	2,414,682,040,998	[3]
8	56,130,437,228,687,557,907,788	[15]
9	286,386,577,668,298,411,128,469,151,667,598,498,812,366	[8]

2 Related Work

[1] presents a procedure to generate all MBFs of n variables using a $2^n \times 2^n$ binary matrix to capture precedence relationships between vectors; element (i, j) in this matrix is 1 iff the ith vector is a predecessor of the jth vector, where vectors are ordered lexicographically. We use this procedure to generate all $D(n)$ MBFs for $n \leq 6$ to evaluate our

heuristics, and we use the precedence matrix to determine predecessors and successors of vectors.

[6] presents a method for ordering vectors that is guaranteed to classify all 2^n vectors in no more than $\binom{n}{\lfloor n/2 \rfloor} + \binom{n}{\lfloor n/2 \rfloor + 1}$ queries. It partitions the elements of a 2^n Boolean lattice into $\binom{n}{\lfloor n/2 \rfloor}$ symmetric chains, considers the chains in non-decreasing order of length, and iteratively queries unclassified vectors in a chain until all its elements are classified. When chains are processed in non-decreasing order of length, each new chain considered contains at most two unclassified elements; this guarantees the upper bound on the number of queries under Hansel's method. We refer to the order in which vectors are queried under Hansel's method as the *Hansel-order*. An MBF with the largest border contains $\binom{n}{\lfloor n/2 \rfloor} + \binom{n}{\lfloor n/2 \rfloor + 1}$ border vectors, and Hansel's method determines such functions without querying any non-border vectors. Results indicate that Hansel's method is second only to the heuristic presented in [13] when ranked on the mean number of queries required to identify an MBF. We use Hansel's method as a baseline in evaluating our regret-minimization heuristics, and the method described in [7] to partition a Boolean lattice into canonical symmetrical chains (see *Definition 2.3* in their paper). [12] presents a method where symmetric chains are considered in decreasing order of length, and vectors in a chain are classified using binary search. While this approach may require fewer queries to infer an MBF if all the border vectors are contained in the longer chains, on average Hansel's method requires fewer queries. Further, Sokolov's method does not guarantee the upper bound on the number of queries provided by the Hansel method.

3   Regret-Minimization Heuristics for Identifying MBSs

The number of queries needed to classify all vectors is determined by the order in which vectors are queried; it equals the number of queries posed until the last of the border vectors is queried. In Fig. 1, the function query_count(f, h) returns the number of queries required to identify an unknown MBF f using a heuristic function h that returns a vector v to be queried; when the value of a vector v is queried, an oracle returns its value $f(v)$.

Hansel's heuristic returns the first unclassified vector $u \in U$ under Hansel's ordering. The remaining heuristics we consider fall under our regret-minimization framework. Let the regret function $r : U \rightarrow \mathbb{R}^{\geq 0}$ measure the regret $r(u)$ for deciding to query the unclassified vector u. We seek some vector $u \in U$ that minimizes regret: $r^*(U) = \text{argmin} \, r(u)$. $\underset{u \in U}{}$ When multiple vectors belong to $r^*(U)$, we choose to query the lexicographically first vector in $r^*(U)$. (When multiple vectors minimize regret, [13] takes the first vector in lexicographic order. Accordingly, we follow the same tie-breaking strategy for each of the heuristics we consider.)

The heuristic proposed in [13] computes $r_{TT}(u) = \left| K_u^0 - K_u^1 \right|$ for each unclassified vector $u \in U$, where K_u^0 and K_u^1 are, respectively, the number of unclassified proper predecessors and proper successors of u. We observe that $r_{TT}(u)$ may

```
query_count(f, h):
  count = 0
  U = set of all 2ⁿ vectors
  while U is not empty:
    v = h(U)
    count = count + 1
    if f(v) is 0:   # query vector v
      C = set of all predecessors of v
    else:
      C = set of all successors of v
    U = U - C
  return count
```

Fig. 1. Function `query_count` returns the number of queries needed to infer MBF f using heuristic h.

be interpreted as a regret function: If the payoff associated with vector u is measured by the number of vectors that get classified by querying u, then selecting u yields the best-case payoff $max(K_u^0, K_u^1)$ and worst-case payoff $min(K_u^0, K_u^1)$. Taking regret to be the difference between the best and worst payoffs, regret is given by $r_{TT}(u) = max(K_u^0, K_u^1) - min(K_u^0, K_u^1) = |K_u^0 - K_u^1|$.

The payoff for selecting vector u may also be measured by the proportion of unclassified vectors classified by querying u. Taking regret to be the difference between the payoffs in these best and worst cases, we obtain a second regret function:
$r_{DP}(u) = max(K_u^0/K_u, K_u^1/K_u) - min(K_u^0/K_u, K_u^1/K_u) = |K_u^0 - K_u^1|/K_u$, where $K_u = K_u^0 + K_u^1 + 1$ is equal to the number of unclassified vectors comparable to u.

The third heuristic we consider uses the *ratio* of the payoffs under the best and worst cases: $r_{RC}(u) = max(K_u^0, K_u^1)/min(K_u^0, K_u^1)$. Note that the ratio of payoffs is the same regardless of whether payoffs are measured by the number of vectors classified or by the proportion of vectors classified. Table 2 summarizes the three regret functions that we evaluate in this paper.

Table 2. Regret-minimization heuristics compared to Hansel's method in this study.

Mnemonic	Regret Function	Description
TT Torvik-Triantaphyllou	$r_{tt}(u) = \left\|K_u^0 - K_u^1\right\|$	Difference in max and min count
DP Difference Proportion	$r_{dp}(u) = \left\|K_u^0 - K_u^1\right\|/K_u$	Difference in max and min proportion
RC Ratio Count	$r_{rc}(u) = max\left(K_u^0, K_u^1\right)/min\left(K_u^0, K_u^1\right)$	Ratio of max and min count

4 Results Computed on All MBFs ($n \leq 6$)

We evaluate the heuristics on all $D(n)$ MBFs for $n = 3, 4, 5$, and 6. Table 3 presents the mean, minimum, and maximum of the number of queries required to identify MBFs, computed over all $D(n)$ MBFs. Results obtained using Hansel's method and the three regret-minimization heuristics appear under the columns *HAN*, *TT*, *DP*, and *RC*, respectively. Ties between multiple vectors with identical regret function values are broken based on the lexicographical ordering of vectors in the reported results. We also ran experiments with two other deterministic tie-breaking criteria: reverse lexicographical ordering and Hansel ordering. While the mean number of queries varied slightly, the observations that follow hold regardless of the tie-breaking criterion. For $n = 3$, the mean number of queries required by the three regret-minimizing heuristics are identical to the mean under Hansel's method. For $n = 4$, the mean number of queries required by the three regret-minimization heuristics are identical, but lower than the mean obtained using Hansel's method. For $n = 5$ and $n = 6$, the mean number of queries under the alternate regret-minimizing heuristics that we consider (*DP* and *RC*) are marginally lower than the mean obtained using the heuristic (*TT*) presented in [13] all three regret-minimizing heuristics perform better than Hansel's method.

Table 3. Number of queries required to identify MBFs ($3 \leq n \leq 6$).

n = 3: D(n) = 6; $|B|_{max}$ = 6			
Heuristic	*HAN*	*TT*	*DP*	*RC*
Mean	4.55	4.55	4.55	4.55
Min	3	3	3	3
Max	6	6	6	6
n = 4: D(n) = 168; $|B|_{max}$ = 10			
Heuristic	*HAN*	*TT*	*DP*	*RC*
Mean	7.767	7.654	7.654	7.654
Min	5	6	6	6
Max	10	10	10	10
n = 5: D(n) = 7,581; $|B|_{max}$ = 20			
Heuristic	*HAN*	*TT*	*DP*	*RC*
Mean	13.96	13.69	13.66	13.68
Min	8	9	9	9
Max	20	20	20	20
n = 6: D(n) = 7,828,354; $|B|_{max}$ = 35			
Heuristic	*HAN*	*TT*	*DP*	*RC*
Mean	24.56	23.98	23.94	23.94
Min	14	15	15	15
Max	35	35	35	35

An MBF of n-variables with the largest border contains $|B|_{max} = \binom{n}{\lfloor n/2 \rfloor} + \binom{n}{\lfloor n/2 \rfloor + 1}$ border vectors. Recall that Hansel's method guarantees that every MBF can be identified in no more than $|B|_{max}$ queries. We observe that all three regret-minimization heuristics also identify every MBF in no more than $|B|_{max}$ queries for $n \le 6$.

Table 4 shows the mean, minimum, and maximum for the number of queries per border element under the four heuristics evaluated. That is, it presents these statistics computed over all $D(n)$ MBFs for the measure $q/|B|$, where q queries are needed to identify an MBF with $|B|$ border vectors. The performance of the heuristics based on this measure is very similar to those obtained using the number of queries, except for $n = 3$. For $n = 3$, the mean number of queries per border element required by the three regret-minimizing heuristics are identical, but higher than the mean under Hansel's method. For $n = 4$, the mean number of queries required by the three regret-minimization heuristics are identical, but lower than the mean obtained using Hansel's method. For $n = 5$ and $n = 6$, the mean number of queries under the alternate regret-minimizing heuristics that we consider (DP and RC) are marginally lower than the mean obtained using the heuristic TT; all three regret-minimizing heuristics perform better than Hansel's method. The maximum number of queries per border element is lower for the regret-minimization heuristics than obtained using Hansel's method for $n > 3$. Also note that the minimum number of queries per border elements equals 1 in every case; we have verified that

Table 4. Number of queries required per border element ($3 \le n \le 6$).

n = 3: D(n) = 6				
Heuristic	*HAN*	*TT*	*DP*	*RC*
Mean	1.670	1.679	1.679	1.679
Min	1	1	1	1
Max	5	5	5	5
n = 4: D(n) = 168				
Heuristic	*HAN*	*TT*	*DP*	*RC*
Mean	1.611	1.585	1.585	1.585
Min	1	1	1	1
Max	9	7	7	7
n = 5: D(n) = 7,581				
Heuristic	*HAN*	*TT*	*DP*	*RC*
Mean	1.568	1.538	1.537	1.538
Min	1	1	1	1
Max	16	11	11	11
n = 6: D(n) = 7,828,354				
Heuristic	*HAN*	*TT*	*DP*	*RC*
Mean	1.491	1.456	1.455	1.455
Min	1	1	1	1
Max	30	17	17	17

for $n < 7$, no non-border vectors get queried for each of the heuristics for MBFs with $|B| = |B|_{max}$.

5 Results Computed on a Subset of MBFs ($7 \leq n \leq 11$)

There are more than 2.4×10^{12} MBFs for $n = 7$, 5.6×10^{22} MBFs for $n = 8$, and 2.8×10^{41} MBFs for $n = 9$. The number of MBFs, $D(n)$, are not known for $n > 9$. The best asymptotic approximation is due to [9] with $\widehat{D}(10) \approx 8.5 \times 10^{78}$ and $\widehat{D}(11) \approx 1.3 \times 10^{144}$. Since comparing heuristics on all $D(n)$ MBFs is computationally unfeasible for $n > 6$, we evaluate them on a small subset of MBFs. To ensure fair comparison, we use the method described in [13] to generate samples and use the same sample sizes as reported in that paper. Specifically, we evaluate heuristics on 2000 samples for $n = 7$ and $n = 8$, and on 200 samples for $n = 9$, $n = 10$, and $n = 11$. Note that for $n = 6$, while [13] report results based on a sample of 2000 MBFs, we report results (in Tables 3 and 4) based on all $D(6)$ MBFs.

Table 5. Number of queries required to identify MBFs ($7 \leq n \leq 11$).

n = 7: D(n) > 2.4 × 10¹²; |B|max = 70			
Heuristic	*HAN*	*TT*	*DP*	*RC*
Mean	51.8	51.4315	51.175	51.2965
Min	39	38	38	38
Max	65	65	66	66

n = 8: D(n) > 5.6 × 10²²; |B|max = 126			
Heuristic	*HAN*	*TT*	*DP*	*RC*
Mean	83.8	79.816	78.876	78.9725
Min	71	72	71	72
Max	96	94	94	94

n = 9: D(n) > 7.6 × 10⁴⁰; |B|max = 252			
Heuristic	*HAN*	*TT*	*DP*	*RC*
Mean	193.	192.7	192.105	192.375
Min	164	167	165	168
Max	222	221	215	218

n = 10: D(n) > 8.5 × 10⁷⁸; |B|max = 462			
Heuristic	*HAN*	*TT*	*DP*	*RC*
Mean	293.	273.685	268.73	269.105
Min	281	259	257	259
Max	307	289	279	281

n = 11: D(n) > 1.3 × 10¹⁴⁴; |B|max = 924			
Heuristic	*HAN*	*TT*	*DP*	*RC*
Mean	783.765	782.65	781.68	781.3
Min	745	744	732	740
Max	824	825	827	834

As expected, the samples generated for $7 \leq n \leq 11$ did not include any MBFs with $|B|_{max} = \binom{n}{\lfloor n/2 \rfloor} + \binom{n}{\lfloor n/2 \rfloor + 1}$ border vectors. Only one of the $D(n)$ MBFs contains $|B|_{max}$ border vectors when n is odd, and only two contain $|B|_{max}$ border vectors when n is even. Accordingly, for each n we tested the four heuristics on all MBFs with $|B|_{max}$ border vectors and confirmed that in each case the MBFs were identified without any non-border elements being queried.

Tables 5 and 6 present our results on subsets of MBFs for $7 \leq n \leq 11$. The relative performance of the heuristics are the same as those observed for $n < 7$. In each case, the regret-minimization heuristics perform better than Hansel's method, and the alternate regret-minimization heuristics that we considered (*DP* and *RC*) perform marginally better than the *TT* heuristic proposed by [13]. This holds, regardless of whether heuristics

Table 6. Number of queries required per border element to identify MBFs ($7 \leq n \leq 11$).

n = 7: D(n) > 2.4 × 10¹²				
Heuristic	*HAN*	*TT*	*DP*	*RC*
Mean	1.3793	1.3685	1.3619	1.3649
Min	1.0755	1.0488	1.0417	1.0625
Max	2	1.8889	1.9231	1.8519
n = 8: D(n) > 5.6 × 10²²				
Heuristic	*HAN*	*TT*	*DP*	*RC*
Mean	1.2372	1.1788	1.1651	1.1666
Min	1.0658	1.0132	1	1
Max	1.6226	1.566	1.6481	1.6481
n = 9: D(n) > 7.6 × 10⁴⁰				
Heuristic	*HAN*	*TT*	*DP*	*RC*
Mean	1.3177	1.3137	1.3096	1.3115
Min	1.1364	1.1299	1.1394	1.1469
Max	1.6283	1.4797	1.5	1.5122
n = 10: D(n) > 8.5 × 10⁷⁸				
Heuristic	*HAN*	*TT*	*DP*	*RC*
Mean	1.163	1.0842	1.0646	1.0661
Min	1.1012	1.0189	1.0155	1.0152
Max	1.2627	1.1598	1.1356	1.1525
n = 11: D(n) > 1.3 × 10¹⁴⁴				
Heuristic	*HAN*	*TT*	*DP*	*RC*
Mean	1.1899	1.1882	1.1868	1.1861
Min	1.1202	1.1175	1.1134	1.112
Max	1.2976	1.2653	1.2735	1.2619

are ranked based on the number queries required to identify an MBF (Table 5), or the number of queries required per border element (Table 6).

6 Conclusion

In many applications that involve identification of an unknown MBF, the cost of inferring the value of a vector using monotonicity is negligible compared to the cost of querying its value. The method proposed in [6] is widely used in such applications because it guarantees an upper bound on the number of queries required. To the best of our knowledge, the heuristic presented in [13] is the only published method that does not violate this guarantee. Furthermore, results indicate that this heuristic, on average, requires fewer queries than alternate methods. We interpret the [13] heuristic as one that selects vectors based on a regret-minimization criterion, and present two alternate regret functions that perform no worse than their heuristic.

Our regret-minimization heuristics identify all $D(n)$ MBFs in no more $|B|_{max}$ queries for $n < 7$. For MBFs of more than 6 variables, we have verified that these heuristics query only border vectors for MBFs with $|B|_{max}$ border vectors. Our results on subsets of MBFs for $n \leq 11$ suggest that this upper limit is not violated. This leads us to conjecture that, like Hansel's method, our regret-minimization heuristics guarantee that any MBF of n variables can be identified in no more than $|B|_{max} = \binom{n}{\lfloor n/2 \rfloor} + \binom{n}{\lfloor n/2 \rfloor + 1}$ queries. Proving this conjecture is an open research challenge.

Since it is not feasible to evaluate heuristics on all $D(n)$ MBFs for $n > 6$, we use subsets of MBFs generated using the method described in [13]. Developing improved methods to generate uniformly distributed random MBFs is another research challenge.

References

1. Bakoev, V.: Combinatorial and Algorithmic Properties of One Matrix Structure at Monotone Boolean Functions (2019). arXiv:1902.06110. [cs.DM]
2. Boros, E., Hammer, P.L., Ibaraki, T., Makino, K.: Polynomial time recognition of 2-monotonic positive Boolean functions given by an oracle. SIAM J. Comput. **26**, 93–109 (1997)
3. Church, R.: Numerical analysis of certain free distributive structures. Duke Math. J. **6**(3), 732–734 (1940)
4. Dedekind, R.: Über Zerlegungen von Zahlen durch ihre größten gemeinsamen Teiler. Gesammelte Werke **2**, 103–148 (1897)
5. Gainanov, D.N.: On one criterion of the optimality of an algorithm for evaluating monotonic Boolean functions. U.S.S.R. Comput. Math. Math. Phys. **24**, 176–181 (1984)
6. Hansel, G.: Sur le nombre des foncions Booleenes monotones de n variables. C. R. Acad. Sci. Paris **262**, 1088–1090 (1966)
7. Hsu, T., Logan, M. J., Shahriari, S., and Towse, C.: Partitioning the boolean lattice into chains of large minimum size. J. Comb. Theory, Ser. A **97**(1), 62–84 (2002). https://doi.org/10.1006/jcta.2001.3197.
8. Jäkel, C.: A computation of the ninth Dedekind number. J. Comput. Algebra **6**, 100006 (2023)
9. Korshunov, A.D.: On the number of monotone Boolean functions. Problemy Kibernetiki **38**, 5–108 (1981)

10. Makino, K., Ibaraki, T.: A fast and simple algorithm for identifying 2-monotonic positive Boolean functions. In: Proceedings of ISAACS'95, Algorithms and Computation, Springer-Verlag, Berlin, Germany, pp. 291–300 (1995)

11. OEIS Foundation Inc. Dedekind numbers, Entry A000372 in The On-Line Encyclopedia of Integer Sequences (2024). https://oeis.org/ A000372

12. Sokolov, N.A.: On the optimal evaluation of monotonic Boolean functions. U.S.S.R. Comput. Math. Math. Phys. **22**, 207–220 (1982)

13. Torvik, V., Triantaphyllou, E.: Minimizing the average query complexity of learning monotone boolean functions. INFORMS J. Comput. **14**, 144–174 (2002). https://doi.org/10.1287/ijoc. 14.2.144.117

14. Ward, M.: Note on the order of the free distributive lattice. Bull. Am. Math. Soc. **52**, 423 (1946)

15. Wiedemann, D.: A computation of the eight Dedekind number. Order **8**, 5 (1991)

Multi-class Classification of Satellite Orbits for Database Quality Control

Richard Peterson[1], Torrey Wagner[1] ⓘ, Paul Auclair[2]([✉]), and Brent Langhals[1]

[1] Air Force Institute of Technology, Wright-Patterson AFB, Dayton, OH 45433, USA
richard.d.peterson90.mil@mail.mil, {torrey.wagner,
brent.langhals}@afit.edu
[2] LinQuest Corporation, Beavercreek, OH 45431, USA
paul.auclair@linquest.com

Abstract. The Joint Spectrum Center (JSC) Equipment, Tactical, and Space (JETS) database contains 9,539 satellite records. When new data is ingested the satellite orbit type needs to be identified, which is currently a manual process. To save time, this work explores automating the process using machine learning. Several statistical machine learning and neural network models were developed and compared using the weighted averages of precision, recall, and F1 score metrics. The number of records used in training and testing was 1,024 with a 60/20/20 train, validation, and test split. Six orbital parameters were initially used to fit the models, but three parameters (the mean motion, eccentricity, and inclination) were most important in determining orbit type. A decision tree model with the three most important orbital parameters as inputs best identified the seven target orbit types. The weighted averages of the precision, recall, and F1 score on the test data were 0.991, 0.990, and 0.990 respectively. This compared favorably to the F1 metrics for a random classifier (0.106) and a model that always predicted the majority class (0.103).

Keywords: Orbits · Satellites · Classification · Machine Learning · Neural Networks · Decision Trees · Logistic Regression

.

1 Introduction & Background

The Spectrum Program Executive Office[1] (PEO Spectrum) of the Defense Information Systems Agency (DISA) maintains the Joint Spectrum Data Repository (JSDR). JSDR is the Joint Authoritative Data Source for all DoD spectrum-related data [1]. As such, it is a repository of spectrum management data sources that provides access to frequency assignments, spectrum certifications, interference reports, engineering characteristics, and equipment data. One segment of the JSDR is the Joint Spectrum Center (JSC) Equipment, Tactical, and Space (JETS) database. The JETS database contains data for DoD and commercial equipment, as well as unit-equipment and platform-equipment relationships.

---

[1] Prior to Oct 2023 PEO Spectrum was the Defense Spectrum Organization (DSO)

D. D. Hodson et al. (Eds.): CSCE 2024, CCIS 2258, pp. 123–133, 2025.
https://doi.org/10.1007/978-3-031-85902-1_13

The roots of JETS began in the 1970s and much of the data is manually entered, which introduces the possibility for human error. The JETS database includes tens of thousands of records stored in over 50 tables, with several tables consisting of over 100 fields. While the base data source is the International Telecommunication Union (ITU), JETS database analysts combine it with data from several other sources. Uploading and joining the various data sources occurs every two weeks as a manual process. With several fields requiring searches through unstructured data to populate them, it typically takes an analyst three days from when the base update is received to publish the updated data in the JETS database [2].

However, in the past decade several of the JETS data sources became unavailable and in 2018 the JETS database was no longer maintained. In 2020 PEO Spectrum was tasked with updating and maintaining the JETS database [3]. Several years later the space component of the JETS database is still being updated because the data map required significant changes. Once the data map is complete, analysts will load all the updates from the past several years. These updates should include key data fields that enable simple and efficient data queries for users. A common field for satellite data is orbit type. Certain orbits are generally used for specific mission types which makes orbit a convenient filtering field [4].

The four most common orbit types are low earth orbit (LEO), medium earth orbit (MEO), geosynchronous orbit (GEO), and highly elliptical orbit (HEO) [4]. These categories are based on the mean motion and eccentricity of the satellite orbit. The mean motion is the number of revolutions the satellite makes in 24 hours. The eccentricity is a measure of how elliptical the orbit is. More specific orbit types (e.g., sun-synchronous, polar, geostationary, and Molniya) are grouped based on additional factors such as the orientation, direction, and inclination of the satellite orbit.

As the satellite data is updated in the JETS database, an automated process to determine orbit type is needed. Currently orbit type is not provided for all satellites so an analyst must search through unstructured data sources to fill in missing data. The purpose of this analysis is to determine how well machine learning and neural network (NN) algorithms can classify satellite orbit type based on orbital parameters. To be applied to new data fed into the JETS database, the model must generalize to unseen data. If successful, the model could save hundreds of man-hours annually.

While the motivation for this analysis is to update a specific and unique database, other orbit classification work has been previously performed for cislunar satellite orbits [5] and asteroid orbits [6]. Machine learning has also been used to classify satellite maneuvers in orbit [7, 8]. The similarity in all these models is classifying an orbit or maneuver based on orbital parameters or changes in parameters for the case of maneuvers.

1.1 Data Acquisition

The data for this analysis was retrieved from the JSDR using the JETS Satellite Query tool. To obtain the entire dataset no filters were specified in the query. The complete dataset contained 55 fields and 9,539 records. Most of the records were incomplete, either lacking orbital parameters or being labeled as "dummy" or "filler." Those records, along with all duplicated records, were removed. The cleaned dataset contained seven data fields and 1,024 records.

1.2 Data Understanding

The seven data fields are listed and described in Table 1. The first six are the orbital parameters that will be the input variables for the classification models. The last field, Orbit Type, is the target variable the models are trained to classify. The distributions for the orbital parameters are shown in Fig. 1. The Argument of Perigee, Mean Anomaly, and Right Ascension of Ascending Node distributions somewhat resemble uniform distributions. All other variables do not resemble common distributions but have discrete spikes at certain values which generally correlate to various orbit types. The Eccentricity is an exception where there appears to be a single spike with no other values. There is a range of eccentricity values from 0 to 0.97 but the proportion above 0 is minimal so they are not visible in the plot.

Table 1. JETS Data Field Descriptions

Variable	Description [9]
Argument of Perigee (deg)	Angle between perigee and the ascending node.
Eccentricity	Distance between foci of the orbital ellipse normalized to the major axis.
Inclination Angle (deg)	Angle between the orbital plane and the Earths equatorial plane.
Mean Anomaly (deg)	Angle between perigee and the satellite position
Mean Motion (revs/day)	Number of revolutions in one day
Right Ascension of Ascending Node (deg)	Angle between the vernal equinox and the point the orbit crosses the equator traveling north.
Orbit Type	Type of Orbit

The Orbit Type data field contained 17 different classes that included variations of LEO, GEO, MEO, and HEO satellite orbits. Three orbit type classes contained over half the records and seven orbit type classes had five or fewer records. With insufficient data to accurately classify several orbital variations or sub-classes, the data was grouped into seven classes: LEO Sun-Synchronous, LEO Polar, LEO Other, MEO, HEO, GEO Stationary, and GEO Inclined. The distribution of the record counts into the broader orbit type classes is shown in Fig. 2. The data is not balanced but all classes are adequately represented with the possible exception of the 43 data points in the HEO class.

The mean motion and eccentricity generally distinguish between the main orbit types of LEO, MEO, HEO, and GEO. With orbit types grouped into broader categories, mean motion and eccentricity are two main factors that should cluster orbit types. Figure 3 shows a scatterplot of orbit classes by mean motion and eccentricity. The LEO classes have a distinguishable cluster with high mean motion and low eccentricity. The GEO

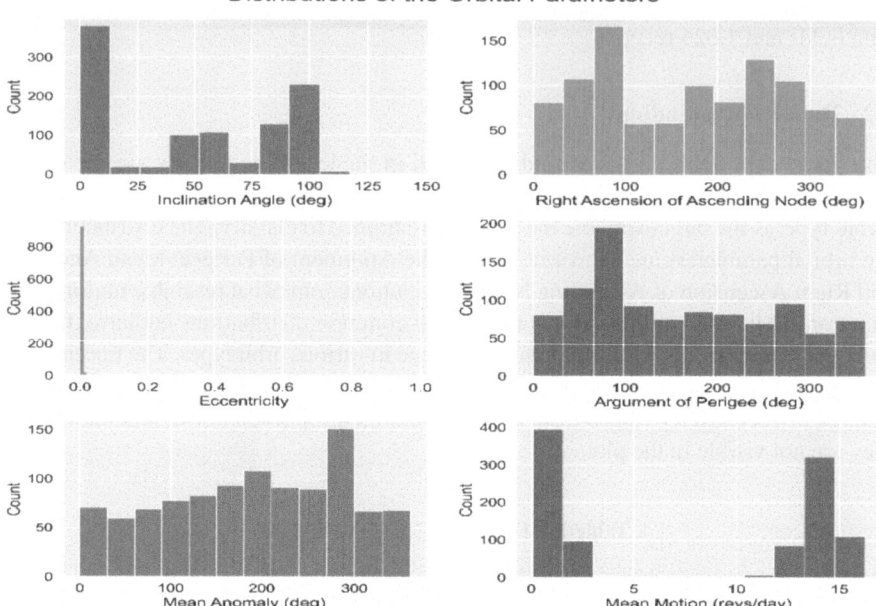

Fig. 1. Histograms for the Orbital Parameters

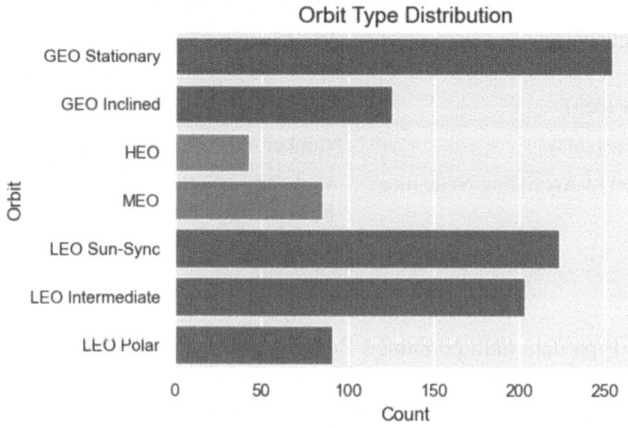

Fig. 2. Distribution of the Orbit Type classes. Colors indicate the general orbit type (LEO, MEO, HEO, and GEO).

classes tend to have an eccentricity less than 0.3 and a mean motion of approximately one revolution per day. The MEO class also tends to have an eccentricity below 0.3, but the mean motion varies between around 2-12 rev/day. It is surprising to see a few data points belonging to the GEO and MEO classes that have eccentricities around 0.8, and those could be errors. The HEO class is distinguishable with eccentricity greater than 0.5.

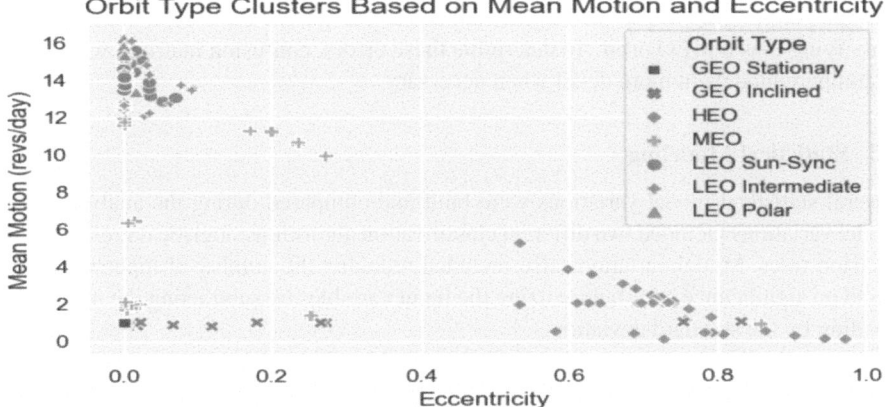

Fig. 3. Scatterplot of orbit types by mean motion and eccentricity.

2   Method

To achieve the goal of classifying orbit types, several models were built and compared. The models included both statistical and NN models.

2.1   Data Preparation

Most of the data preparation was done when initially acquiring the data. As mentioned, the complete JETS satellite database contained 55 fields, but only seven, including the orbit class label, were used in this analysis. The six input variable fields are the orbital parameters that are contained in a two-line element (TLE) set. The TLE is a concise list of mean orbital elements for satellites [10].

The orbital parameters in the TLE can be used to calculate several other orbital parameters including six classic Keplerian orbital elements [11, 12]. Several other orbital parameters are in the JETS database, but data fed into the JETS database will be similar to that contained in TLEs. Therefore, the orbital elements in the TLE were chosen so additional calculations are not needed first when the model is implemented. In addition to filtering the data columns, records with missing data as well as duplicate records were removed.

2.2   Metrics

Since this was an unbalanced multiclass classification model, this analysis used the classification metrics of weighted averages for precision, recall, and F1 score to measure the performance of the statistical and NN models. The support, or number of true instances for each class, was used for weighting the metrics [13]. There were seven orbit classes that were unbalanced so accuracy may not be a good indicator of performance. Most of the classes are equally important, but not all errors are equal. It is better to incorrectly classify an orbit of the same general type rather than another general orbit type. For example, classifying a LEO Sun-Synchronous orbit as a LEO Polar orbit is better than classifying it as a MEO orbit. To determine these errors, confusion matrices were used to compare models in more detail when necessary.

2.3 Statistical Modeling

Several statistical model variations were built and compared during the analysis. The model variations included two different classification algorithms: logistic regression and decision trees. Model variations also included reducing the number of input variables based on significance and standardizing the input variables by subtracting the mean and dividing by the standard deviation.

A train, validation, and test data split was used for all models to prevent overfitting. The models were trained using 60% of the data and validated on 20% of the data. The remaining 20% of the data was held out as a final test set. The same random state was used so all models were trained and validated on the same data. This data partitioning enabled a fair comparison between models and an accurate assessment on unseen data.

2.4 Neural Network Modeling

All the NN models used the same optimization algorithm and loss function. The Adam optimization algorithm was chosen because it is well suited for deep networks. Categorical Cross-entropy was used as the loss function due to having seven classes. To prevent overfitting, the same 60/20/20 training, validation, and testing split used for the statistical models was also used for the NN models. All input variables were standardized prior to training.

Two preliminary models were built; one with all six features, and one with the three features that were most important in the statistical models: mean motion, eccentricity, and inclination. The preliminary models used two hidden layers with 12 neurons per layer, a batch size of 50, and 100 epochs.

Hyperparameter sweeps were performed on the number of layers, number of neurons per layer, number of epochs, and the batch size. The values used in the sweep are shown in Table 2.

Table 2. Hyperparameter Sweep Information

Hyperparameter	Values
Hidden Layers	2, 3, 4
Neurons per Hidden Layer	6, 12, 18
Epochs	50, 100, 200
Batch Size	10, 50, 100

The last variation to the model was investigating the impact of regularization using early stopping. This was implemented by monitoring the validation loss and waiting 10 epochs without improvement prior to stopping.

3 Analysis and Results

The various statistical models were compared against the validation data and the best model selected. That model was then compared to the best NN model. The statistical model results for classifying the validation data are summarized in Table 3. Unless specified the precision, recall, and F1 scores referred to in this section are weighted averages. Table 3 also shows the performance of two trivial models; one which randomly classifies orbit type, and another that always classifies as the majority class, GEO Stationary.

3.1 Statistical Modeling

The first model used logistic regression (LR) with all six features. The model did not converge even when the maximum number of iterations was increased to 100,000. Despite not converging, the model still had good results in classifying the validation data set. The weighted averages of precision, recall, and F1 score were all greater than 0.96. To assist with convergence, the input variables were standardized and another model was fit. The standardized LR model converged in just 82 iterations, but all the metrics decreased. A third LR model was developed by removing the input variables with the smallest coefficients. This provided the best LR model with weighted averages of precision, recall, and F1 score of approximately 0.98. The model used only three features: Mean Motion, Inclination, and Eccentricity.

A decision tree model was then developed using all six features. The criterion used to measure the quality of a split was set to "entropy". The resulting model used only three of the six features. The three features were the same that resulted in the best LR model. The decision tree model had the best performance on the validation dataset. The weighted averages of precision, recall, and F1 score were approximately 0.99. Only two satellite orbits were misclassified. As a result, the decision tree model was selected as the best statistical model.

Table 3. Statistical modeling classification result metrics on validation data. The values for precision, recall and F1 score are the weighted averages.

Model	Precision	Recall	F1	Accuracy
Logistic Regression (LR)	0.965	0.961	0.961	0.961
LR – Standardized	0.895	0.863	0.852	0.863
LR – 3 features	0.976	0.976	0.975	0.976
Decision Tree	0.991	0.990	0.990	0.990
Chance	0.149	0.127	0.134	0.127
Always Classify GEO Stationary	0.040	0.200	0.067	0.200

3.2 Neural Network Modeling

The results for the preliminary NN models, the best model after performing a hyper-parameter sweep, and the model after adding regularization are shown in Table 4. The parameters for the best hyperparameter sweep model were four hidden layers, 12 neurons per layer, a batch size of 10, and 200 epochs. The early stopping regularization stopped the training after 123 epochs.

Table 4. Neural network model performance comparison on validation data. The precision, recall, and F1 score are the weighted averages.

NN Model	Precision	Recall	F1	Accuracy
Preliminary – 6 Features	0.896	0.873	0.862	0.873
Preliminary – 3 Features	0.940	0.927	0.924	0.927
After Hyperparameter Sweep	0.986	0.985	0.985	0.985
After Regularization	0.995	0.995	0.995	0.995

The best NN model used regularization, and included only three input variables: mean motion, inclination, and eccentricity. The hyperparameters were four hidden layers with 12 neurons per layer, and a batch size of 10. Figure 4 shows no divergence between the accuracy for the training and validation data over each epoch, indicating that the NN did not overfit the data.

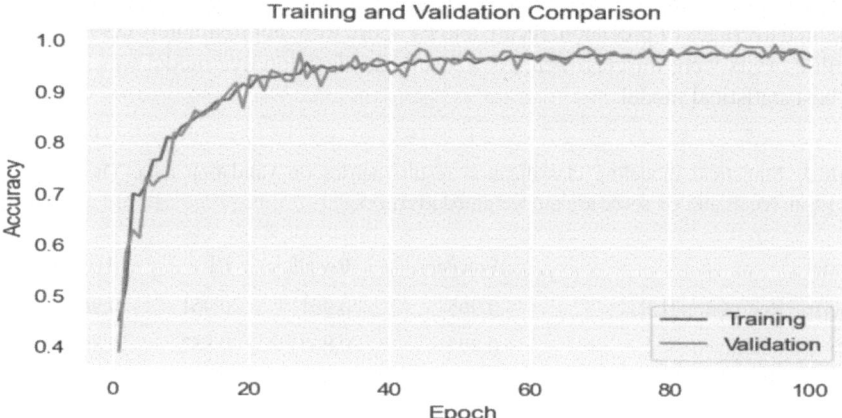

Fig. 4. Neural Net accuracy comparison for training and validation data.

3.3 Model Evaluation

The best NN model, After Regularization, performed better than the best statistical model, Decision Tree, on the validation data. Both models were used to classify the holdout dataset and the results are shown in Table 5. The weighted averages of the precision, recall, and f1 score were all over 0.97, indicating both generalize well to unseen data.

Table 5. Best statistical and NN model performance comparison on test data. The precision, recall, and F1 are the weighted averages.

Model	Precision	Recall	F1	Accuracy
Statistical: Decision Tree	0.991	0.990	0.990	0.990
NN: After Regularization	0.974	0.971	0.971	0.971

Most of the errors in the NN model came from the HEO and MEO classes. The HEO errors tended to be classifying other orbits as HEOs. It should be noted that the sample size for HEOs in the test set was only six. The MEO errors tended to be classifying MEOs as other orbit types. The decision tree model only had two errors. It misclassified a MEO as a GEO Inclined, and a LEO Sun-Synchronous as a LEO Polar.

While either model would be expected to perform well against new data ingested into the JETS database, the decision tree model was selected as the best because of its better performance on the test dataset. The decision tree model has an additional benefit of easily interpretable results. The decision tree logic can be provided to the analysts to show how the model classifies the satellite orbit.

Through the multiple model developments, it was clear that the most important orbital parameters for classifying satellite orbits were mean motion, eccentricity, and inclination.

3.4 Model Application (a.k.a. Deployment)

For successful deployment the model must provide accurate classifications because the database is considered an authoritative data source. To achieve this, two approaches could be used in future work to refine the model. The first is ensuring accurate training data and the second is developing two levels of classification. As mentioned earlier, some orbit type classifications in the data were surprising given their eccentricity and mean motion. It is possible that there could be erroneous data that negatively impacted model training and testing results. To ensure accuracy the possible erroneous data will be investigated with the JETS analyst. The model will then be retrained, and any misclassifications will be investigated to ensure they are correctly labeled. This process will be performed iteratively to refine the model as the database records are corrected (as needed).

The future work in model refinement could also include two levels of classification. The first would be a general orbit classifier into one of the four main orbit types. The second level would consist of be three additional models that focus on identifying the subclass for each particular main orbit type Only three additional models are required because there are no subclasses for MEO orbits. It is hypothesized that the additional level will allow the second-level models to better distinguish between subclasses when fewer overall classes are considered.

4 Conclusion

Several statistical machine learning and NN models were developed and compared to classify orbit type based on six orbital parameters. A common result in the modeling process was that three of the six orbital parameters were the most important for classifying orbit type: mean motion, eccentricity, and inclination.

The best NN model consisted of the three most important parameters as inputs, four hidden layers with 12 neurons each, a batch size of 10, and early stopping to prevent overfitting. The model performed best on the validation dataset, with weighted averages for precision, recall, and f1 score all over 0.99. The same metrics on the test dataset were all over 0.97.

The best statistical model was a decision tree with the same three inputs. The metrics for the validation and test dataset were all approximately 0.99. The decision tree model outperformed the NN model on the test data and was chosen as the best model to classify orbit type from orbital parameters. The model will continue to be refined to ensure the JETS database is updated with accurate records. Once deployed the model will eliminate a manual process and has the potential to save hundreds of man-hours annually.

Authors' Note: The views expressed are those of the authors and do not reflect the official guidance or position of the United States Government, the Department of Defense, the United States Air Force, the United States Space Force or any agency thereof. Reference to specific commercial products does not constitute or imply its endorsement, recommendation, or favoring by the U.S. Government. The authors declare this is a work of the U.S. Government and is not subject to copyright protections in the United States. This article has been cleared with case numbers MSC/PA-2024-0040 and 88ABW-2024-0168.

Disclosure of Interests. The authors have no competing interests to declare that are relevant to the contents of this article.

References

1. U.S. Department of Defense, DODI 8320.05 - Electromagnetic Spectrum Data Sharing, Washington, DC: Chief Information Officer (2017)
2. C. Green, Interviewee, JETS Database Update Process. [Interview], 7 February 2024
3. O'Hehir, J.M.: DSO Data Class: JSC Equipment, Tactical, Space (JETS) (2023)
4. U.S. Department of Defense, Joint Publication 3-14 - Joint Space Operations (2023)
5. Martin, G., et al.: Cislunar periodic orbit family classification from astrometric and photometric observations using machine learning. In: Advanced Maui Optical and Space Surveillance Technologies Conference (AMOS) (2020)
6. López, R.: Classify asteroid orbits using machine learning. Neural Designer, 31 August (2023). https://www.neuraldesigner.com/learning/examples/orbit-class/. Accessed 6 Nov 2023
7. DiBona, P., Foster, J., Falcone, A., Czajkowski, M.: Machine learning for RSO maneuver classification and orbital patern prediction. In: Advanced Maui Optical and Space Surveillance Technologies Conference (AMOS) (2020)
8. Roberts, T.G., Linares, R.: Geosynchronous satellite maneuver classification via supervised machine learning. In: Advanced Maui Optical and Space Surveillance Technologies Conference (AMOS) (2021)

9. O'Hehir, J.M., (ed.) JETS Data Dictionary with codes and structure (2023)
10. Chen, L., Bai, X.-Z., Liang, Y.-G., Li, K.-B.: Orbital Data Applications for Space Objects: Conjunction Assessment and Situation Analysis, Singapore: Springer Nature Singapore (2016)
11. Lefebvre, J.-L.: Space Strategy, Hoboken. Wiley, NJ (2017)
12. Capderou, M.: Handbook of Satellite Orbits: From Kepler to GPS. Springer, New York (2014)
13. 3.3. Metrics and scoring: quantifying the quality of predictions. https://scikit-learn.org/stable/modules/model_evaluation.html. Accessed 2 Feb 2024

Real-Time Motion Planning for Autonomous Vehicles in Dynamic Environments

Mohammad Dehghani Tezerjani$^{(\boxtimes)}$ (D), Deyuan Qu(D), Sudip Dhakal(D), Dominic Carrillo(D), Amir Mirzaeinia(D), and Qing Yang(D)

University of North Texas, Denton, TX 76201, USA
{mike.degany,deyuan.qu,sudip.dhakal,dominic.carrillo,
amir.mirzaeinia,qing.yang}@unt.edu

Abstract. Recent advancements in self-driving car technologies have enabled them to navigate autonomously through various environments. However, one of the critical challenges in autonomous vehicle operation is trajectory planning, especially in dynamic environments with moving obstacles. This research aims to tackle this challenge by proposing a robust algorithm tailored for autonomous cars operating in dynamic environments with moving obstacles. The algorithm introduces two main innovations. Firstly, it defines path density by adjusting the number of waypoints along the trajectory, optimizing their distribution for accuracy in curved areas and reducing computational complexity in straight sections. Secondly, it integrates hierarchical motion planning algorithms, combining global planning with an enhanced A^* graph-based method and local planning using the time elastic band algorithm with moving obstacle detection considering different motion models. The proposed algorithm is adaptable for different vehicle types and mobile robots, making it versatile for real-world applications. Simulation results demonstrate its effectiveness across various conditions, promising safer and more efficient navigation for autonomous vehicles in dynamic environments. These modifications significantly improve trajectory planning capabilities, addressing a crucial aspect of autonomous vehicle technology.

Keywords: Autonomous Vehicles · Dynamic obstacles · Obstacle avoidance · Global planning · Local planning · Timed elastic band · trajectory density

1 Introduction

Today, the advancement of autonomous vehicle technology holds immense promise, offering significant benefits such as heightened safety, doubled efficiency, and increased accessibility, poised to revolutionize transportation systems. A critical aspect of autonomous vehicle development lies in creating a trajectory from the origin to the destination in the streets and places full of cars and pedestrians, which underscores the importance of high safety to prevent fatal accidents

© The Author(s), under exclusive license to Springer Nature Switzerland AG 2025
D. D. Hodson et al. (Eds.): CSCE 2024, CCIS 2258, pp. 134–148, 2025.
https://doi.org/10.1007/978-3-031-85902-1_14

and damages [10]. According to the report of NHTSA, in 2021, 42,939 people died due to road accidents. This number was 39007 in 2020 and 36355 in 2019, which shows the increase in the number of deaths in recent years [17]. Most of the fatal crash were caused by drivers' carelessness and mistakes, and 31% of these accidents are drunk drivers and 10% are distracted drivers [14, 15]. Autonomous vehicles present a groundbreaking opportunity to reduce errors and save lives significantly. They also serve as essential tools for individuals facing physical or visual challenges that hinder private car use. Concurrently, statistical data indicates that 86% of the American workforce relies on private car transportation, spending an average of 25 min driving daily [3]. By adopting autonomous vehicles, people can make more efficient use of their time and reduce the likelihood of experiencing neurological disorders linked to driving. In autonomous driving, three primary components are pivotal: perception, decision-making, and control [4]. The decision-making phase, especially critical in car navigation, is dedicated to generating paths for autonomous vehicles. This task can be segmented into two facets: path planning without temporal constraints and trajectory planning considering time factors. Crafting a path with temporal data entails determining factors like the time needed to reach specific points and the consequent vehicle speed or acceleration. Such planning also necessitates considering vehicle dynamics, dynamic obstacles, and environmental alterations not initially factored into the original mapping process [6]. Achieving autonomous navigation in vehicles relies on accurately describing the environment through mapping, identifying obstacles within it, generating obstacle-free routes from the starting point to the destination, and subsequently adhering to these routes. However, a significant challenge lies in enabling vehicles to navigate through dynamic environments. While current obstacles in trajectory generation primarily revolve around intricate real-time calculations in dynamic settings, this study specifically focuses on real-time motion planning in environments where dynamic obstacles are present. Motion planning strategies can be categorized into four main groups: graph search-based algorithms, sampling-based algorithms, interpolation curve algorithms, and numerical optimization methods [4]. Graph-based algorithms and sampling-based algorithms are commonly employed for global planning purposes [13]. While sampling-based algorithms offer faster performance, they are often probabilistic in nature and may not yield consistent results across iterations. Consequently, this study adopts an enhanced A* graph-based algorithm for global planning. Moreover, recent advancements in the field have introduced several algorithms tailored for local planning to mitigate collisions with moving obstacles. These include the artificial potential field algorithm [5], the dynamic window approach [2], the elastic band algorithm [11], and the timed elastic band algorithm [12]. The well-established elastic band method [11] is a dynamic trajectory planning approach that adapts the path's shape in real-time. Internal forces, predefined within the method, ensure path continuity, while external forces help navigate around obstacles. However, the traditional elastic band method lacks consideration for time-related data and dynamic constraints. Building upon this, a method introduced in [12] extends the classic elastic band approach to incorporate temporal information in two stages. Initially, discrete intermediate way-points are strategically positioned away from obstacles, followed by employing a dynamic movement model to ensure path continuity. In [7], these two stages are integrated to streamline the process. In contrast to the previously mentioned method, alternative approaches such as those utilized in Autoware's waypoint generation process extract waypoints from the 3D map created during mapping and store them in a file [1]. While this file acts as a guide for path tracking, it operates independently of real-time constraints, thus introducing its own draw-backs. Trajectory optimization tasks often entail extensive computational efforts, posing challenges in integrating planning components with control units. Conse-quently, researchers seek efficient solutions for trajectory optimization problems. The dynamic window algorithm, introduced in [2], samples circular trajectories within a search space constrained by permissible linear and rotational speed orders to generate motion. In [8,16], spline paths are continually optimized con-sidering dynamic constraints. Additionally, [12] proposes the time elastic band method, an enhancement of the elastic band method that incorporates time data to optimize trajectories while avoiding obstacles. This study further improves the time elastic band method, enabling dynamic adjustments to trajectory accuracy based on current conditions. Furthermore, it estimates the trajectories of mov-ing obstacles in the environment using the Kalman filter [18]. A combination of local planning algorithms and a predefined global planner facilitates real-time planning for autonomous vehicles in dynamic environments. Initially, motion planning in dynamic environments is conducted without temporal information. As the vehicle progresses along this path, it identifies new obstacles and adjusts the path accordingly. Through a hierarchical approach that integrates planning algorithms, this research aims to design optimal trajectories that minimize travel time while avoiding both stationary and moving obstacles, while adhering to the vehicle's non-holonomic constraints [12].

2   Methodology

In this study, the global planning method employed is the A^* algorithm, enhanced with a gradient descent optimizer. Initially, the A^* algorithm is applied to assign values to all map grids using a function, effectively creating an analo-gous discrete potential field within the environment. Subsequently, the gradient descent method is utilized to extract a favourable path from the origin to the des-tination based on these values. For local planning tasks, the timed elastic band method is preferred due to its numerous advantages over alternative motion planning approaches.

2.1   Proposed Algorithm for Global Planning

The proposed approach for global planning in this research involves utilizing the A^* algorithm to assess a portion of the map and employing a decreasing gradi-ent optimizer to determine the path. The A^* algorithm is adept at finding the shortest path based on the distance criterion from the goal, making it suitable for global planning in both structured and unstructured environments. Incorporating heuristic criteria in this method significantly reduces computational complexity. By employing this approach, higher-probability path segments within the map are prioritized, effectively creating a representation akin to a discrete potential field in the environment. Subsequently, the gradient descent method is employed to derive the shortest path from the starting point to the destination. The A^* algorithm leverages heuristic criteria to streamline calculations, while the use of gradients facilitates the discovery of smoother paths, enhancing its comparative value over other planning methods. The implementation of the A^* algorithm in this research is outlined in Algorithm 1.

2.2 A^* Planner

In the global planning method applied to the generated map, as integrated within the A^* algorithm, the procedure entails receiving the cost map coordinates corresponding to the starting and ending points, and subsequently deriving the path from the end point. Initially, the path finder initializes the path array by placing the destination point. It then examines the eight neighbouring cell, selecting the one with the lowest value as the subsequent waypoint along the path. This iterative process persists until the starting point is reached.

2.3 Gradient Descent Method

In this study, the gradient descent method is employed for path finding. Gradient descent is an iterative mathematical optimization algorithm utilized to locate the minimum of a function. It involves taking steps proportional to the negative gradient (or estimated gradient) of the function at the current point. If steps in the positive gradient direction are taken, the algorithm approaches the maximum of the function, known as the incremental gradient process. Here, the function of interest is discrete and two-dimensional, derived as a map from the A* method. The following pseudocode outlines the process of estimating the gradient on this map and determining the path:

Due to the heuristic criterion employed in the A^* algorithm, only the map regions, where the presence of a path is more probable, are valued. Consequently, a potential error arises at the border between the valued area and the non-valued area when using the decreasing gradient method. This issue is addressed by adding the fourth and fifth lines, thereby rectifying the error.

2.4 Proposed Algorithm for Local Planning

After establishing the global path from the origin to the destination, accounting for static obstacles, the next step involves local planning to fine-tune the final trajectory for the vehicle. In this research, the local trajectory is defined as a sequence of vehicle positions along with the corresponding time intervals. Each position is characterized by four parameters detailing the vehicle's location and orientation.

Algorithm 1 Pseudocode for the modified A^* Algorithm

1: Initialize the overall cost-map with the start and goal locations.
2: Form an array of ordered pairs, where the first component denotes the cell index and the second component represents the cell value.
3: Set the initial value of all map points (except the starting point, which is set to zero) to a large value.
4: Place the starting point with a value of zero in the first position of the queue.
5: **while** the queue is not empty **do**
6:     Extract the cell with the highest value from the queue.
7:     **if** the end point is reached **then**
8:         Terminate the process.
9:     **end if**
10:    **for all** neighboring cells (left, right, top, bottom) **do**
11:        **if** cell value is less than a predefined threshold **then**
12:            Remove the cell from consideration.
13:        **end if**
14:        **if** cell is outside the map boundary **then**
15:            Remove the cell from consideration.
16:        **end if**
17:        Calculate the new value for the cell.
18:        Compute the Euclidean distance from the cell to the end point.
19:        Store the cell index, its new value, and the sum of the new value.
20:    **end for**
21: **end while**

Algorithm 2 Pseudocode for A^* Algorithm

1: Begin from the destination point.
2: Continue until reaching the starting point:
3: **while** not at starting point **do**
4:     **if** each neighboring cell value $= POT\_HIGH^*$ **then**
5:         Move to the neighboring cell with the lowest value.
6:     **else**
7:         Compute the numerical approximation of the potential gradient.
8:         **if** gradient is zero **then**
9:             An error has occurred.
10:        **end if**
11:        Move half a cell in the direction of the negative gradient.
12:    **end if**
13: **end while**

$^*POT\_HIGH$: A very high initial value

2.5 Setting the Trajectory Density

The proposal outlined in this article aims to enhance trajectory quality while mitigating computational burden by augmenting the number of waypoints in critical sections, such as bends or turns. This is achieved by integrating a dynamic term into the time intervals within the fastest time cost function, enabling trajectory accuracy adjustments along specific segments. The cost function for the fastest route is introduced as Eq. 1.

$$f_k = \sum_{k=1}^{n-1} (\Delta T_k)^2 \qquad (1) \qquad\qquad f_k = \sum_{k=1}^{n-1} w_k (\Delta T_k)^2 \qquad (2)$$

By selecting this cost function and employing the Lagrange coefficient, the inclination is to establish uniform time intervals throughout the path. However, assigning specific coefficients to individual time intervals allows for customization of their durations. Thus, the revised cost function is as Eq. 2.

The larger the w_k weight is, the smaller its corresponding time interval ΔT_k will be, and as a result, the accuracy of the trajectory will increase. Since the turns and curves of the route are among its sensitive parts [9], in this research, the accuracy of the path has been increased in the turns and curves of the route, and in the parts where the car moves in a straight line, in order to reduce the computational burden, a smaller number of waypoints have been used. The Eq. 3 is used to identify the path curves, which is obtained according to Fig. 1.

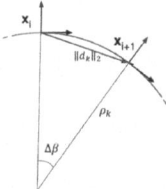

Fig. 1. Calculation of path curvature

$$\rho_k = \frac{\|d_k\|_2}{\left|2 \sin\left(\frac{\Delta\beta_k}{2}\right)\right|} \quad \text{(since } \Delta\beta_k \ll 1) \quad \rho_k = \frac{\|d_k\|_2}{|\Delta\beta_k|} \geq \rho_{\min} \qquad (3)$$

This equation gives the radius of curvature of the path, the smaller the radius of curvature of the path, the more winding the path is. Therefore, according to the Eq. (4), the inverse value obtained from (3) is considered as the weight and is used for w_k in the (5).

$$w_k = \frac{|\Delta\beta_k|}{\|d_k\|_2} \qquad (4)$$

2.6   Obstacle Dynamics in Local Planning

For dynamic obstacle tracking, the position of the obstacle center is calculated every time the cost map is updated and given to the Kalman filter. A critical difference between motion planning for vehicles and mobile robots lies in the nature of the environment they navigate. In the case of vehicles, the planning environment encompasses fast moving vehicles, necessitating consideration of accelerated obstacle movement models. The Kalman filter emerges as a robust tool for providing scientific and engineering predictions regarding the future states of dynamic systems, particularly in scenarios where information about the system is imprecise. Notably, the Kalman filter boasts efficiency, requiring minimal memory as it relies solely on past state information. In this study, the Kalman filter leverages a constant acceleration motion model to estimate obstacle movement, thus yielding the following dynamic system equation.

$$\text{Pos\_est} = \text{Pos\_old} + V_{\text{rel}}\Delta t + \frac{1}{2}A_{\text{rel}}\Delta t^2 \tag{5}$$

where, Pos_est is the estimated position of the obstacle, Pos_old is the previous position of the obstacle, V_{rel} is the relative speed of the obstacle, A_{rel} is the obstacle acceleration and Δt represents the time interval between both iterations of the algorithm. To estimate the position, speed and acceleration of the obstacle, the relationship between these three parameters should be written in a standard way. The following equations contain these relationships.

$$\begin{bmatrix} \text{Pos}_{n+1} \\ \text{Vel}_{n+1} \end{bmatrix} = \begin{bmatrix} 1 & t \\ 0 & 1 \end{bmatrix} \begin{bmatrix} \text{Pos}_n \\ \text{Vel}_n \end{bmatrix} + \begin{bmatrix} \frac{t^2}{2} \\ t \end{bmatrix} \text{Acc}_n + \mathbf{w}_n \tag{6}$$

$$Z_{n+1} = \begin{bmatrix} 1 & 0 \end{bmatrix} \begin{bmatrix} \text{Pos}_{n+1} \\ \text{Vel}_{n+1} \end{bmatrix} + v_{n+1} \tag{7}$$

w_n is process noise and $v_n + 1$ is observation noise, which are considered as white with zero mean. Considering that the above equation has an uncertain input of acceleration, the following equations can be used.

$$\begin{bmatrix} \text{Pos}_{n+1} \\ \text{Vel}_{n+1} \\ \text{Acc}_{n+1} \end{bmatrix} = \begin{bmatrix} 1 & t & \frac{t^2}{2} \\ 0 & 1 & t \\ 0 & 0 & 1 \end{bmatrix} \begin{bmatrix} \text{Pos}_n \\ \text{Vel}_n \\ \text{Acc}_n \end{bmatrix} + \mathbf{w}_n \tag{8}$$

$$Z_{n+1} = \begin{bmatrix} 1 & t & \frac{t^2}{2} \end{bmatrix} \begin{bmatrix} \text{Pos}_n \\ \text{Vel}_n \\ \text{Acc}_n \end{bmatrix} + \mathbf{w}_n + v_{n+1} \tag{9}$$

Table 1 shows the necessary definitions to use in Kalman equations.

The following equations show the Kalman relations necessary to calculate the speed.

Table 1. System Augmented State

System state vector	$x_{\mathrm{aug}}(n) = \begin{bmatrix} \mathrm{Pos}_n \\ \mathrm{Vel}_n \\ \mathrm{Acc}_n \end{bmatrix}$
State transition model matrix	$F_{\mathrm{aug}}(n) = \begin{bmatrix} 1 & t & \frac{t^2}{2} \\ 0 & 1 & t \\ 0 & 0 & 1 \end{bmatrix}$
Effect of noise level	$G_{\mathrm{aug}}(n) = \begin{bmatrix} 1 \\ 1 \\ 1 \end{bmatrix}$
Observation model vector	$H_{\mathrm{aug}}(n) = \begin{bmatrix} 1 & t & \frac{t^2}{2} \end{bmatrix}$
Observation noise	$v_{\mathrm{aug}}(n) = w_n + v_{n+1}$
Process noise covariance	$Q_{\mathrm{aug}}(n) = E\{w_{\mathrm{aug}}(n)w_{\mathrm{aug}}^T(n)\} = Q(n)$
Covariance of observation noise	$R_{\mathrm{aug}}(n) = E\{v_{\mathrm{aug}}(n)v_{\mathrm{aug}}^T(n)\}$ $= H(n)G(n)Q(n)G^T(n)H^T(n) + R(n)$
Correlation matrix of process noise	$T_{\mathrm{aug}}(n) = E\{w_{\mathrm{aug}}(n)v_{\mathrm{aug}}^T(n)\} = Q(n)G^T(n)H^T(n)$

$$\hat{x}_{\mathrm{aug}}(n|n-1) = F_{\mathrm{aug}}(n)\hat{x}_{\mathrm{aug}}(n-1|n-1)$$
$$\Sigma_{\mathrm{aug}}(n|n-1) = F_{\mathrm{aug}}(n)\Sigma_{\mathrm{aug}}(n-1|n-1)F_{\mathrm{aug}}^T(n)$$
$$+ \, G_{\mathrm{aug}}(n)Q_{\mathrm{aug}}(n)G_{\mathrm{aug}}^T(n)$$
$$\hat{y}(n) = Z_{\mathrm{aug}}(n) - H_{\mathrm{aug}}(n)\hat{x}_{\mathrm{aug}}(n|n-1)$$
$$K_{\mathrm{aug}}(n) = [\Sigma_{\mathrm{aug}}(n|n-1)H_{\mathrm{aug}}^T(n)$$
$$+ \, G_{\mathrm{aug}}(n)T_{\mathrm{aug}}(n)]R_{\mathrm{aug}}^{-1}(n)$$
$$\hat{x}_{\mathrm{aug}}(n|n) = \hat{x}_{\mathrm{aug}}(n|n-1) + K_{\mathrm{aug}}(n)\hat{y}(n)$$
$$\Sigma_{\mathrm{aug}}(n|n) = \Sigma_{\mathrm{aug}}(n|n-1)$$
$$- \, K_{\mathrm{aug}}(n)H_{\mathrm{aug}}(n)\Sigma_{\mathrm{aug}}(n|n-1) \qquad (10)$$

In the above equations, $\hat{x}_{\mathrm{aug}}$ is the estimated state vector, Σ_{aug} is the covariance matrix of the estimation error, and K_{aug} is the Kalman gain.

How to design the covariance noise process (Q matrix) is explained below. In practice, a lot of time is spent simulating and evaluating the collected data to choose the right value for Q. In general, the process model will be in the following form:

$$\dot{x} = Ax + Bu + w \qquad (11) \qquad\qquad f(x) = Fx + \Gamma w \qquad (12)$$
where w is the process noise.

The desired dynamic system is modeled using position, speed, and acceleration. Now it is assumed that the acceleration, which is larger than the order, is constant in specific time intervals that are independent of each other and changes at the end of each interval. In other words, the acceleration jumps in each time interval and is modeled as below:

$$F = \begin{bmatrix} 1 & t & \frac{t^2}{2} \\ 0 & 1 & t \\ 0 & 0 & 1 \end{bmatrix} \quad (13) \qquad \Gamma = \begin{bmatrix} \frac{\Delta t^2}{2} \\ \Delta t \\ 1 \end{bmatrix} \quad (14)$$

where Γ is the system noise gain and w is the desired continuous piece acceleration. The transfer matrix of the system is also defined as follows.

Therefore, the covariance matrix of the system will be as follows.

$$Q = \mathbb{E}[\Gamma w(t)w(t)\Gamma^T] = \Gamma \sigma_v^2 \Gamma^T \qquad (15) \qquad Q = \begin{bmatrix} \frac{\Delta t^4}{4} & \frac{\Delta t^3}{2} & \frac{\Delta t^2}{2} \\ \frac{\Delta t^3}{2} & \Delta t^2 & \Delta t \\ \frac{\Delta t^2}{2} & \Delta t & 1 \end{bmatrix} \quad (16)$$

3 Experiments

Figure 2 illustrates the scenario involving a parking lot, showcasing two planning methods: normal A^* and gradient descent. Comparing the paths generated by these methods reveals that the gradient descent approach yields a notably smoother and optimal path compared to the conventional A^* method. It's worth noting that while the global planning may exhibit suboptimal outcomes, the local planner effectively mitigates many of its drawbacks, this means that the imperfections are okay and do not need special care when putting the plan into action. In designing the global planner, the paramount considerations include ensuring completeness, accuracy, and reducing computational complexity. Simulations validate that the proposed algorithm in this study satisfactorily fulfills these criteria, making it well-suited for global path planning.

Figure 3 illustrates the impact of path density enhancement. Here, the origin is located at $(-4, 0)$ and the destination at $(+4, 0)$, while the obstacle has shifted from a position above the horizontal axis to $(0, -4.5)$. Each arrow along the path indicates specific positions and directions for the car to traverse towards reaching the destination. Despite local optimization efforts and the path's continuous shape alteration, without multipath optimization, the resulting path remains suboptimal. This scenario was conducted solely to introduce curvature into the path and evaluate improvements in this aspect. Higher curvature regions entail more waypoints, thus increasing path density accordingly.

To assess the effectiveness of the Kalman filter, various scenarios were examined involving moving obstacles with diverse velocities and accelerations. Their positions were calculated, and this data was subsequently fed into the Kalman filter to extract the motion model of the obstacle.

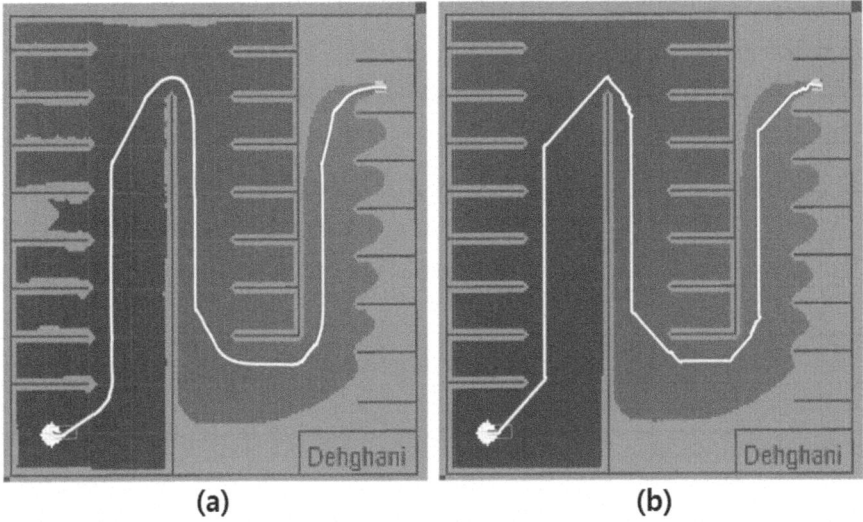

Fig. 2. Comparison of path planning with a) descent gradient and b) normal A^*

Fig. 3. a) normal path planning b) considering density in the bends along the path

3.1 First Scenario: The Obstacle Moves at a Constant Speed in the Vertical (y) Direction

In this scenario, the moving obstacle is positioned ahead of the vehicle and travels along the y-axis (Fig. 4(a)). The obstacle's displacement is such that its linear velocity in the x-axis is zero, while its linear velocity in the y-axis changes completely randomly.

To confine the obstacle within the planning environment, its movement is constrained to a defined interval, with its direction changed upon reaching upper and lower limits. Despite large error in the perception phase and challenges in calculating the obstacle's position, the Kalman filter adeptly estimates the speed and acceleration of the obstacle system (Fig. 4(d)).

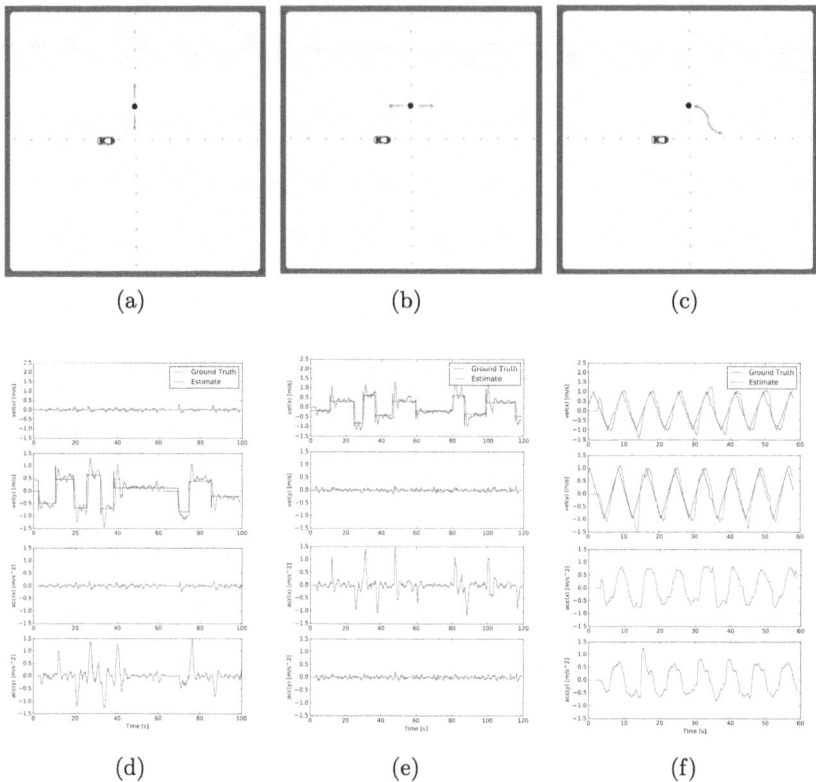

Fig. 4. (a) Path planning in the presence of an obstacle moving in the y direction (b) Evaluation of the Kalman filter for the moving obstacle in the y direction (c) moving obstacle in the x direction (d) Kalman filter for the moving obstacle with constant (e) moving obstacle with different constant accelerations (f) Evaluation of the Kalman filter for an accelerated moving obstacle

3.2 Second Scenario: The Obstacle Moves at a Constant Speed in the Vertical (x) Direction

In this scenario, the obstacle is positioned ahead of the vehicle and travels along the x-axis (Fig. 4(b)). Its displacement is designed so that its linear velocity in the y-direction remains zero while its linear velocity in the x-direction varies randomly. To ensure the obstacle remains within the routing environment, its movement is confined to a specific interval, and its direction is altered upon reaching the left and right boundaries. Despite significant error in calculating the obstacle's position, the Kalman filter effectively estimates the speed and acceleration of the obstacle system (Fig. 4(e)). This scenario was tested to demonstrate the algorithm's robustness to variations in the obstacle's movement direction.

3.3 Third Scenario: The Obstacle Moves with a Constant Acceleration

To assess the Kalman filter's performance in scenarios involving accelerated motion, a moving obstacle was subjected to constant acceleration within the environment. To limit the obstacle's movement within the designated area, its linear velocities in the x and y directions were modulated using triangular functions. Depending on the frequency and amplitude of these functions, the trajectory of the obstacle varied. Despite the challenges in accurately calculating the obstacle's position, the Kalman filter effectively estimated its speed and acceleration, highlighting its robustness even in the presence of significant error in the perception phase (Fig. 4(c)(f)).

4 Motion Planning in the Presence of Moving Obstacles

4.1 First Test: Static Obstacles

In order to test the performance of the algorithm, the initial values specified in Table 2 have been used.

The maximum number of homotopy classes is limited at 5 to control the computational workload. Consequently, 5 trajectories are simultaneously generated, and the one with the lowest cost is chosen. In the Fig. 5(a) red arrows denote the waypoints for the vehicle to traverse from the origin to the destination. The obstacles are considered as points and the circle around them indicates the safety margin. Obstacles can have any shape and be placed in any position. In order to show how the obstacles affect the path, it has been tried to place the obstacles at a point that has the greatest impact on the path. The final trajectory comprises 81 states, with an estimated time of arrival at 20.14 s. The average path computation time is 14.91 ms, which is considered efficient for a computer equipped with a dual-core processor running at 1.8 GHz.

Table 2. Initial conditions for all three tests

Description	Static Obstacle	Obstacle with Constant Speed	Obstacle with Constant Acceleration
Initial position of the vehicle	$[-4,0]$		
Destination location of the vehicle	$[4,0]$		
Initial position of obstacles	$0:[-2,0]$	$1:[2,0]$	$2:[0,0]$
Initial speed of obstacles	$0:[0,0]$	$1:[-0.2,-0.3]$	$2:[0.2,-0.2]$
Initial acceleration of obstacles	$0:[0,0]$	$1:[0,0]$	$2:[-0.02,0.03]$
Dynamic conditions of obstacles	Completely static	Constant velocity	Constant acceleration

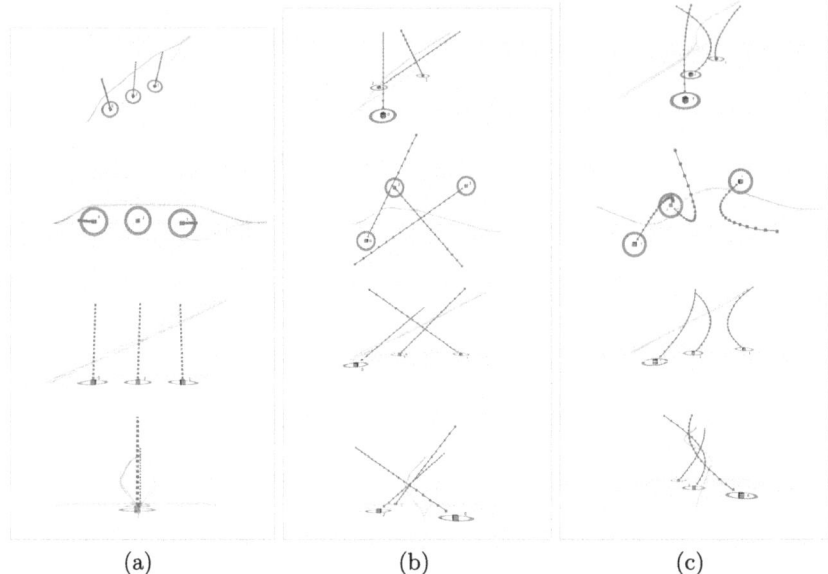

(a)   (b)   (c)

Fig. 5. (a) Two-dimensional position over time, perspective view, from above, from the front, and from the left in the presence of static obstacles (b) n the presence of constant speed obstacles (c) n the presence of constant acceleration obstacles (Color figure online)

4.2   Second Scenario: Moving Obstacles at a Constant Speed

In order to test the performance of the algorithm, the initial values specified in Table 2 have been used in this scenario.

The maximum number of homotopy classes is set to four to avoid the increase in the computational cost. Therefore, four trajectories are designed simultaneously and the one that has a lower cost is selected. In the Fig. 5(b) the red arrows show the situations that the car must go through to go from the origin to the destination. The obstacles are simplified to points, with a surrounding circle denoting the safety margin. These obstacles are versatile, capable of assuming any shape and position. To demonstrate their influence on the path, obstacles are strategically positioned to show their maximum impact. The resulting route includes 75 states and the time to reach the destination will be 19.22 s. The average time required to calculate the path is 23.1 ms, which is a good time for a computer with a dual-core processor with a frequency of 1.8 GHz.

4.3   Third Test: Accelerated Moving Obstacles

In order to test the performance of the algorithm, the initial values specified in Table 2 have been used.

The resulting route includes 85 states and the time to reach the destination will be 21.12 s. The average time required to calculate the route is 27.32 s, which is a good time for a computer with a dual-core processor with a frequency of 1.8 GHz. Figure 5(c) illustrates the scenario of accelerated obstacles.

5   Conclusion

This research introduces the novel concept of "Trajectory density" to assess the quality of generated paths by vehicle motion planning algorithms. By defining a new objective function and applying dynamic coefficients, this criterion is enhanced. Given that increasing the number of track conditions escalates computational load, it's impractical to boost trajectory density throughout its entirety. Hence, the technique proposed in this study detects sensitive areas of the route, such as bends, and adjusts the density accordingly. Motion planning in the proposed method incorporates dynamics of moving obstacles. To identify obstacles and their locations, a new method is employed, amalgamating sensor data to produce a local cost-map. Computer vision methods are then utilized to differentiate between fixed and moving obstacles, with the latter's location provided at a specific frequency enabling dynamic obstacle tracking. This information is integrated into the Kalman filter to estimate speed and acceleration, enabling extraction of obstacle dynamics.

References

1. Dhakal, S., Qu, D., Carrillo, D., Yang, Q., Fu, S.: OASD: an open approach to self-driving vehicle. In: 2021 Fourth International Conference on Connected and Autonomous Driving (MetroCAD), pp. 54–61 (2021). https://doi.org/10.1109/MetroCAD51599.2021.00017
2. Fox, D., Burgard, W., Thrun, S.: The dynamic window approach to collision avoidance. IEEE Rob. Autom. Mag. **4**(1), 23–33 (1997)
3. Gibson, J.: Commuting to work in the US: facts and statistics — Bankrate—bankrate.com (2024). https://www.bankrate.com/insurance/car/commuting-facts-statistics/. Accessed 02 Mar 2024
4. González, D., Pérez, J., Milanés, V., Nashashibi, F.: A review of motion planning techniques for automated vehicles. IEEE Trans. Intell. Transp. Syst. **17**(4), 1135–1145 (2015)
5. Khatib, O.: Real-time obstacle avoidance for manipulators and mobile robots. Int. J. Rob. Res. **5**(1), 90–98 (1986)
6. Kunchev, V., Jain, L., Ivancevic, V., Finn, A.: Path planning and obstacle avoidance for autonomous mobile robots: a review. In: Gabrys, B., Howlett, R.J., Jain, L.C. (eds.) KES 2006. LNCS (LNAI), vol. 4252, pp. 537–544. Springer, Heidelberg (2006). https://doi.org/10.1007/11893004_70
7. Kurniawati, H., Fraichard, T.: From path to trajectory deformation. In: 2007 IEEE/RSJ International Conference on Intelligent Robots and Systems, pp. 159–164. IEEE (2007)

8. Lau, B., Sprunk, C., Burgard, W.: Kinodynamic motion planning for mobile robots using splines. In: 2009 IEEE/RSJ International Conference on Intelligent Robots and Systems, pp. 2427–2433. IEEE (2009)

9. Li, B., Ouyang, Y., Li, L., Zhang, Y.: Autonomous driving on curvy roads without reliance on Frenet frame: a cartesian-based trajectory planning method. IEEE Trans. Intell. Transp. Syst. **23**(9), 15729–15741 (2022)

10. Passmore, J., Yon, Y., Mikkelsen, B.: Progress in reducing road-traffic injuries in the who European region. Lancet Public Health **4**(6), e272–e273 (2019)

11. Quinlan, S.: Real-time modification of collision-free paths. Stanford University (1995)

12. Rösmann, C., Feiten, W., Wösch, T., Hoffmann, F., Bertram, T.: Trajectory modification considering dynamic constraints of autonomous robots. In: ROBOTIK 2012; 7th German Conference on Robotics, pp. 1–6. VDE (2012)

13. Sanchez-Ibanez, J.R., Perez-del Pulgar, C.J., García-Cerezo, A.: Path planning for autonomous mobile robots: a review. Sensors **21**(23), 7898 (2021)

14. Singh, S.: Critical reasons for crashes investigated in the national motor vehicle crash causation survey, February 2018. https://trid.trb.org/view/1507603

15. Singh, S.: Critical reasons for crashes investigated in the national motor vehicle crash causation survey. Technical report (2015)

16. Sprunk, C., Lau, B., Pfaffz, P., Burgard, W.: Online generation of kinodynamic trajectories for non-circular omnidirectional robots. In: 2011 IEEE International Conference on Robotics and Automation, pp. 72–77. IEEE (2011)

17. National Center for Statistics and Analysis: Summary of motor vehicle traffic crashes (2023). https://crashstats.nhtsa.dot.gov/Api/Public/ViewPublication/813515. Accessed 01 Mar 2024

18. Welch, G., Bishop, G., et al.: An introduction to the Kalman filter (1995)

A Novel Deep Learning Method
for Solving PDE's Applied to a Shallow
Water Problem

Jose Palacios-García$^{(\boxtimes)}$ ⓘ, Julio Ibarra-Fiallo ⓘ, and Sevando Espín-Torres ⓘ

Colegio de Ciencias e Ingenierías, Universidad San Francisco de Quito, Cumbayá,
Quito, Ecuador
jpalaciosg@alumni.usfq.edu.ec, {jibarra,lespin}@usfq.edu.ec

Abstract. In this work we explain and implement a method that uses
an artificial neural network to solve differential equations numerically.
The method was applied to a model of the flow of water in an open
channel described by the Saint-Venant Equations (SVE). These equations constitute a system of partial differential equations. The method
was implemented in Python using the libraries Numpy and Pytorch to
manage matrix operations and the construction of the artificial neural network. The results of the method were compared with a common numerical method using RK1, where an average relative error of
4,05% was obtained. The results show that the proposed method has a
promising performance in the resolution of partial differential equations,
especially because of the versatility that it offers to define boundary
conditions in complex geometries. The execution time was comparable
to traditional methods, thanks to common performance enhancements
developed for training artificial neural networks. Possible improvements
for further research are mentioned.

Keywords: Neural Networks · Partial Differential Equations ·
Gradient Descent · Numerical Methods for Partial Differential
Equations

1 Introduction

In the last decade, there has been a considerable increase in the popularity
of different artificial intelligence algorithms and neural networks. Among these
algorithms, the one that has had the most notable applications is that of artificial
neural networks; these represent an abstraction of the theoretical functioning of
neurons in living organisms [11]. The exploration of these models continues to
be a point of research interest, both in the field of optimization from theory [7]
and in applications for prediction and pattern recognition.

On the other hand, methods for solving systems of complex differential equations are a key point of research in most sciences and engineering. However,
analytical methods for solving differential equations are relatively limited and

D. D. Hodson et al. (Eds.): CSCE 2024, CCIS 2258, pp. 149–157, 2025.
https://doi.org/10.1007/978-3-031-85902-1_15

complicated; and in the case of partial differential equations, it is usually more efficient to use numerical methods than to search for an exact solution. That is why research in methods of numerical solution of these systems is of great importance.

In this work we will describe and implement a method for solving differential equations of different types that takes advantage of the advances and architecture designed for the implementation of artificial neural networks and the *universal approximator* characteristics of feed forward neural networks observed in [6]. This method was described in detail in [2,9]. To demonstrate the performance, it will be applied to a system of differential equations describing the flow of water in an open channel, which have been solved numerically in [4]. Finally, the results will be compared with a simple numerical method similar to the one used in [10] and the advantages and limitations of the method will be discussed.

2   Method

A simple feed forward neural network is comprised of layers of *perceptrons* (the analog of neurons in an artificial neural network), which can be represented by the composition of matrix multiplications with *activation functions*. The entries of each matrix in the matrix multiplication are what represents the *weights* of connections between each pair of perceptrons in adjacent layers and the activation functions decide how the output of the matrix multiplication should be translated as an *impulse* (the output vector of the layer) to be sent to the next layer.

The method to be used aims to exploit optimized neural network training mechanisms to find an approximate solution to a differential equation. The first step is to discretize the domain over which a solution is needed. The number of points in this discretization will have an important impact on the execution time of the following steps. Given the discretization, a neural network is created as follows:

- There is only one layer of perceptrons.
- There is the same number of perceptrons as points in the discretized domain.
- The activation function of each of the perceptrons is not bounded or the bounds are wider than those of the differential equation.
- The neural network accepts only one input.
- The output value of each of the perceptrons will be the output value of the neural network.

Once the neural network has been created, an error function must be defined in such a way that once the network has been trained, what it returns is an approximate solution to the differential equation to be solved.

Given a differential equation of degree g of the form:

$$F\left(x, y(x), \nabla y(x), \nabla^2 y(x)\right) = 0 \qquad (1)$$

and with the uniformly discretized domain $X = \{x_0, ..., x_n\}$. A positive error function that, if resulting in zero, would guarantee the fulfillment of the differential equation would be:

$$E(x_0, ..., x_n) = \sum_{i=0}^{n} F\left(x_i, y(x_i), \nabla y(x_i), \nabla^2 y(x_i)\right)^2$$

Using E as the error function in this neural network, where y is the output of the network (a discrete function with a value corresponding to each element of the domain), ensures that the result, if optimized, will comply with the differential equation. However, for applications, it is not enough to find a solution to the differential equation, but it is necessary to find a solution that at the same time meets certain initial or boundary conditions.

That problem can be solved by appropriately using the output of the neural network as in [9]. Let $N_0, ..., N_n$ be the output values of the neural network at each perceptron. Let A be a C^g function (g times continuously differentiable) defined in the domain of the differential equation that satisfies the boundary conditions of the problem, but does not necessarily satisfy the differential equation itself. It is also assumed that f is a C^g function with the same domain that is zero at the boundary, but is nonzero in the rest of the domain. We then define

$$y_T(x_i) = A(x_i) + f(x_i, N_i) \tag{2}$$

this will be the function with which the error function will be calculated. Thus, when the algorithm finds the minimum, it will be known that the differential equation is satisfied as well as the boundary conditions because the neural network is unable to alter the values at the boundary due to the way in which f was constructed. It should be noted that this method can be easily extended dimension-wise by simply changing the domain and discretization, as was done, for example, in [1]. It is also important to remember that since this is a numerical method, the derivatives would have to be replaced by numerical derivatives.

The basic steps of the method then are:

1. Discretize the domain.
2. Create a C^g function, A, that satisfies the boundary conditions.
3. Find a function f that is zero only at the boundary.
4. Create the single layer neural network with appropriate size and activation functions.
5. Define the error function according to the differential equation.
6. Train the neural network using the error function and a suitable optimizer.

An open source Python package that can be used to solve initial-valued first-order ordinary differential equations is currently under development and is described at [2]. However, for equations with more complicated boundary conditions one has to implement the full method as described here.

3 Application Problem

As a concrete example of the use of this algorithm, gradually varying flow in an open channel will be simulated. An open channel is a conduit through which a fluid can pass, but, unlike closed channels, the water is allowed to increase in volume. The easiest example to understand is the flow of water in a river. If the flow increases considerably, the height of the water rises and so does the volume it occupies. On the other hand, if the flow is in a closed channel, this increase in volume is not allowed and must be transformed into an increase in pressure or fluid velocity.

The most appropriate model to represent this phenomenon is the Saint-Venant or shallow water equations. For this paper we will only consider the one-dimensional case that was originally proposed by *Saint-Venant*. A more modern version can be found in "Open-Channel Hydraulics" by Ven Te Chow. The Saint-Venant equations (18.2 and 18.13 in [3, pp. 525-528]) can be written as follows:

$$\frac{\partial A}{\partial t} + \frac{\partial (Q)}{\partial x} = 0 \tag{3}$$

$$g\frac{\partial y}{\partial x} + u\frac{\partial u}{\partial x} + \frac{\partial u}{\partial t} + g(S_f - S_0) = 0 \tag{4}$$

where $Q = Au$ is the flow, u is the velocity, A is the area of the channel cross-section at point x, x is the distance, $y = h$ is the height of the water, t is the time and g is the gravity. S_0 and S_f are the slope of the channel and *friction slope* respectively. S_f and S_0 are simplified assuming a rectangular channel and sensible constants based on [3]. An illustration of the problem can be found in Fig. 1.

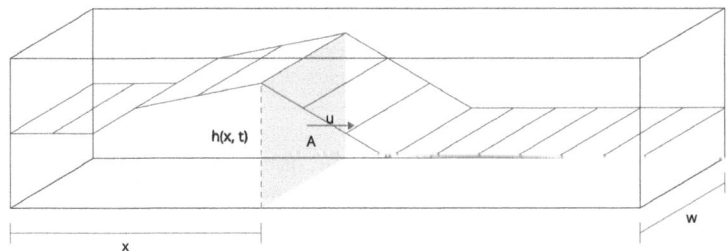

Fig. 1. Illustration of an open channel.

4 Solution

The method described the previous sections will be followed. Recalling that in the differential equation, both functions (u and y) have domains in two-dimensional spaces, x and t. That is to say that, to discretize the domains, we will need two two-dimensional arrays of size k^2, where k is the number of points per dimension. The error function will be defined as follows:

$$E(x_0, ..., x_n) = \sum_{i=0}^{n} \left[\left(\frac{\partial(y)}{\partial t} + \frac{\partial(yu)}{\partial x} \right)^2 \right.$$
$$\left. + \left(g\frac{\partial y}{\partial x} + u\frac{\partial u}{\partial x} + \frac{\partial u}{\partial t} + g\frac{w + 2y}{\rho gwy} \right)^2 \right] \tag{5}$$

We will consider points of the form $(t, x) \in [0, 4] \times [0, 12]$ for the domain and initial conditions $u(0, x) = 0$ and the height:

$$y(0, x) = \begin{cases} 5 & \text{if } x \in [0, 4] \cup [8, 12] \\ -(x - 4)(x - 8) + 5 & \text{otherwise} \end{cases} \tag{6}$$

This function is simply an example of an initial condition for this method and its choice is arbitrary. Strictly it is not differentiable at 4 and 8, but since the mesh is relatively coarse, the derivatives can be approximated at those points.

Then, a valid function for $A_u(t, x)$, as in Eq. 2 would be $A_u(t, x) = 0$ in the whole domain and for the function $A_y(t, x)$, one could take $A_y(t, x) = y(0, x)$, which is the approach taken in [2], but for the moment a function that decreases in time will be used so that the neural network has to adjust more and the performance of the method is more noticeable. We will then take

$$A_y(t, x) = \begin{cases} 5 & \text{if } x \in [0, 4] \cup [8, 12] \\ -(x - 4)(x - 8) \\ \quad \exp(-0.7t) + 5 & \text{otherwise} \end{cases} \tag{7}$$

As functions f_u and f_y, we define $f_u(t, x) = tN_u(t, x)$ and $f_y(t, x) = tN_y(t, x)$ where N_u and N_y are the outputs of the neural network at that point. Thus, all the conditions requested by the method are met. Since the functions A_h and A_u do not change with the training process, they can be computed only once at the beginning. The neural network will be comprised of one single layer, which will be connected to the input node. The output layer will be divided into two parts, which will represent the two functions needed for the solution. See Fig. 2 for a graphical representation of the neural network.

The error function is defined just as in Eq. 5 To take advantage of the parallelization of the torch package, one should use functions and methods from it as much as possible. Fortunately, the package includes functions to compute gradients and partial derivatives.

The training process was done in the standard manner except for the custom loss function. The optimizer Adam, implemented in torch, was used untill a loss of less than 0.0015 was achieved than 0.0015 was achieved. For a comparison, a simple first order method was implemented in a similar manner to [10].

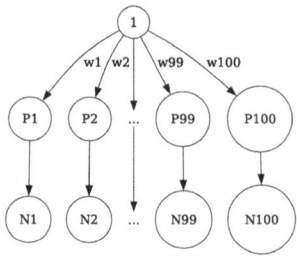

Fig. 2. Graphical representation of the architecture.

5   Results

Once the network was trained, the solution was evaluated with a single input. It was then organized into the two desired domains and plotted in Fig. 3. On the first pair of images, the output of the function $h(x, t)$ is shown together with its heat map, and $u(x, t)$ below it. In $t = 0$, the initial conditions for the height and the velocity of the water, which were discussed previously, can be seen clearly. The results tables can be found on Tables 1 and 2.

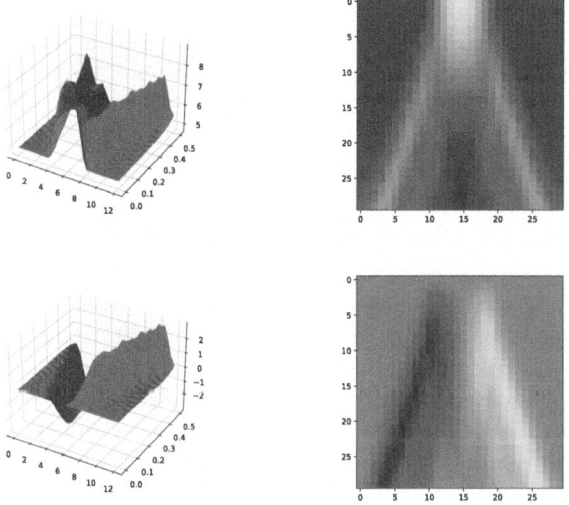

Fig. 3. Output of the neural network after training.

On the other hand, the approximation obtained using a procedure similar to [10] is shown in Fig. 4. It should be noted that this approximation is done using a first order time forward estimation, similar to Euler's method, which is known to be unstable when applied to systems like this one, more complex procedures are typically used for this system of equations as in [5]. For this reason, accuracy should not be compared between these two results, and only the general shape of the output should be considered. The relative average difference taken between each point in both methods was of 4.5% and the general shape of the output is consistent with what a real open channel system would do, starting as an accumulation of water and slowly propagating in waves throughout the length of the channel.

The plot of the error function advancing in time with training can be seen in Fig. 5. In which it should be noted that the convergence is uniform and predictable, which suggests that a different optimization algorithm could improve the efficiency.

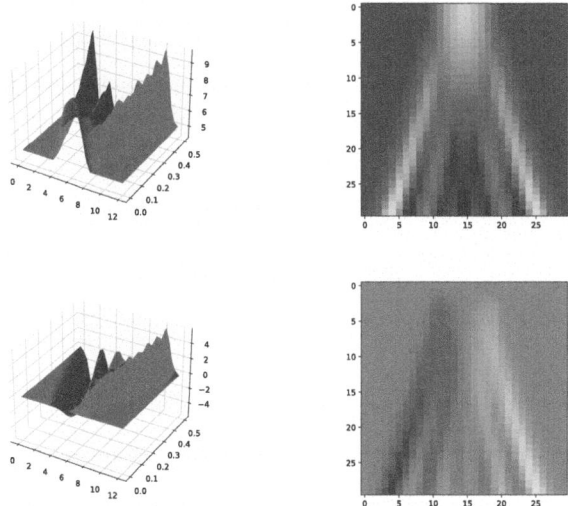

Fig. 4. Results obtained from the time forward Euler's method.

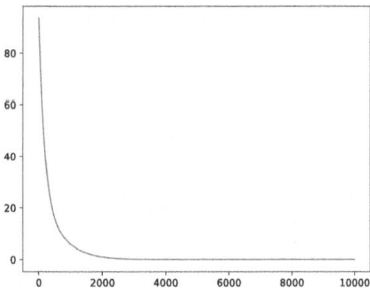

Fig. 5. Plot of the error function.

Table 1. Results table for H.

$t \downarrow \vert x \rightarrow$	0	0.41	0.83	1.24	1.66	2.07	2.48	2.9	3.31	3.72	4.14	4.55	4.97	5.38	5.79	6.21	6.62	7.03	7.45	7.86	8.28	8.69	9.1	9.52	9.93	10.34	10.76	11.17	11.59	12
0	5	5	5	5	5	5	5	5	5	5	5.53	6.9	7.93	8.61	8.96	8.96	8.61	7.93	6.9	5.53	5	5	5	5	5	5	5	5	5	5
0.02	5	5	5	5	5	5	5	5	5	5	5.53	6.9	7.93	8.61	8.96	8.96	8.61	7.93	6.9	5.53	5	5	5	5	5	5	5	5	5	5
0.03	5	5	5	5	5	5	5	5	5.02	5.09	5.65	6.93	7.86	8.53	8.86	8.86	8.53	7.86	6.93	5.65	5.09	5.02	5	5	5	5	5	5	5	5
0.05	5.01	5	5	5	5	5	5	5	5.05	5.19	5.77	6.94	7.8	8.44	8.76	8.76	8.44	7.8	6.94	5.77	5.19	5.05	5	5	5	5	5	5	5	5.01
0.07	5	5	5	5	5	5	5	5.01	5.1	5.36	5.97	6.97	7.67	8.28	8.57	8.57	8.28	7.67	6.97	5.97	5.36	5.1	5.01	5	5	5	5	5	5	5
0.09	5.01	5	5	5	5	5	5	5.02	5.16	5.55	6.17	6.96	7.55	8.12	8.39	8.39	8.12	7.55	6.96	6.17	5.55	5.16	5.02	5	5	5	5	5	5	5.01
0.1	5.01	5	5	5	5	5	5.02	5.05	5.27	5.81	6.39	6.94	7.39	7.93	8.15	8.15	7.93	7.39	6.94	6.39	5.81	5.27	5.05	5.02	5	5	5	5	5	5.01
0.12	5.02	5.01	5	5	5	5.01	5.02	5.08	5.39	6.08	6.6	6.89	7.24	7.73	7.91	7.91	7.73	7.24	6.89	6.6	6.08	5.39	5.08	5.02	5.01	5	5	5	5.01	5.02
0.14	5.01	5	5	5.01	5	5	5.05	5.16	5.56	6.38	6.76	6.8	7.08	7.51	7.64	7.64	7.51	7.08	6.8	6.76	6.38	5.56	5.16	5.05	5	5	5.01	5	5	5.01
0.16	5.02	5.01	5.01	4.99	5	5.02	5.07	5.24	5.76	6.66	6.88	6.7	6.93	7.29	7.38	7.38	7.29	6.93	6.7	6.88	6.66	5.76	5.24	5.07	5.02	5	4.99	5.01	5.01	5.02
0.17	5.03	5	5	5.01	5.01	5.02	5.12	5.39	6.01	6.92	6.92	6.58	6.8	7.06	7.11	7.11	7.06	6.8	6.58	6.92	6.92	6.01	5.39	5.12	5.02	5.01	5.01	5	5	5.03
0.19	5.03	5.02	5.01	5	5	5.05	5.18	5.56	6.28	7.11	6.92	6.49	6.67	6.83	6.85	6.85	6.83	6.67	6.49	6.92	7.11	6.28	5.56	5.18	5.05	5	5	5.01	5.02	5.03
0.21	5.04	5.01	5	5.01	5.03	5.06	5.28	5.8	6.55	7.22	6.84	6.4	6.55	6.59	6.61	6.61	6.59	6.55	6.4	6.84	7.22	6.55	5.8	5.28	5.06	5.03	5.01	5	5.01	5.04
0.22	5.04	5.03	5.02	5.01	5.02	5.12	5.41	6.06	6.79	7.24	6.76	6.36	6.43	6.36	6.37	6.37	6.36	6.43	6.36	6.76	7.24	6.79	6.06	5.41	5.12	5.02	5.01	5.02	5.03	5.04
0.24	5.06	5.03	5	5.01	5.07	5.18	5.58	6.38	6.98	7.16	6.65	6.32	6.31	6.13	6.17	6.17	6.13	6.31	6.32	6.65	7.16	6.98	6.38	5.58	5.18	5.07	5.01	5	5.03	5.06
0.26	5.05	5.03	5.03	5.03	5.08	5.28	5.81	6.68	7.09	7.02	6.57	6.31	6.19	5.92	5.96	5.96	5.92	6.19	6.31	6.57	7.02	7.09	6.68	5.81	5.28	5.08	5.03	5.03	5.03	5.05
0.28	5.08	5.05	5.02	5.03	5.15	5.43	6.07	6.97	7.09	6.83	6.5	6.29	6.05	5.72	5.79	5.79	5.72	6.05	6.29	6.5	6.83	7.09	6.97	6.07	5.43	5.15	5.03	5.02	5.05	5.08
0.29	5.06	5.04	5.05	5.08	5.2	5.6	6.37	7.18	7.03	6.64	6.46	6.28	5.93	5.55	5.61	5.61	5.55	5.93	6.28	6.46	6.64	7.03	7.18	6.37	5.6	5.2	5.08	5.05	5.04	5.06
0.31	5.1	5.08	5.06	5.09	5.32	5.86	6.67	7.31	6.87	6.46	6.43	6.25	5.79	5.4	5.48	5.48	5.4	5.79	6.25	6.43	6.46	6.87	7.31	6.67	5.86	5.32	5.09	5.06	5.08	5.1
0.33	5.08	5.05	5.07	5.18	5.46	6.12	6.94	7.32	6.69	6.33	6.41	6.2	5.67	5.29	5.33	5.33	5.29	5.67	6.2	6.41	6.33	6.69	7.32	6.94	6.12	5.46	5.18	5.07	5.05	5.07
0.34	5.11	5.11	5.12	5.22	5.64	6.47	7.14	7.23	6.49	6.22	6.38	6.12	5.55	5.19	5.21	5.21	5.19	5.55	6.12	6.38	6.22	6.49	7.23	7.14	6.47	5.64	5.22	5.12	5.11	5.11
0.36	5.1	5.08	5.14	5.36	5.9	6.77	7.24	7.05	6.34	6.17	6.33	6.02	5.46	5.13	5.09	5.09	5.13	5.46	6.02	6.33	6.17	6.34	7.05	7.24	6.77	5.9	5.36	5.14	5.08	5.1
0.38	5.13	5.15	5.24	5.49	6.17	7.08	7.23	6.83	6.21	6.12	6.26	5.91	5.39	5.08	5	5	5.08	5.39	5.91	6.26	6.12	6.21	6.83	7.23	7.08	6.17	5.49	5.24	5.15	5.13
0.4	5.14	5.14	5.27	5.71	6.53	7.28	7.1	6.59	6.16	6.11	6.16	5.78	5.33	5.05	4.9	4.9	5.05	5.33	5.78	6.16	6.11	6.16	6.59	7.1	7.28	6.53	5.71	5.27	5.14	5.14
0.41	5.17	5.22	5.45	5.98	6.81	7.39	6.9	6.39	6.12	6.08	6.03	5.66	5.29	5.04	4.83	4.83	5.04	5.29	5.66	6.03	6.08	6.12	6.39	6.9	7.39	6.81	5.98	5.45	5.21	5.17
0.43	5.2	5.26	5.55	6.27	7.13	7.38	6.65	6.23	6.13	6.06	5.89	5.53	5.25	5.03	4.77	4.77	5.03	5.25	5.54	5.89	6.06	6.13	6.23	6.65	7.38	7.13	6.27	5.55	5.26	5.2
0.45	5.23	5.35	5.83	6.65	7.3	7.23	6.41	6.13	6.15	6	5.73	5.42	5.23	5.04	4.72	4.72	5.04	5.23	5.42	5.73	6	6.15	6.13	6.41	7.23	7.3	6.65	5.83	5.35	5.23
0.47	5.31	5.48	6.05	6.94	7.4	7.04	6.21	6.06	6.16	5.94	5.59	5.32	5.21	5.03	4.7	4.7	5.03	5.21	5.32	5.59	5.94	6.16	6.06	6.21	7.04	7.4	6.94	6.05	5.48	5.31
0.48	5.37	5.63	6.41	7.3	7.36	6.75	6.05	6.04	6.17	5.85	5.44	5.23	5.19	5.04	4.68	4.68	5.04	5.19	5.23	5.44	5.85	6.17	6.04	6.05	6.75	7.36	7.3	6.41	5.63	5.37
0.5	5.51	5.88	6.75	7.43	7.16	6.52	5.98	6.03	6.13	5.75	5.33	5.16	5.16	5.04	4.7	4.7	5.04	5.16	5.16	5.33	5.75	6.13	6.03	5.98	6.52	7.16	7.43	6.74	5.87	5.51

Table 2. Result table for U.

$t \downarrow \vert x \rightarrow$	0	0.41	0.83	1.24	1.66	2.07	2.48	2.9	3.31	3.72	4.14	4.55	4.97	5.38	5.79	6.21	6.62	7.03	7.45	7.86	8.28	8.69	9.1	9.52	9.93	10.34	10.76	11.17	11.59	12
0	0	0	0	0	0	0	0	0	0	0	0	0	0	0	0	0	0	0	0	0	0	0	0	0	0	0	0	0	0	0
0.02	0	0	0	0	0	0	0	0	0	−0.1	−0.3	−0.4	−0.3	−0.2	0	0.07	0.21	0.35	0.49	0.39	0.11	0	0	0	0	0	0	0	0	0
0.03	0	0	0	0	0	0	0	0	0	−0.2	−0.7	−0.9	−0.6	−0.4	−0.1	0.14	0.42	0.69	0.98	0.78	0.22	0	0	0	0	0	0	0	0	0
0.05	0	0	0	0	0	0	0	0	0	−0.3	−1.1	−1.3	−0.9	−0.6	−0.2	0.2	0.6	0.99	1.39	1.16	0.37	0.04	0.01	0	0	0	0	0	0	0
0.07	0.01	0	0	0	0	0	0	0	0	−0.5	−1.5	−1.7	−1.2	−0.7	−0.2	0.26	0.79	1.27	1.79	1.55	0.53	0.08	0.02	0	0	0	0	0	0	0
0.09	0	0	0	0.01	0	0	0	0	−0.1	−0.7	−1.9	−2	−1.4	−0.9	−0.3	0.31	0.94	1.47	2.06	1.9	0.76	0.18	0.05	0	0	0	0	0	0	0
0.1	0.02	0.01	0	0	0	0	0	0	−0.3	−1	−2.2	−2.3	−1.6	−1	−0.3	0.35	1.09	1.67	2.32	2.23	1	0.3	0.08	0.01	0	0	0.01	0	0	0
0.12	0.01	0	0	0.01	0	0	0	−0.1	−0.5	−1.3	−2.4	−2.4	−1.7	−1.1	−0.3	0.38	1.19	1.79	2.42	2.48	1.3	0.51	0.15	0.02	0.01	0	0	0	0	0
0.14	0.03	0.01	0	0	0	0	0	−0.2	−0.7	−1.6	−2.6	−2.5	−1.9	−1.2	−0.4	0.4	1.29	1.92	2.51	2.67	1.6	0.73	0.24	0.04	0	0	0.01	0	0	0
0.16	0.03	0	0	0.01	0	0	0	−0.3	−1	−1.9	−2.7	−2.4	−1.9	−1.3	−0.4	0.4	1.33	1.98	2.47	2.76	1.91	1.05	0.37	0.08	0.03	0	0	0.01	0	0
0.17	0.04	0.02	0.01	0	0	0	−0.1	−0.5	−1.3	−2.2	−2.7	−2.4	−2	−1.3	−0.4	0.41	1.39	2.07	2.44	2.75	2.2	1.38	0.54	0.14	0.03	0.01	0.01	0	0	0
0.19	0.05	0.01	0	0.01	0	0	−0.2	−0.7	−1.7	−2.4	−2.6	−2.6	−2	−1.3	−0.3	0.30	1.37	2.09	2.35	2.65	2.41	1.77	0.76	0.24	0.08	0	0	0.01	0	0
0.21	0.05	0.03	0.02	0	0	−0.1	−0.3	−1	−2.1	−2.5	−2.4	−2.2	−2.1	−1.3	−0.3	0.39	1.36	2.12	2.28	2.49	2.55	2.13	1.03	0.35	0.1	0.03	0	0	0	0
0.22	0.07	0.03	0	0	0	−0.1	−0.5	−1.3	−2.4	−2.5	−2.2	−2.2	−2	−1.3	−0.3	0.37	1.3	2.09	2.2	2.29	2.57	2.48	1.35	0.55	0.18	0.03	0.01	0.01	0	0
0.24	0.06	0.04	0.03	0	0	−0.2	−0.7	−1.7	−2.7	−2.5	−2.1	−2.1	−2	−1.2	−0.3	0.37	1.24	2.04	2.13	2.1	2.51	2.74	1.71	0.77	0.26	0.08	0	0	0	0
0.26	0.1	0.06	0	0	−0.1	−0.4	−1	−2	−2.8	−2.3	−1.9	−2	−1.9	−1.1	−0.3	0.36	1.15	1.94	2.06	1.91	2.37	2.89	2.06	1.09	0.4	0.1	0.03	0	0	−0.1
0.28	0.07	0.04	0.03	0	−0.1	−0.5	−1.4	−2.3	−2.9	−2.2	−1.7	−1.9	−1.8	−1	−0.3	0.36	1.07	1.8	1.97	1.78	2.21	2.91	2.38	1.41	0.58	0.18	0.02	0	0	0
0.29	0.12	0.08	0.01	0	−0.2	−0.8	−1.8	−2.6	−2.8	−2	−1.6	−1.8	−1.6	−0.9	−0.3	0.37	0.98	1.63	1.87	1.67	2.02	2.81	2.63	1.83	0.8	0.26	0.09	0	0	−0.1
0.31	0.09	0.05	0.01	0	−0.4	−1.1	−2.2	−2.7	−2.6	−1.8	-1.6	−1.7	−1.4	−0.8	−0.3	0.37	0.89	1.44	1.75	1.62	1.88	2.62	2.76	2.2	1.11	0.4	0.09	0	0	0
0.33	0.14	0.1	0.01	−0.2	−0.5	−1.4	−2.5	−2.7	−2.3	−1.7	−1.5	−1.6	−1.2	−0.8	−0.3	0.38	0.82	1.24	1.6	1.58	1.77	2.37	2.76	2.57	1.43	0.59	0.2	0	−0.1	−0.1
0.34	0.11	0.05	0	−0.2	−0.8	−1.8	−2.8	−2.6	−2.1	−1.7	−1.5	−1.4	−1	−0.7	−0.3	0.37	0.72	1.03	1.43	1.56	1.71	2.11	2.63	2.83	1.84	0.82	0.24	0.04	0	−0.1
0.36	0.15	0.1	0	−0.4	−1.1	−2.2	−2.9	−2.4	−1.8	−1.6	−1.5	−1.2	−0.8	−0.6	−0.3	0.37	0.66	0.83	1.23	1.52	1.68	1.88	2.42	2.98	2.2	1.16	0.42	0.04	−0.1	−0.1
0.38	0.12	0.03	−0.1	−0.5	−1.4	−2.5	−2.9	−2.1	−1.6	−1.6	−1.4	−1	−0.6	−0.5	−0.3	0.34	0.56	0.64	1.04	1.47	1.68	1.69	2.15	2.98	2.56	1.48	0.58	0.15	0	−0.1
0.4	0.13	0.06	−0.1	−0.8	−1.9	−2.7	−2.8	−1.8	−1.5	−1.6	−1.3	−0.8	−0.4	−0.4	−0.3	0.32	0.49	0.48	0.84	1.39	1.69	1.56	1.88	2.82	2.79	1.93	0.84	0.18	0	−0.1
0.41	0.12	0	−0.3	−1.1	−2.2	−2.9	−2.5	−1.6	−1.4	−1.6	−1.2	−0.6	−0.3	−0.3	−0.2	0.27	0.38	0.34	0.66	1.28	1.67	1.48	1.67	2.59	2.9	2.27	1.15	0.39	0.02	−0.1
0.43	0.1	0	−0.5	−1.4	−2.6	−2.8	−2.2	−1.4	−1.4	−1.6	−1.1	−0.5	−0.2	−0.3	−0.2	0.22	0.3	0.23	0.51	1.16	1.64	1.44	1.49	2.28	2.87	2.67	1.48	0.51	0.06	0
0.45	0.08	−0.1	−0.8	−1.9	−2.8	−2.6	−1.9	−1.4	−1.4	−1.5	−1	−0.3	−0.1	−0.1	−0.1	0.15	0.19	0.13	0.38	1.02	1.55	1.42	1.41	1.98	2.65	2.88	1.93	0.84	0.17	0
0.47	0	−0.3	−1.1	−2.2	−3	−2.4	−1.7	−1.3	−1.3	−1.4	−0.8	−0.2	0	0	0	0.09	0.09	0.07	0.29	0.88	1.44	1.39	1.35	1.73	2.4	3	2.25	1.1	0.31	0
0.48	0	−0.4	−1.5	−2.6	−2.9	−2	−1.5	−1.3	−1.3	−1.2	−0.7	−0.2	0	0.02	0	0.02	0	0.02	0.22	0.72	1.29	1.38	1.37	1.51	2.04	2.94	2.66	1.52	0.48	0.06
0.5	−0.2	−0.7	−1.9	−2.7	−2.6	−1.7	−1.4	−1.3	−1.3	−1.1	−0.5	−0.1	0.01	0.11	0.05	0	−0.1	0	0.18	0.59	1.11	1.31	1.39	1.4	1.75	2.7	2.79	1.92	0.76	0.21

6   Conclusion

As shown, the proposed method is capable of solving differential equations with acceptable accuracy with respect to the traditional numerical method. Theoretically, the exposed method is slower than other methods for solving partial differential equations such as Runge-Kutta of different orders, since it requires a larger amount of more complex operations and it depends on the initial state of the parameters. However, thanks to the parallelization capability offered by neural networks, it is possible to obtain execution time and accuracy comparable to those of other methods.

A considerable advantage of this method is the ease of defining boundary conditions. In addition, thanks to the iterative nature of the method, the order of approximation of the function values in the domain becomes less important, and because the error function is calculated at each step, it is trivial to find out whether the function satisfies the boundary conditions and the differential equation.

It is important to remember that this method is relatively new and requires further research into possible functions for A, optimization algorithms and neural network architectures, as was recently explored in [8]. In addition, the method can be made even more efficient by further use of parallelization or divergence acceleration algorithms such as Richardson Extrapolation.

References

1. de Almeida, G.A.M., Maldonado, S.: Physics informed neural networks for solving flow problems modeled by the shallow water equations (2023)
2. Chen, F., et al.: NeuroDiffEq: a Python package for solving differential equations with neural networks. J. Open Source Softw. **5**(46), 1931 (2020)
3. Chow, V.T.: Open-Channel Hydraulics. McGraw-Hill Book Company, Inc. (1959)
4. Fauzi, R., Wiryanto, L.H.: Predictor-corrector scheme for simulating wave propagation on shallow water region. IOP Conf. Ser. Earth Environ. Sci. **162**, 012047 (2018)
5. Garcia, R., Kahawita, R.A.: Numerical solution of the St. Venant equations with the MacCormack finite-difference scheme. Int. J. Numer. Methods Fluids **6**(5), 259–274 (1986)
6. Hornik, K., Stinchcombe, M., White, H.: Multilayer feedforward networks are universal approximators. Neural Netw. **2**(5), 359–366 (1989)
7. Kingma, D.P., Ba, J.: Adam: A method for stochastic optimization (2017)
8. Luo, T., Yang, H.: Two-layer neural networks for partial differential equations: optimization and generalization theory. arXiv preprint arXiv:2006.15733 (2020)
9. Yadav, N., Yadav, A., Kumar, M.: An Introduction to Neural Network Methods for Differential Equations. SAST, Springer, Dordrecht (2015). https://doi.org/10.1007/978-94-017-9816-7
10. Sukron, M., Habibah, U., Hidayat, N.: Numerical solution of Saint-Venant equation using Runge-Kutta fourth-order method. J. Phys. Conf. Ser. **1872**, 012036 (2021)
11. Veelenturf, L.: Analysis and Applications of Artificial Neural Networks. Prentice Hall International (1995)

Exploring the Impact of Social Media on Mental Health and Well-Being: A Multi-dimensional Analysis

Vasit Ali[1](✉), Cristina Hava Muntean[1], and Abid Yaqoob[2]

[1] School of Computing, National College of Ireland, Dublin, Ireland
vasit517@gmail.com, cristina.muntean@ncirl.ie
[2] School of Electronic Engineering, Dublin City University, Dublin, Ireland
abid.yaqoob@dcu.ie

Abstract. Over the past decade, the popularity and adoption of social media have increased globally, making it an inevitable part of daily communication and connection. However, the widespread use of social platforms introduces significant challenges to mental well-being. Ongoing state-of-the-art research demonstrates a robust correlation between extensive social media usage and the worsening of medical conditions such as depression and anxiety. These approaches often struggle because they fail to adequately model key health-related information and screen usage frequency in their analyses. Moreover, most of the existing methods do not fully leverage data analytics and machine learning technologies to effectively model the influence of social media algorithms on different age groups. In this paper, we employ a multi-model analysis, utilizing techniques such as decision trees, random forests, support vector machines (SVMs), and convolutional neural networks (CNNs), to gain a deeper understanding of the intricate relationship between social media use and mental health. In particular, we present four case studies exploring demographic risk factors, broader health consequences and specific health behaviors, and depression predictors associated with the use of social media. These analyses provide a comprehensive view of social media's multi-dimensional impact on mental health and offer critical understandings for designing targeted interventions and policies.

Keywords: Machine learning · Data analysis · CNN · Social media · E-health

1 Introduction

In recent years, social media platforms have completely changed the way individuals exchange information, communicate, and develop relationships. These platforms have raised questions about their impact on mental health and general well-being, even though they present never-before-seen possibilities for communication and community development. The way that digital communication is

D. D. Hodson et al. (Eds.): CSCE 2024, CCIS 2258, pp. 158–172, 2025.
https://doi.org/10.1007/978-3-031-85902-1_16

developing needs an in-depth investigation of the social and psychological effects of heavy social media use [35]. The widespread usage of social media in today's digital environment has emerged as a key characteristic of modern interaction and communication. As the number of people using virtual spaces continues to rise, concerns about how social media affects psychological, emotional, and social health also increase.

The digital landscape and social media platforms have experienced explosive growth, raising significant concerns about their impact on mental health and social connections. With these platforms competing for attention, it's crucial to dissect the complex relationship between social media use and well-being. This paper examines the challenging impacts of social media on relationship quality, psychological, social, and emotional health. In particular, we employ machine learning models, such as decision tree, random forest, support vector machine (SVM), and convolutional neural network (CNN), on an open-source dataset collected from young adults. In this context, we present the following four case studies with distinct objectives to explore the impact of social media on mental health considering demographic details and general and mental health information, including depression:

1. **Case Study 1** explores how age, gender, and student status, i.e., local or international, correlate with mental health outcomes, particularly depression risk.
2. **Case Study 2** examines broader health implications by analyzing general and specific mental health data to identify social media's impact patterns.
3. **Case Study 3** focuses on the relationship between social media usage and specific medical conditions, determining if certain health behaviors are more prevalent among heavy social media users.
4. **Case Study 4** investigates the predictors of depression, utilizing machine learning to analyze which factors most strongly predict mental health issues related to social media use.

Together, these case studies provide a comprehensive view of how social media impacts mental health across different dimensions, offering insights that are critical for developing targeted interventions and policies.

The rest of the paper is organized as follows: Section 2 reviews the most recently published closest works. Section 3 outlines data handling and analysis methods, including modeling techniques, tools, and analysis used. Section 4 presents case studies to assess model efficacy. Section 5 concludes with key insights and future research directions, followed by a comprehensive references list for further exploration.

2   Related Works

Machine learning can be applied to various domains, such as medical image recognition [27], education [3,8,10,12,13], video streaming [9,24–26], recommender systems [22], air flights [20], sports [23] and more. Various machine learning and deep learning techniques have also been implemented in the health-care domain. This research investigates the complex impact of social media on mental health, addressing concerns like addiction, social comparison, and cyber-bullying. It aims to understand the effects of extended social media use and find ways to foster healthy online behaviors [11]. Starting with the significance of social media in modern life, this work covers the psychological impacts on ado-lescents, the application of machine learning in analyzing mental health through social media data, and patterns of social media addiction. Through integrating insights across these areas, the research seeks to offer a deeper understanding of social media's role in mental health [2].

This research delves into the psychological effects of social media on adoles-cents and young adults, drawing insights from several studies to understand its impact on well-being. [1] focuses on digital media's influence on young people's psychological and lifestyle changes, using a survey to capture the nuanced rela-tionship between digital engagement and youth well-being. Our paper extends this inquiry to specifically examine social media's effects on psychological, social, and emotional health. [21] highlights the medical risks of social media addiction, underscoring the importance of exploring beyond medical perspectives to include psychological and emotional factors in our research. [7,32] further inform our investigation by emphasizing the adverse and beneficial impacts of social media usage, from self-esteem issues to the broadening of viewpoints.

This research explores the application of machine learning in mental health analysis through social media studies. [18] utilized over 1.2 million social media posts from platforms like Weibo and Instagram for mental health stigma analysis, achieving significant results with logistic regression and sentiment analysis. Our study, while focusing on survey data, similarly employs advanced techniques for a broad mental health analysis. [4] analyzed mental well-being during COVID-19 using data mining, paralleling our use of machine learning models for mental health predictions. [17] conducted sentiment analysis on Twitter data related to COVID-19, using Naïve Bayes and Logistic Regression, highlighting the poten-tial for algorithmic improvements. [6] focused on identifying suicidal tendencies through NLP techniques, achieving notable precision with SVM and accuracy with Logistic Regression. [15] examined the role of machine learning in detecting mental health issues on social media, suggesting the need for more comprehen-sive datasets and the incorporation of advanced techniques like BERT. Each study contributes to the broader understanding of mental health through the lens of data science, with our research adding to this body of work by analyzing survey responses alongside these methodologies.

[30] discuss the economic and diagnostic challenges of social media addic-tion. They call for more sophisticated predictive models to improve diagnostic accuracy. [33] use NLP and ML to analyze Reddit posts for depression indica-tors, employing a variety of classifiers with MLP demonstrating notable effec-tiveness. The study notes limitations in generalizability and accuracy due to the sole reliance on Reddit data. [31] develop computational models to predict depression and PTSD from Twitter data, underscoring social media's value in

mental health early warning systems. Both studies emphasize the potential of social media data in mental health screening but caution about the challenges in ensuring accuracy and representativeness.

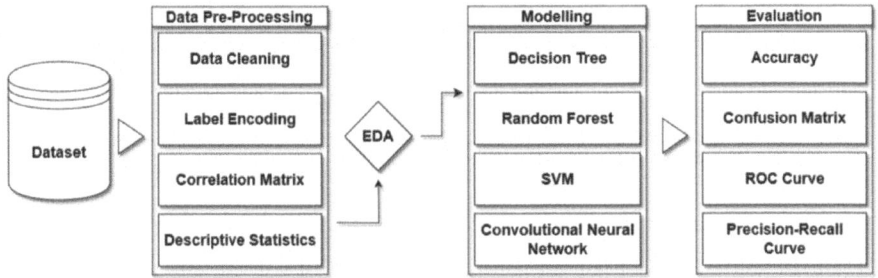

Fig. 1. Proposed System Workflow

3   System Design and Proposed Architecture Modelling

For this research, data was obtained from a survey on social media's effects on mental health, part of the "Social Media and Mental Health" project. The dataset [28] includes responses from young adults on demographics, engagement, and mental health. The analysis focused on data offering insights into how social media influences mental health outcomes [5]. This analytical process is outlined in the Proposed System Workflow in Fig. 1, which illustrates the stages of data handling and analysis employed in our study.

3.1   Data Exploration and Preparation

In this paper, we embarked on a detailed exploration of a survey dataset examining social media's impact on mental health, focusing on identifying patterns, trends, and anomalies within demographic and engagement data. Data exploration involved assessing response patterns and analyzing demographic data, especially focusing on age distribution depicted in Fig. 2 and Fig. 3, to understand the survey's primary audience [34]. We evaluated engagement metrics like response duration and analyzed the dataset's composition, including data types and memory usage, ensuring a thorough understanding of statistical analysis.

Data Preparation, conducted via Jupyter Notebook, began with importing the raw data and included steps for cleaning and transforming the data to suit our analysis needs. This phase was critical for maintaining the dataset's accuracy and reliability. Data cleaning steps included creating a DataFrame, removing irrelevant or non-essential columns (e.g., 'Start Date', 'End Date'), and encoding categorical variables for analysis [29]. A correlation matrix heatmap was used

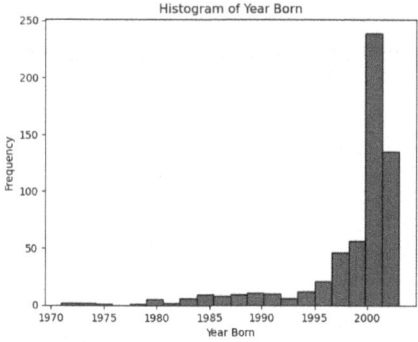

Fig. 2. Histogram of Year Born

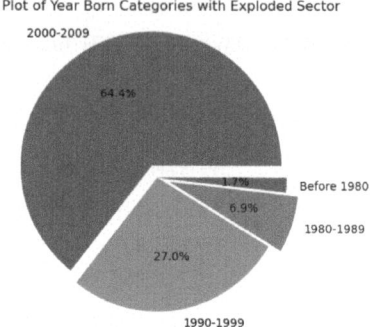

Fig. 3. Pie Chart of Year Born

to refine our variable selection, enhancing the dataset's structure for effective analysis. These steps laid a solid foundation for our subsequent analysis, ensuring the dataset was meticulously prepared for examining the nuanced impacts of social media on mental health.

3.2 Exploratory Data Analysis (EDA)

In our work, we implemented feature engineering to enhance the dataset's relevance for analysis and modeling, focusing on techniques like label encoding of categorical variables and correlation analysis for feature selection [16,19]. This process streamlined the dataset by converting categorical data into numerical formats and refining the feature set based on variable relationships. Exploratory Data Analysis (EDA) played a crucial role, utilizing visualization tools (Figs. 4 and 5) and statistical methods to identify patterns, anomalies, and relationships within the data. This included generating descriptive statistics and using visualizations to elucidate the data's structure and the interdependencies among variables.

The dataset was then split into an 80/20 ratio for training and testing, ensuring a broad training base and an unbiased performance evaluation. Model training involved the use of various models (decision trees, random forests, SVMs, CNNs) to analyze the data, with a focus on predicting depression diagnoses. Models were evaluated based on accuracy scores and detailed through confusion matrices and ROC curves among other metrics. The model evaluation highlighted the comparative effectiveness of each model in diagnosing depression, using visual and statistical analyses to underscore the predictive accuracy and the significance of key variables Fig. 4 and Fig. 5.

This methodology, underpinned by rigorous feature engineering and EDA, laid the groundwork for insightful model training and evaluation, driving towards reliable mental health diagnosis through social media data analysis.

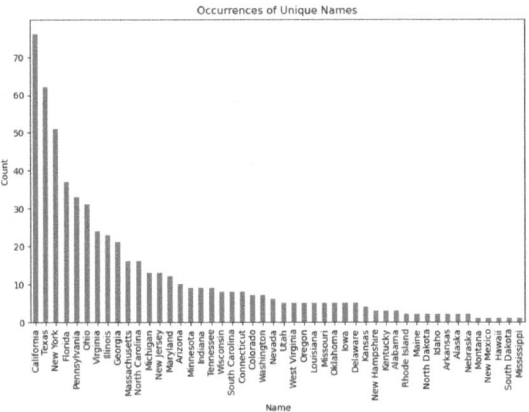

Fig. 4. Region wise data

3.3   Modelling Techniques

This subsection outlines the system specifications designed to conduct a comprehensive and rigorous analysis of how demographic characteristics and mental health symptoms influence depression diagnosis. The methodology integrates various statistical and machine-learning techniques to model and evaluate these relationships. This work employs a mix of statistical and machine learning techniques tailored to understand and predict mental health conditions effectively.

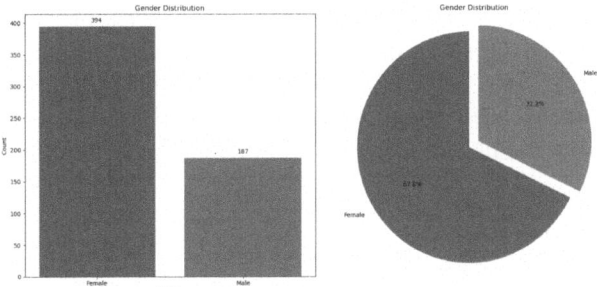

Fig. 5. Gender based data

Decision Tree. Utilizing a decision tree classifier, this model facilitates the visualization and understanding of decision-making processes related to depression prediction. It is configured to handle the complexities of the dataset, focusing on demographic and symptom variables to determine their influence on depression. The model's tree-like structure displays key decision nodes and outcomes, simplifying the interpretation of influential factors. Additionally, the Decision Tree model offers an intuitive approach to handle missing values and interactions between features, further increasing its utility in exploratory data analysis.

Random Forest. As an extension of the decision tree model, the random forest classifier aggregates multiple trees to enhance prediction accuracy and address overfitting. It is configured with parameters optimized for medical datasets, such as the number of trees and maximum depth, to balance bias and variance effectively. This model provides an important ranking of features, which is crucial for identifying significant predictors within the health-related dataset. The ensemble nature of the Random Forest also allows it to provide estimates of feature importance, offering insights into which variables are most critical in predicting depression outcomes.

Support Vector Machine. SVM is applied to distinguish between patients with and without depression based on a high-dimensional space of features, including both demographic and symptom data. By configuring it with a suitable kernel, the SVM effectively manages the complexities inherent in mental health datasets. This model excels in forming robust decision boundaries, crucial for dealing with varied and intricate data patterns. SVM's use of kernel tricks further enhances its ability to manage complex, non-linear data interactions effectively.

Convolutional Neural Network. In this paper, CNNs are adapted to process structured data from medical records to identify patterns indicative of mental health conditions. Through layers that capture hierarchical pattern complexities, the CNN model discerns subtle signs that may suggest depression, utilizing configurations like filter sizes and layer depths tailored to the specificity and scale of input data. CNNs excel in identifying key patterns in large datasets that traditional models might miss, thanks to their deep learning architecture.

4   Implementation

The implementation phase of our machine learning model involved several key steps, utilizing Python and its libraries for data handling, model development, and visualization.

Utilized Python and libraries like pandas, sci-kit-learn, Keras, Matplotlib, and Seaborn for data analysis and model development. Focused on a dataset from a depression prevalence survey, refining it to emphasize features critical to our study, with depression diagnosis as the target variable. Adjusted model parameters to optimize performance, employing GridSearchCV for random forests, selecting the linear kernel for SVMs, and configuring CNNs with ReLU and sigmoid functions and the Adam optimizer.

5   Evaluation

We evaluated and visualized model performances using accuracy scores, classification reports, confusion matrices, ROC curves, and precision-recall curves. Random forests were further analyzed for feature importance. Model accuracies and learning curves were compared to identify the most effective model for predicting depression, ensuring the development of a functional, deployable model for real-world application.

Accuracy was the primary metric for assessing model performance in depression diagnosis. Classification reports provided precision, recall, and F1 scores for each class, while confusion matrices highlighted false positives and negatives, enhancing our understanding of model effectiveness.

The evaluation phase focused on strategies to address class imbalance and the division of data for training and testing. We acknowledged the class imbalance in depression diagnosis datasets and implemented oversampling and class weighting to ensure balanced learning [14]. An 80:20 split was adopted using sklearn, with 80% of the data for training and 20% for testing, allowing thorough pattern learning and unbiased evaluation [16].

This methodology ensures our models are evaluated effectively, and prepared for potential real-world deployment.

5.1   Case Study 1

In the evaluation of classification models on demographic data, the decision tree classifier achieved 58% accuracy, showing balanced precision but lower recall for the positive class, as detailed in Table 1. The random forest and support vector machine classifiers both recorded a 62% accuracy, with the former better identifying the negative class but struggling with the positive class, indicating possible class imbalance issues. The SVM exhibited similar tendencies, particularly with a lower precision for the positive class, leading to more false positives. The CNN outperformed others with approximately 65.81% accuracy Fig. 6, showing significant strength in identifying the negative class but, like the others, it also had limitations in accurately detecting the positive class Fig. 7, underscoring challenges in model performance across varying demographics.

Table 1. CNN - Classification Report

	Precision	Recall	F1-score	Support
Negative	0.67	0.93	0.78	76
Positive	0.55	0.15	0.23	41
Accuracy	0.66			Total: 117
Macro average	0.61	0.54	0.51	Total: 117
Weighted average	0.63	0.66	0.59	Total: 117

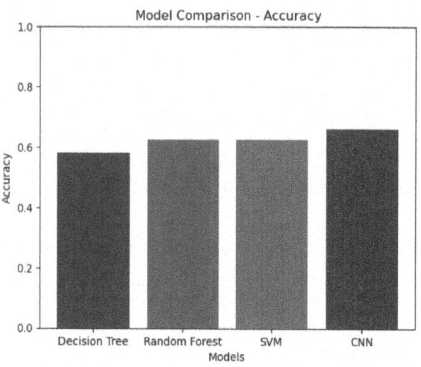

Fig. 6. Model Accuracy Case Study 1

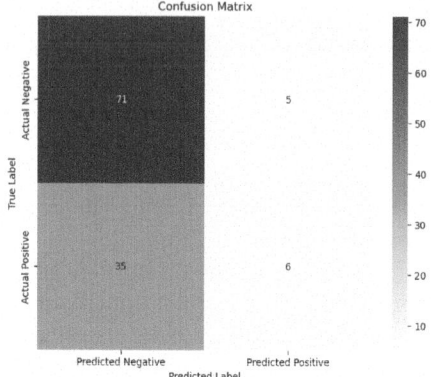

Fig. 7. Confusion Matrix CNN - Case Study 1

5.2   Case Study 2

In Case Study 2, evaluating general and mental health assessments, the decision tree classifier showed moderate accuracy (59%, Table 2), effectively identifying true negatives but less so for positives. The random forest classifier improved accuracy to 67%, excelling in negative class predictions but faltered with positives, indicating difficulty in recognizing actual positive cases. The support vector machine classifier, at 65% accuracy, was notably precise in negative predictions but failed to identify any positives, suggesting possible overfitting or limitations in handling dataset complexities. CNN led with the highest accuracy (72%, Fig. 8), presenting balanced precision and recall across classes, particularly excelling in the negative class while maintaining respectable precision for positives, despite some missed true positives Fig. 9. While random forest and SVM showed a negative class bias, CNN offered a more balanced approach, proving the most effective for the task due to its comprehensive dataset handling.

Table 2. CNN - Classification Report

	Precision	Recall	F1-score	Support
Negative	0.71	0.93	0.82	76
Positive	0.79	0.27	0.40	41
Accuracy	0.72			Total: 117
Macro average	0.75	0.61	0.61	Total: 117
Weighted average	0.74	0.72	0.67	Total: 117

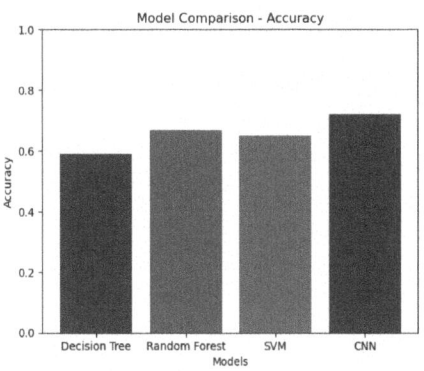

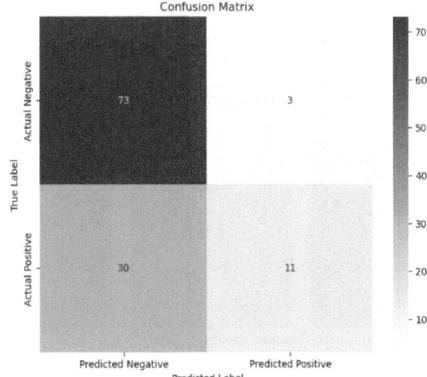

Fig. 8. Model Accuracy Case Study 2

Fig. 9. Confusion Matrix CNN - Case Study 2

5.3   Case Study 3

In Case Study 3's medical and health conditions analysis, the decision tree classifier achieved a 72% accuracy, displaying balanced performance with notable precision and recall for the negative class Table 3. The random forest classifier topped performance charts with a 77% accuracy Fig. 10, excelling in identifying both classes but showing a slight preference for the negative class Fig. 11. The SVM classifier, at 68% accuracy, demonstrated a bias towards the negative class, with high precision but low recall for positives, indicating difficulty in identifying true positive cases. Similarly, the CNN model, also with 68% accuracy, effectively identified the negative class but struggled with accurately pinpointing positive cases due to lower recall. Among the models, the random forest stood out for its balanced and effective performance, with the decision tree also showing a good balance. In contrast, SVM and CNN exhibited imbalances, particularly in positively classifying cases accurately.

Table 3. Random Forest classifier - Classification Report

	Precision	Recall	F1-score	Support
Negative	0.79	0.88	0.83	76
Positive	0.72	0.56	0.63	41
Accuracy	0.77			Total: 117
Macro average	0.75	0.72	0.73	Total: 117
Weighted average	0.76	0.77	0.76	Total: 117

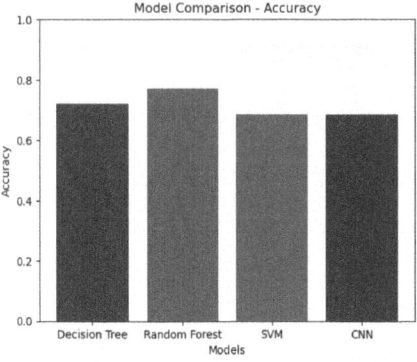

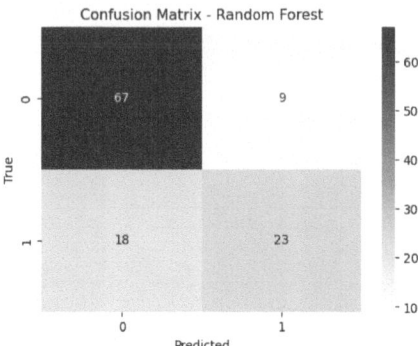

Fig. 10. Model Accuracy Case Study 3

Fig. 11. Confusion Matrix Random Forest - Case Study 3

5.4 Case Study 4

In Case Study 4, analyzing depression diagnosis and health variables, the decision tree classifier displayed robustness with an 87% accuracy, showing high precision and recall across classes as detailed in Table 4. The random forest classifier excelled, achieving a 91% accuracy Fig. 12, with nearly equal precision and recall for both classes, indicating a strong balance in prediction capabilities Fig. 13. The SVM classifier matched the random forest in accuracy at 91%, excelling in negative case precision but showing variability in positive case recall, indicating a propensity for correct negative predictions but with room for improvement in positive case identification. The CNN model, with an 89% accuracy, demonstrated balanced performance, slightly favoring the negative class but still effectively identifying both. This analysis revealed the random forest and SVM as top performers, offering the most balanced approach to depression diagnosis, with the random forest slightly ahead due to its overall performance balance. The decision tree and CNN also showed strong capabilities, especially in managing negative cases, underscoring the varied strengths of each model in handling complex health-related data.

Table 4. Random Forest classifier - Classification Report

	Precision	Recall	F1-score	Support
Negative	0.93	0.93	0.93	76
Positive	0.88	0.88	0.88	41
Accuracy	0.91			Total: 117
Macro average	0.91	0.91	0.91	Total: 117
Weighted average	0.91	0.91	0.91	Total: 117

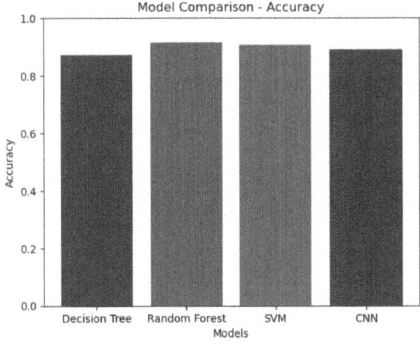

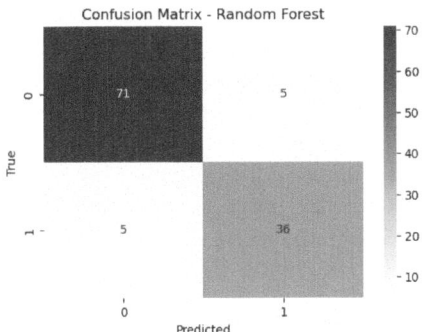

Fig. 12. Model Accuracy Case Study 4

Fig. 13. Confusion Matrix Random Forest - Case Study 4

5.5 Discussion

In our analysis of four key machine learning models to predict depression diagnoses, the random forest classifier emerged as the most effective, achieving an accuracy of 91%. Its strength lies in its ensemble approach, which integrates multiple decision trees to enhance prediction accuracy and robustness, effectively managing the challenge of overfitting common in complex mental health data. In contrast, the SVM matched the random forest in accuracy but lacked effectiveness in class recall, highlighting a need for more precise hyperparameter adjustments. The decision tree, while less complex, tended to overfit, suggesting limitations in handling nuanced data without adjustments such as pruning. The CNN, requiring extensive dataset and careful parameter tuning, offered a balanced 89% accuracy, showcasing its potential in diverse data environments. The standout performance of the random forest, however, was primarily due to its ability to maintain high accuracy while mitigating overfitting, marking it as particularly suitable for the intricate nature of mental health datasets.

6 Conclusions and Future Works

In this paper, we delve into the significant role that social media plays in daily interactions and its profound impact on mental health. By applying machine learning models, we investigate how social media can intensify mental health issues such as depression and anxiety, providing a nuanced analysis of this critical issue. Specifically evaluated decision tree, random forest, SVM, and CNN models for depression diagnosis prediction in the context of social media use. Decision trees were accurate but prone to overfitting while considering the distinct demographics and health-related variables. The random forest model performs accurately but requires significant computational resources and improved interpretability. SVM showed promise in high-dimensional data handling but necessitated careful tuning for optimal performance. CNNs, on the other hand, excelled in pattern recognition but demanded large datasets and faced challenges in complexity management. These insights underscore the importance of model selection in mental health data analysis and contribute to the application of machine learning in healthcare, especially in mental health diagnosis. Future research will focus on enhancing model performance and interpretability, broadening dataset diversity, and integrating ethical AI practices in healthcare. This groundwork paves the way for incorporating AI-driven diagnostics in clinical settings, advancing AI's role in healthcare.

References

1. Abirami, S.: Psychological effects and changes in the lifestyle of young individuals due to exposure to digital media. Int. J. Clinicopathological Correl. **6**(2), 4–8 (2022)
2. Andreassen, C.S.: Online social network site addiction: a comprehensive review. Curr. Addict. Rep. **2**(2), 175–184 (2015)
3. Bogusevschi, D., Muntean, C., Gorji, N., Muntean, G.: Earth course: a primary school large-scale pilot on stem education. In: EDULEARN18 Proceedings, 10th International Conference on Education and New Learning Technologies, IATED, 2–4 July 2018, pp. 3769–3777 (2018). https://doi.org/10.21125/edulearn.2018.0958
4. Boy, F.: Google trendstexttrademark dynamics for the guidance of open-source intelligence: augmentation of social-media and survey surveillance of population mental health. In: 2023 IEEE International Symposium on Technology and Society (ISTAS), pp. 1–9 (2023). https://doi.org/10.1109/ISTAS57930.2023.10305931
5. Bryman, A.: Social Research Methods. Oxford University Press (2016)
6. Chadha, A., Gupta, A., Kumar, Y.: Suicidal ideation detection on social media: a machine learning approach. In: 2022 2nd International Conference on Technological Advancements in Computational Sciences (ICTACS), pp. 685–688 (2022). https://doi.org/10.1109/ICTACS56270.2022.9988722
7. Chukwuere, G., Chukwuere, J.: The difficulties posed by digital technology: understanding the psychological consequences of social media use on young adults' body image and self-esteem. Acad. J. Interdisc. Stud. **12**, 379 (2023). https://doi.org/10.36941/ajis-2023-0176
8. Comşa, I.S., et al.: A machine learning resource allocation solution to improve video quality in remote education. IEEE Trans. Broadcast. **67**(3), 664–684 (2021)
9. Comşa, I.S., Muntean, G.M., Trestian, R.: An innovative machine-learning-based scheduling solution for improving live UIID video streaming quality in highly dynamic network environments. IEEE Trans. Broadcast. **67**(1), 212–224 (2021)
10. Comşa, I.S., et al.: Improved quality of online education using prioritized multi-agent reinforcement learning for video traffic scheduling. IEEE Trans. Broadcast. **69**(2), 436–454 (2023)
11. De Choudhury, M., De, S.: Mental health discourse on reddit: self-disclosure, social support, and anonymity. In: Proceedings of the International AAAI Conference on Web and Social Media, vol. 8, pp. 71–80 (2014)
12. El Mawas, N., Ghergulescu, I., Moldovan, A.N., Muntean, C.H.: Pedagogical based learner model characteristics. In: Ireland International Conference on Education, Dublin, Ireland, October 2018. https://hal.science/hal-02251323
13. Ghergulescu, I., Muntean, C.H.: Motivation monitoring and assessment extension for input-process-outcome game model. Int. J. Game-Based Learn. **4**(2), 15–35 (2014)

14. He, H., Garcia, E.A.: Learning from imbalanced data. IEEE Trans. Knowl. Data Eng. **21**(9), 1263–1284 (2009). https://doi.org/10.1109/TKDE.2008.239

15. Illahi, M., Siddiqui, I.F., Ali, Q., Alvi, F.A.: Ensemble machine learning approach for stress detection in social media texts. Quaid-E-Awam Univ. Res. J. Eng. Sci. Technol. Nawabshah **20**(02), 123–128 (2022)

16. James, G., Witten, D., Hastie, T., Tibshirani, R.: An Introduction to Statistical Learning. STS, Springer, New York (2021). https://doi.org/10.1007/978-1-0716-1418-1

17. Khasnis, N.S., Sen, S., Khasnis, S.S.: A machine learning approach for sentiment analysis to nurture mental health amidst covid-19. In: Proceedings of the International Conference on Data Science, Machine Learning and Artificial Intelligence, DSMLAI 2021, pp. 284–289. Association for Computing Machinery, New York, NY, USA (2022). https://doi.org/10.1145/3484824.3484877

18. Kim, J., Lee, D., Park, E., et al.: Machine learning for mental health in social media: bibliometric study. J. Med. Internet Res. **23**(3), e24870 (2021)

19. Kotsiantis, S.B., Zaharakis, I., Pintelas, P., et al.: Supervised machine learning: A review of classification techniques. In: Emerging Artificial Intelligence Applications in Computer Engineering, vol. 160(1), pp. 3–24 (2007)

20. Lal, V., Stynes, P., Muntean, C.: An investigation into predicting flight fares in India using machine learning models. In: Younas, M., Awan, I., Benbernou, S., Petcu, D. (eds.) Deep-BDB 2023. LNNS, vol. 768, pp. 106–118. Springer, Cham (2023). https://doi.org/10.1007/978-3-031-42317-8_9

21. Luca, L., Ciubara, A.B., Antohe, M.E., Peterson, I., Ciubara, A.: Social media addiction in adolescents and young adults-psychoeducational aspects (2023)

22. Marigowda, C., Moldovan, A.N., Siddig, A., Muntean, C.H., Pathak, P., Stynes, P.: A novel hybrid machine learning framework to recommend e-commerce products. In: Proceedings of the 5th International Conference on Information Technology and Computer Communications, ITCC 2023, pp. 59–67. Association for Computing Machinery, New York, NY, USA (2023)

23. Menon, A., Siddig, A., Muntean, C.H., Pathak, P., Jilani, M., Stynes, P.: A machine learning framework for shuttlecock tracking and player service fault detection. In: Conte, D., Fred, A., Gusikhin, O., Sansone, C. (eds.) Deep Learning Theory and Applications, pp. 71–83. Springer, Cham (2023). https://doi.org/10.1007/978-3-031-39059-3_5

24. Moldovan, A.N., Ghergulescu, I., Muntean, C.H.: A novel methodology for mapping objective video quality metrics to the subjective mos scale. In: 2014 IEEE International Symposium on Broadband Multimedia Systems and Broadcasting, pp. 1–7 (2014)

25. Moldovan, A.N., Muntean, C.H.: Personalisation of the multimedia content delivered to mobile device users. In: IEEE International Symposium on Broadband Multimedia Systems and Broadcasting, pp. 1 – 6 (2009)

26. Moldovan, A.N., Muntean, C.H.: Towards personalised and adaptive multimedia in m-learning systems. In: AACE E-Learn: World Conference on E-Learning in Corporate, Government, Healthcare, and Higher Education, pp. 782–791 (2011)

27. Muntean, C.H., Chowkkar, M.: Breast cancer detection from histopathological images using deep learning and transfer learning. In: Proceedings of the 2022 7th International Conference on Machine Learning Technologies (2022)

28. OpenICPSR: Mental health survey data (2022). https://www.openicpsr.org/openicpsr/project/175582/version/V1/view?path=/openicpsr/175582/fcr:versions/V1. Accessed 27 Aug 2024

29. Osborne, J.: Is data cleaning and the testing of assumptions relevant in the 21st century? Front. Psychol. **4** (2013). https://doi.org/10.3389/fpsyg.2013.00370. https://www.frontiersin.org/articles/10.3389/fpsyg.2013.00370

30. Priya, P.L., Prakash, R.V.: A broad survey on detection of depression in societal platforms using machine learning model for the public health care system. In: 2023 4th International Conference on Electronics and Sustainable Communication Systems (ICESC), pp. 1643–1649 (2023). https://doi.org/10.1109/ICESC57686.2023.10193515

31. Reece, A.G., Reagan, A.J., Lix, K.L., Dodds, P.S., Danforth, C.M., Langer, E.J.: Forecasting the onset and course of mental illness with twitter data. Sci. Rep. **7**(1), 13006 (2017)

32. Satyaninrum, I.R., Rumondor, P., Kurniawati, H., Aziz, A.M., et al.: Promoting mental health in the digital age: exploring the effects of social media use on psyhcological well-being. West Sci. Interdisc. Stud. **1**(06), 248–256 (2023)

33. Tadesse, M.M., Lin, H., Xu, B., Yang, L.: Detection of depression-related posts in reddit social media forum. IEEE Access **7**, 44883–44893 (2019). https://doi.org/10.1109/ACCESS.2019.2909180

34. Trochim, W.M., Donnelly, J.P.: Research Methods Knowledge Base, vol. 2. Atomic Dog Publishing Macmillan Publishing Company, New York (2001)

35. Twenge, J.M., Campbell, W.K.: Associations between screen time and lower psychological well-being among children and adolescents: evidence from a population-based study. Prev. Med. Rep. **12**, 271–283 (2018)

The Strategic Optimization of a Tabletop Role-Playing Game

Zhi Zheng$^{(\boxtimes)}$, Nicholas Porter, Toby Hilliard, and Feng-Jen Yang

Florida Polytechnic University, Lakeland, FL 33805, USA
{zhizheng0889,nporter2168,thilliard2096,fyang}@floridapoly.edu
https://floridapoly.edu/index.php

Abstract. Globally, Warhammer 40k TRPG (Tabletop Role-Playing Game) enthusiasts often find that the most time-consuming aspect of the game is setting up their loadout. In this project, we employ genetic algorithms to streamline the optimization of a Space Marine Squad's weapon loadout, tailored to combat various adversaries. This endeavor is not just an exercise in game preparation but a deep dive into the intricate interplay between strategy and probability. It parallels significant AI research in game playing, reinforcing the notion that games serve as an excellent proving ground for AI research. Our ultimate goal is to connect genetic algorithms with practical tabletop warfare games, transforming the way players strategize and engage with the game. This project is more than a study; it is an exploration of the complex balance of strategy and chance.

Keywords: Tabletop Role-Playing Games · Genetic Algorithms · Optimization · Evolutionary Computations

1 Introduction

In the beautiful and dark world of Warhammer 40k TRPG (Table Role Playing Game), an eternal war rages on in the 41st millennium across galaxies. For players around the globe, setting up the loadout has always been the most time-consuming part of the game. In this project, we focus on using genetic algorithms to optimize a Space Marine Squad weapon loadout against different opponents. This demonstration can be thought of as analogous to other significant AI research in game playing, as games are among the best testing grounds for AI research.

The project is more than just a research project on mere game preparation; it is an adventure into the sophisticated balance between strategy and probability. The complex and rich universe of Warhammer 40K is an excellent subject for integrating computational power with tabletop role-playing games. We seek to create a bridge between genetic algorithms and practical tabletop warfare.

The challenge of optimizing a Space Marine Squad loadout is the prerequisite of understanding the complex rules and lore of Warhammer 40K. It is

D. D. Hodson et al. (Eds.): CSCE 2024, CCIS 2258, pp. 173–181, 2025.
https://doi.org/10.1007/978-3-031-85902-1_17

like navigating through a complex labyrinth that can only be solved with deep understanding and thorough analysis. The initial task at hand is to identify the optimal combination of gear that can adapt to and triumph over numerous possible battlefield scenarios.

This optimization analysis is not just about picking the most dangerous weapon; it requires balancing firepower, versatility, and adaptability. The diversity of enemies, each with unique traits, vulnerabilities, and equipment, demands a loadout strategy that considers armor penetration, weapon range, and tactical flexibility. We will be facing hordes of Orks, forces of Chaos, hives of Tyranids, technologically advanced Tau, and many more malicious threats of the 40K universe.

The project approaches the problem domain using genetic algorithms tailored to evolve and refine loadout configurations through successive iterations. Our goal is to approximate the global optimal loadout. This methodology aligns with our analytical needs to enrich our understanding of the strategic puzzle of Warhammer 40K. We plan to contribute to the broader community for the optimization of gaming, offering insights into methodologies that can be applied to various strategic games dealing with strategy and probability.

2   Literature Review

The idea for this project originated from a video on how AlphaGo defeated a professional Go player, inspiring research into how AI is used in modern tabletop board games. Warhammer 40K was chosen due to its complexity and growing popularity. Initial research confirmed the plausibility of applying a genetic algorithm to optimize squad loadouts for 40K. Barros et al. demonstrated how genetic algorithms (GAs) could improve AI gameplay in checkers with mutation strategies like sub-exchange and replacement to enhance genetic operations [1]. Tao et al. used GAs for search tree optimization in computer games, applying genetic operations such as selection, crossover, and mutation to the search tree, providing valuable insights into improving search efficiency [4]. Silver et al.'s research on AlphaGo, which combined deep neural networks with Monte Carlo Tree Search (MCTS) to outperform human professionals in Go, suggests potential future enhancements by combining neural networks with optimization techniques [5]. These studies guided the development of the project's genetic algorithms, focusing on parameters like population size, crossover probability, and mutation probability.

3   Warhammer 40K Optimization Project Review

Genetic algorithms (GAs) are a subset of evolutionary algorithms inspired by natural selection and genetics. GAs simulate natural evolution, employing mechanisms like selection, crossover, and mutation for evolutionary optimization and search problems. GAs are particularly adept at navigating large and complex search spaces, making them ideal for challenges where traditional optimization methods are inadequate. The critical formula that represents the GA process is:

$$\text{New Generation} = \text{Mutate(Crossover(}$$
$$\text{Select(Current Generation)))} \tag{1}$$

3.1 Representation of Chromosomes

Each chromosome in our genetic algorithm represents a potential loadout for a Space Marine Squad. The loadout is encoded as a sequence of genes, where each gene corresponds to a specific weapon. The weapon and unit data used to encode these chromosomes are obtained from the comprehensive dataset provided in [11].

$$C = [w_1, w_2, w_3, w_4] \tag{2}$$

3.2 Algorithm Parameters

We assign the following parameters for the genetic algorithm:

- **Population Size (N)**: Set at 200, 500, and 1000 as parameters that influence the diversity of loadout combinations.
- **Crossover Probability (Pc)**: At 0.6, 0.7, and 0.9, these rates determine how frequently chromosomes combine their genetic material, thus affecting population diversity.
- **Mutation Probability (Pm)**: At 0.01, 0.05, and 0.1, these rates control the frequency of random changes in the genes, allowing for the introduction of new weapons at a controlled rate.

3.3 Fitness Function

Our fitness function evaluates the effectiveness of a weapon loadout in a single attack sequence against a diverse range of enemies. The fitness is determined by the number of enemies destroyed, which is a function of several parameters, including weapon strength, armor penetration, target toughness, and additional factors such as range bonuses. The fitness function $f(w, t)$ is mathematically defined as follows:

$$f(w, t) = \text{ceil}(w_n \cdot 0.5) \cdot \text{wounds}(w_s, t_t)$$
$$\cdot \left(\frac{ts - 1 + w_{ap}}{6} \right) \cdot w_d + r_b(w) \tag{3}$$

where:

- w represents the weapon.
- t represents the test case (enemy unit).
- w_n is the number of weapons.

- w_s is the weapon strength.
- t_t is the target toughness.
- t_s is the target save.
- w_{ap} is the weapon armor penetration.
- w_d is the weapon damage.
- *ceil* denotes the ceiling function, ensuring that fractional values are rounded up.
- wounds(w_s, t_t) is a function that calculates the number of wounds inflicted based on weapon strength and target toughness.
- $r_b(w)$ is a function that adds a bonus for weapons with a range greater than 24 units or penalizes melee weapons.

Additionally, the fitness function incorporates a range bonus and constraint to increase weapon diversity. The total number of enemies destroyed (t_d) is then calculated by dividing the fitness score by the total toughness of the target:

$$t_d = \frac{f(w,t)}{t_t} \tag{4}$$

3.4   Implementation

The initial population is a set of chromosomes, each representing a potential weapon loadout solution. Mathematically, this is expressed as:

$$\text{Population}_{\text{initial}} = \{C_1, C_2, \ldots, C_N\} \tag{5}$$

where $C_i = [g_1, g_2, \ldots, g_m]$ is a chromosome consisting of m genes, and each gene g represents a weapon type. These genes are randomly selected from a predefined set of weapons, ensuring diversity within the initial population. The population size N is a predetermined parameter that influences the genetic diversity available for evolution.

To ensure diversity and strategic variability for optimizing the squad building, we impose a maximum repetition constraint on each weapon type in the chromosome. This constraint is defined as:

$$\forall w \in W, \ \text{count}(w, L) \leq 2 \tag{6}$$

Crossover and Mutation Mechanisms: The crossover operation combines genetic material from two parent chromosomes to produce new offspring. For two parents, C_{parent1} and C_{parent2}, the crossover operation is defined as:

$$C_{\text{child1}} = C_{\text{parent1}}[0 : x] \cup C_{\text{parent2}}[x : n] \tag{7}$$

$$C_{\text{child2}} = C_{\text{parent2}}[0 : x] \cup C_{\text{parent1}}[x : n] \tag{8}$$

Here, x is a randomly chosen crossover point within the chromosome's length. This operation is applied with a probability P_c (crossover probability), which governs the frequency of crossover events. The resulting offspring are subjected to the weapon repetition constraint to ensure no weapon type exceeds the allowed repetition limit.

Mutation introduces new genetic variations into the population, enhancing the algorithm's ability to explore the solution space. The mutation operation for a chromosome C is mathematically described as:

$$C_{\text{mutated}}[i] = \begin{cases} \text{random weapon} & \text{if rand}(0,1) < P_m \\ C[i] & \text{otherwise} \end{cases} \tag{9}$$

Termination Criteria: The termination criteria for the genetic algorithm can be mathematically formalized as follows:

$$\text{Term if } (G = MG) \text{ or } (\varDelta f \leq \epsilon \text{ for } T \text{ generations}) \tag{10}$$

where:

- G is the current generation number.
- MG is the maximum number of generations allowed.
- $\varDelta f$ is the change in the maximum fitness value across generations.
- ϵ is a small threshold value indicating stagnation in fitness.
- T is the number of generations for which fitness changes are below the threshold.

These mathematical formulations provide a clear and precise framework for the implementation of the genetic algorithm, enhancing the understanding of its operational mechanics.

3.5 Results

Interim Findings: The genetic algorithm's initial runs have shown a progressive improvement in fitness scores, indicating an evolution toward more effective weapon combinations. The best fitness scores achieved for different population sizes and mutation rates were consistently high, with the best score being 1157.2 across multiple configurations. Initially, the GA frequently selected loadouts with 'Thunder Hammer'; after implementing a range bonus and a weapon repetition constraint, the GA now favors two 'Assault Cannons' and two 'Autocannons' loadouts. By generation three, the best fitness score achieved was 1048.6, and by generation seven, it had reached 1157.2. The algorithm converged around the sixth generation for smaller populations and around the fourth to seventh generation for larger ones. The result indicates a need for greater diversity and balance in weapon choices, suggesting that the GA could be improved to be more dynamic and adaptive for various scenarios.

Performance Metrics: The evaluation of loadouts relies on a fitness function that assesses their combat effectiveness against a range of enemy units based on the following:

- **Expected Damage Output**: This metric is crucial, as it measures each weapon's potential impact in various combat scenarios, considering its strength, armor penetration, damage, and rate of fire.

– **Versatility**: The algorithm evaluates the loadout's ability to handle different enemy types, ensuring that it can adapt to diverse battlefield situations.
– **Combat Efficiency**: This aspect considers the potential of a loadout to maximize damage while minimizing vulnerabilities based on the strategic combination of weapons.

Performance Metrics: The evaluation of loadouts relies on a fitness function that assesses their combat effectiveness against a range of enemy units based on the following:

– **Expected Damage Output**: This metric is crucial, as it measures each weapon's potential impact in various combat scenarios, considering its strength, armor penetration, damage, and rate of fire.
– **Versatility**: The algorithm evaluates the loadout's ability to handle different enemy types, ensuring that it can adapt to diverse battlefield situations.
– **Combat Efficiency**: This aspect considers the potential of a loadout to maximize damage while minimizing vulnerabilities based on the strategic combination of weapons.

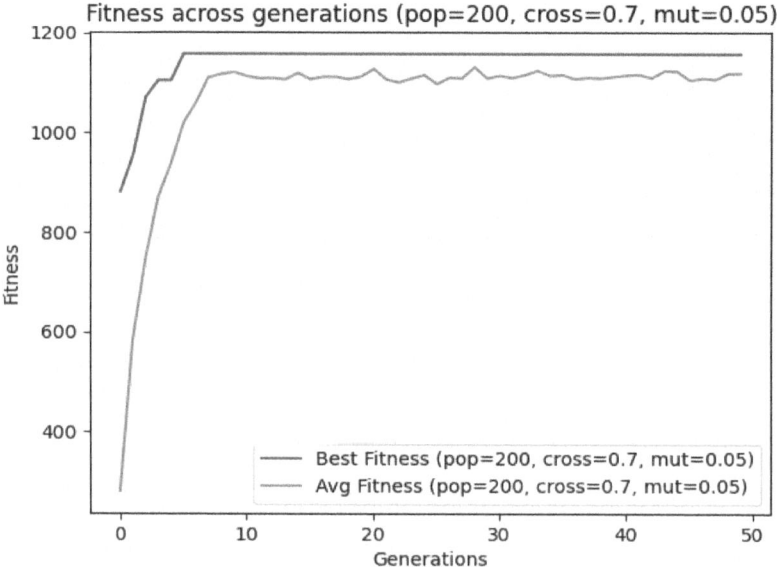

Fig. 1. Fitness across generations (pop = 200, cross = 0.7, mut = 0.05)

Ongoing Analysis: While the current results are promising in terms of fitness score improvement, they also highlight the need for further analysis and potential adjustments:

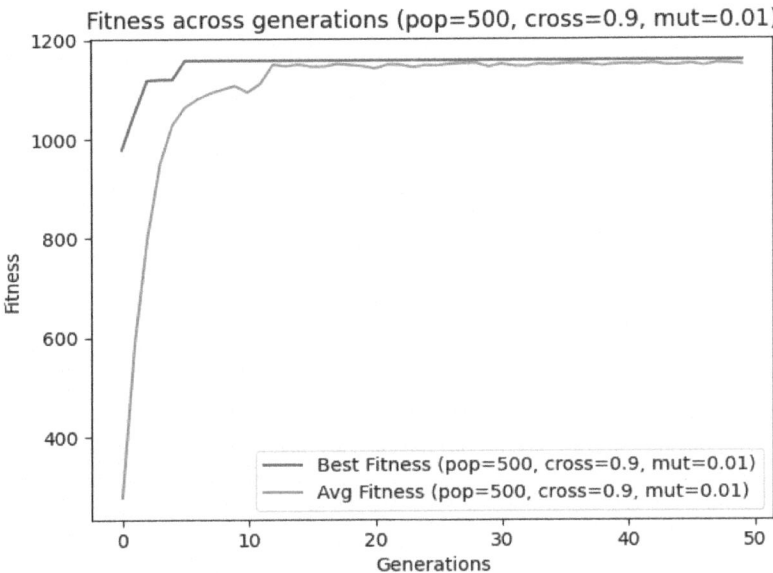

Fig. 2. Fitness across generations (pop = 500, cross = 0.9, mut = 0.01)

- **Diversity in Weaponry:** The dominance of 'Autocannons' and 'Assault Cannons' in the optimal loadout suggests a need to re-examine the balance of weapon attributes and their representation in the fitness function.
- **Strategic Balance:** Future iterations will explore how different combinations of weapons can offer a more balanced approach to combat, considering factors like range, rate of fire, adaptability, and weapon unique ability.
- **Algorithm Tuning:** Adjustments to parameters such as mutation rate and selection process will be considered to encourage a broader exploration of the solution space.
- **Fitness Function Refinement:** The fitness function will be reassessed to ensure it accurately evaluates the strategic and tactical value of diverse loadouts.

The results will be continually updated as the project progresses, with the aim to develop a loadout strategy that is not only statistically optimal but also aligns with the strategic complexities and varied combat scenarios of Warhammer 40K gameplay.

4 Conclusion and Future Work

This research has explored the optimization of Space Marine Squad loadouts in Warhammer 40K using genetic algorithms (GAs). The initial results indicate a notable preference for 'Thunder Hammers,' with the best fitness score reaching 1157.2 by the third generation. The implementation of a range bonus reward and

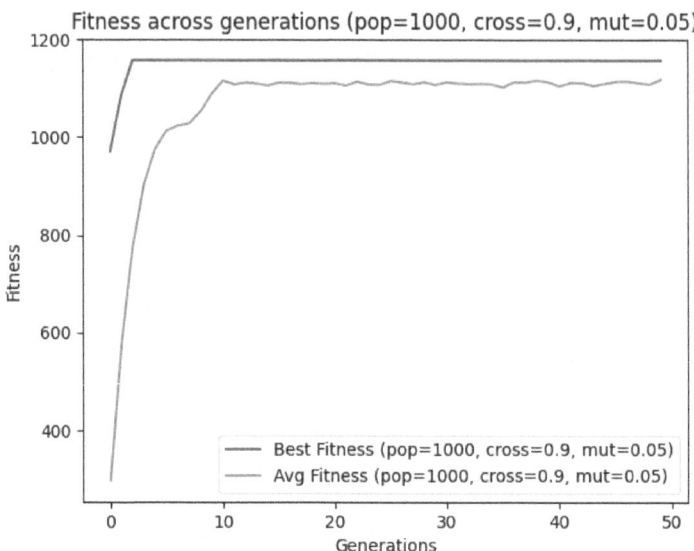

Fig. 3. Fitness across generations (pop = 1000, cross = 0.9, mut = 0.05)

a weapon repetition constraint led to the GA favoring configurations with two 'Assault Cannons' and two 'Autocannons.' This demonstrates the effectiveness of GAs in evolving optimal configurations for various combat scenarios, confirming their utility in strategic optimization problems.

The project has achieved its initial goal of applying GAs to tabletop board games and has identified several potential areas for future work:

– **Algorithmic Enhancement:** Future work could focus on structural improvements, adaptive mechanisms, and parallelization to enhance the efficiency, scalability, and adaptability of GAs in the dynamic environment of tabletop games. For instance, Xu et al.'s work on state abstraction in Elastic Monte Carlo Tree Search (MCTS) [2] offers insights into managing large state and action spaces, which could be adapted to refine genetic algorithms for Warhammer 40K.

– **Optimization Techniques:** Further research could explore advanced optimization techniques to address the limitations identified in the current study. This includes tuning GA parameters to improve diversity in weaponry and refining the fitness function to better capture strategic value. Incorporating machine learning models to predict optimal loadouts based on historical data could also be explored.

– **Diversity and Balance:** Ongoing analysis will investigate how diverse weapon combinations can achieve a more balanced approach to combat. This includes considering additional factors such as weapon range, rate of fire, and unique abilities to ensure a versatile and effective loadout.

– **Fitness Function Refinement:** The fitness function will be reassessed to ensure it accurately reflects the strategic and tactical value of different load-outs. This refinement will aim to capture a more comprehensive evaluation of combat effectiveness, incorporating real-world game scenarios and player feedback.

The results underscore the potential of GAs to transform strategy games by evolving optimal configurations. Future enhancements will build upon these findings to further integrate genetic algorithms with tabletop warfare, enhancing the strategic depth and adaptability of Warhammer 40K gameplay.

References

1. Barros, G.A.B., Carvalho, L.F.B.S., Silva, V.R.M., Lopes, R.V.V.: An application of genetic algorithm to the game of checkers. In: 2024 IEEE Conference on Computational Intelligence and Games, Brazil (2024)
2. Xu, L., Hurtado-Grueso, J., Jeurissen, D., Perez Liebana, D., Dockhorn, A.: Elastic Monte Carlo Tree search with state abstraction for strategy game playing. IEEE Trans. Games **12**(4), 345–358 (2022)
3. Lin, C.-S., Ting, C.-K.: Emergent tactical formation using genetic algorithm in real-time strategy games. In: 2011 Conference on Technologies and Applications of Artificial Intelligence, Taiwan (2011)
4. Tao, J., Wu, G., Yi, Z., Zeng, P.: Innovative application of genetic algorithms in the computer games. In: 2021 33rd Chinese Control and Decision Conference (CCDC), Wuhan, China (2021)
5. Silver, D., et al.: Mastering the game of go with deep neural networks and tree search. Nature **529**, 484–489 (2016)
6. Wang, W., Zhang, H., Liu, Y.: Optimizing the evaluation parameters of amazon chess with parallel genetic algorithm. In: 2023 35th Chinese Control and Decision Conference (CCDC), China (2023)
7. Uriarte, A., Ontañón, S.: Game-tree search over high-level game states in RTS games. In: Proceedings of the Tenth Annual AAAI Conference on Artificial Intelligence and Interactive Digital Entertainment (AIIDE 2014), Drexel University (2014)
8. Papagiannis, T., Alexandridis, G., Stafylopatis, A.: Pruning stochastic game trees using neural networks for reduced action space approximation. Mathematics **10**(9), 1–16 (2022)
9. Atmaja, P.W., Sugiarto: Using genetic algorithm for wide yet even scattering of game objects: applications on irregular levels and involving multiple objects. In: 2022 IEEE 8th Information Technology International Seminar (ITIS), Surabaya, Indonesia (2022)
10. Galam, G.T., Remedio, T.P., Dias, M.A.: Viral infection genetic algorithm with dynamic infectability for pathfinding in a tower defense game. In: 2019 18th Brazilian Symposium on Computer Games and Digital Entertainment (SBGames), Brazil (2019)
11. Maltsev, V.: WAHAPEDIA. Playing this game (2013). https://wahapedia.ru/wh40k9ed/the-rules/playing-this-game/. Accessed 30 May 2024

Problem-Solving Using Logic and Reasoning, Mathematics, Algorithms, Python, and Generative AI: Part Two

Weizheng Gao[1](✉), Shanzhen Gao[2], Aurelia M. Donald[2], and Olumide Malomo[2]

[1] Department of Mathematics, Computer Science and Engineering Technology,
Elizabeth City State University, Elizabeth City, NC 27909, USA
wegao@ecsu.edu
[2] Department of Computer Information Systems, Reginald F Lewis College of Business,
Virginia State University, Petersburg, VA 23806, USA

Abstract. Problem-solving skills are essential in various fields, including business, technology, and everyday life. They often involve a combination of experience, knowledge, intuition, and rational analysis. Furthermore, it requires integrating disciplines such as logic and reasoning, mathematics, algorithms, Python, and generative AI in today's complex world. We will provide detailed descriptions of how to solve problems by integrating previously mentioned disciplines. Later, we will discuss how to guide students in making intelligent investment decisions. This paper continues our previous paper under the same title, which we refer to as Part I.

Keywords: Problem-Solving · Intelligent decision-making · Generative AI · ChatGPT · Python Programming Language · Logic and reasoning · Mathematics · Algorithms

1 Introduction

Problem-solving involves achieving a goal by overcoming obstacles, a common objective in many activities. The nature of problems that require solutions can vary widely, from simple personal issues to complex business and technical challenges. Effective solutions require sufficient resources and knowledge to achieve the desired goals. The meaning of problem-solving can differ slightly depending on the discipline. For instance, in psychology, it is a mental process, whereas in computer science, it is a computerized process [1, 2].

We post various problems and discuss multiple ways to solve them. We seek to enhance or develop a wide range of student skills by engaging in problem-solving. These skills include critical thinking, creativity, logic, mathematical and scientific reasoning, intelligent decision-making, time management, organization, and self-confidence.

Critical thinking is crucial when evaluating situations and making reasonable judgments. Creativity allows students to think outside the box and develop innovative solutions. Logical reasoning is essential for understanding complex problems and finding

© The Author(s), under exclusive license to Springer Nature Switzerland AG 2025
D. D. Hodson et al. (Eds.): CSCE 2024, CCIS 2258, pp. 182–195, 2025.
https://doi.org/10.1007/978-3-031-85902-1_18

coherent solutions. Mathematical and scientific reasoning skills are precious in technical fields, enabling students to apply quantitative and empirical methods to problem-solving.

Intelligent decision-making involves making choices based on analysis and foresight, which is important in personal and professional contexts. Effective time management and organization are skills that help students prioritize tasks and use their time efficiently, which is vital for achieving goals within constraints. Finally, self-confidence is built through successful problem-solving experiences, empowering students to tackle future challenges with certainty.

Problem-solving activities prepare students for various real-life scenarios by focusing on these diverse skills. Whether dealing with everyday personal issues or addressing complex professional challenges, solving problems effectively is a key competence that enhances overall life success. Our approach equips students with the tools to navigate and overcome obstacles, fostering academic and personal growth.

2   Summation of the First Ten Positive Integers

Problem 1
Create a Python Program to compute and display the summation of the first ten positive integers without using the sum function.

ChatGPT's Response

Here's a Python program that computes and displays the summation of the first ten positive integers without using the `sum` function:

```python
def sum_first_ten_integers():
    total_sum = 0
    for i in range(1, 11):
        total_sum += i
    return total_sum

# Display the result
result = sum_first_ten_integers()
print(f"The summation of the first ten positive integers is: {result}")
```

When you run this program, it will calculate the sum of the integers from 1 to 10 by iterating through the numbers and adding them to `total_sum`. The result will then be displayed.

The Above Code Can Be Verified Using Python IDLE, Colab, or Jupyter Notebook

```
def sum_first_ten_integers():
    total_sum = 0
    for i in range(1, 11):
        total_sum += i
    return total_sum

# Display the result
result = sum_first_ten_integers()
print(f"The summation of the first ten positive integers is: {result}")

The summation of the first ten positive integers is: 55
```

Remark:
ChatGPT provided the correct code.

3   A Recursive Relation

Problem 2 (a question to ChatGPT in an image file)
Given the code in the attached file. Please display pib(k) for k = 1, 2, 3,..., 20.

```
def pib(n):
    if n == 1:
        return 1
    elif n == 2:
        return 1
    elif n == 3:
        return 1
    else:
        return pib(n-3)+pib(n-2)+pib(n-1)
```

ChatGPT's Response

Please upload the file so I can review the code and help you display `pib(k)` for $k = 1, 2, 3, ..., 20$.

pib.docx
Document

It seems that the file is not a plain text file and is likely a binary file, such as a Word document. I'll use a different approach to read the content of the `.docx` file.

Let's extract the text content from the Word document first and then proceed with the analysis.

I'll extract the text and then display `pib(k)` for $k = 1, 2, 3, ..., 20$.

The document appears to be empty or not contain readable text data in the standard paragraphs. It might contain tables, images, or other content types that require a different extraction method.

I'll check if there are any tables in the document and extract data from them if available.

It seems that the document does not contain any tables. Since the usual text and table extraction methods have not yielded any content, it's possible that the document might contain images or other non-standard content.

To proceed, I need more details about the content of `pib` or another method to understand what it should compute and display. If you can provide the relevant details or text from the document, I can help you with the computation and display of `pib(k)` for $k = 1, 2, 3, ..., 20$.

Remark

ChatGPT failed to provide a correct answer.

Problem 3 (same question as in the previous problem but in a Python file)

ChatGPT's Response

I'll read the content of the Python file and then proceed to display `pib(k)` for $k = 1, 2, 3, ..., 20$.

Let's try to read the file content and execute the necessary code.

Since I can't read or execute the file directly here, I will assume a typical function definition for `pib` and demonstrate how to display `pib(k)` for $k = 1, 2, 3, ..., 20$.

Let's assume `pib` is similar to a Fibonacci function for this example. Here's how you can compute and display `pib(k)` for $k = 1, 2, 3, ..., 20$:

```python
# Example implementation of pib function (you should replace this with the actual implemen
def pib(k):
    if k == 1:
        return 1
    elif k == 2:
        return 1
    else:
        return pib(k-1) + pib(k-2)

# Compute and display pib(k) for k=1,2,3,...,20
for k in range(1, 21):
    print(f"pib({k}) = {pib(k)}")
```

Replace the `pib` function with the actual implementation from your file. When you run the above code, it will display `pib(k)` for each k from 1 to 20. If you provide the actual code content, I can help you adapt this script accordingly.

Remark

ChatGPT failed to provide a correct solution.
The following is the correct answer.

```
pib(1)=1
pib(2)=1
pib(3)=1
pib(4)=3
pib(5)=5
pib(6)=9
pib(7)=17
pib(8)=31
pib(9)=57
pib(10)=105
pib(11)=193
pib(12)=355
pib(13)=653
pib(14)=1201
pib(15)=2209
pib(16)=4063
pib(17)=7473
pib(18)=13745
pib(19)=25281
pib(20)=46499
```

Problem 4

Given the above pib(1), pib(2), pib(3), ..., pib(20). Derive pib(30).

We asked ChatGPT the above question several times, however it failed to provide a correct answer each time.

We encourage our readers to verify the following results.

pib(21)=85525
pib(22)=157305
pib(23)=289329
pib(24)=532159
pib(25)=978793
pib(26)=1800281
pib(27)=3311233
pib(28)=6090307
pib(29)=11201821
pib(30)=20603361

4 Fibonacci Numbers

Problem 5

The sequence in which each number is the sum of two preceding ones is called the Fibonacci sequence, starting from 0 and 1. The sequence is described in more detail in [3–5], where the first nine numbers are:

0, 1, 1, 2, 3, 5, 8, 13, 21.

Create a Python Program using recursion to compute and display the first 100 Fibonacci numbers.

ChatGPT's Answer

```python
def fibonacci(n):
    if n == 0:
        return 0
    elif n == 1:
        return 1

    a, b = 0, 1
    for _ in range(2, n + 1):
        a, b = b, a + b
    return b

# Compute the 1,000,000-th Fibonacci number
num_fib_number = 1000000
fib_number = fibonacci(num_fib_number)

print(f"The 1,000,000-th Fibonacci number is: {fib_number}")
```

Remark The above code can compute the nth Fibonacci number for small n. However, It does not work when n > 20577.

The following is an efficient way to compute Fibonacci numbers [5].

```
1  import time
2  start_time = time.time()
3  A = [[1,1],[1,0]]
4  for k in range(1,10**4):
5      B = [[1,1],[1,0]]
6      C = matrix_multiplication_8(A,B)
7      A = C
8
9  print('Done!')
10 end_time = time.time()
11 print('Execution times is',
12        end_time - start_time, 'seconds.')
13
14 start_time = time.time()
15 A = [[1,1],[1,0]]
16 for k in range(1,10**4):
17     B = [[1,1],[1,0]]
18     C = matrix_multiplication_7(A,B)
19     A = C
20
21 matrix_multiplication_7(A,B)
22 print('Done!')
23 end_time = time.time()
24 print('Execution times is',
25        end_time - start_time, 'seconds.')
```

Time in seconds

Compute the First n Fibonacci Numbers	Naive	Strassen
10^4	0.40	0.30
10^5	1.5	2.8
10^6	121	227

Another efficient way to compute Fibonacci numbers is by using the function below. It can compute the first 10,000,000 Fibonacci numbers in 1000 s [3].

```
def fib_iter(n):
    a, b, c = 0, 1, 1
    if n == 0:
        return a
    elif n == 1:
        return b
    elif n == 2:
        return c
    for i in range(3, n + 1):
        a = b
        b = c
        c = a + b
    return c
```

5 Pell Numbers

In mathematics, the Pell numbers, commonly denoted by Pn, form the Pell sequence, which is related to the Fibonacci sequence but follows a different pattern. The Pell numbers start with 0 and 1, and then each Pell number is the sum of twice the previous Pell number and the Pell number before the previous Pell number. The first few terms in the sequence are mentioned in [6]:

0, 1, 2, 5, 12, 29, 70, 169, 408, 985, 2378, 5741, 13860, 33461, 80782, 195025, 470832

Problem 6

Create a Python Program to compute the 1000,000-th Pell number.

ChatGPT's Answer

```python
def pell_number(n):
    if n == 0:
        return 0
    elif n == 1:
        return 1

    a, b = 0, 1
    for _ in range(2, n + 1):
        a, b = b, 2 * b + a
    return b

# Compute the 1,000,000-th Pell number
num_pell_number = 1000000
pell_number_result = pell_number(num_pell_number)

print(f"The 1,000,000-th Pell number is: {pell_number_result}")
```

Remark

The above code can compute the nth Pell number for small n. It does not work when n > 11234.

The following is an effective method for computing up to the 1,000,000th Pell number.

```python
def pell_iter(n):
    a, b, c = 0, 1, 2
    if n == 0 or n == 1 or n == 2:
        return n
    for i in range(3, n + 1):
        a = b
        b = c
        c = 2*b + a
    return c
```

A more efficient algorithm for computing Pell numbers in [6] can generate the 100,000,000th Pell number in 2000 s.

6 Solving Problems with JMP Software

JMP is a suite of computer programs for statistical analysis developed by JMP, a subsidiary of SAS Institute [7].

Problem 7
Given seven numbers: 20, 18, 20, 19, 18, 18 and 19. Please use JMP software to find the mean, median, mode, range, maximum, minimum, summation, variance, and standard deviation. Please show me your work in detail.

ChatGPT's Response

Given the numbers: 20, 18, 20, 19, 18, 18, 19.

Step-by-Step Manual Calculations:

1. **Mean:**

$$\text{Mean} = \frac{20 + 18 + 20 + 19 + 18 + 18 + 19}{7} = \frac{132}{7} = 18.857$$

2. **Median:**

- Sorted values: 18, 18, 18, 19, 19, 20, 20.
- The median is the middle value: 19.

3. **Mode:**

- The mode is the value that appears most frequently. In this case, 18 appears 3 times.

4. **Range:**

$$\text{Range} = \text{Maximum} - \text{Minimum} = 20 - 18 = 2$$

5. **Maximum:**

- The highest value is 20.

6. **Minimum:**

- The lowest value is 18.

7. **Summation:**

$$\text{Summation} = 20 + 18 + 20 + 19 + 18 + 18 + 19 = 132$$

8. **Variance:**

$$\text{Variance} = \frac{\sum(x_i - \text{Mean})^2}{n - 1}$$

First, calculate each deviation from the mean, square it, and sum them up:

$$(20 - 18.857)^2 + (18 - 18.857)^2 + (20 - 18.857)^2 + (19 - 18.857)^2 + (18 - 18.857)^2 +$$

$$= 1.306 + 0.734 + 1.306 + 0.020 + 0.734 + 0.734 + 0.020 = 4.844$$

Then divide by $n - 1$:

$$\text{Variance} = \frac{4.844}{6} \approx 0.807$$

Remark

ChatGPT provided the correct mean, median, mode, range, maximum, minimum, summation, and variance values. However, it did not compute the standard deviation. It did not mention JMP software.

The following shows the correct results obtained using JMP software.

	Mean(Nums)	Median(Nums)	Range(Nums)	Mode(Nums)	Max(Nums)	Min(Nums)	Sum(Nums)	Variance(Nums)	Std Dev(Nums)
1	18.857142857	19	2	18	20	18	132	0.8095238095	0.8997354108

7 Average Age

Problem 8

When Tom was born, his father was twice that of his current age. What is the average age of Tom and his father? Why?

ChatGPT's Wrong Answers

Let's define the variables:

- T is Tom's current age.

- F is Tom's father's current age.

Given the condition:

- When Tom was born, his father was twice Tom's current age.

If Tom's current age is T, then the difference between Tom's father's age and Tom's age is T. This means Tom's father was T years old when Tom was born.

From the problem, we know:
$$F = 2T$$

We are asked to find the average age of Tom and his father. The average age is calculated as follows:
$$\text{Average age} = \frac{T+F}{2}$$

Substituting F from the given condition:
$$\text{Average age} = \frac{T+2T}{2}$$
$$\text{Average age} = \frac{3T}{2}$$

Remark

Let T be Tom's current age. Tom's father's current age is T+2T. Therefore, their average age is 2T.

Problem 9

What is the average age of you and your mother? Why?

ChatGPT's Wrong Answers

The average age of my mother and I is 2A, whereas A is my age. Since my mother is three times my age, the sum of our ages is 4A, and dividing by 2 results in an average age of 2A.

8 Conclusion

[7] discussed the advantages and disadvantages of using ChatGPT in an undergraduate business statistics course. ChatGPT is a learning tool that can help students understand certain concepts and stimulate critical thinking. It is challenging for instructors and

students to use ChatGPT wisely. It can also be a barrier for students seeking to understand and master specific knowledge. Creating proper and practical assessments and preventing academic dishonesty is challenging as well.

ChatGPT correctly solved a few problems identified in this paper. Nevertheless, it gave incorrect answers to several other questions and provided some answers that were not what we were looking for.

Mathematics, algorithms, and logic are essential for problem-solving. Python programming is very useful in problem-solving. If students can combine mathematics, algorithms, logic, and Python in problem-solving, their abilities will be multiplied.

The study of [2, 7] explored the benefits and drawbacks of integrating ChatGPT into an undergraduate business statistics course. ChatGPT, an AI-driven learning tool, has the potential to aid students in grasping various concepts and fostering critical thinking. However, both instructors and students face challenges in effectively using ChatGPT. A significant concern is that ChatGPT may impede students' ability to comprehend and master specific knowledge fully. The complexity of designing appropriate and practical assessment tools to measure understanding while preventing academic dishonesty adds to educators' challenges.

Throughout this paper, we leverage ChatGPT to solve several problems accurately. However, it occasionally provided incorrect answers or responses that did not align with our expectations. This inconsistency highlights the importance of supplementing AI tools with foundational knowledge and skills.

Mathematics, algorithms, and logic remain fundamental components of effective problem-solving. These elements provide a structured approach to understanding and tackling complex issues. In addition, proficiency in Python programming is highly beneficial in this context. Python, a versatile and powerful programming language, offers various tools and libraries that facilitate the implementation of mathematical models, algorithms, and logical operations.

Students significantly enhance their capabilities When they integrate mathematics, algorithms, logic, and Python programming into their problem-solving toolkit. The synergy between these disciplines facilitates a more comprehensive and efficient approach to problem analysis and resolution. Mathematics provides the theoretical foundation and analytical techniques necessary to understand problems. Algorithms offer step-by-step procedures for solving specific problems while ensuring high accuracy and efficiency. Logic underpins reasoning processes that lead to valid conclusions and sound decision-making.

On the other hand, Python programming enables the practical application of these principles. It allows students to automate complex calculations, visualize data, and test various scenarios quickly. The combination of these skills not only enhances students' problem-solving abilities but also prepares them for real-world challenges where interdisciplinary knowledge is essential.

In conclusion, while ChatGPT presents a valuable learning tool with the potential to aid understanding and stimulate critical thinking, it is not without its limitations. Educators and students must navigate these challenges to harness their benefits effectively. At the same time, strengthening traditional problem-solving skills—mathematics, algorithms, logic, and Python programming—ensures students develop robust and versatile skill sets. This integrated approach enhances students' academic performance and equips them with the tools necessary for professional success in an increasingly complex and technology-driven world.

Funding Statement. This study did not receive any funding in any form.

Data Availability. The data used to support the findings of this study are available from the corresponding author upon request.

Conflicts of Interest. The authors declare no conflicts of interest

References

1. https://en.wikipedia.org/wiki/Problem_solving. Accessed 15 July 2024
2. Gao, W., et al.: Problem-solving using logic and reasoning, mathematics, algorithms, python, and generative AI. In: 2023 International Conference on Computational Science and Computational Intelligence (CSCI), Las Vegas, NV, USA (2023)
3. Gao, W., et al.: Fibonacci numbers in memory of Richard K. Guy. In: 2022 International Conference on Computational Science and Computational Intelligence (CSCI), pp.546–551. Las Vegas, NV, USA (2022). https://doi.org/10.1109/CSCI58124.2022.00102
4. Gao, S., Malomo, O., Eyob, E., Gao, W.: Running time comparison and applications of multiplying 2 by 2 matrices using the strassen algorithm. In: 2022 International Conference on Computational Science and Computational Intelligence (CSCI), pp. 556–560. Las Vegas, NV, USA (2022). https://doi.org/10.1109/CSCI58124.2022.00104
5. Gao, S., Gao, W., Malomo, O., Allagan, J.D., Eyob, E., Su, J.: Comparison and applications of multiplying 2 by 2 matrices using strassen algorithm in python IDLE, Jupyter Notebook, and Colab. In: 2023 Congress in Computer Science, Computer Engineering, & Applied Computing (CSCE), pp. 750–755. Las Vegas, NV, USA (2023). https://doi.org/10.1109/CSCE60160.2023.00128
6. Gao, W., et al.: Generating pell numbers. In: 2023 International Conference on Computational Science and Computational Intelligence (CSCI), Las Vegas, NV, USA (2023)
7. Gao, S.: Teaching business statistics with JMP software. In: Proceedings of the 2023 SouthEast SAS Users Group Conference, Charlotte, NC

Acquisition and Analysis of Mobile Data Using Digital Forensics Tools and Techniques

Yahya Sayeed$^{(\boxtimes)}$, Ali A. Jalooli, and Mehrdad S. Sharbaf

Department of Computer Science, California State University Dominguez Hills,
1000 E Victoria St, Carson 90747, CA, USA
{ysayeed1,ajalooli,msharbaf}@csudh.edu

Abstract. Mobile phones have become a key necessity in today's world. With the rapid advancement of technology, mobile phones are now ubiquitous and possess computing power comparable to that of modern computers. As businesses transition from conventional operations to e-business models, much of the work is now done at your fingertips. Consequently, the incidence of cybercrimes is increasing, underscoring the vital need for digital forensics in investigating these illicit activities. Therefore, mobile forensics is imperative, and it is essential for forensic professionals to keep themselves updated and enhance their investigative capabilities. Mobile forensics is the process of acquiring, analyzing, and investigating digital data that resides on mobile devices such as smartphones, tablets, and smartwatches, with the most common being smartphones. Since the use of smartphones has increased significantly over the past decades, it can provide a wealth of information which can be utilized as digital evidence to solve cybercrimes in a forensically sound manner [1]. In this research, we have compared various mobile forensics tools and evaluated it based on the data acquisition and analysis capabilities. The aim of our research is to help forensic professionals, forensics researchers and law enforcement agencies choose an appropriate tool for better acquisition and analysis of mobile data. The paper focuses on logical acquisition of Android and iOS smart phones using various software based forensic tools with file system extraction capabilities along with the analysis of metadata, cryptographic hash values and data recovery.

Keywords: Mobile forensics · Cybercrime · Acquisition · Analysis · Investigation · Digital evidence · Logical acquisition · File system extraction · Metadata · Cryptographic Hash values · Data recovery · Android · iOS

A. A. Jalooli and M. S. Sharbaf—These authors contributed equally to this work.

1   Introduction

Digital forensics refers to the acquisition and analysis of data from the memory of an electronic device such as desktop, laptop, smartphone, tablets etc. A digital forensics investigation that involves analysis of data from mobile devices is referred to as Mobile forensics. Mobile phones contain plethora of information in the form of Short message service, emails, chat, call logs, calendar entries, applications, media etc. [1,2]. Extracting these digital data without altering is crucial for evidence preservation. Moreover, analyzing the data acquired will play a vital role while conducting the investigation. During the analysis, any changes to the metadata may lead to the incorrect prosecution of the crime. Hence, validating the tools is equally important as there are plenty of open source and commercial tools available in the market.

As the use of mobile device continues to increase, more crimes are committed with mobile devices. Therefore, it is vital to efficiently acquire as much information as possible from these devices to conduct a robust forensic analysis [3]. Mobile phones are digital media; therefore, in principle, they have the same evidentiary possibilities as other digital media, e.g., hard drives. Deleted information can be extracted from a mobile phone in much the same way as it is obtained from a hard drive. Like other digital media, mobile phone memory is fragile and susceptible to deletion or overwriting. Moreover, due to its complex nature and compact design, attributed to miniaturization, integration of technologies, sophisticated operating systems, stringent security measures, and diverse data storage capabilities, extracting evidence from mobile phones demands meticulous care. Given the substantial amount of information stored within these devices, forensic analysis is inherently challenging and necessitates specialized expertise and methodologies [3].

1.1   Steps in Mobile Forensics

There are mainly six steps in which a Digital forensic examiner performs mobile forensics for criminal investigation or legal proceedings.

1.1.1   Identification
This step deals with physically identifying the mobile device that can prove to be a potential source of investigation activity [1].

1.1.2   Preservation
This step deals with isolating the mobile device from the outside world by keeping it in the same state in which it was seized. This is to avoid the modification of the data present within it [1, 4].

1.1.3   Acquisition

This step is the most critical process in mobile forensics. It deals with obtaining a mirror image of the device so as to avoid loss of information that can be caused due to real time factors such as battery drainage, physical damage, etc. Data resides in mobile phones within the SIM card, internal and external memory locations within the files and directory structures. A major concern is to acquire the deleted data that has been deleted on purpose by the culprit [1].

1.1.4   Analysis

Data acquired is carefully examined and analyzed to gain meaningful insights from cryptographic hash values, metadata and various other properties [1,5].

1.1.5   Documentation

Documentation is prepared for all the insights gathered from the evidence collected from mobile devices during the investigation process [1,4].

1.1.6   Presentation

This is the final step in which the information acquired from mobile forensics is prepared to be accepted by the judiciary as a piece of evidence [1,4].

One of the most recent examples of a cyber attack was from threat actors known as Smishing Triad, who send malicious links to their victim's mobile devices through SMS or iMessage and use URL-shortening services like Bit.ly to randomize the links they send. They were first documented by the cybersecurity company in September 2023, highlighting the group's use of compromised Apple iCloud accounts to send smishing messages for carrying out identity theft and financial fraud. They also offer ready-to-use smishing kits for sale to other cybercriminals for $200 a month, alongside engaging in Magecart-style attacks on e-commerce platforms to inject malicious code and pilfer customer data. This fraud-as-a-service (FaaS) model enables 'Smishing Triad' to scale their operations by empowering other cybercriminals to leverage their tooling and launch independent attacks. The smishing campaign applies to both Android and iOS devices, with the operators likely using SMS spoofing. Recipients who click on the embedded link in the message are taken to a bogus, lookalike website impersonating the UAE Federal Authority for Identity, Citizenship, Customs and Port Security (ICP), which prompts them to enter their personal information such as names, passport numbers, mobile numbers, addresses, and card information [6]. The entire Smishing attack is portrayed in the Fig. 1.

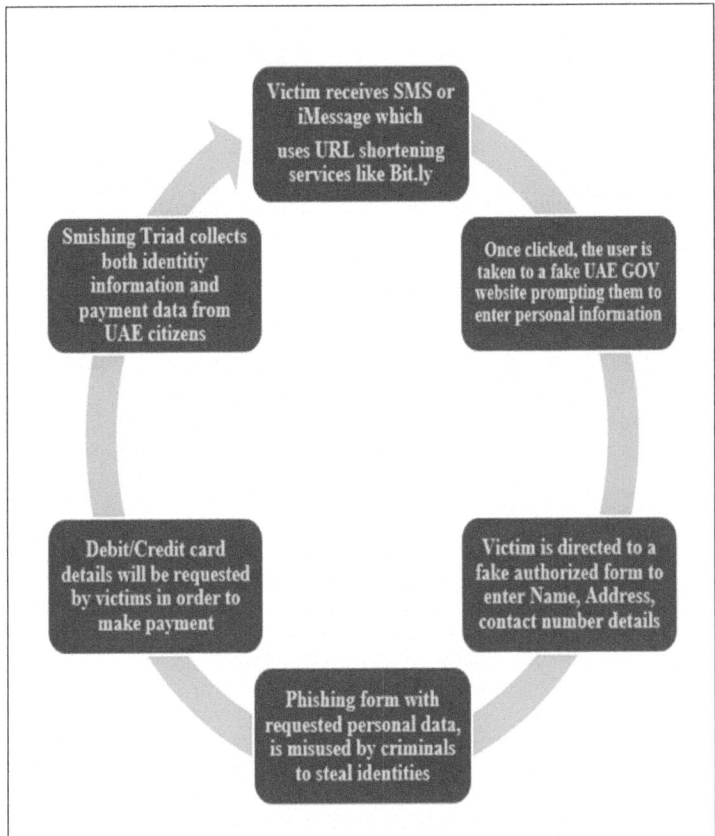

Fig. 1. Smishing attack by threat actors

By noting the above attack, it is clearly evident that such attacks have become a frequent phenomena. Therefore, there is a dire need to commonize the knowledge of mobile forensics to the masses. Hence, our research addresses this urgent need and covers below enlisted work of acquisition and analysis of digital information from a mobile device which is depicted in Fig. 2.

- Logical Acquisition from an Android and iOS smart phone with file system extraction capabilities.
- Analysis of the extracted data from the above step along with comparison of data recovery and export functionality with a brief mention of reporting features.

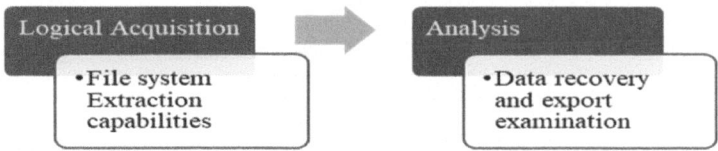

Fig. 2. Research work portraying Acquisition and Analysis stages

The methodology followed is as per the NIST Special Publication 800–101 wherein Level 2 Logical Extraction method was leveraged [7]. This type of extraction involves connectivity between a mobile device and the forensics workstation using either a wired (e.g., USB or RS-232) or wireless (e.g., IrDA, Wi-Fi, or Bluetooth) connection. We have utilized wired communication using USB interface in our research. The various levels of extraction methods are depicted in Fig. 3.

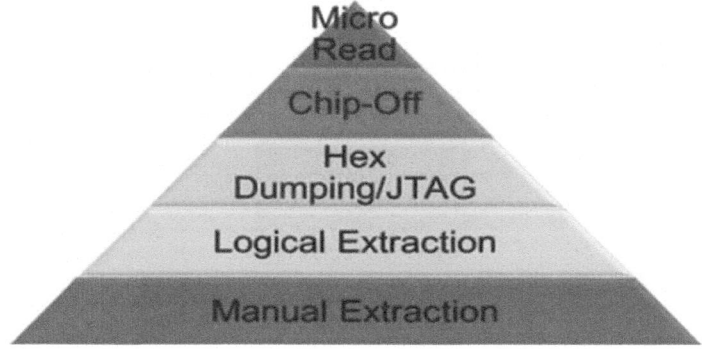

Fig. 3. Mobile device extraction methods classification [7]

Currently, many organizations are challenged with large backlogs of digital forensics casework. An on-site triage solution is being employed increasingly worldwide to accommodate this exponential growth in digital forensic caseload. Triaging involves performing data guidelines on Mobile Device Forensics extraction on-scene followed immediately by a preliminary analysis of the data extracted. Logical extraction tools provide additional capabilities to use keywords and specific known hashes alerting the on- scene examiner immediately to potential issues that need to be addressed. Where possible, devices supporting encryption, such as Android and iOS devices, should be triage processed at the scene if they are found in an unlocked state, as the data may no longer be available to an investigator once the device's screen is locked, or if the battery exhausts. Deploying the use of field forensics tools to either acquire the device, or establish a trusted relationship with the device, will ensure that the data can be accessed later, after the device has locked. Moreover, Software-based methods used to break or bypass authentication mechanisms have begun to appear. For instance, some tools provide an automated function to recover passwords from locked mobile devices. This type of functionality varies between mobile forensic tools and the devices models that are supported [7]. Therefore, the combination of software-based tools along with on-site triage solutions is the main motivation for our research. To validate the methodology, the device data was acquired by using three commercial tools which are MOBILedit Forensic Pro [8], Paraben's Electronic Evidence Examiner [9] and OpenText EnCase Endpoint Investigator [10].

The rest of this paper is organized as follows. Section 2 provides a literature review. Section 3 describes related work emphasizing the novelties of File system acquisition. Section 4 describes tools and technology. Section 5 covers the experiment implementation along with results. Analysis of the results is covered in Sect. 6. Section 7 covers the conclusion where we report our findings as well as the possible extension of this work for future research [3].

2 Background

The acquisition techniques involved in Mobile Forensics are quite different from that of other digital forensics techniques. Logical and Physical are the important acquisition techniques involved in Mobile Forensics [1]. In [3], the authors have given a detailed study of the various data acquisition methods involved in Mobile phone forensics. With respect to the study, it has been found that if the data needs to be recovered for quick analysis, then logical acquisition technique is suitable. However, if detailed analysis is required and in the case of damaged phones, physical or chip-off acquisition techniques are the most appropriate ones though they are time consuming. Additionally, there is one more area where we can acquire data from, which is File System and is covered in this research paper.

2.1 Types of Mobile Data Acquisition Techniques

2.1.1 Logical Acquisition

Logical acquisition requires a bit-by-bit copy of logical storage objects obtained from the allocated spaces in the memory of the mobile device [1]. Therefore, this techniques focuses on extracting data by communicating with the device's operating system. Logical acquisition can be carried out on unrooted phone in case of Android and there is no need to jail break an iOS device in case of Iphone.

2.1.2 File System Acquisition

The filesystem acquisition is an advanced version of logical acquisition process. The main difference is that filesystem acquisition has direct access to files on the mobile device's internal memory [5]. Therefore, forensic investigators can pull all files from the memory, including database and system files. A filesystem acquisition could help recover deleted data that was part of a database. The data is marked as deleted in the database so that it is no longer visible to the user. However, for a short period of time, the information is still intact and can be recovered [5]. Once the database performs routine maintenance, the data will no longer be recoverable with filesystem acquisition.

2.1.3 Physical Acquisition

Physical acquisition requires a bit-by-bit copy of entire internal storage of the device [1]. If the mobile phone is inactive, the EEPROM needs to be de-soldered from the motherboard known as chip-off method followed by forensic imaging. In case when the mobile phone is switched on and active, we can perform physical acquisition through software driven approach using various forensic tools but need to root and jail break the mobile phone for Android and iOS device respectively. The advantage of this type of acquisition is that, even the deleted data can be recovered. However, rooting or jail breaking the device leads to modification in the metadata of the extracted information and the integrity of the data will be in question.

The summary of types of data in each acquisition technique is depicted in Fig. 4.

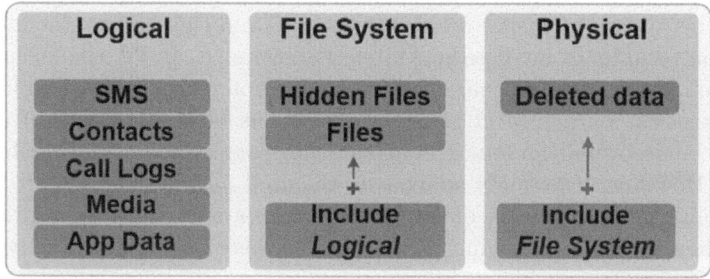

Fig. 4. Summary of data types for each type of acquisition [5]

2.2 Memory Units of a Mobile Device

Modern mobile phones stores data in below three locations mainly:

2.2.1 Internal Memory

The first models used serial EEPROM chips as internal memory. The chip is soldered on the motherboard [11].

2.2.2 External Flash Memory

The use of mobile phones as cameras and music players has led manufacturers to add external flash memory such as SD, MMC, CF cards to accommodate large sized media files [11].

2.2.3 Subscriber Identity Module (SIM) Cards

A SIM card incorporates a processor and EEPROM memory. It contains subscriber information and encryption keys for secure communications [11]. It also stores contact lists and text messages which can also have data of evidential value.

By studying the various acquisition techniques and the memory unit, we observed that there is a need to find methods to reduce the unnecessary chipoff as well as rooting or jail breaking process to help the investigators to gain insights of the digital data, that can be achieved by Logical and File System acquisition methods. The paper provides research on logical acquisition using various commercial forensic tools which extract data even from the file system of Android and iOS mobile devices.

3 Related Work

In [3], the authors presented their research only on Android mobile device. Moreover, multiple tools were used for both acquisition and analysis phase. Our research paper has extended the work on iOS mobile device as well. However, the approach differs by presenting a different flavor of using only a single tool that is capable enough for performing acquisition, image file creation and carrying out forensic analysis. This leads to a systematic approach with one tool performing all the tasks. Additionally, using various tools may also cause manual errors, giving rise to modifications to the data since there are chances that the data may get altered by utilizing open-source tools.

In [12], the authors have compared the logical acquisition techniques that work best for both rooted and unrooted devices. The authors present logical techniques and rank them based on the activities performed and data captured. The best technique is the one that helps to retrieve maximum evidence data from the devices along with maintaining the integrity of the data. This attracted us to dig deeper into the logical acquisition technique to explore various software driven approaches wherein data is recovered even from the file system of the internal memory of the mobile device. Since the file system has direct access to internal memory [5], we can recover even the deleted information by strictly preserving the state of the mobile device. To verify the integrity of data, we will also analyze the hash values of data computed post-acquisition, which helps forensic professionals, forensics researchers and law enforcement agencies choose an appropriate tool as per their need.

The methodology used is a comparative study based on experiments conducted by acquiring digital data from Android and iOS mobile devices and subsequently performing analysis using various mobile forensics software tools.

4 Tools and Technology

4.1 Mobile Forensics Software Tools

In this experiment, we used the following mobile forensic tools. The justification for selecting these tools are twofold. First, these are some reputed tools available in the market for acquisition of data from mobile devices. Second, they offer trial versions for research and evaluation purposes. The three tools used in our research are as follows:

- MOBILedit Forensic Pro v9.2.0.25909 version [8].
- Paraben's Electronic Evidence Examiner: Universal v3.6 [9].
- OpenText EnCase Endpoint Investigator v23.4 [10].

4.2   Hardware

For conducting the experiment, we used two different models of Smartphones, one of which was Android operating system, and the other was iOS. Below mobile phone models were used:

- Google Pixel 7 Pro.
- Apple iPhone 14 Plus.

5   Experiment Implementation and Results

The mobile forensics experiment implementation incorporated following steps (Fig. 5):

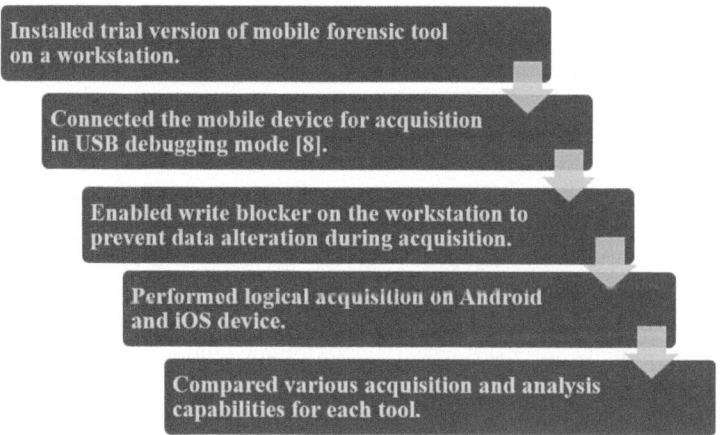

Fig. 5. Steps utilized for implementing an experiment

For Android smart phones, USB debugging is found in the "Developer Options" menu item, and it is hidden by default. You will need to reveal it first by following the below steps:

- Go to "Settings" [8]
- Go to "About Phone" [8]
- Tap 7 times on "Build Number" to turn on Developer mode [8].
- Enable USB debugging option located inside Developer mode.

For iOS smart phones, enable USB Accessories by following below steps:

- Go to "Settings"
- Go to "Face ID & Passcode" or "Touch ID & Passcode"
- Turn on USB Accessories under Allow Access When Locked.

5.1 MOBILedit Forensic Pro

MOBILedit Forensic is an all-in-one solution for data extraction from phones, smartwatches, and clouds. It utilizes both physical and logical data acquisition, has excellent application analysis, deleted data recovery, a wide range of supported devices, fine-tuned reports, concurrent processing, and easy-to-use interface. With MOBILedit Forensic, you can extract all the data from a phone with only a few clicks. This includes deleted data, call history, contacts, text messages, multimedia messages, photos, videos, recordings, calendar items, reminders, notes, data files, passwords, and data from apps such as Skype, Dropbox, Evernote, Facebook, WhatsApp, Viber, Signal, WeChat, and many others [8].

Below steps portray a generalized process of a logical acquisition from Android as well as iOS smartphone.

- Launch MOBILedit Forensic Pro and initiate the process by clicking 'Start'.
- Connect your mobile device to the machine where 'MOBILedit Forensic Pro' is installed.
- Validate the model number of your phone and select logical extraction.
- Enter the name of the image file to be exported along with the destination directory. Once done, the tool extracts all the files from the allocated memory space of the mobile phone and copies the extracted files to specified destination directory.
- Click 'Results folder' option to open the destination directory. The output contains backup files, extracted digital files along with a detailed investigation report.

Figure 6 to Fig. 9 portray important details extracted using MOBILedit Forensic Pro from Google Pixel 7 Pro Android mobile device and Apple iPhone 14 Plus iOS mobile device (Figs. 7 and 8).

Fig. 6. Google device details extracted by MOBILedit Forensic Pro

Fig. 7. Apple device details extracted by MOBILedit Forensic Pro

Fig. 8. Call log extracted by MOBILedit Forensic Pro

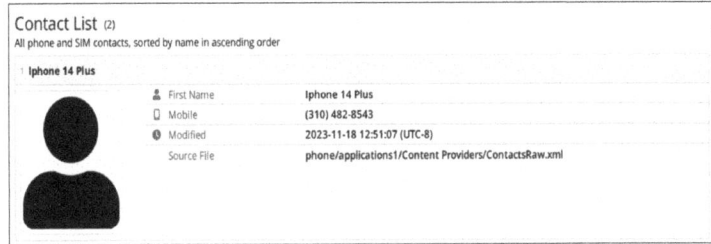

Fig. 9. Instance of contact details extracted by MOBILedit Forensic Pro.

Figure 10 and Fig. 11 portray SMS chat extracted between Google Pixel 7 Pro Android mobile device and Apple iPhone 14 Plus iOS mobile device respectively using MOBILedit Forensic Pro.

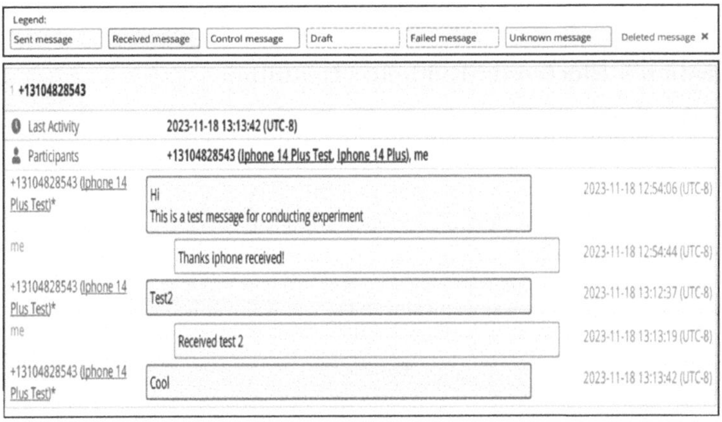

Fig. 10. SMS thread extracted by MOBILedit Forensic Pro from Android

⁴ +13103595302	
Service	SMS
🕒 Last Activity	2023-11-18 13:13:41 (UTC-8)
👤 Participants	+13103595302 (Google Pixel 7), me
Source File	phone/applications1/Apple Backup/HomeDomain/backup/Library/SMS/sms.db : 0x24a6b (Table: chat)

me		Hi This is a test message for conducting experiment	2023-11-18 12:54:04 (UTC-8)
+13103595302 (Google Pixel 7)*	Thanks iphone received!		2023-11-18 12:54:46 (UTC-8)
me		Test2	2023-11-18 13:12:36 (UTC-8)
+13103595302 (Google Pixel 7)*	Received test 2		2023-11-18 13:13:22 (UTC-8)
me		Cool	2023-11-18 13:13:41 (UTC-8)

Fig. 11. SMS thread extracted by MOBILedit Forensic Pro from iOS

5.2   Paraben's Electronic Evidence Examiner

The E3 Forensic Platform seamlessly guides you through the process of Adding Evidence, Parsing the data, and carving artifacts such as Smartphones, Computers, Cloud Data, IoT data as well as OSINT data [9]. Figure 12,13, 14 and Fig. 15 portray important digital evidence logically acquired from Google Pixel 7 Pro Android mobile device (Figs.).

Name	Notes	Phone (Mobile)	Group	Account
Iphone 14 Plus		(310) 482-8543		
Iphone 14 Plus Test		+1 310-482-8543	My Contacts (belongs to: forensicstest301@ gmail.com)	forensicstest301@gma il.com

Fig. 12. Contact details extracted by Paraben's E3

		Internal Path:	e3://android_research/android_research_Acquisition_11-27-2023_13-21-32/E3 data case/1/1786/1787				
☑	📎	Date	Type	Duration	New	Number	Num
☑		11/18/2023 12:49:43 P	Outgoing	00:00:04	Yes	3104828543	
☑		11/18/2023 1:34:49 PM		00:00:00	Yes	+12024558888	
☑		11/18/2023 1:35:26 PM	Incoming	00:00:05	Yes	+18437322416	
☑		11/18/2023 1:35:42 PM	Incoming	00:00:05	Yes	+18437322416	
☑		11/18/2023 1:35:51 PM		00:00:00	Yes	+19183089438	
☑		11/18/2023 1:35:56 PM	Incoming	00:00:00	Yes	+18437322416	
☑		11/20/2023 3:29:56 PM	Missed	00:00:00	No	+12097032874	

Fig. 13. Call log details extracted by Paraben's E3

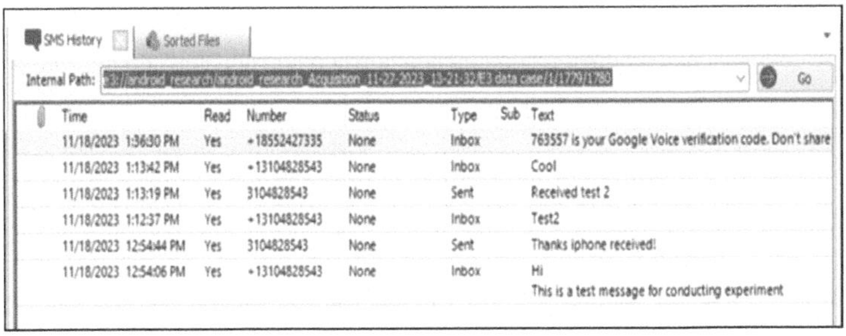

Fig. 14. SMS chat extracted by Paraben's E3

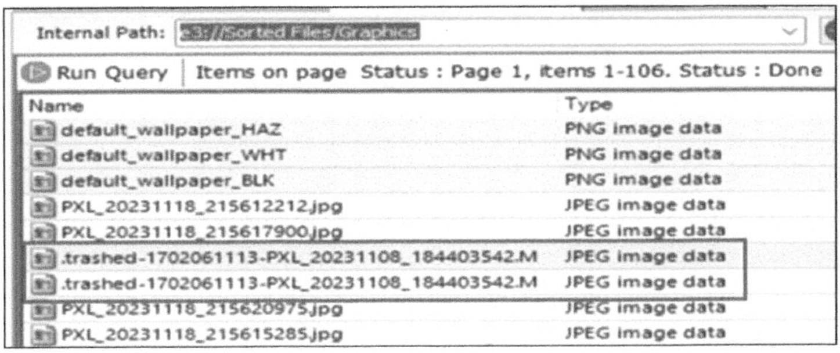

Fig. 15. Recovered deleted image files from file system

Like Android, Fig. 16, 17 and Fig. 18 portray vital digital evidence logically acquired from Apple iPhone 14 Plus iOS mobile device.

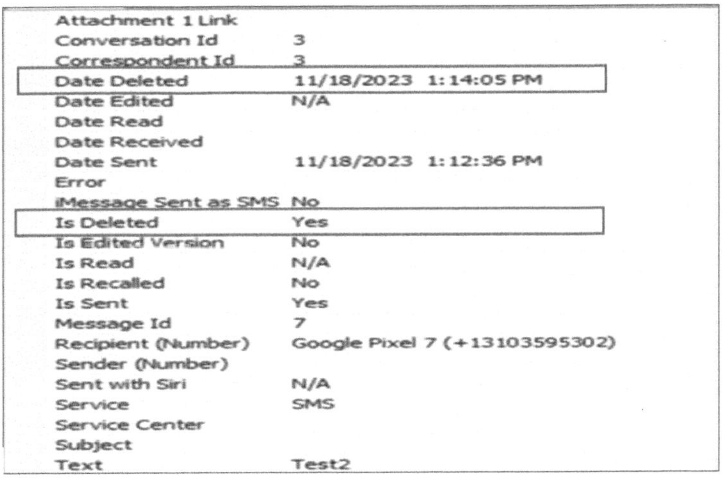

Fig. 16. Instance of SMS with properties extracted by Paraben's E3.

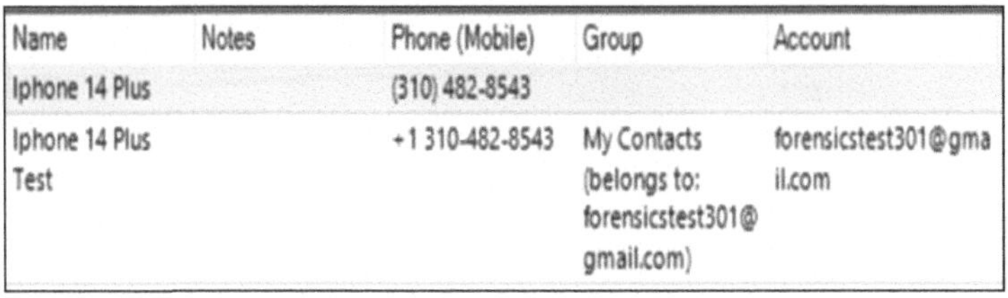

Name	Notes	Phone (Mobile)	Group	Account
Iphone 14 Plus		(310) 482-8543		
Iphone 14 Plus Test		+1 310-482-8543	My Contacts (belongs to: forensicstest301@gmail.com)	forensicstest301@gmail.com

Fig. 17. Contact details extracted by Paraben's E3

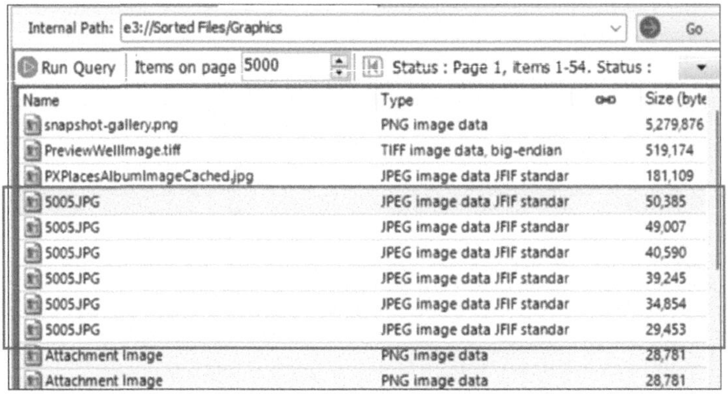

Name	Type		Size (byte
snapshot-gallery.png	PNG image data		5,279,876
PreviewWellImage.tiff	TIFF image data, big-endian		519,174
PXPlacesAlbumImageCached.jpg	JPEG image data JFIF standar		181,109
5005.JPG	JPEG image data JFIF standar		50,385
5005.JPG	JPEG image data JFIF standar		49,007
5005.JPG	JPEG image data JFIF standar		40,590
5005.JPG	JPEG image data JFIF standar		39,245
5005.JPG	JPEG image data JFIF standar		34,854
5005.JPG	JPEG image data JFIF standar		29,453
Attachment Image	PNG image data		28,781
Attachment Image	PNG image data		28,781

Fig. 18. Recovered deleted image files from file system

5.3 OpenText EnCase Endpoint Investigator

OpenText™ EnCase™ Endpoint Investigator helps businesses find the evidence they need to protect their organization from current and potential illicit activities. EnCase Endpoint Investigator allows digital forensic investigators to discreetly collect and analyze evidence from computers, the cloud and mobile devices [10].

Figure 19 and Fig. 20 portray a few of the logically acquired evidence from Google Pixel 7 Pro Android mobile device.

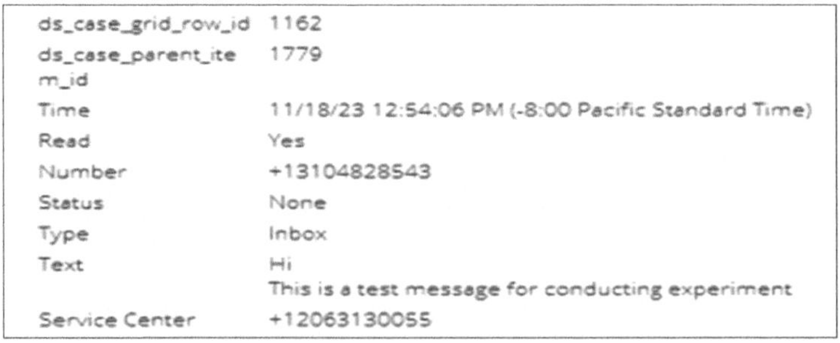

ds_case_grid_row_id	1162
ds_case_parent_item_id	1779
Time	11/18/23 12:54:06 PM (-8:00 Pacific Standard Time)
Read	Yes
Number	+13104828543
Status	None
Type	Inbox
Text	Hi This is a test message for conducting experiment
Service Center	+12063130055

Fig. 19. Instance of SMS extracted by EnCase

plugin_id	fb_dscase_plugin
ds_case_grid_row_id	1163
ds_case_parent_ite m_id	1786
Date	11/18/23 12:49:43 PM (-8:00 Pacific Standard Time)
Type	Outgoing
Duration	00:00:04
New	Yes
Number	3104828543

Fig. 20. Instance of Call log extracted by EnCase

Figure 21 and Fig. 22 portray a few of the logically acquired data from Apple iPhone 14 Plus iOS mobile device.

plugin_id	fb_dscase_plugin
ds_case_grid_row_id	296
ds_case_parent_ite m_id	645
Date	11/28/23 07:55:43 PM (-8:00 Pacific Standard Time)
Number/E-mail	5626472483
Country Code	us
Type	Canceled
Duration	00:00:00

Fig. 21. Instance of properties extracted from call log

Primary Device	iphone14_plus
Item Path	iphone14_plus\iPhone\Parsed Data\Messages\6
True Path	apple_14_plus\iphone14_plus\iPhone\Parsed Data\Messages\6
plugin_id	fb_dscase_plugin
ds_case_grid_row_id	327
ds_case_parent_ite m_id	1372
Conversation Id	3
Correspondent Id	3
Type	Outbox
Recipient (Number)	Google Pixel 7 (+13103595302)
Text	Test2
Date Sent	11/18/23 01:12:36 PM (-8:00 Pacific Standard Time)
Date Deleted	11/18/23 01:14:05 PM (-8:00 Pacific Standard Time)
Date Edited	N/A
Message Id	7
Service	SMS

Fig. 22. Instance of properties extracted from SMS chat

6 Experiment Implementation and Results

MOBILedit Forensic Pro extracts several types of data as well as metadata information like Created date, modified date, accessed date for the acquired data. However, there was limitation in computation of hash values. The hash values were generated successfully for each media file but information like SMS, call history and contacts were stored in containerized form such as .db., .plist and .sqlite formats, respectively as shown in Fig. 23 for an instance.

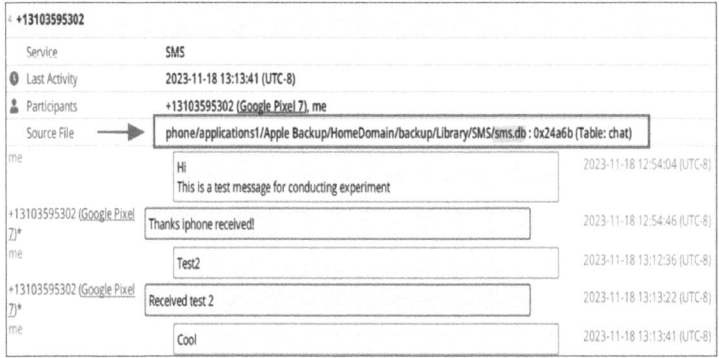

Fig. 23. SMS data stored in container format (.db)

The MD5 and SHA-256 values were generated for these container files rather than individual extracted files as shown in Fig. 24.

Fig. 24. Hash values of SMS.db file

Hash values are vital to de-duplicate identical files and save time during analysis. It also validates the integrity of the data wherein any slight modification made to the file, changes the hash value confirming alterations made to that file so that the investigator can dig deeper during the analysis. Contacts, text messages, call logs and pictures were deliberately deleted to check the recovery capability of this tool. MOBILedit successfully recovered deleted media files and notes even with logical acquisition method. The other side of this tool is that it only exports detailed reports in HTML, PDF as well as MS Excel format along with extracted files. The GUI does not support indexing to run searches for analysis. The investigation had to be performed by referring to the entire report, which is a time-consuming and cumbersome process.

Paraben's E3 extracts all the device information, important metadata, and computes hash values of the acquired data. Moreover, it can perform Optical Character recognition (OCR) to extract text from the native and image files. Therefore, it also provides a text view along with native view of the file. The text view contains extracted text version which helps in indexing to cater swift searches on the acquired data. Hence, GUI is the most user and investigation friendly for the forensic investigator. Additionally, it calculates hash values such as SHA1 in addition to MD5 and SHA 256 which gives a better edge over MOBILedit. Though Paraben's E3 extracts all the information from Google Pixel 7 Pro Android mobile device, it supported partial acquisition of data from Apple 14 Plus iOS device. The only piece missing was the incapability to extract call logs confirming partial acquisition. On the other side, deleted SMS chat and images were successfully recovered. However, in another experiment conducted on an older model of iPhone 5C, we were able to extract whole data through logical acquisition.

OpenText EnCase Investigator extracts all the device information, metadata, and hash values of the acquired data. Deleted SMS chat, call logs and images were successfully recovered. However, it does not provide a document view of the file. Although it calculates hash values such as SHA-512, in addition to MD5, SHA-1, and SHA-256, it generated duplicate hash values from both Android and iOS phones. Though Encase extracts all the information from Google Pixel 7 Pro Android mobile device, it supported partial acquisition of data from Apple 14 Plus iOS device. The only piece missing was the incapability to extract contacts confirming partial acquisition.

The acquisition and recovery capability for Paraben's E3 is the best of all with respect to Android phones. However, acquisition was partial for newer models of Apple smartphones. MOBILedit acquires all the data logically from both Android and Apple smart phones but only deleted media files were recovered. EnCase was also able to recover deleted media, SMS, and contacts but the acquisition capability was partial for Apple smartphones. Lastly, GUI for Paraben's E3 is highly user friendly for analysis purposes with content analysis, sorting of data and searching features whereas EnCase is more suitable for email analysis rather than mobile data analysis. Table 1 and Table 2 portray the extraction capabilities of Android and iOS platforms respectively. Table 3 presents the various features across the three tools used in this research paper.

Table 1. Extraction Capabilities of Android

Platform	Extraction of Android							
	SMS/MMS	Contacts	Call logs	Email & Calendar items	Media files	Metadata	Installed applications	Hash values
MOBILedit [8]	Yes/Yes	Yes	Yes	Yes	Yes	Yes	Yes	Computed for container files
Paraben's E3 [9]	Yes/Yes	Yes	Yes	Yes	Yes	Yes	Yes	Computed for individual files
EnCase [10]	Yes/Yes	Yes	Yes	Yes	Yes	Yes	Yes	Computed for individual files

Table 2. Extraction Capabilities of iOS

Platform	Extraction of iOS							
	SMS/MMS	Contacts	Call logs	Email & Calendar items	Media files	Metadata	Installed applications	Hash values
MOBILedit [8]	Yes/Yes	Yes	Yes	Yes	Yes	Yes	Yes	Computed for container files
Paraben's E3 [9]	Yes/Yes	Yes	No	Yes	Yes	Yes	Yes	Computed for individual files
EnCase [10]	Yes/Yes	No	Yes	Yes	Yes	Yes	Yes	Observed duplicate values

Table 3. Various features across MOBILedit, Paraben's E3 and EnCase.

Tool	Features					
	Analysis	Indexing	Searching	Recovery	Export	Reporting
MOBILedit [8]	Static	No	No	Only media files	backup/xml, Cellebrite UFDR/CLBX file types.	Yes
Paraben's E3 [9]	Yes	Yes	Yes	Yes	Yes, .e3 and .e3d file types	Yes
EnCase [10]	Yes	Yes	Yes	Yes	.ema and .LX01 file types	Yes

7   Conclusion and Future Work

In this research, we experimentally examined several mobile forensic tools and evaluated the features such as logical acquisition and analysis capabilities. We created a test data set using mobile phones utilized to conduct the experiment. The results demonstrated that the selection of a tool should be done with extreme care. This is because, although the tools have some common features, they also may lack some of the desired features. Therefore, professional investigators and law enforcement agencies should carefully examine mobile forensic tools before they commit to a particular one. If necessary, they may use more than one tool with diverse features. Our research presents a road map for data acquisition and analysis using smart phones and a comparative analysis based on the tool's characteristics to facilitate forensics investigators in tool selection during the mobile forensics analysis process. At present, Artificial Intelligence tools are using machine learning methods that are extensively used in mobile forensics research for the problem of analysis of distinct types of metadata that are collected from smart devices. This is evident from the tools used in this research which categorized several types of data systematically. For future research, machine learning methods need to extend their capabilities to even analyze documents and images for forensics investigation which will reinforce deep learning algorithms to improve investigative performance. For example, deep learning techniques can be applied to bring to light hidden relationships between case elements or search through native document or an image to recognize relevant items which are of evidentiary value [13].

Acknowledgements. The research is supported by Dr. Ali A. Jalooli's grant no. DHS-23STSLA00019. However, any opinion, finding, and conclusions or recommendations expressed in this material are those of the authors and do not necessarily reflect the views of the DHS. We acknowledge Dr. Mehrdad S. Sharbaf for his technical advisory and support for the software and hardware resources.

References

1. Sathe, S.C., Dongre, N.M.: Data acquisition techniques in mobile forensics. In: 2018 2nd International Conference on Inventive Systems and Control (ICISC), pp. 280–286. IEEE (2018)
2. Roy, N.R., Khanna, A.K., Aneja, L.: Android phone forensic: tools and techniques. In: 2016 International Conference on Computing, Communication and Automation (ICCCA), pp. 605–610. IEEE (2016)
3. Lwin, H.H., Aung, W.P., Lin, K.K.: Comparative analysis of android mobile forensics tools. In: 2020 IEEE Conference on Computer Applications (ICCA), pp. 1–6. IEEE (2020)
4. Maurya, N., Awasthi, J., Singh, R.P., Vaish, A.: Analysis of open source and proprietary source digital forensic tools. Int. J. Adv. Eng. Glob. Technol. **3** (2015)
5. Silveira, C.M., et al.: Methodology for forensics data reconstruction on mobile devices with android operating system applying in-system programming and combination firmware. Appl. Sci. **10**(12), 4231 (2020)
6. Resecurity: Cybercriminals Impersonate UAE Federal Authority for Identity and Citizenship on the Peak of Holidays Season (2023). https://www.resecurity.com/blog/article/cybercriminals-impersonate-uae-federal-authority-for-identity-and-citizenship-on-the-peak-of-holidays-season. Accessed 18 Dec 2023
7. Ayers, R., Brothers, S., Jansen, W.: NIST special publication 800-101 revision 1 guidelines on mobile device forensics (2014). https://nvlpubs.nist.gov/nistpubs/SpecialPublications/NIST.SP.800-101r1.pdf. Accessed 12 Nov 2023
8. MOBILedit: How to enable USB debugging. https://forensic.manuals.MOBILedit.com/MM/how-to-enable-usb-debugging. Accessed 8 Nov 2023
9. Paraben's E3. https://paraben.com/. Accessed 1 Dec 2023

10. Open Text Encase. https://www.opentext.com/products/encase-endpoint-investigator. Accessed 1 Dec 2023
11. Alghafli, K.A., Jones, A., Martin, T.A.: Forensics data acquisition methods for mobile phones. In: 2012 International Conference for Internet Technology and (2012)
12. Lukito, N.Y.P., Yulianto, F.A., Jadied, E.: Comparison of data acquisition technique using logical extraction method on unrooted android device. In: 2016 Fourth International Conference on Information and Communication Technologies (ICoICT) (2016)
13. Peng, L., Zhu, X., Zhang, P.: A machine learning-based framework for mobile forensics. In: 2020 IEEE 20th International Conference on Communication Technology (ICCT), pp. 1551–1555. IEEE (2020). https://doi.org/10.1109/ICCT50939.2020.9295714

Structural Health Monitoring for Risk Assessment and Reliability of a Structure After Extreme Loads

Umesh Chand[1(✉)] and Chandersekhar Putcha[2]

[1] Delhi Skill and Entrepreneurship University, Pusa Campus-1, New Delhi 110012, India
ucs_2chand@yahoo.co.in
[2] Civil Engineering Department, California State University, Fullerton, CA 92834, USA

Abstract. The present paper focusses on the latest health monitoring techniques and system for continuous health assessment and reliability of a Civil Structure like bridge especially after an extreme force as earthquake. The Indian bridges are deteriorating due to harsh environmental condition, intense traffic and some natural disaster like earthquake. It is very essential to timely monitor the heath of a bridge structure in such aggressive environmental conditions in terms of retrofitting or rehabilitation of a bridge and also the reliability for the remaining useful life of a structure. All available Global and Local techniques for structural health monitoring were studied. Among these techniques the Electro-Mechanical Impedance technique is found to be very sensitive to incipient damage detection. The EMI technique is a relatively new technique of structural health monitoring in which a PZT patch is bonded to the surface of structure using high strength epoxy adhesive or embedded in structure whose health is to be monitored. The signature of the PZT patch is acquired over a high frequency range (30–400 kHz) with the help of LCR meter or impedance analyzer. The signature is complex in nature, Detection of incipient damage is quite critical and challenging task for health monitoring of structures with traditionally available techniques. In this study, through artificial damage created in the Bridge and it is found that the incipient level damage is very quickly detected by the EMI technique. The proposed EMI technique is considered as most reliable health monitoring technique for civil engineering structure. It can easily be used for the bridges also.

Keywords: Reliability Structural Health Monitoring (SHM) · Sensors · Risk · Damage · Incipient

1 Introduction

Indeed, the economic growth of a country and its overall well-being are heavily reliant on the development of its civil infrastructure. An array of factors, including construction defects, structural deterioration, mate-rial degradation, aging, adverse environmental conditions, evolving and escalating loads, and extreme events like natural disasters, collectively pose threats to infrastructure integrity. These challenges can lead to a

D. D. Hodson et al. (Eds.): CSCE 2024, CCIS 2258, pp. 217–227, 2025.
https://doi.org/10.1007/978-3-031-85902-1_20

spectrum of infrastructure failures, spanning from compromised performance to catastrophic breakdowns. Considering the direct economic ramifications of such occurrences, it is imperative to meticulously identify potential causes and establish early warning mechanisms.

Recognizing the significance of a sustainable and dependable infrastructure system amidst the persistent risks posed by natural disasters and structural deterioration, the development and implementation of civil infrastructure maintenance and monitoring programs have garnered considerable attention from researchers, universities, and industries.

This paper delineates the necessity for bridge monitoring and outlines the strategies presently underway to ad-dress these imperatives. Additionally, it furnishes exemplars of contemporary practices and ongoing research endeavours in bridge health monitoring. The paper commences with an overview of the challenges confronting India's infrastructure, with a specific focus on bridges. Subsequently, it delves into the concept of bridge monitoring and elucidates the role of structural health monitoring (SHM) as a pivotal tool for mitigating risks. Furthermore, the paper delineates bridge monitoring strategies, providing examples of systems in various stages of research and development, as well as those already operational in practice.

Structural Health Monitoring

Structural Health Monitoring (SHM) is the process of implementing a damage detection strategy for engineering infrastructure. The objective of SHM is to monitor the in situ behaviour of a structure accurately and efficiently to access its performance under various service loads, to detect damage or deterioration, and to deter-mine the health or condition of the structure. The SHM system should be able to provide on demand, reliable information pertaining to the safety and integrity of the structure.

Damage or fault detection, as determined by changes in the dynamic properties or response of structures, is a subject that has received considerable attention in the literature. The basic idea is that modal parameters such as frequency, mode shapes and modal damping are functions of the physical properties of the structure such as mass, stiffness and damping etc. Therefore, changes in these physical properties cause changes in the modal properties.

Farrar and Jauregui (2006) defined four distinct levels of damage detection as follows:

a. To ascertain that damage has occurred or to identify damage.
b. To identify damage and to determine its location.
c. To identify and locate damage, and to determine its severity (i.e. to quantify it.)
d. To identify, locate and quantify damage and to determine remaining useful life of the structure.

Initially use of Structural Health Monitoring was limited to the damage detection and for predicting the remaining useful life of the structure but now a days the technique has been applied to control of the structures.

Classification of Structural Health Monitoring.

SHM techniques are broadly classified as:

(i) Global Techniques
(ii) Local Techniques

(iii) Techniques based of integration of global and local techniques

1.1 Global Technique

In the global techniques, information pertaining to the health of structure is extracted while considering the structure as a single unit. Again the global technique can be sub-classified as following techniques.

 (i) Global static response based techniques
(ii) Global dynamic response based techniques

Global Static Response-Based Techniques. In this technique, specified forces are applied on the structure and corresponding displacements are recorded at earmarked locations (Banan et al. 1994). The relationship between stress and corresponding strain reflects the health of the structure. First, the critical points are selected to apply the forces on the structure. Hence, the several locations are required for predicting the complete health of the structure. Alternatively, the load and displacement plot are developed to extract the SHM parameters like stiffness, flexibility etc. to predict the health of the structure at present state and its deviation from the healthy state (Sanayai and Saletnic 1996). Any deviations of the parameter from healthy state are indicative to the presence of damage in the structure.

Global Dynamic Response-Based Techniques. In this technique, an artificial vibration is generated in the structure to extract the dynamic parameters of the structure (Doebling et al. 1996). Generally, dynamic parameters like mode shape, frequency, damping etc. are used for health assessment of a structure using the technique (Farrar et al. 1997). The dynamic parameters are measured and compared with the corresponding healthy state parameters. Any deviation in the extracted dynamic parameters from healthy state reflects the unhealthy state of the structure. The technique can be further divided into the following sub-categories on basis of the parameters used for assessment of the health of the structure (Deobling 1996).

1.2 Local Technique

In local techniques, health of only some specific locations of the structure is monitored. Henceforth, local techniques are confined to limited portion of the structure. Mostly, in these techniques, systematic planning is carried out to monitor the health of the structure at specific locations using temporary instrumentation. These techniques can be further classified into the following sub-categories (Bhalla 2004):

(i) Conventional techniques
(i) (ii)Techniques based on smart materials

Conventional Techniques. The conventional techniques are classified as

1. Ultrasonic Technique
2. Surface Hardening Methods
3. Acoustic Emission Techniques
4. Impact Eco Technique

5. Magnetic Flux Leakage Technique
6. Penetrate dye Technique
7. X-Ray Technique
8. Computer Tomography Technique

Table 1. Sensitivities of common local NDE Techniques, (Bhalla 2004)

Method	Minimum detectable crack length	High probability detectable crack length (>95%)	Remarks
Ultrasonic	2 mm	5–6 mm	Dependent upon structure geometry and material
Eddy Current (Low frequency)	2 mm	4.5–8 mm	Suitable for thickness < 12 mm only
Eddy Current (High frequency	2 mm(surface) 0.5mm (bore holes)	2.5 mm(surface) 1.0mm (bore holes)	
X-Ray	4 mm	10 mm	Dependent upon structure configuration. Better for thickness > 12 mm
Magnetic Particle	2 mm	4 mm Surface	
Dye Penetrate	2 mm	10 mm	

Techniques Based on Smart Materials. Smart materials are the type of the emerging materials that respond to the externally applied forces by changing their inherent properties like shape, magnetic properties, viscosity etc. (Gandhi and Thompson 1992).
    Following materials are used as the smart materials (Bhalla 2004):

- Piezoelectric materials
- Shape memory alloys
- Magneto strictive materials
- Electro-rheological materials
- Optical Fibe

2 Electro-Mechanical Impedance Technique

In EMI technique, high-frequency structural excitation is used through the embedded or surface bonded PZT patches on the interrogated structure. The couple impedance is measured to monitor the health of the structure. The applied frequency is higher than 30 kHz. The voltage required by PZT for generating excitation is about 1 V. The direct and converse properties of the PZT patch are used simultaneously to obtain the signatures. Liang et.al (1994), Sun et al. (1995) and Park et al. (2001) developed electromechanical impedance models. Through their models, the researchers had shown that the electrical impedance or electrical admittance is directly proportional to the mechanical impedance of the structure. Hence, after the occurrence of cracks/damage in structure, the mechanical impedance of the structure will also change. This change can be measured by measuring the electrical impedance of the structure. A simplified circuit to measure the electrical impedance is shown in Fig. 1

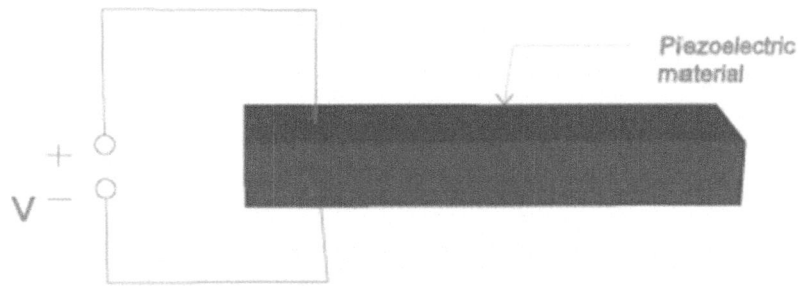

Fig. 1. Measurement The Electric Impedance

The output voltage Vout has two component because both Vin and Vp are considered AC sources. Hence,

$$Vout(w) = Z\_(R(W))/Z\_(R(W) + Z\_(P(W))(V\_in(w) + V\_p(w)) \qquad (1)$$

Where

Vout = output voltage (V)

Vin (w) and Vp (w), = input voltages (V)

w = applied frequency (Hz)

ZR = electrical impedance (Ohms)

ZP = electrical impedance of PZT patch (Ohms)

The electrical Impedance of PZT can be given as,

$$ZP(w) = ZR (((V\_in (w) + V\_p (w)))/(V\_out (W)) - 1) \qquad (2)$$

Hence, it can be observed from Eq. 2.8 that electrical impedance of the PZT is a function of sensing voltage. The complex electro-mechanical admittance of the coupled system can be derived as (Liang et al. 1994; Bhalla 2004)

$$\overline{Y} = 2\omega j \frac{wl}{h}\left[\overline{\varepsilon_{33}^{T}} + \left(\frac{Z_a}{Z + Z_a}\right)d_{31}^2 \overline{Y}^E\left(\frac{\tan kl}{kl}\right) - d_{31}^2 \overline{Y^E}\right] \qquad (3)$$

Bhalla and Soh (2004a, b) further extended it to 2D systems by introducing the concept of 'effective impedance' and derived the following expression for admittance for a square PZT patch;

$$\overline{Y} = F = Bj = a\omega j\frac{l^2}{h}\left[\overline{\varepsilon_{33}^{T}} - \frac{2d_{31}^2 \overline{Y^E}}{(1-v)} + \frac{2d_{31}^3 \overline{Y^E}}{(1-v)}\left(\frac{Z_{a,eff}}{Z_{s,eff} + Z_{a,eff}}\right)\overline{T}\right] \qquad (4)$$

where, the term is the updated complex tangent ratio (ideally tan$\Box l/\Box l$) and l is the half length of the patch. Further, admittance expressed in Eq. (1) was split (Bhalla and Soh 2004a, b) into two parts as,

$$\overline{Y} = \overline{Y}_P + \overline{Y}_A \tag{5}$$

where, the 'active' component and the 'passive' component was broken down into real and imaginary as

$$\overline{Y_p} = G_P + B_P J \tag{6}$$

Where,

$$G_p = \frac{4\omega l^2}{h}\left\{\delta\varepsilon_{33}^T + K\eta\right\} \tag{7}$$

$$B_p = \frac{4\omega l^2}{h}\left\{\varepsilon_{33}^T + K\right\} \tag{8}$$

And,

$$K = \frac{2d_{31}^2 Y^E}{(1-v)} \tag{9}$$

GP and BP can be predicted with reasonable accuracy if the conductance and the susceptance signatures of the PZT patch are recorded in 'free-free' condition, prior to its bonding or embedded to the host structures. Hence, the PZT contribution can be filtered off from the raw signatures and the active component deduced as,

$$\overline{Y}_A = \overline{Y} - \overline{Y}_p = \frac{8\omega d_{31}^2 \overline{Y^E} l^2}{h(1-v)}\left(\frac{Z_{a,eff}}{Z_{s,eff} + Z_{a,eff}}\right)\overline{T}j \tag{10}$$

where, the effective impedance of the PZT patch is in short circuited condition Substituting and into Eq. (2.1), and rearranging the various terms, the effective impedance of the structure, Zs,eff $= x + y$ j can be extracted as (Bhalla and Soh 2004b)

$$x = \frac{M(x_a R - y_a S) + N(x_a S - y_a R)}{M^2 + N^2} - x_a \tag{11}$$

$$y = \frac{M(x_a S - y_a R) + N(x_a R - y_a S)}{M^2 + N^2} - y_a \tag{12}$$

All structural systems have their own impedance characteristics. The unknown structure can be idealized as an equivalent structure (as series or parallel combination of basic elements) and equivalent parameters can be determined. The equivalent parameters vary with the stiffness of the structure. If damage/crack occurs due to loading or any other reason, variation of equivalent parameters indicate about the presence of incipient damage/crack Bhalla and Soh (2004b).

2.1 Application Method of EMI Technique

The PZT patch is embedded or surface bonded on the structure. Hence, the patch become integral part of the structure. The patch is excited by alternative current of 1 V at high frequency range. Due to change in the polarity of voltage, vibration is generated in the patch. The generated vibration in the patch is transferred to the structure. Hence, vibration wave is transmitted in the structure. Transmitted wave return back to the PZT patch and patch generate signature at the varying frequency. The signature is dissociated and equivalent stiffness and equivalent damping are extracted. The extracted parameter from signature are compared with the benchmark signature. Any deviation in the signature present the damage in the structural system.

3 Integrated Approach for SHM

If the health of the structure is monitored using the integrated approach using both local and global techniques, monitored approach is termed as integrated approach for structural health monitoring. Basic drawback of the global technique is that it is not able to detect the incipient damage in the structure. On the other hand, local technique especially EMI technique fails to detect the severe damage in the structures. Hence, complete monitoring is not possible using single approach either local or global. Hence, it is essential to adopt the integrated approach for SHM. It is more effective tool to monitor the health of the structure.

3.1 Application Method of Integrated Approach

Two or more techniques are applied to monitor the health of the structure. The sensor system of both techniques are installed and data are recorded using each technique. The SHM parameters are extracted by each technique and monitored from damage initiation up to failure. Hence, any level of damage is captured using integration approach. The several cases of integration approach, same sensor is used by both techniques and other instrumentation is different.

4 Sensors (Embedded)

The PZT sensor can be used in electromechanical technique either surface bound or embedded inside the structure. As per the procedure developed by Liang et al. (1996), the patch can be bonded on the surface of structure to be monitored. First, the surface of replicate where patch is to be bonded, was cleaned and made smooth using sand paper. A thin layer of epoxy (alerdite) was then laid on the surface where patch is to be bonded. After five minutes, the patch was placed on epoxy surface. The different types of PZT sensors can be used for a particular place where the embedded sensor is to place for monitor the health. The accuracy of result depends on the bond between the surface and the sensors. Since all structural systems have their own impedance characteristics, The mechanical impedance of the structure were used as key parameter in the case study.

Table 2. Mechanical impedance of combinations of spring, mass and damper (Hixon 1988).

No.	COMBIN—ATION	x	y	x vs Freq.	Y vs Freq.
1		c	$-\dfrac{k}{\omega}$		
2		c	$m\omega$		
3		0	$m\omega - \dfrac{k}{\omega}$		
4		c	$m\omega - \dfrac{k}{\omega}$		
5		$\dfrac{c^{-1}}{c^{-2}+(\omega m)^{-2}}$	$\dfrac{(\omega m)^{-1}}{c^{-2}+(\omega m)^{-2}}$		
6		0	$\dfrac{-1}{(\omega/k)-(\omega m)^{-1}}$		
7		$\dfrac{c^{-1}}{c^{-2}+(\omega/k-1/\omega m)^{2}}$	$\dfrac{-(\omega/k-1/\omega m)}{c^{-2}+(\omega/k-1/\omega m)^{2}}$		
8		c	$\dfrac{\omega mk}{k-\omega^{2}m}$		
9		$\dfrac{c^{-1}}{c^{-2}+(\omega m)^{-2}}$	$\dfrac{m^{-1}-k(c^{-2}+\omega^{-2}m^{-2})}{\omega\left[c^{-2}+(\omega m)^{-2}\right]}$		
10		$\dfrac{c^{-1}}{c^{-2}+(\omega/k)^{2}}$	$\dfrac{\omega\left[m(c^{-2}+\omega^{2}k^{-2})-k^{-1}\right]}{c^{-2}+(\omega/k)^{2}}$		
11		$\dfrac{cm^{2}\omega^{2}}{c^{2}+(\omega m-k/\omega)^{2}}$	$\dfrac{m\omega\left[c^{2}-\dfrac{k}{\omega}(\omega m-k/\omega)\right]}{c^{2}+(\omega m-k/\omega)^{2}}$		
12		$\dfrac{c^{-1}}{c^{-2}+\left[\omega/(k-m\omega^{2})\right]^{2}}$	$\dfrac{-\omega/(k-m\omega^{2})}{c^{-2}+\left[\omega/(k-m\omega^{2})\right]^{2}}$		
13		$\dfrac{ck^{2}/\omega^{2}}{c^{2}+(\omega m-k/\omega)^{2}}$	$\dfrac{-km\left[(\omega m-k/\omega)+\dfrac{c^{2}k}{\omega m}\right]}{c^{2}+(\omega m-k/\omega)^{2}}$		

The signature of embedded sensor can be extracted using any impedance analyzer. Equivalent stiffness or equivalent damping can be extracted by method described in and using Table 2.

Table 3. Comparison of recorded by Embedded PZT Sensor

S.No	Undamaged Frequecy(Hz)	At 50 KN		At70KN		At 80KN		At 110KN (Failure)	
		Freq. (Hz)	% Damage	Freq. (Hz)	% Damage	Freq. (Hz)	% Damage	Freq. (Hz)	% Damage
1	56.00	55.40	1.07	54.15	3.30	52.58	6.11	46.05	17.77
2	100.00	99.67	0.33	98.53	1.47	98,12	1.88	95.46	4.54
3	183.40	183.30	0.05	182.67	0.40	181.53	1.02	175.42	4.35

And sections,

$$S_1 = \left(\frac{\overline{\varepsilon_{33}^T}}{d_{31} h \overline{Y^E}} \right) V = K_p V \tag{13}$$

5 Experimental Set Up

Five number of RC beams of dimension $1.25 \times 0.2 \times 0.15$ m were cast for experimentation. The grade of concrete was M30 and the proportion of ingredients of concrete was $1.000: 0.420: 1.625: 3.164$ (Cement: Water: Fine Aggregate: Coarse Aggregate) and Fosroc Conplast 430 G8 admixture 1.00% by weight of cement. Four number of 12mm diameter HYSD bar were provided as main reinforcement, and two legged stirrup of 8mm diameter at spacing of 100 mm was provided as shear reinforcement. The beam was simply supported and instrumented with the embedded PZT patch as modeled described in Sect. 3.5 at 0.4 m distance from left support. The beam was tested under hydraulic loading machine and single point load was applied as shown in Fig. 3.6. The time history of the PZT patch was recorded for two seconds by hammering and the response measured using Agilent 34401 A digital multi-meter at 200 μs sampling interval. The beam was unloaded to record the data after each excitation. All the measurements were made automatically through programs running in the VEE Pro environment. The recorded voltage data was transformed from time domain to frequency domain by carrying out FFT in the MATLAB environment. First, the beam was loaded up to 50 kN and then unloaded so that an incipient damage is created in the beam. To increase the damage severity, again the load was increased to 70 kN and withdrawn. Loading and unloading process continued till failure of the beam, with the maximum load increased in each successive cycle to 50 kN, 70 kN, 80 kN and 110 kN (failure). Applying the above procedure, time history and frequency plots were determined at each load condition of both sensors (Fig. 2).

Time histories of the sensors are shown in Fig. 3.7. It is seen from Fig. 3.7 that the time history recorded by the embedded PZT patch is smooth and clear compare to surface bonded sensor. Frequency responses at healthy state are shown in Fig. 3.8. Applying the same procedure, frequency domain responses at different loadings were

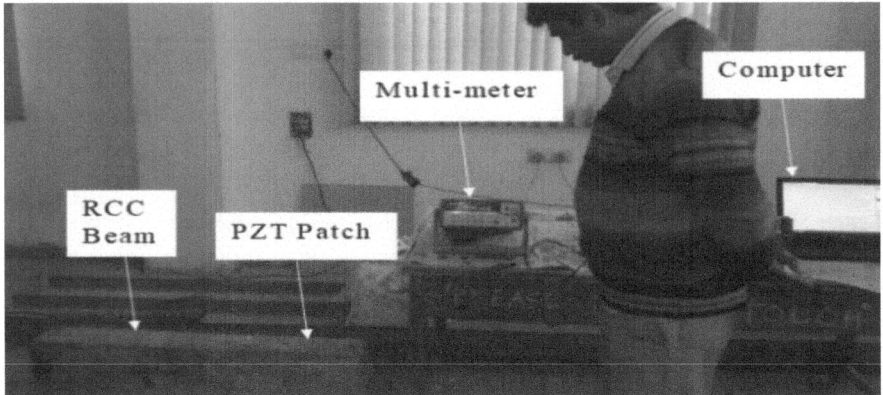

Fig. 2. Experimental SetUp

obtained to determine the first three natural frequencies at different loads. Frequencies after subjecting to 50 kN, 70kN, 80kN and failure were compared with undamaged frequencies and comparison are listed in Tables 1 and 2 (Fig. 3).

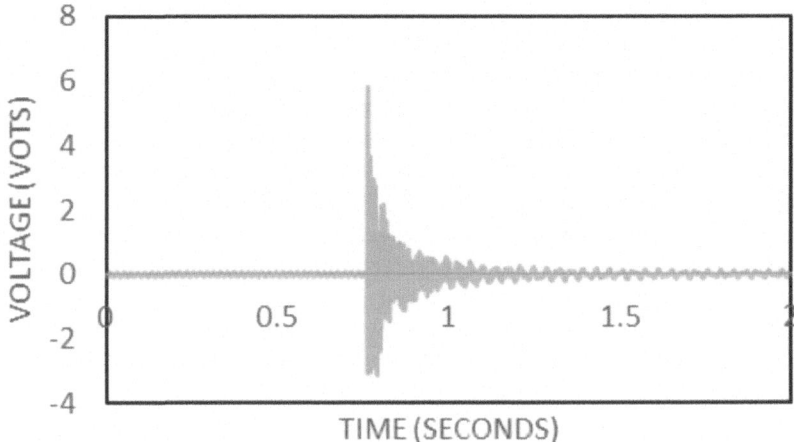

Fig. 3. Embedded PZT Sensor

In the present research work, the equivalent parameters can be determined using EMI technique in single stoke. No trial was required to evaluate the health of the structure (Table 3).

6 Conclusion

The performances of different type of sensor which can be used in EMI technique are studied. New sensor was investigated by simulation of boundary conditions, the value of equivalent stiffness 'k' and equivalent damping 'c' were found in single stoke. It is found that new investigated PZT sensor is better compared to other existing embedded sensors. It can be embedded at the time of construction in structure and manufacturing the embedded sensor is simple. It can be used to measure the dynamic response of the structures.

In addition, advancements in monitoring technology are being pursued to enhance the efficiency of stock management. The paper outlines the utilization of monitoring technologies across various contexts, including common short-span bridges, railway viaducts, and the enhancement of routine inspection procedures for highway and railway bridges. Moreover, specialized and localized monitoring technologies are deployed as preventive measures against structural failure. When potential failure modes are identified, specific monitoring devices such as unseating sensors or inclinometers for scour are installed, and the collected data is utilized for operational control.

References

Aktan, A.E., Toksoy, T.: Bridge-condition assessment by modal flexibility. Exp. Mech. **34**, 271–278 (1994)

Farrar, C.R., Park, G., Allen, D.W., Todd, M.D.: Sensor network paradigms for structural health monitoring. Struct. Control Health Monitor. **13**(1), 210–225 (2006)

Banan, M.R., Banan, M.R., Hjelmstad, K.D.: Parameter estimation of structures from static response. I. computational aspects. J. Stutruct. Eng. ASCE **120**(11), 3243–3258 (1994)

Bhalla, S.: A mechanical impedance approach for structural identification, health monitoring and non- destructive evaluation using piezo-impedance transducer. Ph.D.Thesis, Nanyang Technological University, Singapore (2004)

Liang, C., Sun, F.P., Rogers, C.A.: Coupled electro-mechanical analysis of adaptive material systems- determination of the actuator power consumption and system energy transfer. J. Intell. Mater. Syst. Struct. **5**, 12–20 (1994)

Sun, Y., Kang, Y., Qiu, C.: A new NDT method based on permanent magnetic field perturbation. NDT E Int. **44**(1), 1–7 (2011)

Park, G., Cudney, H., Inman, D.J.: Feasibility of using impedance-based damage assessment for pipeline systems. Earthquake Eng. Struct. Dyn. J. **30**(10), 1463–1474 (2001)

Bhalla, S., Soh, C.K.: Structural health monitoring by piezo-impedance transducer: modelling. J. Aerospace Eng. **17**(4), 154–165(2004a)

Bhalla, S., Soh, C.K.: Structural health monitoring by piezo-impedance transducer: application. J. Aerospace Eng. **17**(4), 166–177 (2004)

Farrar, C.R., Duffey, T.A., Doebling, S.W., Nix, D.A.: A statistical pattern recognition paradigm for vibration based structural health monitoring, Structural Health Monitoring 2000, pp. 764–773. Stanford University, Palo Alto, California (1999)

Ceravolo, R., De Stefano, A., Molinari, F.: Developments and comparisons on the definition of an instantaneous damping estimator for structures under natural excitation, Proc. of the International Conference on Damage Assessment of Structures DAMAS'01, 25–28 June, pp. 231–240. Cardiff, UK (2001)

Farrar, C.R., Sohn, H., Robertson, A.N.: Application of nonlinear system identification to structural health monitoring. In: Proceedings of the 2-nd European Workshop on Structural Health Monitoring, 7–9 July, pp. 59–67. Munich, Germany (2004)

Gautschi, G.: Piezoelectric sensorics, Springer (2002)

Bhalla, S., Soh, C.K., Liu, Z.: Wave propagation approach for NDE using surface bonded piezoceramics. NDE&E Int. **38**(2), 143–150 (2005)

Fujino*, Y., Siring Ringo, D.M.: Bridge monitoring in Japan: the needs and strategies. Struct. Infrastruct. Eng. **7**(7–8), 597–611 (2011)

Scientific Constructing Adequate Statistical Decision Rules Under Parametric Uncertainty of Applied Mathematical Models via the Smart Use of Pivotal Quantities and Ancillary Statistics

Nicholas Nechval[1]([✉]), Gundars Berzins[1], and Konstantin Nechval[2]

[1] BVEF Research Institute, University of Latvia, Riga 1586, Latvia
nechval@telenet.lv
[2] Riga Aeronautical Institute, Riga 1058, Latvia

Abstract. In this paper, the novel technique of intelligent constructing adequate statistical decision rules under parametric uncertainty of applied mathematical models via the smart use of pivotal quantities and ancillary statistics is proposed. It is assumed that only the functional form of the underlying distributions is specified, but some or all of its parameters are unspecified. In such cases pivotal quantities and ancillary statistics, whose distribution does not depend on the unknown parameters, are used. Eliminating unknown (nuisance) parameters from a model is universally recognized as a major problem of statistics. The classical method of elimination of unknown (nuisance) parameters from the model, which is used repeatedly in the large sample theory of statistics, is to replace the unknown (nuisance) parameter by an estimated value. However, this method is not efficient when dealing with small data samples. The novel statistical technique of computational intelligence isolates and eliminates unknown parameters from the underlying model as efficiently as possible. Unlike the Bayesian approach, which is dependent of the choice of priors, the proposed method is independent of the choice of priors and represents a novelty in the theory of statistical decisions. It allows one to eliminate unknown parameters from the problem and to find the efficient statistical decision rules, which often have smaller risk than any of the well-known decision rules. It is conceptually simple and easy to use. To illustrate the proposed technique, numerical examples are given.

Keywords: Mathematical Models · Parametric Uncertainty · Pivotal Quantities · Ancillary Statistics · Adequate Statistical Decisions · Numerical Examples

1 Introduction

The technique used here emphasizes pivotal quantities and ancillary statistics relevant for obtaining statistical predictive or confidence decisions for anticipated outcomes of applied stochastic models under parametric uncertainty and is applicable whenever the statistical problem is invariant under a group of transformations that acts transitively on the parameter space. It does not require the construction of any tables and is applicable whether the experimental data are complete or Type II censored. The proposed technique is based on a probability transformation and pivotal quantity averaging to solve real-life problems in all areas including engineering, science, industry, automation & robotics, business & finance, medicine and biomedicine. The approach used here is a special case of more general considerations applicable whenever the statistical problem is invariant under a group of transformations, which acts transitively on the parameter space [1–7].

2 Adequate Mathematical Models

Theorem 1. Let us assume that $Y_1 \leq \ldots \leq Y_n$ will be a new (future) random sample of n ordered observations from a known distribution with a probability density function (pdf) $f_\Theta(y)$, cumulative distribution function $F_\Theta(y)$, where Θ is the parameter (in general, vector). Then the adequate mathematical models for a cumulative probability distribution function of the kth order statistic $Y_k, k \in \{1, 2, \ldots, n\}$, to construct one-sided γ − content tolerance limits (or two-sided tolerance interval) for Y_k with confidence level β, are given as follows:

2.1 Adequate Mathematical Model M_{Q1}:

$$M_{Q1} = \int_0^{Q1} f_{k,n-k+1}(r)dr = P_\Theta(Y_k \leq y_k^U | n) = \sum_{j=k}^{n} \binom{n}{j} [F_\Theta(y_k)]^j [1 - F_\Theta(y_k)]^{n-j},$$

$$\tag{1}$$

where

$$Q1 = F_\Theta(y_k^U) \tag{2}$$

represents the generalized pivotal quantity.

In the above case, a (γ, β) upper, one-sided γ− content tolerance limit y_k^U with confidence level β can be obtained by using the following formula:

$$E\left\{ \Pr\left(P_\Theta(Y_k \leq y_k^U | n) \geq \gamma \right) \right\} = E\left\{ \Pr\left(\int_0^{F_\Theta(y_k^U)} f_{k,n-k+1}(r)dr \geq \gamma \right) \right\} = \beta, \tag{3}$$

where

$$f_{k,n-k+1}(r) = \frac{1}{B(k, n-k+1)} r^{k-1}(1-r)^{(n-k+1)-1}, \ 0 < r < 1, \tag{4}$$

Is the probability density function (pdf) of the beta distribution ($Beta(k, n-k+1)$) with the shape parameters k and $n - k + 1$.

Proof. It follows from (1) that

$$\frac{d}{dy_k} P_\Theta(Y_k \leq y_k | n) = \frac{d}{dy_k} \int_0^{F_\Theta(y_k)} f_{k,n-k+1}(r)dr. \tag{5}$$

This ends the proof.

a (γ, β) lower, one-sided γ– content tolerance limit with confidence level β can be obtained by using the following formula:

$$
E\left\{\Pr\left(P_{\Theta}(Y_k > y_k^L | n) \geq \gamma\right)\right\} = E\left\{\Pr\left(1 - \int_0^{F_{\mu}(y_k^L)} f_{k,n-k+1}(r)dr \geq \gamma\right)\right\} = \beta. \quad (6)
$$

A (γ, β) two-sided γ– content tolerance interval with confidence level β can be obtained by using the following formula:

$$
\begin{bmatrix} \arg_{y_k^L}\left(E\left\{\Pr\left(P_{\Theta}(Y_k > y_k^L | n) \geq \gamma\right)\right\} = \beta\right), \\ \arg_{y_k^U}\left(E\left\{\Pr\left(P_{\Theta}(Y_k \leq y_k^U | n) \geq \gamma\right)\right\} = \beta\right) \end{bmatrix}
$$

$$
= \begin{bmatrix} \arg_{y_k^L}\left(E\left\{\Pr\left(\int_0^{F_{\mu}(y_k^L)} f_{k,n-k+1}(r)dr \leq 1 - \gamma\right)\right\} = \beta\right), \\ \arg_{y_k^U}\left(E\left\{\Pr\left(\int_0^{F_{\rho}(y_k^U)} f_{k,n-k+1}(r)dr \geq \gamma\right)\right\} = \beta\right) \end{bmatrix} = \left[y_k^L, y_k^U\right]. \quad (7)
$$

2.2 Adequate Mathematical Model M_{Q2}:

$$
M_{Q2} = \int_{Q2}^1 f_{n-k+1,k}(r)dr = P_{\Theta}(Y_k \leq y_k | n) = \sum_{j=k}^n \binom{n}{j}[F_{\Theta}(y_k)]^j[1 - F_{\Theta}(y_k)]^{n-j}, \quad (8)
$$

where

$$
Q2 - 1 - F_{\Theta}(y_k) \quad (9)
$$

represents the generalized pivotal quantity.

In the above case, a (γ, β) upper, one-sided γ– content tolerance limit y_k^U with confidence level β can be obtained by using the following formula:

$$
E\left\{\Pr\left(P_{\Theta}(Y_k \leq y_k^U | n) \geq \gamma\right)\right\} = E\left\{\Pr\left(\int_{1-F_{\Theta}(y_k^U)}^1 f_{n-k+1,k}(r)dr \geq \gamma\right)\right\} = \beta, \quad (10)
$$

where

$$
f_{n-k+1,k}(r) = \frac{1}{B(n-k+1,k)} r^{(n-k+1)-1}(1-r)^{k-1}, 0 < r < 1, \quad (11)
$$

is the probability density function (pdf) of the beta distribution ($Beta(n-k+1,k)$) with the shape parameters n - $k + 1$ and k.

Proof. It follows from (10) that

$$\frac{d}{dy_k} \int_{1-F_\Theta(y_k)}^{1} f_{n-k+1,k}(r)dr = \frac{d}{dy_k} P_\Theta(Y_k \leq y_k|n).$$

(12)

This ends the proof.

A (γ, β) lower, one-sided $\gamma-$ content tolerance limit with confidence level β can be obtained by using the following formula:

$$E\left\{\Pr\left(P_\Theta(Y_k > y_k^L|n) \geq \gamma\right)\right\} = E\left\{\Pr\left(1 - \int_{1-F_\Theta(y_k^L)}^{1} f_{n-k+1,k}(r)dr \geq \gamma\right)\right\} = \beta.$$

(13)

A (γ, β) two-sided $\gamma-$ content tolerance interval with confidence level β can be obtained by using the following formula:

$$\begin{bmatrix} \arg_{y_k^L}\left(E\left\{\Pr\left(P_\Theta(Y_k > y_k^L|n) \geq \gamma\right)\right\} = \beta\right), \\ \arg_{y_k^U}\left(E\left\{\Pr\left(P_\Theta(Y_k \leq y_k^U|n) \geq \gamma\right)\right\} = \beta\right) \end{bmatrix}$$
$$= \begin{bmatrix} \arg_{y_k^L}\left(E\left\{\Pr\left(\int_{1-F_\Theta(y_k^L)}^{1} f_{n-k+1,k}(r)dr \leq 1 - \gamma\right)\right\} = \beta\right), \\ \arg_{y_k^U}\left(E\left\{\Pr\left(\int_{1-F_\Theta(y_k^U)}^{1} f_{n-k+1,k}(r)dr \geq \gamma\right)\right\} = \beta\right) \end{bmatrix} = \left[y_k^L, y_k^U\right].$$

(14)

3 Two-Parameter Exponential Distribution

Let $\mathbf{X} = (X_1 \leq \ldots \leq X_h)$ be the first h ordered observations (order statistics) in a sample of size m from the two-parameter exponential distribution with the probability density function

$$f_\Theta(x) = \vartheta^{-1}\exp\left(-\frac{x-\upsilon}{\vartheta}\right), \quad \vartheta > 0, \upsilon \geq 0,$$

(15)

and the cumulative probability distribution function

$$F_\Theta(x) = 1 - \exp\left(-\frac{x-\upsilon}{\vartheta}\right), \overline{F}_\Theta(x) = 1 - F_\Theta(x) = \exp\left(-\frac{x-\upsilon}{\vartheta}\right),$$

(16)

where $\Theta = (\upsilon, \vartheta)$, υ is the shift parameter and ϑ is the scale parameter. It is assumed that these parameters are unknown. In Type II censoring, which is of primary interest here, the number of survivors is fixed and X is a random variable. In this case, the likelihood function is given by

$$
\begin{aligned}
L(\upsilon, \vartheta) &= \prod_{i=1}^{h} f_\Theta(x_i)\big(\overline{F}_\Theta(x_h)\big)^{m-h} = \frac{1}{\vartheta^h} \exp\left(-\left[\sum_{i=1}^{h}(x_i - \upsilon) + (m-h)(x_h - \upsilon)\right]\bigg/\vartheta\right) \\
&= \frac{1}{\vartheta^h} \exp\left(-\sum_{i=1}^{h} \frac{(x_i - x_1 + x_1 - \upsilon)}{\vartheta}\right) \exp\left(-\frac{(m-h)(y_h - y_1 + y_1 - \upsilon)}{\vartheta}\right) \\
&= \frac{1}{\vartheta^{h-1}} \exp\left(-\frac{\sum_{i=1}^{h}(y_i - y_1) + (m-h)(y_h - y_1)}{\vartheta}\right) \frac{1}{\vartheta} \exp\left(-\frac{m(x_1 - \upsilon)}{\vartheta}\right) \\
&= \frac{1}{\vartheta^{h-1}} \exp\left(-\frac{s_h}{\vartheta}\right) \times \frac{1}{\vartheta} \exp\left(-\frac{m(s_1 - \upsilon)}{\vartheta}\right),
\end{aligned}
\tag{17}
$$

where

$$
\mathbf{S} = \left(S_1 = X_1,\ S_h = \sum_{i=1}^{h}(X_i - X_1) + (m-h)(X_h - X_1) \right)
\tag{18}
$$

is the complete sufficient statistic for $\Theta = (\upsilon, \vartheta)$,. The probability density function of $\mathbf{S} = (S_1, S_h)$ is given by

$$
\begin{aligned}
f_\Theta(s_1, s_h) &= \frac{\frac{1}{\vartheta^{h-1}}\exp\left(-\frac{s_h}{\vartheta}\right) \times \frac{1}{\vartheta}\exp\left(-\frac{h(s_1-\upsilon)}{\vartheta}\right)}{\frac{1}{s_h^{h-2}}\int_0^\infty \frac{s_h^{h-2}}{\vartheta^{h-1}}\exp\left(-\frac{s_h}{\vartheta}\right)ds_1 \times \frac{1}{m}\int_0^\infty \frac{m}{\vartheta}\exp\left(-\frac{m(s_1-\upsilon)}{\vartheta}\right)ds_1} \\
&= \frac{\frac{1}{\vartheta^{h-1}}\exp\left(-\frac{s_h}{\vartheta}\right) \times \frac{1}{\vartheta}\exp\left(-\frac{m(s_1-\upsilon)}{\vartheta}\right)}{\frac{\Gamma(h-1)}{s_h^{h-2}} \times \frac{1}{m}} = \frac{1}{\Gamma(h-1)\vartheta^{h-1}} s_h^{h-2}\exp\left(-\frac{s_h}{\vartheta}\right) \\
&\quad \times \frac{m}{\vartheta}\exp\left(-\frac{m(s_1-\upsilon)}{\vartheta}\right) = f_\vartheta(s_h)f_\Theta(s_1),
\end{aligned}
\tag{19}
$$

where

$$
f_\Theta(s_1) = \frac{m}{\vartheta}\exp\left(-\frac{m(s_1 - \upsilon)}{\vartheta}\right),\quad s_1 \geq \upsilon,
\tag{20}
$$

$$
f_\vartheta(s_h) = \frac{1}{\Gamma(h-1)\vartheta^{h-1}} s_h^{h-2}\exp\left(-\frac{s_h}{\vartheta}\right),\quad s_h \geq 0,
\tag{21}
$$

$$
V_1 = \frac{S_1 - \upsilon}{\vartheta}
\tag{22}
$$

is the pivotal quantity, the probability density function of which is given by

$$
f_1(v_1) = m\exp(-mv_1),\quad v_1 \geq 0,
\tag{23}
$$

$$V_h = \frac{S_h}{\vartheta} \tag{24}$$

is the pivotal quantity, the probability density function of which is given by

$$f_h(v_h) = \frac{1}{\Gamma(h-1)} v_h^{h-2} \exp(-v_h), \ v_h \geq 0. \tag{25}$$

3.1 Constructing a (γ, β) Upper, One-Sided $\gamma-$ Content Tolerance Limit with Confidence Level β for the Case of Model M_{Q1}

Theorem 2. Let $X_1 \leq \dots \leq X_h$ be the first h ordered observations from the preliminary sample of size m from a two-parameter exponential distribution defined by the probability density function (15). Then a (γ, β) upper one-sided γ-content tolerance limit (with a confidence level β) y_k^U on the kth order statistic Y_k from a set of n future ordered observations $Y_1 \leq \dots \leq Y_n$ also from the distribution (15), which satisfies.

$$E\left\{ \Pr\left(P_\rho(Y_k \leq y_k^U | n) \geq \gamma \right) \right\} = \beta, \tag{26}$$

is given by

$$y_k^U = \begin{cases} S_1 + \frac{S_h}{m} \left[1 - \left(\frac{\Omega_\gamma^m}{\beta} \right)^{\frac{1}{h-1}} \right], \text{ if } \left(\frac{\Omega_\gamma^m}{\beta} \right)^{\frac{1}{h-1}} \leq 1, \\[4mm] S_1 + \frac{S_h}{m} \left[\left(\frac{\Omega_\gamma^m}{\beta} \right)^{\frac{1}{h-1}} - 1 \right], \text{ if } \left(\frac{\Omega_\gamma^m}{\beta} \right)^{\frac{1}{h-1}} > 1, \end{cases} \tag{27}$$

where

$$\Omega_\gamma = 1 - q_{(k,n-k+1),\gamma} (Beta(k, n-k+1), \gamma \text{ quantile}). \tag{28}$$

Proof. It follows from (1) and (3) that

$$E\left\{\Pr\left(P_\rho(Y_k \leq y_k^U | n) \geq \gamma\right)\right\} = E\left\{\Pr\left(\int_0^{F_\rho(y_k^U)} f_{k,n-k+1}(r)dr \geq \gamma\right)\right\}$$

$$= E\left\{\Pr\left(1 - \exp\left(-\frac{y_k^U - \upsilon}{\vartheta}\right) \geq q_{k,n-k+1;\gamma}\right)\right\} = E\left\{\Pr\left(\exp\left(-\frac{y_k^U - \upsilon}{\vartheta}\right) \leq 1 - q_{k,n-k+1;\gamma}\right)\right\}$$

$$= E\left\{\Pr\left(-\frac{y_k^U - \upsilon}{\vartheta} \leq \ln(1 - q_{k,n-k+1;\gamma})\right)\right\} = E\left\{\Pr\left(\frac{y_k^U - \upsilon}{\vartheta} \geq -\ln(1 - q_{k,n-k+1;\gamma})\right)\right\}$$

$$= E\left\{\Pr\left(\frac{y_k^U - S_1}{S_h}\frac{S_h}{\vartheta} + \frac{S_1 - \upsilon}{\vartheta} \geq -\ln(1 - q_{k,n-k+1;\gamma})\right)\right\}$$

$$= E\left\{\Pr\left(\frac{S_1 - \upsilon}{\vartheta} \geq -\frac{y_k^U - S_1}{S_h}\frac{S_h}{\vartheta} - \ln(1 - q_{k,n-k+1;\gamma})\right)\right\}$$

$$= E\left\{\Pr\left(V_1 \geq -\eta_k^U V_h - \ln \Omega_\gamma\right)\right\} = E\left\{1 - \Pr\left(V_1 \leq -\eta_k^U V_h - \ln \Omega_\gamma\right)\right\}$$

$$= E\left\{1 - \int_0^{-\eta_k^U V_h - \ln \Omega_\gamma} f_1(v_1)dv_1\right\},$$

(29)

where

$$\eta_k^U = \frac{y_k^U - S_1}{S_h}. \tag{30}$$

It follows from (29) and (30) that

$$E\left\{1 - \int_0^{-\eta_k^U V_h - \ln \Omega_\gamma} f_1(v_1)dv_1\right\} = E\left\{1 - \int_0^{-\eta_k^U V_m - \ln \Omega_\gamma} m\exp(-mv_1)dv_1\right\}$$

$$= E\left\{1 - \left[1 - \exp\left(-m\left[-\eta_k^U V_h - \ln \Omega_\gamma\right]\right)\right]\right\}$$

$$= E\left\{\exp\left(m\eta_k^U V_h\right)\exp\left(\ln \Omega_{\gamma'}^m\right)\right\} = E\left\{\Omega_{\gamma'}^m \exp\left(m\eta_k^U V_h\right)\right\} \tag{31}$$

$$= \int_0^\infty \left(\Omega_\gamma^m \exp\left(m\eta_k^U v_h\right)\right)f_h(v_h)dv_h = \int_0^\infty \left(\Omega_\gamma^m \exp\left(m\eta_k^U v_h\right)\right)\frac{1}{\Gamma(h-1)}v_h^{h-2}\exp(-v_h)dv_h$$

$$= \Omega_\gamma^m \int_0^\infty \frac{1}{\Gamma(h-1)}v_h^{h-2}\exp\left(-v_h\left[1 - m\eta_k^U\right]\right)dv_h = \frac{\Omega_\gamma^m}{\left[1 - m\eta_k^U\right]^{h-1}} = \beta.$$

It follows from (30) and (31) that

$$\eta_k^U = \frac{y_k^U - S_1}{S_h} = \frac{1}{m}\left(1 - \left[\frac{\Omega_\gamma^m}{\beta}\right]^{\frac{1}{h-1}}\right). \tag{32}$$

It follows from (32) that

$$y_k^U = S_1 + \frac{S_h}{m}\left(1 - \left[\frac{\Omega_\gamma^m}{\beta}\right]^{\frac{1}{h-1}}\right). \tag{33}$$

Then (27) follows from (33). This ends the proof.

3.2 Constructing a (γ, β) Lower, One-Sided $\gamma-$ Content Tolerance Limit with Confidence Level β for the Case of Model M_{Q1}

Theorem 3. Let $X_1 \leq \dots \leq X_h$ be the first h ordered observations from the preliminary sample of size m from a two-parameter exponential distribution defined by the probability density function (15). Then the lower one-sided γ-content tolerance limit (with a confidence level β)y_k^L on the kth order statistic Y_k from a set of n future ordered observations $Y_1 \leq \dots \leq Y_n$ also from the distribution (15)), which satisfies.

Proof. It follows from (3) and (5) that

$$E\left\{\Pr\left(P_\mu(Y_k > y_k^L|n) \geq \gamma\right)\right\} = \beta, \tag{34}$$

is given by

$$y_k^L = \begin{cases} S_1 + \dfrac{S_h}{m}\left[1 - \left(\dfrac{\Omega_{1-\gamma}^m}{1-\beta}\right)^{\frac{1}{h-1}}\right], & \text{if } \left(\dfrac{\Omega_{1-\gamma}^m}{1-\beta}\right)^{\frac{1}{h-1}} \leq 1, \\[4mm] S_1 + \dfrac{S_h}{m}\left[\left(\dfrac{\Omega_{1-\gamma}^m}{1-\beta}\right)^{\frac{1}{h-1}} - 1\right], & \text{if } \left(\dfrac{\Omega_{1-\gamma}^m}{1-\beta}\right)^{\frac{1}{h-1}} > 1, \end{cases} \tag{35}$$

where

$$\Omega_{1-\gamma} = 1 - q_{(k,n-k+1),1-\gamma}\ (Beta(k, n-k+1), 1-\gamma \text{ quantile}). \tag{36}$$

$$\begin{aligned} E\left\{\Pr\left(P_\rho(Y_k > y_k^L|n) \geq \gamma\right)\right\} &= E\left\{\Pr\left(\int_0^{F_\rho(y_k^L)} f_{k,n-k+1}(r)dr \leq 1-\gamma\right)\right\} \\ &= E\left\{\Pr\left(\exp\left(-\frac{y_k^L - \upsilon}{\vartheta}\right) \geq 1 - q_{k,n-k+1;1-\gamma}\right)\right\} \\ &= E\left\{\Pr\left(\frac{y_k^L - S_1}{S_h}\frac{S_h}{\vartheta} + \frac{S_1 - \upsilon}{\vartheta} \leq -\ln\left(1 - q_{k,n-k+1;1-\gamma}\right)\right)\right\} \\ &= E\left\{\Pr\left(\frac{S_1 - \upsilon}{\vartheta} \leq -\frac{y_k^L - S_1}{S_h}\frac{S_h}{\vartheta} - \ln\left(1 - q_{k,n-k+1;1-\gamma}\right)\right)\right\} \\ &= E\left\{\Pr\left(V_1 \leq -\eta_k^L V_h - \ln\Omega_{1-\gamma}\right)\right\} = E\left\{\int_0^{-\eta_k^L V_h - \ln\Omega_{1-\gamma}} f_1(v_1)dv_1\right\}, \end{aligned} \tag{37}$$

where

$$\eta_k^L = \frac{y_k^L - S_1}{S_h}. \tag{38}$$

It follows from (23) and (37) that

$$E\left\{\int_0^{-\eta_k^L V_h - \ln \Omega_{1-\gamma}} f_1(v_1)dv_1\right\} = E\left\{\int_0^{-\eta_k^L V_h - \ln \Omega_{1-\gamma}} m\exp(-mv_1)dv_1\right\}$$

$$= E\left\{1 - \exp\left(-m\left[-\eta_k^L V_h - \ln \Omega_{1-\gamma}\right]\right)\right\}$$

$$= E\left\{1 - \exp\left(m\eta_k^L V_h\right)\exp\left(m\ln \Omega_{1-\gamma}\right)\right\} = E\left\{1 - \Omega_{1-\gamma}^m \exp\left(m\eta_k^L V_h\right)\right\}$$

$$= \int_0^\infty \left(1 - \Omega_{1-\gamma}^m \exp\left(m\eta_k^L v_m\right)\right) f_h(v_h)dv_h$$

$$= \int_0^\infty \left(1 - \Omega_{1-\gamma}^m \exp\left(m\eta_k^L v_h\right)\right) \frac{1}{\Gamma(h-1)} v_h^{h-2} \exp(-v_h)dv_h$$

$$= 1 - \Omega_{1-\gamma}^m \int_0^\infty \frac{1}{\Gamma(h-1)} v_h^{h-2} \exp\left(-v_h\left[1 - m\eta_k^L\right]\right)dv_h = 1 - \frac{\Omega_{1-\gamma}^m}{\left[1 - m\eta_k^L\right]^{h-1}} = \beta. \tag{39}$$

It follows from (38) and (39) that

$$\eta_k^L = \frac{y_k^L - S_1}{S_h} = \frac{1}{m}\left(1 - \left[\frac{\Omega_{1-\gamma}^m}{1-\beta}\right]^{\frac{1}{h-1}}\right). \tag{40}$$

It follows from (40) that

$$y_k^L = S_1 + \frac{S_h}{m}\left(1 - \left[\frac{\Omega_{1-\gamma}^m}{1-\beta}\right]^{\frac{1}{h-1}}\right). \tag{41}$$

3.3 Constructing a (γ, β) Lower, One-Sided $\gamma-$ Content Tolerance Limit with Confidence Level β for the Case of Model M_{Q1}

Let us assume that $k = 5$, $h = 8$, $m = 10$, $n = 12$, $\gamma = \beta = 0.95$,

$$\mathbf{S} = \left(S_1 = Y_1 = 9, \ S_h = \sum_{i=1}^h (Y_i - Y_1) + (m-h)(Y_h - Y_1)\right) \tag{42}$$

$$= (S_1 = 9, \ S_h = 0 + 1 + 2 + 4 + 6 + 10 + 15 + 23 + (10-8)23 = 107),$$

then, the ($\gamma = 0.95$, $\beta = 0.95$) upper, one-sided $\gamma -$ content tolerance limit y_k^U with confidence level β can be obtained from (27), where the quantile of $Beta(k, n-k+1), \gamma$ is given by

$$q_{(k,n-k+1),\gamma} = 0.609138, \tag{43}$$

$$\Omega_{1-\gamma} = 1 - q_{(k,n-k+1),1-\gamma} = 1 - 0.609138 = 0.390862. \tag{44}$$

It follows from (27), (42) and (44) that

$$y_k^U = S_1 + \frac{S_h}{m}\left[1 - \left(\frac{\Omega_\gamma^m}{\beta}\right)^{\frac{1}{h-1}}\right] = 9 + \frac{107}{10}\left[\left(1 - \frac{[0.390862]^{10}}{0.95}\right)^{\frac{1}{8-1}}\right] \tag{45}$$

$$= 9 + 7.883285 = 16.883285.$$

The ($\gamma = 0.95$, $\beta = 0.95$) lower, one-sided $\gamma -$ content tolerance limit y_k^U with confidence level β can be obtained from (35), where the quantile of $Beta(k, n - k + 1), 1 - \gamma$ is given by

$$q_{(k,n-k+1),1-\gamma} = 0.181025, \tag{46}$$

$$\Omega_{1-\gamma} = 1 - q_{(k,n-k+1),1-\gamma} = 1 - 0.181025 = 0.818975. \tag{47}$$

It follows from (35), (42) and (47) that

$$y_k^L = S_1 + \frac{S_h}{m}\left[\left(\frac{\Omega^m}{1-\beta}\right)^{\frac{1}{h-1}} - 1\right] = 9 + \frac{107}{10}\left[\left(\frac{[0.818975]^{10}}{1 - 0.95}\right)^{\frac{1}{8-1}} - 1\right] \tag{48}$$

$$= 9 + \frac{107}{10}[1.15335326 - 1] = 10.64088.$$

The ($\gamma = 0.95$, $\beta = 0.95$) two-sided $\gamma -$ content tolerance interval with confidence level β can be obtained by using (6), (45) and (48):

$$\left[y_k^L, y_k^U\right] = [10.64088, 16.883285]. \tag{49}$$

4 Intelligent Derivation of the Density Function of the Student's T Distribution

Theorem 4. If $W_1 \in N(0, 1)$ and $W_2 \in \chi^2(\nu)$ are independent random variables, then

Proof.
$$W_1/\sqrt{W_2/\nu} = T(\nu), \tag{50}$$

where $t(\nu)$ follows the student's t distribution with ν degrees of freedom,

$$t(\nu) \sim f(t) = \frac{\Gamma\big((\nu + 1)/2\big)}{\sqrt{\pi \nu}\,\Gamma(\nu/2)}\left[1 + \frac{t^2}{\nu}\right]^{-(\nu+1)/2}, \quad -\infty < t < \infty. \tag{51}$$

$$w_1 \sim f_1(w_1) = \frac{1}{\sqrt{2\pi}} \exp\left(-\frac{w_1^2}{2}\right), \quad -\infty < w_1 < \infty, \tag{52}$$

where

$$w_1 = t\left[\frac{w_2}{v}\right]^{1/2}, \quad dw_1 = \left[\frac{w_2}{v}\right]^{1/2} dt. \tag{53}$$

It follows from (52) and (53) that

$$f_1(w_1)dw_1 = \frac{1}{\sqrt{2\pi}} \exp\left(-\frac{w_1^2}{2}\right)dw_1 = \frac{1}{\sqrt{2\pi}} \exp\left(-\frac{t^2[w_2/v]}{2}\right)\left[\frac{w_2}{v}\right]^{1/2} dt \tag{54}$$

$$= f(t|w_2)dt, \quad -\infty < t < \infty.$$

$$w_2 \sim f_2(w_2) = \frac{1}{\Gamma(v/2)2^{v/2}} w_2^{(v/2)-1} \exp\left(-\frac{w_2}{2}\right), \quad 0 < w_2 < \infty. \tag{55}$$

It follows from (54) and (55) that

$$f(t) = \int_0^\infty f(t|w_2)f_2(w_2)dw_2$$

$$= \int_0^\infty \frac{1}{\sqrt{2\pi}} \exp\left(-\frac{t^2[w_2/v]}{2}\right)\left[\frac{w_2}{v}\right]^{1/2} \times \frac{1}{\Gamma(v/2)2^{v/2}} w_2^{(v/2)-1} \exp\left(-\frac{w_2}{2}\right)dw_2 \tag{56}$$

$$= \int_0^\infty \frac{1}{\sqrt{\pi v}\Gamma(v/2)2^{(v+1)/2}} w_2^{(v+1)/2)-1} \exp\left(-\frac{w_2}{2}\left[1+\frac{t^2}{v}\right]\right)dw_2$$

$$= \frac{\Gamma((v+1)/2)}{\sqrt{\pi v}\,\Gamma(v/2)}\left[1+\frac{t^2}{v}\right]^{-(v+1)/2}, \quad -\infty < t < \infty.$$

This ends the proof.

5   Confidence Interval for the Difference of Means of Two Different Normal Populations

In most applications, two populations are compared using the difference in the means. Let $U_1, U_2,..., U_m$ be a sample of size m from a normal population having mean μ_m and variance σ_m^2 and let $Z_1,..., Z_n$ be a sample of size n from a different normal population having mean μ_n and variance σ_n^2 and suppose that the two samples are independent of each other. We are interested in constructing a confidence interval for $\mu_m - \mu_n$. To obtain this confidence interval, we need the distribution of $\overline{U}_m - \overline{Z}_n$, where

$$\overline{U}_m = \sum_{i=1}^m U_i \bigg/ m \sim N\left(\mu_m, \sigma_m^2/m\right), \overline{Z}_n = \sum_{i=1}^m Z_i \bigg/ n \sim N\left(\mu_n, \sigma_n^2/n\right). \tag{57}$$

It follows from (57) that

$$\overline{U}_m - \overline{Z}_n \sim N\left(\mu_m - \mu_n, \frac{\sigma_m^2}{m} + \frac{\sigma_n^2}{n}\right).$$ (58)

It follows from (58) that

$$\frac{\overline{U}_m - \overline{Z}_n - (\mu_m - \mu_n)}{\sqrt{\sigma_m^2/m + \sigma_n^2/n}} = W_1 \sim N(0, 1).$$ (59)

This is independent of

$$\sum_{i=1}^{m}\left(U_i - \overline{U}_m\right)^2 \Big/ \sigma_m^2 = \frac{(m-1)\sum_{i=1}^{m}\left(U_i - \overline{U}_m\right)^2}{\sigma_m^2 \quad (m-1)} = \frac{(m-1)S_m^2}{\sigma_m^2} \sim \chi_{m-1}^2$$ (60)

and

$$\sum_{i=1}^{n}\left(Z_i - \overline{Z}_n\right)^2 \Big/ \sigma_n^2 = \frac{(n-1)\sum_{i=1}^{n}(Z_i - \overline{Z}_n)^2}{\sigma_n^2 \quad (n-1)} = \frac{(n-1)S_n^2}{\sigma_n^2} \sim \chi_{n-1}^2,$$ (61)

where

$$\frac{(m-1)S_m^2}{\sigma_m^2} + \frac{(n-1)S_n^2}{\sigma_n^2} = W_2 \sim \chi^2(m+n-2).$$ (62)

Taking (50), (59) and (62) into account, we have that

$$\frac{W_1}{\sqrt{W_2/(m+n-2)}} = \frac{\dfrac{\overline{U}_m - \overline{Z}_n - (\mu_m - \mu_n)}{\sqrt{\sigma_m^2/m + \sigma_n^2/n}}}{\sqrt{\left(\dfrac{(m-1)S_m^2}{\sigma_m^2} + \dfrac{(n-1)S_n^2}{\sigma_n^2}\right)\Big/(m+n-2)}}$$ (63)

$$= \frac{\overline{U}_m - \overline{Z}_n - (\mu_m - \mu_n)}{\sqrt{(m-1)S_m^2/\sigma_m^2 + (n-1)S_n^2/\sigma_n^2}}\sqrt{\frac{m+n-2}{\sigma_m^2/m + \sigma_n^2/n}} = T(m+n-2) \sim f(t),$$

where $T(m+n\;2)$ is a t random variable with $m\;|\;n\;\;2$ degrees of freedom,

$$f(t) = \frac{\Gamma\big((m+n-1)/2\big)}{\sqrt{\pi(m+n-2)}\,\Gamma((m+n-2)/2)}$$

$$\times \left[1 + \frac{t^2}{m+n-2}\right]^{-(m+n-1)/2}, \quad -\infty < t < \infty.$$ (64)

Using (63) and (64), it can be obtained a $100(1 - \alpha)\%$ confidence interval for $\overline{U}_m - \overline{Z}_n - (\mu_m - \mu_n)$ from

$$P(t_1 \leq T(m+n-2) \leq t_2)$$

$$= P\left(t_1 \leq \frac{\overline{U}_m - \overline{Z}_n - (\mu_m - \mu_n)}{\sqrt{(m-1)S_m^2/\sigma_m^2 + (n-1)S_n^2/\sigma_n^2}} \frac{\sqrt{m+n-2}}{\sqrt{\sigma_m^2/m + \sigma_n^2/n}} \leq t_2 \right)$$

$$= P\left(\begin{array}{c} t_1 \sqrt{\dfrac{(m-1)S_m^2/\sigma_m^2 + (n-1)S_n^2/\sigma_n^2}{m+n-2}} \sqrt{\sigma_m^2/m + \sigma_n^2/n} \\ \leq \overline{U}_m - \overline{Z}_n - (\mu_m - \mu_n) \\ \leq t_2 \sqrt{\dfrac{(m-1)S_m^2/\sigma_m^2 + (n-1)S_n^2/\sigma_n^2}{m+n-2}} \sqrt{\sigma_m^2/m + \sigma_n^2/n} \end{array} \right) = 1 - \alpha \qquad (65)$$

by suitably choosing the decision variables t_1 and t_2. Hence, the statistical confidence interval for $\overline{U}_m - \overline{Z}_n - (\mu_m - \mu_n)$ is given by

$$\left(\begin{array}{c} t_1 \sqrt{\dfrac{(m-1)S_m^2/\sigma_m^2 + (n-1)S_n^2/\sigma_n^2}{m+n-2}} \sqrt{\sigma_m^2/m + \sigma_n^2/n}, \\ t_2 \sqrt{\dfrac{(m-1)S_m^2/\sigma_m^2 + (n-1)S_n^2/\sigma_n^2}{m+n-2}} \sqrt{\sigma_m^2/m + \sigma_n^2/n} \end{array} \right), \qquad (66)$$

The length of the statistical confidence interval for $\overline{U}_m - \overline{Z}_n - (\mu_m - \mu_n)$ is given by

$$L\left(t_1, t_2 | \sqrt{\dfrac{(m-1)S_m^2/\sigma_m^2 + (n-1)S_n^2/\sigma_n^2}{m+n-2}} \sqrt{\sigma_m^2/m + \sigma_n^2/n} \right)$$

$$= (t_2 - t_1) \left(\sqrt{\dfrac{(m-1)S_m^2/\sigma_m^2 + (n-1)S_n^2/\sigma_n^2}{m+n-2}} \sqrt{\sigma_m^2/m + \sigma_n^2/n} \right). \qquad (67)$$

In order to find the confidence interval of shortest-length for $\overline{U}_m - \overline{Z}_n - (\mu_m - \mu_n)$, we should find a pair of decision variables t_1 and t_2 such that (67) is minimum. It follows from (64) and (65) that

$$\int_{t_1}^{t_2} f(t)dt = \int_0^{t_2} f(t)dt - \int_0^{t_1} f(t)dt = (1 - \alpha + p) - p = 1 - \alpha, \qquad (68)$$

where p $(0 \leq p \leq \alpha)$ is a decision variable,

$$\int_0^{t_2} f(t)dt = 1 - \alpha + p \qquad (69)$$

and

$$\int_0^{t_1} f(t)dt = p. \tag{70}$$

Then t_2 represents the $(1 - \alpha + p)$- quantile, which is given by

$$t_2 = q_{1-\alpha+p;(t(m+n-2))}, \tag{71}$$

t_1 represents the p- quantile, which is given by

$$t_1 = q_{p;(t(m+n-2))}. \tag{72}$$

The shortest length confidence interval for $\overline{U}_m - \overline{Z}_n - (\mu_m - \mu_n)$ can be found as follows:

Minimize

$$(t_2 - t_1)^2 = \left(q_{1-\alpha+p;(t(m+n-2))} - q_{p;(t(m+n-2))}\right)^2 \tag{73}$$

subject to

$$0 \le p \le \alpha, \tag{74}$$

The optimal numerical solution minimizing $(t_2 - t_1)^2$ can be obtained using the standard computer software "Solver" of Excel 2016. If $\sigma_m^2 = \sigma_n^2$, it follows from (67) that

$$L\left(t_1, t_2 \middle| \sqrt{\frac{(m-1)S_m^2 + (n-1)S_n^2}{m+n-2}} \sqrt{\frac{m+n}{mn}}\right) = (t_2 - t_1)\sqrt{\frac{(m-1)S_m^2 + (n-1)S_n^2}{m+n-2}} \sqrt{\frac{m+n}{mn}}. \tag{75}$$

If, for example, $m = 58$, $n = 27$, $\alpha = 0.05$, $\overline{U}_m = 70.7$, $\overline{Z}_n = 76.13$, $S_m^2 = (1.8)^2$, $S_n^2 = (2.42)^2$, then the optimal numerical solution of (73) is given by

$$p = 0.025, \ t_1 = q_{p;(t(m+n-2))} = -1.98896, \ t_2 = q_{1-\alpha+p;(t(m+n-2))} = 1.98896 \tag{76}$$

and it follows from (65) and (75) that the $100(1 - \alpha)\%$ confidence interval of shortest-length (or equal tails) for $\mu_m - \mu_n$ is given by

$$(\mu_m - \mu_n)$$

$$\in \left(\begin{array}{c} (\overline{U}_m - \overline{Z}_n) - t_2\sqrt{\dfrac{(m-1)S_m^2 + (n-1)S_n^2}{m+n-2}} \sqrt{\dfrac{m+n}{mn}}, \\[2ex] (\overline{U}_m - \overline{Z}_n) - t_1\sqrt{\dfrac{(m-1)S_m^2 + (n-1)S_n^2}{m+n-2}} \sqrt{\dfrac{m+n}{mn}} \end{array} \right) = (-6.330947, -4.52905) \tag{77}$$

or

$$-6.330947 \le \mu_m - \mu_n \le -4.52905. \tag{78}$$

6 Confidence Interval for the Ratio of Means of Two Different Normal Populations

Ratio in the means is used to compare two populations of positive data. Let $U_1, U_2, \ldots, U_m$ be a sample of size m from a normal population having mean μ_m and variance σ_m^2 and let $U_1, \ldots, U_n$ be a sample of size n from a different normal population having mean μ_n and variance σ_n^2 and suppose that the two samples are independent of each other. We are interested in constructing a confidence interval for the ratio of means (μ_m, μ_n) of two different normal populations To obtain this confidence interval, we need the distribution of $\overline{U}_m - \kappa \overline{U}_n$, where

$$\overline{U}_m = \sum_{i=1}^{m} U_i \Big/ m \sim N\left(\mu_m, \sigma_m^2/m\right), \ \overline{U}_n = \sum_{i=1}^{n} U_i \Big/ n \sim N\left(\mu_n, \sigma_n^2/n\right). \tag{79}$$

It can be shown that

$$\overline{U}_m - \kappa \overline{U}_n \sim N\left(\mu_m - \kappa \mu_n, \ \frac{\sigma_m^2}{m} + \frac{\kappa^2 \sigma_n^2}{n}\right) \tag{80}$$

or

$$\frac{\overline{U}_m - \kappa \overline{U}_n - (\mu_m - \kappa \mu_n)}{\sqrt{\frac{\sigma_m^2}{m} + \frac{\kappa^2 \sigma_n^2}{n}}} = W_1 \sim N(0, 1). \tag{81}$$

This is independent of

$$\sum_{i=1}^{m} \left(U_i - \overline{U}_m\right)^2 \Big/ \sigma_m^2 = \frac{(m-1)}{\sigma_m^2} \frac{\sum_{i=1}^{m} \left(U_i - \overline{U}_m\right)^2}{(m-1)} = \frac{(m-1)S_m^2}{\sigma_m^2} \sim \chi_{m-1}^2 \tag{82}$$

and

$$\sum_{j=1}^{n} \left(U_j - \overline{U}_n\right)^2 \Big/ \sigma_n^2 = \frac{(n-1)}{\sigma_n^2} \frac{\sum_{j=1}^{n} \left(U_j - \overline{U}_n\right)^2}{(n-1)} = \frac{(n-1)S_n^2}{\sigma_n^2} \sim \chi_{n-1}^2, \tag{83}$$

where

$$\frac{(m-1)S_m^2}{\sigma_m^2} + \frac{(n-1)S_n^2}{\sigma_n^2} = W_2 \sim \chi^2(m+n-2). \tag{84}$$

It follows from (50), (81) and (84) that

$$
\frac{W_1}{\sqrt{W_2/(m+n-2)}} = \frac{\overline{U}_m - \kappa \overline{U}_n - (\mu_m - \kappa \mu_n)}{\sqrt{\frac{\sigma_m^2}{m} + \frac{\kappa^2 \sigma_n^2}{n}}} \frac{1}{\sqrt{\left[\frac{(m-1)S_m^2}{\sigma_m^2} + \frac{(n-1)S_n^2}{\sigma_n^2}\right] / (m+n-2)}}
$$

$$
= \frac{\overline{U}_m - \kappa \overline{U}_n - (\mu_m - \kappa \mu_n)}{\sqrt{(m-1)S_m^2/\sigma_m^2 + (n-1)S_n^2/\sigma_n^2}} \sqrt{\frac{m+n-2}{\sigma_m^2/m + \kappa^2 \sigma_n^2/n}} = T(m+n-2) \sim f(t),
$$
(85)

where $T(m+n\text{-}2)$ is a t-random variable with $m+n-2$ degrees of freedom. Taking (64) into account, we have that

$$
f(t) = \frac{\Gamma((m+n-1)/2)}{\sqrt{\pi(m+n-2)}\,\Gamma((m+n-2)/2)} \left[1 + \frac{t^2}{m+n-2}\right]^{-(m+n-1)/2}, \quad -\infty < t < \infty.
$$
(86)

Using (85) and (86), it can be obtained a $100(1-\alpha)\%$ confidence interval for $\overline{U}_m - \kappa \overline{U}_n - (\mu_m - \kappa \mu_n)$ from

$$
P\big(t_1 \le T\big(m+n-2|\overline{U}_m - \kappa \overline{U}_n - (\mu_m - \kappa \mu_n)\big) \le t_2\big)
$$

$$
= P\left(t_1 \le \frac{\overline{U}_m - \kappa \overline{U}_n - (\mu_m - \kappa \mu_n)}{\sqrt{(m-1)S_m^2/\sigma_m^2 + (n-1)S_n^2/\sigma_n^2}} \frac{\sqrt{m+n-2}}{\sqrt{\sigma_m^2/m + \kappa^2 \sigma_n^2/n}} \le t_2\right)
$$

$$
= P\left(\begin{array}{l} t_1\sqrt{\dfrac{(m-1)S_m^2/\sigma_m^2 + (n-1)S_n^2/\sigma_n^2}{m+n-2}}\sqrt{\sigma_m^2/m + \kappa^2 \sigma_n^2/n} \\[2mm] \le \overline{U}_m - \kappa \overline{U}_n - (\mu_m - \kappa \mu_n) \\[2mm] \le t_2\sqrt{\dfrac{(m-1)S_m^2/\sigma_m^2 + (n-1)S_n^2/\sigma_n^2}{m+n-2}}\sqrt{\sigma_m^2/m + \kappa^2 \sigma_n^2/n} \end{array}\right) = 1-\alpha
$$
(87)

by suitably choosing the decision variables t_1 and t_2. An analytical expression for determining the optimal value of κ (the ratio in means of two different normal populations) can be obtained from (87), where it is assumed that $\sigma_m^2 = \sigma_n^2$ and $(\mu_m - \kappa \mu_n) = 0$:

$$
\begin{pmatrix} t_1 \sqrt{\dfrac{(m-1)S_m^2 + (n-1)S_n^2}{m+n-2}} \sqrt{1/m + \kappa^2/n} \\ \leq \overline{U}_m - \kappa \overline{U}_n \\ \leq t_2 \sqrt{\dfrac{(m-1)S_m^2 + (n-1)S_n^2}{m+n-2}} \sqrt{1/m + \kappa^2/n} \end{pmatrix}
$$

$$
= \begin{pmatrix} \kappa \leq \dfrac{\overline{U}_m}{\overline{U}_n} - t_1 \dfrac{\sqrt{\frac{(m-1)S_m^2 + (n-1)S_n^2}{m+n-2}}}{\overline{U}_n} \sqrt{1/m + \kappa^2/n}, \\ \kappa \geq \dfrac{\overline{U}_m}{\overline{U}_n} - t_2 \dfrac{\sqrt{\frac{(m-1)S_m^2 + (n-1)S_n^2}{m+n-2}}}{\overline{U}_n} \sqrt{1/m + \kappa^2/n} \end{pmatrix}
$$

$$
= \begin{pmatrix} \kappa \leq 0.926656 + 2.306 \dfrac{10.6}{126.8} \sqrt{1/6 + \kappa^2/4}, \\ \kappa \geq 0.926656 - 2.306 \dfrac{10.6}{126.8} \sqrt{1/6 + \kappa^2/4} \end{pmatrix} \tag{88}
$$

$$
= \begin{pmatrix} \kappa \leq 0.926656 + 0.192773 \sqrt{0.166667 + 0.25\kappa^2}, \\ \kappa \geq 0.926656 - 0.192773 \sqrt{0.166667 + 0.25\kappa^2} \end{pmatrix}
$$

$$
\Rightarrow \begin{pmatrix} \text{minimize:} \\ \left(\kappa - 0.926656 - 0.192773 \sqrt{0.166667 + 0.25\kappa^2} \right)^2, \\ \left(\kappa - 0.926656 + 0.192773 \sqrt{0.166667 + 0.25\kappa^2} \right)^2, \\ \text{subject to: } \kappa \geq 0. \end{pmatrix}
$$

$$
= (\kappa \leq 1.05526, \ \kappa \geq 0.815431).
$$

Thus, it follows from (88) that

$$
\kappa \in (0.815431, \ 1.05526). \tag{89}
$$

7 Conclusion

The new intelligent computational models proposed in this paper are conceptually simple, efficient, and useful for constructing accurate statistical tolerance or prediction limits and shortest-length or equal-tailed confidence intervals under the parametric uncertainty of applied stochastic models. The methods listed above are based on adequate computational models of the cumulative distribution function of order statistics and constructive use of the invariance principle in mathematical statistics. These methods can be used to solve real-life problems in all areas including engineering, science, industry, automation & robotics, machine learning, business & finance, medicine and biomedicine, optimization, planning and scheduling.

Acknowledgments. None.

Conflicts of Interest. The authors declare that there is no conflict of interest.

References

1. Nechval, N., Vasermanis, E.: Improved decisions in statistics. Izglitibas soli, Riga (2004)
2. Nechval, N., Berzins, G., Purgailis, M., Nechval, K.: Improved estimation of state of stochastic systems via invariant embedding technique. WSEAS Trans. Math. **7**, 141–159 (2008)
3. Nechval, N., Nechval, K., Danovich, V., Liepins, T.: Optimization of new-sample and within-sample prediction intervals for order statistics. In: Proceedings of the 2011 World Congress in Computer Science, Computer Engineering, and Applied Computing, WORLDCOMP'11, July 18–21, pp. 91−97. Las Vegas Nevada, USA, CSREA Press (2011)
4. Nechval, N., Nechval, K., Berzins, G.: A new unified computational method for finding confidence intervals of shortest length and/or equal tails under parametric uncertainty. In: Proceedings of the 2021 International Conference on Computational Science and Computational Intelligence (CSCI), 15–17 December 2021, pp. 533–539. IEEE, Las Vegas, NV, USA (2021)
5. Nechval, N., Berzins, G., Nechval, K.: Intelligent computational approach to constructing adequate statistical decisions under parametric uncertainty of applied stochastic models. In: Proceedings of the 2022 International Conference on Computational Science and Computational Intelligence, 14–16 December 2022, pp. 522–529. IEEE, Las Vegas, United States (2023)
6. Nechval, N., Berzins, G., Nechval, K.: Adequate mathematical models of the cumulative distribution function of order statistics to construct accurate tolerance limits and confidence intervals of the shortest length or equal tails. WSEAS Trans. Math. **20**, 154–166 (2023)
7. Nechval, N., Berzins, G., Nechval, K.: Optimal statistical estimation and dynamic adaptive control of airline seat protection levels for several nested fare classes under parametric uncertainty of customer demand models. WSEAS Trans. Math. **22**, 395–408 (2023)

A Smart Air Quality Analysis and Pollutant Diffusion Detection and Prediction System Based on Tree Canopy Shape Research Using Machine Learning and Artificial Intelligence

Mingyuan Liu[1]([⊠]) and Ang Li[2]

[1] Montverde Academy Shanghai, Shanghai, China
2549979963@qq.com
[2] EECS Department, California State University, Long Beach, USA

Abstract. This project represents a significant foray into the intersection of computational fluid dynamics (CFD), machine learning, and environmental science [1]. By integrating CFD results with the predictive capabilities of computer vision and AI, we have crafted a multifaceted approach that not only serves environmental sciences by forecasting air quality but also advances the field of machine learning with its interdisciplinary applications [2].

The developed model stands as a testament to this synergy, exhibiting high levels of accuracy in its predictions, albeit with occasional outliers. Recognizing the model's substantial promise, we are committed to its ongoing refinement. Future efforts will be channeled into expanding its data foundation and exploring innovative algorithmic strategies, underscoring our long-term commitment to enhancing the project's contribution to both scientific domains. This sustained investment is poised to solidify and extend the practical and theoretical benefits of our interdisciplinary methodology.

Keywords: Tree Canopy · Machine Learning · Air Quality

1 Introduction

Air quality in urban areas is a pressing issue, affecting the health and quality of life of residents. The dynamics of air quality are influenced by a variety of factors, including vehicle emissions, the design of urban streets, and prevailing weather conditions, particularly within "street canyons" formed by high buildings along narrow streets [3]. These elements interact in complex ways, making the task of assessing and forecasting urban air quality particularly challenging.

Furthermore, the dynamic nature of urban traffic flow and its correlation with industrial activities contribute to fluctuating levels of air pollution [4]. The presence of green spaces and local topography also play pivotal roles in determining air circulation patterns, which in turn affect pollutant dispersal and concentration in urban areas. Understanding these intricate relationships is essential for developing effective air quality management strategies that can mitigate health risks and enhance the urban living environment [5].

Our approach enhances these methodologies by integrating real-time IoT air quality sensor data, detailed phenological data on tree canopies, and weather conditions into a machine learning model [19]. This enables not only real-time analysis but also predictive insights based on current environmental conditions, offering a more adaptive and comprehensive tool for urban air quality management.

Machine learning has increasingly become an invaluable tool across various research disciplines, particularly in projects focusing on environmental protection and public health within urban settings. In this study, we employ machine learning models, trained using TensorFlow, to assess and predict Air Quality Index (AQI) levels in urban street canyons [20]. These areas, characterized by their unique architectural configurations that can trap pollutants, present specific challenges for environmental modeling.

To address these challenges, we integrated Computational Fluid Dynamics (CFD) modeling with our machine learning algorithms to enhance our understanding of how various environmental factors influence AQI levels [1]. The synthesis of CFD modeling with AI technologies allows for more precise predictions and deeper insights into pollutant distribution patterns in confined urban spaces [6].

In subsequent sections of this paper, we will detail the processes involved in acquiring and analyzing our dataset, which includes multiple variables impacting urban air quality. We will also describe the specific machine learning algorithms we utilized, explaining how they contribute to our ability to forecast AQI with greater accuracy [23]. This approach not only advances our methodological framework but also significantly bolsters our capability to devise more effective strategies for mitigating air pollution in densely populated areas.

Our model's capacity to forecast the Air Quality Index with a margin of error of 5.53 within a 95% confidence interval underscores its proficiency [22]. With this narrow margin, the model stands as a valuable tool for accurate AQI prediction, a testament to the success of the innovative methodology we've introduced. By synthesizing artificial intelligence, specifically machine learning, with environmental science, we've taken a step toward quantitative predictions that can inform and enhance real-world applications. This interdisciplinary fusion not only enriches the field of environmental science with advanced analytical tools but also expands the practical applications of machine learning, paving the way for more informed decision-making in public health and environmental policy.

2 Challenges

2.1 Collect Data

One of the initial challenges we encountered was how to efficiently collect the vast amount of data required for the machine learning component of our project. Initially, we attempted to manually gather screenshots from Google Map Satellite View and Air Quality Indexes (AQI) [21]. However, it quickly became apparent that this method was too labor-intensive and time-consuming.

To streamline this process, we shifted to utilizing Google Map APIs, which allowed us to automatically capture screenshots at various coordinates. Simultaneously, we sourced the corresponding AQI data from official weather forecast websites. This approach significantly reduced our workload and improved the efficiency of data collection, enabling us to focus more on the analysis and application of the data.

2.2 Integrate Image and Numerical Data

The next step in our project involved developing a machine learning model that efficiently integrates image and numerical data. We chose a Convolutional Neural Network (CNN) for this task, given its effectiveness in computer vision applications [7]. CNNs are well-suited for our needs due to their deep learning architecture, which processes data through multiple layers. These layers are capable of extracting and learning from complex patterns in the data, making CNNs ideal for handling the mixed data types in our study. In subsequent sections, we will detail the configuration of our CNN, its training process, and the optimizations made for enhanced performance with our specific dataset.

2.3 Enhance Model Accuracy

Later in the project, we faced the challenge of enhancing model accuracy and avoiding overfitting. To tackle this, we implemented a train-test-validation split, organizing the datasets into three distinct groups. This method allowed us to train the model on one set of data, test its performance on another, and validate it on a third set. By employing this approach, we were able to monitor the model's real-time accuracy and stability through graphs generated from the testing and validation datasets. This continuous evaluation helped us identify and implement improvements, ensuring the model's robustness and reliability.

3 Solution

The project initiated with an exploration of the identified problem and proposed methodologies before transitioning into the data collection phase, which marks the formal beginning of our study. We utilized the Google Map Satellite View API and sourced AQI data from official meteorological websites to create a combined image-numerical dataset. This dataset underpins our machine learning model constructed using a Convolutional Neural Network (CNN).

To ensure the model's accuracy and stability, we implemented a train-test-validation cycle. This method not only allows for ongoing adjustments based on performance feedback but also helps in mitigating the risk of overfitting.

Further in our research, we employed the Google Maps' Satellite View, accessed via the Google Maps API, to pinpoint exact geographical coordinates for street-level air quality analysis. We enhanced these data points by overlaying them with historical Air Quality Index (AQI) data, allowing us to study the correlation between atmospheric conditions and observed satellite imagery over time.

Our predictive models are powered by TensorFlow, a robust machine learning library, which trains on datasets that integrate visual data from Google Maps with corresponding AQI values. The objective is to identify patterns in environmental quality across urban canyons, providing insights into pollution trends.

To evaluate our models effectively, we analyze various performance metrics such as Model Loss, Mean Squared Error (MSE), Mean Squared Logarithmic Error (MSLE), R-Square, and Mean Absolute Error (MAE) [8]. We also employ heat maps to visually represent pollutant concentrations, offering an intuitive understanding of air quality variations across different regions. This comprehensive approach enhances our model's reliability for real-world applications, deepening our understanding of urban air quality dynamics and facilitating better environmental management strategies (Figs. 1 and 2).

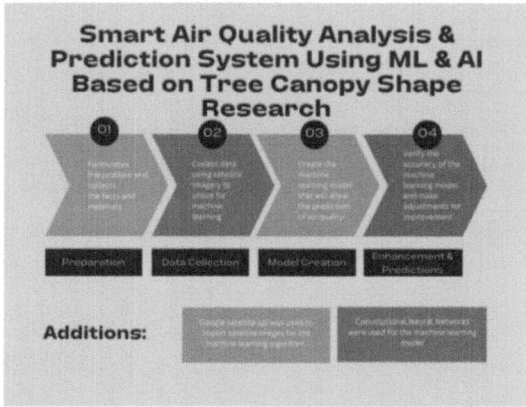

Fig. 1. The overview of the solution

The code demonstrates how to use a pre-trained deep learning model to predict the Air Quality Index (AQI) from images using Python, OpenCV, and TensorFlow. Here's a breakdown of its functionalities:

Imports and Setup: The code begins by importing necessary libraries. os for interacting with the operating system, cv2 (OpenCV) for image processing, numpy for numerical operations, and TensorFlow's load_model function to load the pre-trained model along with backend for custom metric functions.

Custom Metric Functions: Two functions, mse_metric and r_square, are defined to evaluate the model's predictions. mse_metric calculates the Mean Squared Error between the true and predicted values, a common measure of prediction accuracy. r_square, or the coefficient of determination, provides a measure of how well observed outcomes are replicated by the model.

Model Loading: The pre-trained model is loaded from a specified path with the custom metrics defined earlier. This model is trained to predict AQI from images.

Image Preprocessing: The preprocess_image function reads an image from a given path, resizes it to 128x128 pixels (a requirement of the model), and normalizes its pixel values to the range [0,1], preparing it for prediction.

```
# Load images and labels directly into arrays
images = []
labels = []

for index, row in df.iterrows():
    filename = row['File_Name']
    image_path = os.path.join(path_to_images, filename)
    img = cv2.imread(image_path)  # Use cv2 for image loading
    if img is None:
        print(f"Error: Unable to read the image: {image_path}")
        continue  # Skip to the next iteration
    img = cv2.resize(img, (128, 128))
    img_array = img / 255.0  # Normalize to [0, 1]
    label = row['AQI']
    print(f"Original Image Size: {img.shape}")

    images.append(img_array)
    labels.append(label)
# Define the architecture of the model
model = keras.Sequential([
    layers.Conv2D(32, (3, 3), activation = 'relu', input_shape = (128, 128, 3)),
    layers.MaxPooling2D((2, 2)),
    layers.Conv2D(64, (3, 3), activation = 'relu'),
    layers.MaxPooling2D((2, 2)),
    layers.Conv2D(128, (3, 3), activation = 'relu'),
    layers.MaxPooling2D((2, 2)),
    layers.Flatten(),
    layers.Dense(128, activation = 'relu'),
    layers.Dropout(0.5),
    layers.Dense(64, activation = 'relu'),
    layers.Dropout(0.5),
    layers.Dense(1)
])

# Define custom metrics
def mse_metric(y_true, y_pred):
    return K.mean(K.square(y_true - y_pred))

def r_square(y_true, y_pred):
    SS_res = K.sum(K.square(y_true - y_pred))
    SS_tot = K.sum(K.square(y_true - K.mean(y_true)))
    r2 = 1 - SS_res / (SS_tot + K.epsilon())
    return K.clip(r2, 0, 1)
```

Fig. 2. Screenshot of code 1

Prediction Function: predict_aqi takes an image path and the loaded model, preprocesses the image using the previously defined function, expands its dimensions (to fit the model's input requirements), and predicts the AQI. The prediction is then returned.

Prediction Loop: The code iterates over all image files in a specified directory, predicts the AQI for each using the predict_aqi function, and prints the results. Predictions are stored in predicted_aqi_list for later use or analysis (Fig. 3).

The code is designed to automate the process of capturing satellite imagery for specific locations and correlating these images with Air Quality Index (AQI) data for environmental analysis.

Imports and Setup: The code begins by importing necessary Python libraries—requests for HTTP requests, os for operating system interactions, and pandas for data manipulation.

```
# Predict AQI from image/images
def predict_aqi(image_path,model):
    img_array = preprocess_image(image_path)
    if img_array is None:
        return None
    img_array = np.expand_dims(img_array, axis=0)
    prediction = model.predict(img_array)
    return prediction[0][0]

predicted_aqi_list = []
for filename in os.listdir(imageToPredictFolder):
    if filename.endswith(('.png', '.jpg', '.jpeg')):
        image_path = os.path.join(imageToPredictFolder, filename)
        predicted_aqi = predict_aqi(image_path, model)
        if predicted_aqi is not None:
            print(f"Image: {filename}, Predicted AQI: {predicted_aqi}")
            predicted_aqi_list.append((filename, predicted_aqi))
# Main function
def main():
    # Read coordinates and AQI data from the CSV file
    csv_file_path = 'data_to_retrieve.csv'
    coordinate_aqi_data = read_coordinates_aqi(csv_file_path)

    # Initialize empty lists
    file_names = []
    aqi_list = []

    # Iterate through the coordinates list
    for i, row in enumerate(coordinate_aqi_data):
        latitude = float(row['Latitude'])
        longitude = float(row['Longitude'])
        aqi = int(row['AQI'])

        # Take screenshot and get the image path
        screenshot_path = take_screenshot(api_key, latitude, longitude, zoom_level, image_size, map_

        # Update lists
        if screenshot_path:
            file_names.append(os.path.basename(screenshot_path))
            aqi_list.append(aqi)
```

Fig. 3. The screenshot of code 2

Google Maps API Setup: It sets up variables for accessing the Google Maps API, including an API key, desired zoom level for the images, image size, and map type (satellite in this case).

Reading Coordinates and AQI Data: The read_coordinates_aqi function reads a CSV file containing latitude, longitude, and AQI data using pandas. It converts this data into a list of dictionaries for easier processing.

Capturing Satellite Imagery: The take_screenshot function constructs a URL to request a static map image from the Google Maps API for given coordinates [9]. It saves the image to a "screenshots" directory, naming the file with a unique index and the AQI value.

Updating a CSV File: After capturing images, update_csv creates a new CSV file or updates an existing one with the filenames of the saved images and their corresponding AQI values.

Main Function Execution: In the main function, the script reads the initial CSV file for coordinates and AQI data, captures satellite images for each location, and updates a new CSV file with the image filenames and AQI data (Fig. 4).

The code calculates the mean and standard deviation of a list of predicted AQI (Air Quality Index) values [15]. It then computes the 95% confidence interval for the mean

```
import numpy as np

predicted_aqi_values = [55.17, 75.52, 57.31, 63.44, 61.50, 62.26, 60.60, 73.67, 46.11]

std_deviation = np.std(predicted_aqi_values)

mean_aqi = np.mean(predicted_aqi_values)

n = len(predicted_aqi_values)
z_score = 1.96
confidence_interval = z_score * (std_deviation/ np.sqrt(n))

lower_bound = mean_aqi - confidence_interval
upper_bound = mean_aqi + confidence_interval

print(f"Mean AQI: {mean_aqi}")
print(f"Standard Deviation: {std_deviation}")
print(f"95% Confidence Interval: {confidence_interval}")
```

Fig. 4. Screenshot of code 3

AQI using the formula for the confidence interval, where the z-score for 95% confidence is 1.96. This interval gives us a range in which we can be 95% confident that the true mean of the population from which these samples were drawn falls.

Mean AQI is calculated as the average of the predicted AQI values.

Standard Deviation measures the amount of variation or dispersion from the mean.

Confidence Interval provides a range around the mean that likely contains the true mean of the overall population. The width of this interval depends on the standard deviation and the number of observations, reflecting the precision of the estimate.

Lower Bound and Upper Bound represent the limits of this interval, indicating the interval within which the true mean is likely to lie with 95% confidence [18].

Given a list of AQI values, the script will accurately provide these statistical insights [10]. Unfortunately, I encountered a hiccup in executing the code to produce the actual results. However, based on the formula, you can expect outputs indicating the mean AQI value, its standard deviation, the 95% confidence interval, and the specific lower and upper bounds of this interval, offering valuable statistical insight into the AQI data's central tendency and variability.

4 Experiment

4.1 Experiment 1

The trends observed in the Model Loss graph are encouraging, indicating that our machine learning model is enhancing its predictive capabilities over time. From epochs 20 to 35, the graph shows a moderate decline in loss, interspersed with several peaks. These peaks suggest variability in learning, which is typical as the model encounters new complexities within the training data. Similarly, the validation loss mirrors this pattern with its own periodic spikes, yet it consistently trends downward, reinforcing the gradual improvement in model performance.

The Mean Squared Error (MSE) metric reveals significant learning challenges particularly evident around the 7th and 16th epochs, where pronounced errors occur. These spikes are indicative of the hurdles the model initially faces. However, the reduction in these peaks over subsequent epochs is a positive sign, pointing to the model's ability to adapt and enhance its accuracy progressively.

As for the Mean Squared Logarithmic Error (MSLE), a notable correction around the 9th epoch appears to be a pivotal moment in the training process. Following this adjustment, the MSLE stabilizes, suggesting that the model has achieved a consistent understanding of the data patterns it's analyzing. This stabilization is crucial for ensuring that the model's predictions are reliable and robust.

These observations are vital as they guide the ongoing refinement of our model, ensuring that each iteration brings us closer to a more accurate and reliable predictive tool. Such detailed monitoring of the model's learning curve and error metrics not only helps in pinpointing specific areas for improvement but also validates the effectiveness of our training methodology (Fig. 5).

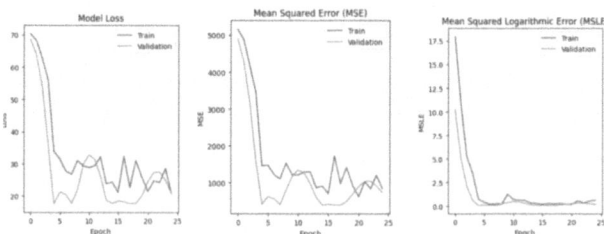

Fig. 5. Figure of experiment 1

Model Loss and Mean Absolute Error (MAE) are critical indicators in predictive model performance, measuring the deviation of the model's predictions from the actual values [17]. Model Loss reflects the overall health of the model's predictions, capturing how well the model performs across the entire dataset. MAE provides a straightforward arithmetic average of the absolute errors, offering a clear measure of prediction accuracy without overly penalizing larger discrepancies, making it intuitive and easily interpretable. Mean Squared Error (MSE) delves deeper by squaring the differences before averaging, amplifying the impact of larger errors. This characteristic makes MSE a more sensitive measure that signals the need for model adjustment when dealing with significant prediction errors.

Mean Squared Logarithmic Error (MSLE) modifies this approach by first transforming the prediction and actual values through a logarithmic scale, then computing the squared difference. This process dampens the influence of large numerical ranges, making MSLE particularly useful when predicting exponential growth or when dealing with data across vast scales. Each of these metrics serves a distinct purpose, providing a nuanced view of a model's performance to guide the refinement of predictive algorithms (Fig. 6).

4.2 Experiment 2

Over successive training sessions, our model's predictive accuracy has demonstrated considerable improvement, achieving closer alignment between predicted and actual AQI values. This suggests a more precise model calibration over time.

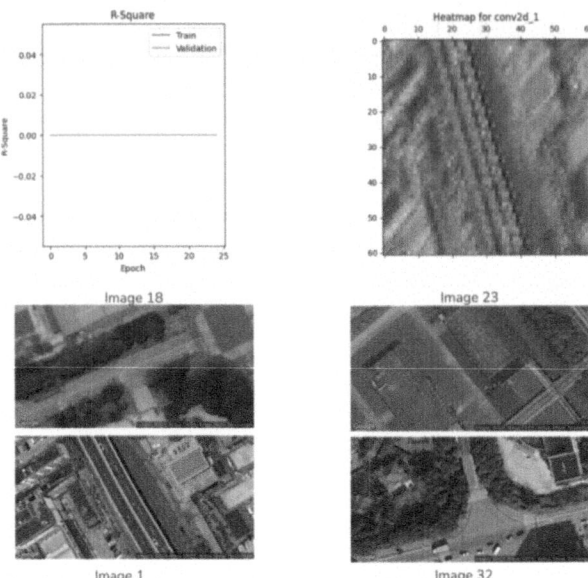

Fig. 6. Figure of experiment 2

The Mean Squared Error (MSE) provides insight into challenges faced during specific training intervals, notably around the 7th and 16th epochs, where we observed spikes in error magnitude [8]. The squaring of differences within the MSE calculation amplifies these errors, indicating that the model particularly struggled to learn from the data at these points.

Meanwhile, the Mean Squared Logarithmic Error (MSLE) has effectively moderated the volatility of error peaks, resulting in a smoother error landscape across epochs. A notable exception is the epoch around 9, where there is a discernible fluctuation. Outside of this, the MSLE maintains a relative consistency, indicating that, on a logarithmic scale, the model is learning with a stable error rate, pointing to effective training on the datasets for most epochs.

Overall, while there are epochs where the model has faced learning challenges, the general trend towards lower error rates in both MSE and MSLE confirms the maturation of the model's learning capability.

4.3 Data Source

At the beginning of this research, in order to understand the realistic condition of urban air quality and various factors, including tree canopy size, traffic level, street width, building height and so on, we have arrived at different sites in different cities to manually measure the parameters above to gain a primary conception about their impacts to urban environment, mostly with the help of Computational Fluid Dynamics (CFD) applications Gambit and Fluent. Subsequent to that process and prior to our machine learning analysis, we utilized the CFD tools with known environmental properties to understand and generate data in conditions with adjusted simulated parameters. All the procedures above, integrated together, helped form our original datasets.

5 Related Work

"In our research, we build on the work of Zhang, who used remote sensing data to explore the impact of tree canopy structures on urban air quality [11]. Zhang's method maps tree densities with satellite imagery and correlates these with ground-level air pollution measurements. Despite demonstrating a reduction in particulate matter around large tree canopies, this approach is limited by its coarse spatial resolution and inability to capture seasonal and meteorological changes affecting pollutants.

We refine Zhang's methodology by incorporating a dynamic machine learning model that analyzes air quality and meteorological data alongside high-resolution satellite imagery. Our enhanced system not only assesses current pollutant levels but also predicts future changes, making it a valuable tool for urban planning and environmental management.

Additionally, we extend the static model used by Kim [12], which relates urban tree canopies to pollution absorption rates. Our approach updates Kim's model by integrating live data from IoT-enabled sensors and weather stations. This real-time analysis, powered by machine learning, dynamically adjusts predictions and provides deeper insights into the environmental impact of urban greenery, supporting more effective public health policies and urban planning strategies."

Li have provided sufficient review and analysis on how CNN can be applied as a general means to treat and solve problems in different fields, as well as providing a reference to various kinds of convolutions [7]. Therefore, we've harnessed their provision of insights into different CNN frameworks and utilized CNN well as an important tool in our study.

In the aspect of street canyon geometry, the study by Huang et al. have provided an insight to roadside air pollution management, thus giving our study the access to this field of knowledge and information. In this way, we are able to combine this aspect of air pollution with our methodology to form a more advanced strategy in monitoring and managing urban street air quality.

An additional reference pertinent to our study is the work of Liu, which developed a GIS-based model to assess the impact of urban greenery on air quality improvement [13]. This model utilizes geographic data to map vegetation and analyze its correlation with pollution reduction. However, while effective in establishing static correlations, Liu et al.'s approach does not account for the dynamic nature of air pollution, such as daily fluctuations and acute pollution events, nor does it explore the specific morphological characteristics of tree canopies.

Our project enhances Liu's foundational research by applying a machine learning framework that incorporates not only GIS data but also continuous air quality monitoring and detailed phenological data on tree canopies.

6 Conclusion

Our model, while advancing in accuracy, still encounters instances of temporary outliers or inaccuracies that can impact its real-world utility. To enhance the model's performance for future applications, we are considering two primary improvements:

Enriching our datasets by incorporating a more extensive array of data points will serve to bolster the model's training foundation. A richer dataset can provide a more detailed context for the model, improving its ability to identify patterns and reduce the impact of outliers.

Exploring a variety of machine learning algorithms and potentially integrating them could yield a model with composite accuracy [14]. By testing different algorithms, we can identify which one—or which combination—best addresses the specificities of our dataset and task.

These refinements aim to improve the robustness of our model and its applicability in accurately predicting air quality indices in various settings. The integration of a larger dataset, alongside the implementation of a diversified machine learning strategy, is anticipated to substantially mitigate the current limitations of the model.

Our project capitalizes on the latest advances in machine learning and AI to offer a comprehensive analysis and prediction system for urban air quality management. By incorporating dynamic data and detailed canopy shapes, we provide a significant enhancement over existing models, promoting smarter urban planning and healthier communities [16].

References

1. Lomax, H., et al.: Fundamentals of computational fluid dynamics. Appl. Mech. Rev. **55.4**, B61–B61 (2002)
2. Zhang, Y., et al.: Real-time air quality forecasting, part I: history, techniques, and current status. Atmosph. Environ. **60**, 632–655 (2012)
3. Vardoulakis, S., et al.: Modelling air quality in street canyons: a review. Atmosph. Environ. **37.2**, 155–182 (2003)
4. Kampa, M., Castanas, E.: Human health effects of air pollution. Environ. Pollut. **151**(2), 362–367 (2008)
5. Xu, J., et al.: Effects of urban living environments on mental health in adults. Nat. Med. **29.6**, 1456–1467 (2023)
6. Steinman, D.A.: Image-based computational fluid dynamics modeling in realistic arterial geometries. Ann. Biomed. Eng. **30**, 483–497 (2002)
7. Li, Z., et al.: A survey of convolutional neural networks: analysis, applications, and prospects. IEEE Trans. Neural Networks Learn. Syst. **33.12**, 6999–7019 (2021)
8. Wang, Z., Bovik, A.C.: Mean squared error: love it or leave it? A new look at signal fidelity measures. IEEE Signal Process. Mag. **26**(1), 98–117 (2009)
9. Tim, B.-L., Masinter, L., McCahill, M.: Uniform resource locators (URL). No. rfc1738 (1994)
10. Kumari, S., Jain, M.K.: A critical review on air quality index. Environmental Pollution: Select Proceedings of ICWEES-2016, pp. 87–102 (2018)
11. Anderson, J.R.: A land use and land cover classification system for use with remote sensor data, vol. 964. US Government Printing Office (1976)
12. Dwyer, M.C., Miller, R.W.: Using GIS to assess urban tree canopy benefits and surrounding greenspace distributions. J. Arboric. **25**, 102–107 (1999)

13. Crosetto, M., Tarantola, S.: Uncertainty and sensitivity analysis: tools for GIS-based model implementation. Int. J. Geogr. Inf. Sci. **15**(5), 415–437 (2001)
14. Singh, A., Thakur, N., Sharma, A.: A review of supervised machine learning algorithms. In: 2016 3rd International Conference on Computing for Sustainable Global Development (INDIACom). IEEE (2016)
15. Sowlat, M.H., et al.: A novel, fuzzy-based air quality index (FAQI) for air quality assessment. Atmosph. Environ. **45.12**, 2050–2059 (2011)
16. Zhou, Q., Simmhan, Y., Prasanna, V.: Incorporating semantic knowledge into dynamic data processing for smart power grids. In: The Semantic Web–ISWC 2012: 11th International Semantic Web Conference, Boston, MA, USA, 11–15 November 2012, Proceedings, Part II 11. Springer Berlin Heidelberg (2012)
17. Hodson, T.O.: Root mean square error (RMSE) or mean absolute error (MAE): when to use them or not." Geoscientific Model Development Discussions **2022**, 1–10 (2022)
18. Shinmura, S.: The 95% confidence intervals of error rates and discriminant coefficients. Stat. Optim. Inform. Comput. **3**(1), 66–78 (2015)
19. Benammar, M., et al.: A modular IoT platform for real-time indoor air quality monitoring. Sensors **18.2**, 581 (2018)
20. Huang, Y., et al.: A review of strategies for mitigating roadside air pollution in urban street canyons. Environ. Poll. **280**, 116971 (2021)
21. Zamir, A.R., Shah, M.: Accurate image localization based on google maps street view. In: Computer Vision–ECCV 2010: 11th European Conference on Computer Vision, Heraklion, Crete, Greece, September 5–11, 2010, Proceedings, Part IV 11. Springer Berlin Heidelberg (2010)
22. Zhu, S., et al.: Daily air quality index forecasting with hybrid models: a case in China. Environ. Pollution **231**, 1232–1244 (2017)
23. Mahesh, B.: Machine learning algorithms-a review. Int. J. Sci. Res. **9.1**, 381–38 (2020)

A High Order Scheme for Modelling Viscous Incompressible Fluid Flow in a Channel with a Step

Saeed M. Dubas[(✉)]

Engineering and Computer Science Division, University of Pittsburgh at Johnstown, Johnstown, PA 15904, USA
dubasis@pitt.edu

Abstract. The viscous incompressible fluid flow in a channel with a step is studied under steady state conditions. An earlier work [3] employed a fourth order scheme with second order boundary conditions to obtain very accurate results which were in close agreement with various other studies in channel flow problems. The present work employs a fifth order scheme using 13-point grid. Moreover, it uses fourth order boundary conditions to further improve the accuracy of results. Two well-known workshop problems are chosen for the comparison of results, the problems of contraction and expansion flows. The results compare favorably with the literature from experimental and numerical view-point.

Keywords: Reynold's number · Taylor's series expansions · Channel problem

1 Introduction

The flow in a channel with a step is a classic benchmark problem in fluid dynamics and has been the subject of numerous studies [1, 2]. These problems involve expansion and contraction flows and pulsating inlet flow conditions in a channel. Contraction flows in a channel with a step has been a focus of considerable attention and a subject of a major international workshop [8]. Valencia [1] studied the laminar flow in a channel with a backward-facing step under steady and pulsatile conditions. He reported good agreement of results on his predictions of reattachment location with the experimental results of Armaly et al. [7] up to Reynolds number R = 500, beyond which differences arose due to different velocity profiles in the channel.

Boger [6] provided a comprehensive review of the flows of viscoelastic fluids for both Newtonian and non-Newtonian fluid mechanics. His experimental data suggests the formation of a "trailing edge" vortex downstream of the step, which was also detected in the stream function and plotted at selected values of R between 100 and 1000 by Dubas et al. [3]. Dennis and Smith [9] were able to infer qualitatively the presence of this vortex through grid refinement. Hawken et al. [4] used a Taylor-Galerkin algorithm, and were

"Regular Research Paper"

D. D. Hodson et al. (Eds.): CSCE 2024, CCIS 2258, pp. 258–270, 2025.
https://doi.org/10.1007/978-3-031-85902-1_23

able to visually detect the trailing edge vortex at the Reynolds number R = 450. They obtained converged results up to Reynolds number R = 100 for the expansion case and R = 800 for the contraction case.

This paper uses a fifth order scheme involving Taylor Series expansion to discretize the convective term, which comprises the highly non-linear part of the problem. It uses sixth order central difference approximation for the terms involving the second order partial derivatives in the given system of equations. We obtained converged results up to Reynolds number R = 1000. The fifth order scheme used a fourth order vorticity function at the boundary whereas the fourth order scheme [3] used second order accurate vorticity function there. The present scheme is also more accurate and efficient than the fourth order scheme, especially at lower values of Reynolds number R.

2 Mathematical Formulation

The Navier-Stokes equations governing the fluid flow in the channel are given by

$$\psi_{xx} + \psi_{yy} = -\omega \tag{1}$$

$$\omega_{xx} + \omega_{yy} + R(\psi_x \omega_y - \psi_y \omega_x) = 0 \tag{2}$$

These two equations form a coupled system in which ψ and ω are the stream and the vorticity functions respectively, and the flow parameter R is the Reynolds number.

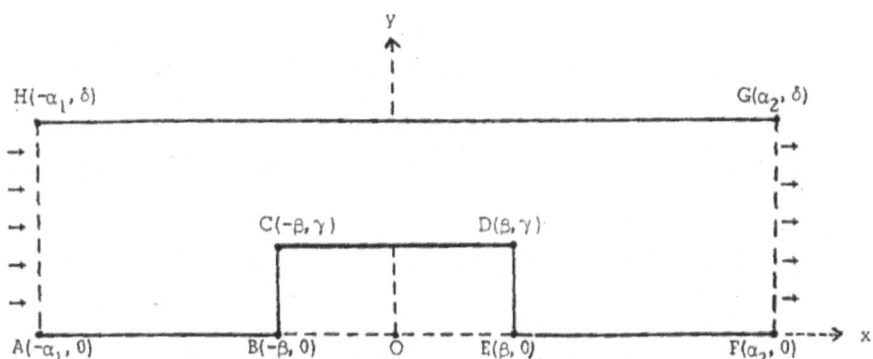

Fig. 1. The channel with a step

The boundary conditions are given by

$$\psi = 1, \quad \psi_y = 0, \quad on \;\; HG \tag{3}$$

$$\psi = 0, \quad \psi_y = 0, \quad on \;\; AB, \; CD, \; EF \tag{4}$$

$$\psi = 0, \quad \psi_x = 0, \quad on \;\; BC, \; DE \tag{5}$$

$$\psi = 3y^2 - 2y^3, \quad \omega = 12y - 6, \quad on \ AH \tag{6}$$

$$\psi_x = 0, \quad \omega_x + R\psi_y(\omega + \psi_{yy}) = 0 \ on \ FG \tag{7}$$

3 Numerical Solution Technique

(1) and (2) form a coupled system of partial differential equations such that (1) is usually regarded as the stream equation and (2) as the vorticity equation. Using sixth order central difference approximation for the stream equation, we obtain

$$\sum_{i=0}^{12} A_i \psi_i + \omega_0 = 0 \tag{8}$$

$$A_0 = -49/9h^2, \quad A_j = 3/h^2, \ 1 \leq j \leq 4,$$

$$A_k = -3/20h^2, \ 5 \leq k \leq 8, \quad A_l = 1/90\,h^2, \ 9 \leq l \leq 12.$$

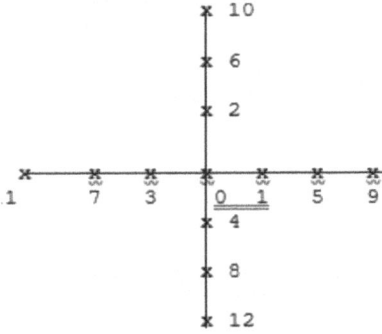

Fig. 2. The grid.

The numerical scheme for the vorticity equation is developed by using the sixth order central difference approximation for the Laplacian term $\Delta\omega \equiv \omega_{xx} + \omega_{yy}$.

For the convective term
$R(\psi_x\omega_y - \psi_y\omega_x)$, we use the expression
$\sum_{i=0}^{12} B_i\omega_i$ to write the Taylor Series
expansions for each ω_i, $1 \leq i \leq 12$ up to order 5 by utilizing the grid shown in Fig. 2. The resulting system of equations can be solved to obtain

$$(-980 + 180h^2\alpha_0)\omega_0 + \sum_{i=1}^{4} (270 + 180h^2\alpha_i)\omega_i +$$

$$\sum_{i=5}^{8}(-27 + 180h^2\alpha_i)\omega_i+$$

$$\sum_{i=9}^{12}(2 + 180h^2\alpha_i)\omega_i = 0 \tag{9}$$

Note that (9) includes the sixth order central difference approximation for the discretization of the Laplacian term $\Delta\omega$ and therefore it gives the numerical scheme for the vorticity Eq. (2). The coefficients of ω_i in (9) can be denoted as follows

$$\Gamma_0 = -980 + 180\,h^2\alpha_0, \quad \Gamma_i = 270 + 180\,h^2\alpha_i, \ 1 \le i \le 4,$$
$$\Gamma_j = -27 + 180\,h^2\alpha_j, \ 5 \le j \le 8, \Gamma_k = 2 + 180h^2\alpha_k,$$
$$9 \le j \le 12. \tag{10}$$

Set

$$\alpha_0 = -R(|\psi_x| + |\psi_y|)/h \tag{11}$$

The coefficients $\alpha_i, \ 1 \le i \le 12$ in (10) are given by the following four cases.
Case 1 : $\psi_x \ge 0, \ \psi_y \ge 0$:
$\alpha_1 = 0, \quad \alpha_2 = 3R\psi_x/2h, \quad \alpha_3 = 3R\psi_y/2h,$
$\alpha_4 = 0, \quad \alpha_5 = -3R\psi_y/20h,$
$\alpha_6 = -9R\psi_x/20h, \quad \alpha_7 = 9R\psi_y/20h,$
$\alpha_8 = -3R\psi_x/20h, \quad \alpha_9 = R\psi_y/30h,$
$\alpha_{10} = R\psi_x/15h, \quad \alpha_{11} = R\psi_y/15h, \quad \alpha_{12} = R\psi_x/30h.$
Case 2: $\psi_x \ge 0, \ \psi_y < 0$:
$\alpha_1 = -4R\psi_y/2h, \quad \alpha_2 = 3R\psi_x/3h,$
$\alpha_3 = \alpha_4 = 0, \quad \alpha_5 = 9R\psi_y/20h,$
$\alpha_6 = -9R\psi_x/20h, \quad \alpha_7 = 3R\psi_y/20h,$
$\alpha_8 = -3R\psi_x/20h, \quad \alpha_9 = -R\psi_y/15h,$
$\alpha_{10} = R\psi_x/15h, \quad \alpha_{11} = -R\psi_y/30h,$
$\alpha_{12} = R\psi_x/30h.$
Case 3: $\psi_x < 0, \ \psi_y < 0$:
$\alpha_1 = -3R\psi_y/2h, \quad \alpha_2 = 0, \quad \alpha_3 = 0,$
$\alpha_4 = -3R\psi_x/2h, \quad \alpha_5 = 9R\psi_y/20h,$
$\alpha_6 = 3R\psi_x/20h, \alpha_7 = 3R\psi_y/20h,$
$\alpha_8 = 9R\psi_x/20h, \quad \alpha_9 = -R\psi_y/15h,$
$\alpha_{10} = -R\psi_x/30h, \alpha_{11} = -R\psi_y/30h,$
$\alpha_{12} = -R\psi_x/15h.$
Case 4: $\psi_x < 0, \ \psi_y \ge 0$:
$\alpha_1 = 0, \quad \alpha_2 = 0, \quad \alpha_3 = 3R\psi_y/2h,$
$\alpha_4 = -3R\psi_x/2h, \quad \alpha_5 = -3R\psi_y/20h,$
$\alpha_6 = 3R\psi_x/20h, \quad \alpha_7 = -9R\psi_y/20h,$
$\alpha_8 = 9R\psi_x/20h, \quad \alpha_9 = R\psi_y/30h,$
$\alpha_{10} = -R\psi_x/30h, \quad \alpha_{11} = R\psi_y/15h,$
$\alpha_{12} = -R\psi_x/15h.$

Note that in each of the four cases above, the ratio of the sum of the absolute values of the off-diagonal coefficients α_i, $(i \neq 0)$ to the absolute value of the main diagonal coefficient α_0 is 2.2. This ratio is also known as diagonal ratio.

To see that this is indeed the case, we consider, without loss of generality, the case of $\psi_x \geq 0$, $\psi_y < 0$.

With $\alpha_0 = -R(|\psi_x| + |\psi_y|)/h$,

$$\sum_{i=1}^{12} |\alpha_i| = -3R\psi_y/2h + 3R\psi_x/2h - 9R\psi_y/20h + 9R\psi_x/20h$$
$$- 3R\psi_y/20h + 3R\psi_x/20h - R\psi_y/15h + R\psi_x/15h - R\psi_y/30h$$
$$+ R\psi_x/30h = -132R\psi_y/60h + 132R\psi_x/60h$$

$$\sum_{i=1}^{12} |\alpha_i| = -3R\psi_y/2h + 3R\psi_x/2h.$$

Therefore, the diagonal ratio is given by

$$\sum_{i=1}^{12} |\alpha_i|/|\alpha_0| = 2.2. \tag{12}$$

The diagonal ratio is a measure of the diagonal dominance of a system of linear equations

$$AX = b \tag{13}$$

From a well-known result from linear algebra, the existence and uniqueness of solution to (13) requires matrix A to have diagonal dominance, negative elements on the main diagonal and positive elements elsewhere.

In general, it is desirable to get the diagonal ratio to be as large as possible.

In addition to achieving diagonal dominance of A by (12), the development of the numerical scheme (10) ensures that A has negative elements on the main diagonal. This is done by the choice of α_0 in (11). The matrix A in this discussion results from the application of the numerical scheme (10) to the differential equation for the vorticity function given by (2).

Substituting the values of $\alpha_i \geq 0$, $1 \leq i \leq 12$ from above four cases and α_0 from (11), the values of Γ_i in (10) is given as follows.

With $\Gamma_0 = -980 + 180\,h^2\alpha_0 = 980 - 180\,hR(|\psi_x| + |\psi_y|)$, the coefficients Γ_i in (10) are given as follows.

Case 1': $\psi_x \geq 0$, $\psi_y \geq 0$:
$\Gamma_1 = 270$, $\Gamma_2 = 270 + 270\,hR\psi_x$
$\Gamma_3 = 270 + 270\,hR\psi_y$, $\Gamma_4 = 270$
$\Gamma_5 = -27 - 27\,hR\psi_y$, $\Gamma_6 = -27 - 81\,hR\psi_x$
$\Gamma_7 = -27 - 81\,hR\psi_y$, $\Gamma_8 = 27 - 27hR\psi_x$
$\Gamma_9 = 2 + 6\,hR\psi_y$, $\Gamma_{10} = 2 + 12\,hR\psi_x$
$\Gamma_{11} = 2 + 12hR\psi_y$, $\Gamma_{12} = 2 + 6hR\psi_x$.

$\Gamma_{12} = 2 + 6\,hR\psi_x.$

Case 2: $\psi_x \geq 0, \quad \psi_y < 0$:

$\Gamma_1 = 270 - 270\,hR\psi_y, \quad \Gamma_2 = 270 + 270\,hR\psi_x$

$\Gamma_3 = \Gamma_4 = 270, \quad \Gamma_5 = -27 + 81\,hR\psi_y$

$\Gamma_6 = -27 - 81\,hR\psi_x, \quad \Gamma_7 = -27 + 27\,hR\psi_y$

$\Gamma_8 = -27 - 27\,hR\psi_x, \quad \Gamma_9 = 2 - 12\,hR\psi_y$

$\Gamma_{10} = 2 + 12\,hR\psi_x, \quad \Gamma_{11} = 2 - 6\,hR\psi_y$

$\Gamma_{12} = 2 + 6\,hR\psi_x$

Case 3: $\psi_x < 0, \quad \psi_y < 0$:

$\Gamma_1 = 270 - 270\,hR\psi_y, \Gamma_2 = \Gamma_3 = 270$

$\Gamma_4 = 270 - 270\,hR\psi_x, \quad \Gamma_5 = -27 + 81\,hR\psi_y$

$\Gamma_6 = -27 + 27\,hR\psi_x, \quad \Gamma_7 = -27 + 27hR\psi_y$

$\Gamma_8 = -27 + 81\,hR\psi_x, \quad \Gamma_9 = 2 - 12hR\psi_y$

$\Gamma_{10} = 2 - 6\,hR\psi_x, \quad \Gamma_{11} = 2 - 6\,hR\psi_y$

$\Gamma_{12} = 2 - 12hR\psi_x.$

Case 4: $\psi_x < 0, \quad \psi_y \geq 0$:

$\Gamma_1 = \Gamma_2 = 270, \quad \Gamma_3 = 270 + 270\,hR\psi_y$

$\Gamma_4 = 270 - 270\,hR\psi_x, \quad \Gamma_5 = -27 - 27\,hR\psi_y$

$\Gamma_6 = -27 + 27\,hR\psi_x, \quad \Gamma_7 = -27 - 81\,hR\psi_y$

$\Gamma_8 = -27 + 81\,hR\psi_x, \quad \Gamma_9 = 2 + 6\,hR\psi_y$

$\Gamma_{10} = 2 - 6\,hR\psi_x, \quad \Gamma_{11} = 2 + 6\,hR\psi_y$

$\Gamma_{12} = 2 - 12\,hR\psi_x.$

We can finally give the finite difference scheme to approximate (2) as

$$\sum_{i=0}^{12} \Gamma_i \omega_i = 0 \tag{14}$$

where Γ_i are given by (10).

3.1 Order of the Numerical Scheme

To check the order of the numerical scheme (14) for the vorticity equation given by (2), we set up

$$
\begin{aligned}
\Gamma_i \omega_i =& \Big[\sum_{i=1}^{6} \Gamma_{2i-1} \omega_{2i-1}\Big] + \Big[\sum_{i=1}^{6} \Gamma_{2i} \omega_{2i}\Big] + \sum_{i=3}^{4} (-27 + 180\,h^2 \alpha_{2i-1}\,\omega_{2i-1}) \\
&+ \sum_{i=5}^{6} (2 + 180h^2 \alpha_{2i-1}\,\omega_{2i-1})\Big] + \Big[\sum_{i=1}^{2} (270 + 180\,h^2 \alpha_{2i}\,\omega_{2i}) \\
&+ \sum_{i=3}^{4} (-27 + 180h^2 \alpha_{2i}\omega_{2i}) + \sum_{i=5}^{6} (2 + 180h^2 \alpha_{2i}\omega_{2i})\Big]
\end{aligned}
$$

Referring to the grid shown in Fig. 2 for ω_i, $0 \le i \le 12$, this becomes

$$= [(270 + 180\,h^2\alpha_1)\,\omega(x+h, y) + (270 + 180h^2\,\alpha_3)\,\omega(x-h, y) + (-27 + 180h^2\alpha_5)\omega(x+2h, y)$$
$$+ (-27 + 180\,h^2\alpha_7)\,\omega(x-2h, y) + (2 + 180h^2\alpha_9)\,\omega(x+3h, y) + (2 + 180h^2\alpha_{11})\,\omega(x-3h, y)]$$
$$+ [(270 + 180\,h^2\alpha_2)\,\omega(x, y+h) + (270 + 180h^2\alpha_4)\omega(x, y-h) + (-27 + 180h^2\alpha_6)\,\omega(x, y+2h)$$
$$+ (-27 + 180\,h^2\alpha_8)\,\omega(x, y-2h) + (2 + 180h^2\alpha_{10})\,\omega(x, y+3h) + (2 + 180h^2\alpha_{12})\,\omega(x, y-3h)].$$

Without any loss of generality, we can use the α_i for the case of $\psi_x \ge 0$, $\psi_y \ge 0$. This is because the other three cases which result from the signs of the first partial derivatives of the stream function can be handled similarly.

Therefore, the above expression becomes

$$[270\omega(x+h, y) + (270 + 270hR\psi_y)\omega(x-h, y) - (27 + 7hR\psi_y)\omega(x+2h, y) - (27 + 81hR\psi_y)$$
$$+ \omega(x-2h, y) + (2 + 6hR\psi_y)\omega(x+3h, y) + (2 + 12hR\psi_y)\omega(x-3h, y)] + [(270 + 270hR\psi_x)\omega(x, y+h)$$
$$+ 270\omega(x, y-h) - (27 + 81hR\psi_x)\omega(x, y+2h) - (27 + 27hR\psi_x)\omega(x, y-2h) + (2 + 12hR\psi_x)\omega(x, y+3h)$$
$$+ (2 + 6hR\psi_x)\omega(x, y-3h)]$$

Expanding the above expression in Taylor Series about the point (x_0, y_0) up to and including h^6 terms and combining like terms, we get a simplified expression

$$(980 + 180\,hR\psi_x + 180\,hR\psi_y\omega(x, y) - 180\,h^2R\psi_y\omega_x(x, y) + 180\,h^2\omega_{xx}(x, y)$$
$$+ 9h^7R\psi_y\omega_{xxxxxxx}(\zeta_7, y) + 180\,h^2R\psi_x\omega_y(x, y) + 180h^2\omega_{yy}(x, y) + 9h^7R\psi_x\omega_{yyyyyyy}(\eta_7, y)$$

where $\zeta_7 \in (\zeta_5, \zeta_6)$, $\eta_7 \in (\eta_5, \eta_6)$, such that $\zeta_{2n-1} \in (x, x+nh)$, $\zeta_{2n} \in (x-nh, x,)$, $\eta_{2n-1} \in (y, y+nh)$, $\eta_{2n} \in (y-nh, y,)$, for $1 \le n \le 3$.

Also note that

$$O(h^6) = h^6 \Big/ 720[(w_x^{(vi)}(\zeta_1, y) + (w_x^{(vi)}(\zeta_2, y)] + 4h^6 \Big/ 45[(w_x^{(vi)}(\zeta_3, y) + (w_x^{(vi)}(\zeta_4, y)]$$
$$+ 81h^6 \Big/ 80[(w_x^{(vi)}(\zeta_5, y) + (w_x^{(vi)}(\zeta_6, y)] + h^6 \Big/ 720[(w_y^{(vi)}(x, \eta_1) + (w_y^{(vi)}(x, \eta_2)]$$
$$+ 4h^6 \Big/ 45[(w_y^{(vi)}(x, \eta_3) + (w_y^{(vi)}(x, \eta_4)] + 81h^6 \Big/ 80[(w_y^{(vi)}(x, \eta_5) + (w_y^{(vi)}(x, \eta_6)].$$

Since $\sum_{i-0}^{12} \Gamma_{2i}\omega_{2i} = 0$ is the finite difference equation approximating the vorticity Eq. (2) and $\Gamma_0 = -980 - 180hR(\psi_x + \psi_y)$, the above expression leads to the following equation

$$-180\,h^2R\psi_y\omega_x(x, y) + 180\,h^2\omega_x^{(ii)}(x, y) + 9h^7R\psi_y\omega_x^{(vii)}(\zeta_7, y) + 180\,h^2R\psi_x\omega_y(x, y)$$
$$+ 180\,h^2\omega_{yy}(x, y) + 9h^7R\psi_x\omega_y^{(vi)}(x, \eta_7) = 0$$

Dividing by $180\,h^2$, we obtain.
$R(\psi_x\omega_y - \psi_y\omega_x) + \omega_{xx} + \omega_{yy} + O(h^5) = 0$, such that

$$O(h^5) = -h^5 \Big/ 20R(\psi_y\omega_x^{(vi)}(\zeta_7, y) + 180\,h^2R\psi_x\omega_y^{(vi)}(x, \eta_7).$$

It follows that we have obtained a fifth order finite difference scheme for the vorticity Eq. (2).

3.2 Boundary Conditions for Vorticity

With the exception of the sides AH and FG in Fig. 1, ω on the lower boundary and the top boundary is given by (1). On the side BC, we have $\psi_{yy} = 0$,

Therefore from (1), we have

$$-\omega_0 = \psi_{xx} \qquad (15)$$

Using the grid in Fig. 2, we next develop the fourth order backward approximation for ψ_{xx} by setting

$$\psi_{xx} = \sum_{i=0}^{5} \alpha_i \psi_i \qquad (16)$$

Writing Taylor Series expansions up to $O(h^6)$ for ψ_i, $1 \le i \le 5$ in the backward direction and comparing coefficients for the partial derivatives of ψ, the resulting system of equations can be solved for α_i, $1 \le i \le 5$, whence

$$\omega_0 = 1/h^2[-8\psi_1 + 3\psi_2 - (1/9)\psi_3 + (1/8)\psi_4] + O(h^4) \qquad (17)$$

where

$$O(h^4) = h^4 \big/ 720 \psi_x^{(Vi)}[-77/6 + 3424/3 - 9477 + 24949/12 - 2625/6]$$

which is a fourth order approximation and is valid everywhere on the lower boundary AB, BC, CD, DE, and EF.

For the top boundary GH, since $\psi_0 = 1$, we obtain

$$\omega_0 = 1/h^2[-8\psi_1 + 3\psi_2 - 8/9\psi_3 + (1/8)\psi_4 + 415/72] + O(h^4) \qquad (18)$$

ω on the right boundary FG is defined by the following equation

$$\omega_x + R\psi_y(\omega + \psi_{yy}) = 0 \qquad (19)$$

To obtain a fourth order approximation for this equation, we use a similar approach to (17) resulting in the following discretized equation

$$(25/12h\,\omega_0 - 4/h\,\omega_1 + 3/h\,\omega_2 - 4/3h\,\omega_3 + 1/h\,\omega_4)$$
$$+ R(-5/6h\psi_0 - 1/4h\,\psi_1 + 3/2h\,\psi_2 - 1/2h\,\psi_3 + 1/2h\,\psi_4)[\omega_0 + 1\big/h^2\,(5/4\psi_0 + 5/6\psi_1 - 1/3\psi_2$$
$$+ 7/6\psi_3 - 1/2\psi_4 + 1/12\psi_5)] = 0 \qquad (20)$$

The approximation of each of the partial derivative in (19) resulted in a 4th order error term $O(h^4)$, which is being omitted for the sake of simplicity, and (20) is a 4th order approximation.

4 Examples and Comparisons

The present scheme is 5th order in the interior and 4th order on the boundaries of the channel. The earlier scheme [3] is 4th order in the interior and 2nd order on the boundaries of the channel. Referring to Fig. 1, the present scheme was run for the following cases. $\beta_1 = 4, \beta_2 = 4, \gamma = 0.5, \zeta = 1$ and the following parameters.

- For R = 10, the method converged for all h = 0.1,.0 5 and the results are given in Table set 1.
- For R = 10, the method converged for all h =.025,.0215 and the results are given in Table set 1.
- For R = 50, the method converged for all h =.01,.05 and the results are given in Table set 2.
- For R = 50, the method converged for all h =.025,.0125 and the results are given in Table set 2.
- For R = 100, the method converged for all h = 0.1,.05 and the results are given in Table set 3.
- For R = 100, the method converged for all h =.05,.025,.0125 and the results are given in Table set 3.

The graphs for the examples were essentially the same as given in [3]. However, for the stream function with R = 10, we obtained three digits accuracy at step size h = 0.1 with the present scheme. The scheme in [3] required h =.025 and the Greenspan method [5] required an h =.00625 to obtain the same accuracy.

For the vorticity function, at the same points x = 0.1, y = 0.1 and x = 1.9, y = 0.8 in the region for R = 10, we obtained three digits accuracy at step size h = 0.1 by using the present scheme. The numerical scheme in [3] required h =.025 and the Greenspan method [5] did not converge. See Table Set1.

When we compared the two methods at the same points x = 0.1, y = 0.1 with R = 50 for the vorticity function, we obtained three digits accuracy for h = 0.1 by the present scheme. The scheme in [3] also converged for the same point, but it required h =.05, whereas Greenspan scheme [5] did not converge. See Table Set2.

For the comparison between the two methods at the same points x = 0.1, y = 0.1 and x 1.9, y = 0.8, but with R = 100 for the vorticity function, we obtained three digits accuracy for h =.025 by the present scheme, but the scheme in [3] required h =.05 to obtain the same results whereas Greenspan scheme [5] did not converge. For the stream function the results for h =.05 were better than the results from [3] with h =.025.

5 Conclusion

The results with the present fifth order scheme for R = 10, 50, 100 and h = 0.1,.05,.025,.0125 are more accurate than the results of numerical scheme given in [3].

The present scheme is very efficient for lower values of R.

Tables below give the results of the fourth order scheme [3], the present scheme and Greenspan scheme [5].

Table 1A. $R = 10, \psi(0.1, 0.1)$

h	4th order	Present scheme	Greenspan scheme
0.1	.0279	.0028	.02869
.05	.02799	.0028	.02820
.025	.02800	.0028	.02805
.0125	.02800	.0028	.02801

Table 1B. $R = 10, \psi(1.8, , 0.9)$

h	4th order	Present scheme	Greenspan scheme
0.1	0.8887	0.8910	0.8882
.05	0.8906	0.8910	0.8903
.025	0.8909	0.8910	0.8908
.0125	0.8908	0.8910	0.8909

Table 1C. $R = 10, \omega(0.1, , 0.1)$

h	4th order	Present scheme	Greenspan scheme
0.1	−4.798	−4.80	−4.707
.05	−4.799	−4.80	−4.707
.025	−4.80	−4.80	−4.792
.0125	−4.80	−4.80	−4.798

Table 1D. $R = 10, \omega(1.98, , 0.8)$

h	4th order	Present scheme	Greenspan scheme
0.1	3.633	3.687	3.622
.05	3.680	3.687	3.672
.025	3.685	3.687	3.684
.0125	3.686	3.687	3.687

Table 2A. $R = 50$, $\psi(0.1, 0.1)$

h	4th order	Present scheme	Greenspan scheme
0.1	.0278	.02799	.02841
.05	.02797	.02798	.02813
.025	.02797	.02797	.02802
.0125	.02797	.02797	.02798

Table 2B. $R = 50$, $\psi(1.9, 0.8)$

h	4th order	Present scheme	Greenspan scheme
0.1	0.8812	0.8839	0.8775
.05	0.8825	0.8833	0.8815
.025	0.8829	0.8832	0.8824
.0125	0.8831	0.8832	0.8829

Table 2C. $R = 50$, $\omega(0.1, , 0.1)$

h	4th order	Present scheme	Greenspan scheme
0.1	−4.800	−4.798	−4.732
.05	−4.798	−4.798	−4.776
.025	−4.798	−4.799	−4.792
.0125	−4.799	−4.799	−4.797

Table 2D. $R = 50$, $\omega(1.9, , 0.8)$

h	4th order	Present scheme	Greenspan scheme
0.1	3.567	3.632	3.529
.05	3.609	3.614	3.593
.025	3.610	3.613	3.608
.0125	3.611	3.612	3.612

Table 3A. $R = 100$, $\psi(0.1, 0.1)$

h	4th order	Present scheme	Greenspan scheme
0.1	.02800	.02797	.02822
.05	.02794	.02795	.02805
.025	.02794	.02794	.02797
.0125	.02794	.02794	.02795

Table 3B. $R = 100$, $\psi(1.9, 0.8)$

h	4th order	Present scheme	Greenspan scheme
0.1	0.8765	0.8795	0.8801
.05	0.8772	0.8783	0.8757
.025	0.8777	0.8782	0.8772
.0125	0.8779	0.8781	0.8776

Table 3C. $R = 100$, $\omega(0.1, 0.1)$

h	4th order	Present scheme	Greenspan scheme
0.1	−4.801	−4.797	−4.749
.05	−4.797	−4.798	−4.782
.025	−4.799	−4.799	−4.794
.0125	−4.799	−4.799	−4.798

Table 3D. $R = 100$, $\omega(1.9, 0.8)$

h	4th order	Present scheme	Greenspan scheme
0.1	3.495	3.559	3.417
.05	3.510	3.524	3.494
.025	3.516	3.520	3.512
.0125	3.517	3.520	3.517

References

1. Valencia, A.: Pulsating flow in a channel with a backward-facing step. Appl. Mech. Rev. **50**(11), part 2 (1997)
2. Hickmott, S., Smith, R.M.: A finite element prediction of laminar flow over an upstream facing step in a channel
3. Dubas, S.M., Bouthellier, P., Siriwardana, N., Weiserman, L.: Numerical modelling of a viscous incompressible fluid flow in a channel with a step. Advances in Parallel & Distributed Processing, and Applications (2021)
4. Hawken, D.M., Townsend, P., Webster, M.F.: Numerical simulations of viscous flows in channels with a step. J. Comput. Fluids **20**(1), 59–75 (1991)
5. Greenspan, D.: Numerical studies of steady, viscous, incompressible flow in a channel with a step. J. Eng. Math. **3**, 21–28 (1969)
6. Boger, D.V.: Viscoelastic flow through contractions. Ann. Rev. Fluid. Mech. 157–182 (1987)
7. Armaly, B.F., Durst, F., Pereira, J.C.F., Schonung, B.: Experimental and theoretical investigation of backward-facing step flow
8. Proceedings of the 6th Meeting of IAHR Working Group on Refined Modelling of Flows, Karisruhe, Germany (1983)
9. Dennis, S.C.R., Smith, F.T.: Steady flow through a channel with a symmetrical constriction in the form of a step. Proc. Royal Soc. Lond. **A327**, 393 (1980)

Feasibility Study of Neutron Mammography Using MCNPX with a Breast Voxel Anthropomorphic Phantom

Ali A. A. Alghamdi[1]($\boxtimes$) (iD), Andy K. W. Ma[2] (iD), M. H. A. Mhareb[3] (iD),
Gameel Saleh[4] (iD), E. Abuelhia[1] (iD), Hamed A. Alshammari[1] (iD), and D. A. Bradley[5,6] (iD)

[1] Department of Radiological Sciences, College of Applied Medical Science, Imam
Abdulrahman Bin Faisal University, P.O. Box 2435, Dammam 31441, Saudi Arabia
{alalghamdi,aabuelhia,halshammari}@iau.edu.sa

[2] School of Medicine, Royal College of Surgeons in Ireland-Bahrain, P.O. Box 15503, Adliya,
Bahrain
ama@rcsi-mub.com

[3] Department of Physics, College of Science, Imam Abdulrahman Bin Faisal University, P.O.
Box 1982, Dammam 31441, Saudi Arabia
mhsabumhareb@iau.edu.s

[4] Department of Biomedical Engineering, College of Engineering, Imam Abdulrahman Bin
Faisal University, P.O. Box 1982, Dammam 31441, Saudi Arabia
gsmohammed@iau.edu.sa

[5] Center for Applied Physics and Radiation Technologies, School of Engineering and
Technology, Sunway University, 47500 Bandar Sunway, Selangor Darul Ehsan, Malaysia

[6] Department of Physics, University of Surrey, Guildford GU2 7XH, UK
d.a.bradley@surrey.ac.uk

Abstract. Neutron radiography represents a nondestructive testing method using neutron beams instead of X-rays or gamma rays for imaging purposes. This approach offers distinct advantages, particularly in its enhanced interaction with light atoms and materials, facilitating the visualization of concealed structural intricacies. This study investigated the applicability of neutron radiography in mammography. Monte Carlo simulations, employing voxel phantoms, are pivotal in analyzing neutron interactions within objects or biological bodies. Specifically, this study uses MCNPX 2.5.0 alongside a high-resolution breast voxel phantom. Grayscale postprocessing methods were implemented to refine image contrast. The findings underscore the contrast enhancement achieved through influence of varied neutron energies. Notably, fast neutrons sourced from the fission spectrum manifest better overall contrast. However, further investigations are warranted to optimize possible in-beam collimation, conduct dose assessments, and juxtapose neutron radiography with conventional photon mammography. This study underscores the potential of neutron radiography in medical imaging and delineates pathways for future research and development endeavors.

Keywords: Neutron radiography · Breast voxel phantom · Postprocessing

© The Author(s), under exclusive license to Springer Nature Switzerland AG 2025
D. D. Hodson et al. (Eds.): CSCE 2024, CCIS 2258, pp. 271–279, 2025.
https://doi.org/10.1007/978-3-031-85902-1_24

1 Introduction

Neutron radiography is a potent nondestructive testing instrument, employing neutrons instead of X-rays or gamma-rays for imaging. The fundamental principle underlying neutron radiography involves the disparate absorption of neutrons by various materials, akin to conventional radiography, albeit using a neutron beam as the radiation source. Unlike X-rays, neutrons exhibit a heightened propensity to interact with light atoms and materials, unveiling concealed structural nuances that might evade detection through other radiographic modalities [1, 2]. The application of neutron radiography spans diverse domains, including life sciences, industrial engineering, environmental surveying, and security inspections, with its utilization rising steadily. This surge can largely be attributed to the availability of compact sources, notable advancements in detector systems, neutron dosimetry and the refinement of postprocessing techniques [3–8].

The exceptional penetration and contrasting capabilities of neutron imaging render it particularly well-suited for analyzing material structures and defects. Moreover, its utility extends to medical applications, particularly in areas with light elements such as soft tissues. Neutron imaging facilitates identifying and quantifying hydrogen-rich substances within biological samples, thereby enabling direct visualization with high sensitivity, resolution, and accuracy [9].

Neutron radiography and imaging hold significant promise in medical applications owing to their unique interactions with light elements and substantial penetration depth, enabling examining structures obscured by other imaging modalities. Ongoing research and development endeavors augur continued advancements and expanded applications in the medical realm, encompassing areas such as cancer treatment, diagnosis, drug delivery, and tissue engineering [9–11].

Therefore, Monte Carlo simulations have emerged as a cornerstone in neutron radiography and imaging, offering a robust approach to modeling complex transport systems with precision. Central to this methodology is the voxel phantom, a three-dimensional representation of a system or subject in cubic form, which serves as a critical tool for realistically simulating neutron interactions within objects or biological entities [12]. Monte Carlo simulations using voxel phantoms play a crucial role in neutron imaging because these phantoms can accurately depict various tissue types and organs. These phantoms aid in determining the distribution of neutron radiation doses within biological tissues using Monte Carlo simulations, minimizing radiation exposure while maximizing diagnostic efficacy.

This study used MCNPX 2.5.0 with a high-resolution breast voxel phantom to investigate neutron radiography resulted from different energy bands and the effects employing grayscale postprocessing techniques.

2   Material and Methods

2.1   Simulation Setup

Figure 1 illustrates the distinctive attributes of the computational breast voxel phantom employed in this study. The phantom comprised skin, adipose tissue, and muscle components. Notably, fibroglandular tissues, predominant within the breast, were delineated by 49 cells exhibiting realistic densities and elemental compositions, as detailed in the pertinent literature [13]. The simulation configuration specified key distances: 48.8 cm from the source to the surface of the breast voxel phantom, and 60 cm from the source to the radiography tally. Collimation assumed a pivotal role in sculpting and directing neutron beams. The collimation ratio (L/D), defined as the ratio of the distance from the aperture to the image plane (L) to the aperture diameter (D), delineated beam divergence and intensity reduction in accordance with the inverse square law [14]. The source definition in MCNPX entailed a radial distribution spanning 0 to 0.5 cm, thereby establishing an (L/D) ratio of 120. The neutron radiography tally F5 in MCNPX operated with the NOTRN card for direct contributions from the source to the imaging grid [15]. Neutron energy sources were modeled to encompass a thermal neutron energy of 2.53e−8 MeV, a fast neutron energy of approximately 0.5 MeV and using an MCNPX multi-in function that characterizes the Maxwellian fission spectrum of the source with a mean neutron energy of 1.26 MeV. Cell number 110 (Fig. 1) within the fibroglandular tissues was changed to a density of 0.441 gm/cm^3 for comparative analysis, simulating the density and elemental composition characteristic of cancerous tissue [16]. All cells within the simulation were assigned equal importance, with the sole variance reduction implemented being the biasing of the source to impart a directional orientation towards the imaging plane.

The dose to breast tissues is typically referred to as Mean Glandular Dose (MGD). Several factors are taken into account when calculating MGD, including the dose received by glandular tissues, the granularity and thickness of the breast, and the number and orientation of the views. Additionally, X-ray machine specific factors such as entrance dose and Half Value Layer (HVL) are considered for normalization.

Several combinations of measurements and calculation methods have been reported to assess and investigate these factors in X-ray mammography, such as Dance (1990) [17], Boone (1999) [18], and Ma et al. (2009) [19]. However, it should be noted that applying these methods to neutron radiography may be inadequate due to the unique nature of neutron energy interactions and their dependence on the elemental composition of the breast tissues.

In this study, we report the total equivalent dose (HT) received by all tissues simulated in the breast voxel phantom. Furthermore, a separate future study will focus on developing a method for calculating MGD expected from neutron radiography of the breast voxel phantom.

Total collision heating tally (+F6) were used to calculate the amount of energy deposited in the breast voxel phantom from neutron, secondary gamma, and possible light-ion production. Adjustments are made to the MODE card, PHYS cards, and energy CUT cards to consider the potential contributions of different particles to the dose calculations. The results are initially obtained per neutron, representing the energy deposition per gram (MeV/g). These results are then converted to absorbed dose in (mGy) and multiplied by the neutron energy dependent radiation weighting factor to obtain the final result in terms of equivalent dose in (mSv).

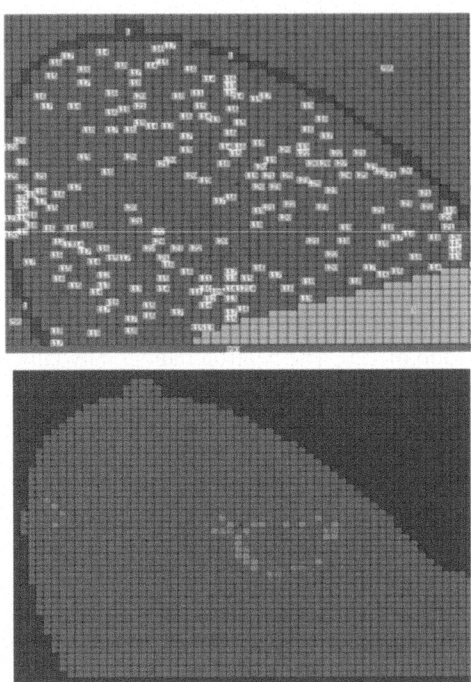

Fig. 1. MCNPX plot window displaying several distinctive features of the breast voxel phantom. (Top) cells numbering (1) skin tissue, (2) adipose tissues, (3) muscle tissue, (100-149) fibro-glandular tissues. (Below) the altered density position for cell universe 110.

2.2 Grayscale Postprocessing

Figure 2 depicts the flowchart delineating the steps encompassing simulation and grayscale postprocessing. Initially, the MCNPX output MCTAL file containing the radiography tally F5 underwent processing using the external graphics program GRIDCONV, an integral component of the MCNPX package. GRIDCONV facilitated the conversion of radiography tally results from the MCTAL file into a text file, incorporating header information alongside arrays for radiography tally F5 and associated bins error values. Subsequently, the resultant files from the aforementioned steps were parsed using Python code, encompassing two primary operations: 1. Converting the raw text data into an image format (image.png). 2. Enhancing the image contrast using Python functions for equalizing the histogram of the image files.

The Python code used the np.loadtxt() function to read the text file generated by GRIDCONV, enabling the skipping of header information lines. The plt.imshow() function was employed to exclude the associated error array while enabling feature plotting, subsequently saving the image in the desired format. The code in the second step computed a histogram of the input image using the np.histogram() function, representing the frequency distribution of pixel intensities within the image. The cumulative distribution function (CDF) was computed by summing the histogram values subsequently normalized to a range of 0–1. Intensity-mapping lookup tables were applied to map input image intensities to output intensities using histogram equalization facilitated by the cv2.LUT() function. Specifically, a lookup table was generated by scaling the normalized CDF values to the range of 0–255. The code computed the histogram of the equalized image employing the same methodology as the input image.

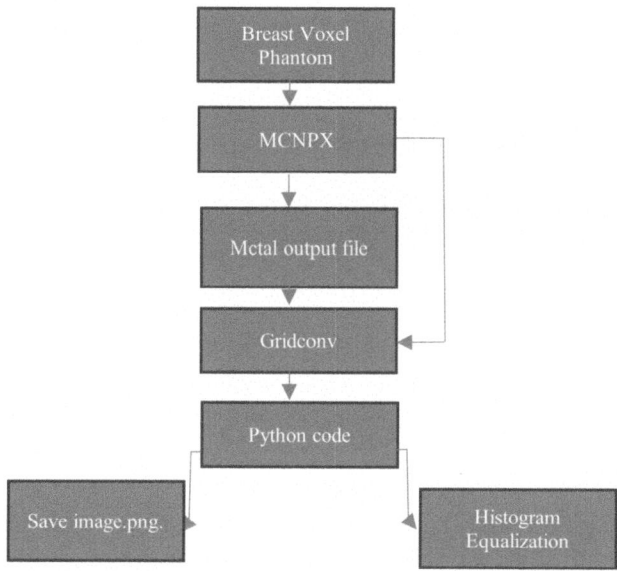

Fig. 2. Flowchart delineates the steps and processes of simulating and postprocessing neutron radiography using MCNPX, GIRCONV, and Python

3   Results and Discussion

The results of F5 radiography were promptly recorded using the NORTN card. Figure 3 showcases the histogram-equalized output. The figure illustrates the outcomes of the Python code, which reads input row data from GRIDCONV, computes the histogram of the input grayscale image, and proceeds to map to output intensities using histogram equalization, as demonstrated with the "viridis" color mapping option using the Python plotting function in imshow().

Figure 4 presents the distinct images obtained from three neutron energies sources explored in this study. Figure 4 were obtained as a direct contribution from the beam passing through the breast voxel phantom. Most of the neutrons were absorbed by the breast tissues owing to thermal energy of 2.53e−8 MeV (Fig. 4 (top)). The MCNPX (output

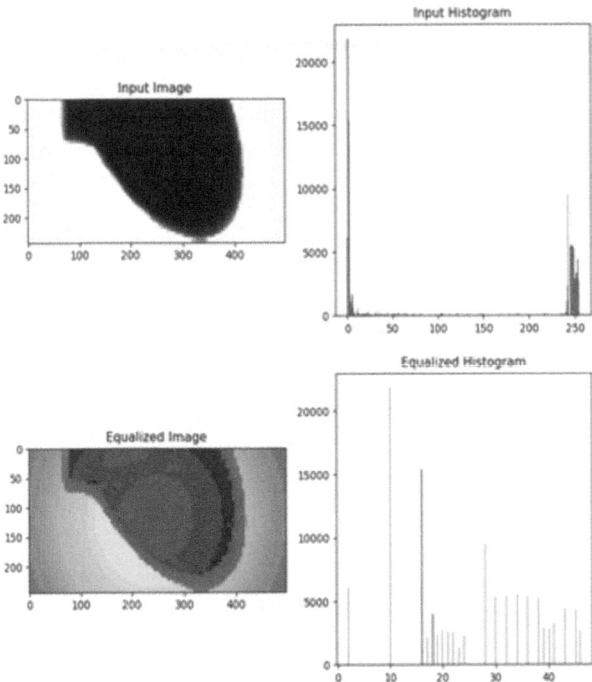

Fig. 3. Selected results depict histograms from a neutron source of the fission spectrum with a mean energy of 1.26 MeV. This image represents the outcomes of the F5 radiography tally conducted with the presence of NORTN card

table 126) estimated an average neutron mean free path of approximately 0.5 cm, whereas the compressed breast voxel phantom thickness was 4 cm. This disparity explains the reduced contrast in the image from thermal neutron energy because fewer neutrons reach the imaging grid of the F5 tally. Figure 4 (middle), obtained from a neutron energy of 0.5 MeV, demonstrates slightly improved contrast compared to Fig. 4 (top), with an average neutron mean free path of 1.16 cm. This resulted in the absorption of most neutrons, while some underwent attenuation in the breast, yielding contrast in Fig. 4(middle) for the edited cell number 110 with a low density of 0.441 g/cm^3. Figure 4(down), obtained from an energy source resembling the fission spectrum with a mean energy of 1.26 MeV, exhibits enhanced contrast compared to images provided in Figs. 4(top) and 6(middle). Neutron energy in this range exhibited an average mean free path of 2.5 cm, resulting in greater attenuation and improved contrast appearance for the edited cell number 110 with a low density of 0.441 g/cm^3.

Previous results suggested that fast neutrons were a more favorable option for neutron radiography in potential medical diagnostic applications. Given the predominance of light elements in the human body, thermal neutrons were swiftly absorbed within a few centimeters. This study does not preclude the possibility of using in-beam collimation to enhance final image contrast and warrants further investigation, alongside dose calculations and comparisons with normal photon mammography.

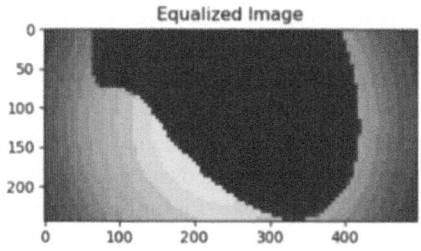

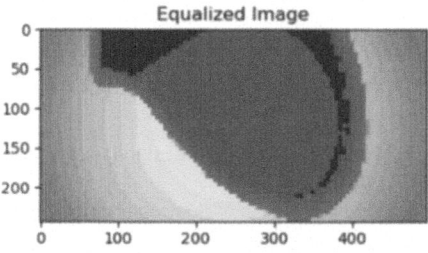

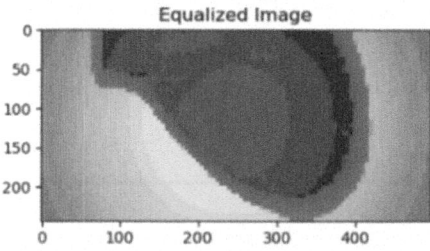

Fig. 4. Equalized neutron radiography tallies (top) from thermal neutron energy, (middle) from 0.5 MeV neutron energy and (down) from fission spectrum with mean energy of 1.26.

The results from +F6 tally from running 2e+8 particles history show that the equivalent dose from neutron energies of 2.53e−8 MeV, 0.5 MeV, and a Maxwell energy spectrum are 4.64e−7 mSv/s, 3.88e−5 mSv/s, and 1.9e−4 mSv/s, respectively. These results indicate the dependence of equivalent doses on neutron energy, which can be used as a reference for balancing image quality and received dose in future investigations on MGD.

4 Conclusion

This study used a realistic breast voxel phantom to investigate the influence of neutron energy range on neutron radiography. Simulations were conducted using the MCNPX 2.5.0 code, and images were processed using Python postprocessing functions. Among the settings explored, fast neutrons from the fission spectrum, with an average energy of 1.26 MeV yielded superior overall contrast than the other energies configurations.

The application of neutron radiography for medical imaging purposes may encounter several challenges in achieving real-world testing and evaluation. While some limitations have been addressed, such as advancements in neutron source availability, detector sensitivity, and enhancements in image postprocessing techniques, additional obstacles persist. Fast neutrons prove more adept at attenuating breast tissue thickness despite the potentially low overall neutron flux reaching the detector plate for thermal energy. This pilot investigation underscores the necessity for further exploration to determine optimal neutron energy, assess the impact of various possible in-beam collimation designs and potential effect of contrast agent i.e. Gadolinium on image contrast.

Disclosure of Interests. The authors declare no competing interests.

References

1. Kardjilov, N., Manke, I., Woracek, R., Hilger, A., Banhart, J.: Advances in neutron imaging. Mater. Today **21**(6), 652–672 (2018)
2. Alghamdi, A.A.: Monte Carlo simulation of neutron tomography for palm weevil detection. J. Radioanal. Nucl. Chem. **291**, 359–364 (2012)
3. Otake, Y., et al.: Research and development of a non-destructive inspection technique with a compact neutron source. J. Disaster Res. **12**(3), 585–592 (2017)
4. Lehmann, E.H.: Neutron imaging methods and applications. Neutron Applications in Earth, Energy and Environmental Sciences, 1st edn, pp. 319–48. Springer, Boston, MA (2009)
5. Smith, T., Bilheux, H., Ray, H., Bilheux, J.C., Yan, Y.: High resolution neutron radiography and tomography of hydrided Zircaloy-4 cladding materials. Phys. Procedia **69**, 478–482 (2015)
6. Hashim, S., Bradley, D.A., Saripan, M.I., Ramli, A.T., Wagiran, H.: The thermoluminescence response of doped SiO2 optical fibres subjected to fast neutrons. Appl. Radiat. Isot. **68**(4–5), 700–703 (2010)
7. Alghamdi, A.A.: Machine learning for predicting neutron effective dose. Appl. Sci. **14**(13), 5740 (2024)
8. Minniti, T., Tremsin, A.S., Vitucci, G., Kockelmann, W.: Towards high-resolution neutron imaging on IMAT. J. Instrum. **13**(01), C01039 (2018)
9. Medich, D.C., Currier, B.H., Karellas, A.: Feasibility of small animal anatomical and functional imaging with neutrons: a monte carlo simulation study. IEEE Trans. Nucl. Sci. **61**(5), 2480–2488 (2014)
10. Karihtala, P.H.: The current status and future perspectives of clinical boron neutron capture therapy trials. Health Technol. 1–5 (2024)
11. Guillaume, F., et al.: Neutron microtomography to investigate the bone-implant interface—comparison with histological analysis. Phys. Med. Biol. **66**(10), 105006 (2021)
12. Alghamdi, A.A., Ma, A., Tzortzis, M., Spyrou, N.M.: Neutron-fluence-to-dose conversion coefficients in an anthropomorphic phantom. Radiat. Prot. Dosimetry **115**, 606–611 (2005)
13. Alghamdi, K.W.A.: Development of a realistic computational breast phantom for dosimetric simulations. Nuclear Sci. Technol. **2**, 147–152 (2011)
14. MacGillivray, G.: Neutron radiography collimator design. Nray Services Inc., Petawa, Ontario, Canada (2011)
15. Pelowitz, D.B.: MCNPX user's manual version 2.5.0. Los Alamos National Laboratory, vol. 76, p. 473 (2005)
16. Saleh, G., et al.: Heterogeneous breast phantom for computed tomography and magnetic resonance imaging. PLoS ONE **18**(4), e0284531 (2023)

17. Dance, D.R.: Monte Carlo calculation of conversion factors for the estimation of mean glandular breast dose. Phys. Med. Biol. **9**, 1211–1219 (1990)
18. Boone, J.M.: Glandular breast dose for monoenergetic and high-energy x-ray beams: Monte Carlo assessment. Radiology **213**, 23–37 (1999)
19. Ma, A., Darambara, D.G., Stewart, A., Gunn, S., Bullard, E.: Mean glandular dose estimation using MCNPX for a digital breast tomosynthesis system with tungsten/aluminum and tungsten/aluminum+silver x-ray anode-filter combinations. Med. Phys. **35**, 5278–5289 (2008)

An Evaluation Tool for Cybersickness Mitigation Techniques in a Virtual Reality Environment

Guang Wei Too[1(✉)], Alan Yuan[1], Ziqian Dong[2], and Huanying Gu[1]

[1] Department of Computer Science, New York Institute of Technology, New York, NY, USA
{gtoo,ayuan01,hgu03}@nyit.edu
[2] Department of Electrical and Computer Engineering, New York Institute of Technology, New York, NY, USA
ziqian.dong@nyit.edu

Abstract. This study proposes a ball-hunting game to evaluate techniques for mitigating cybersickness in a virtual reality (VR) environment. As VR technology evolves, lower costs and more compact systems will require developers to create high-quality content. Integrated cybersickness countermeasures are often necessary to ensure safety and comfort for all users. However, different countermeasures may have varying effectiveness. Our proposed application assesses various cybersickness mitigation techniques through an experimental simulation and includes automatic user interaction data collection. The tool provides a method for quantifying simulation sickness questionnaire (SSQ) to assess cybersickness.

Keywords: Virtual reality · cybersickness mitigation techniques · simulation tool · simulator sickness questionnaire · automated data collection

1 Introduction

Virtual reality (VR) is a technology with enormous potential and numerous applications across various fields, including entertainment, manufacturing, and business, to name just a few [16]. For instance, VR can be utilized for medical simulation training, virtual classrooms [13], and visual meetings, showcasing its wide range of potential applications. However, the concept of this technology is not new. Many have worked to enhance it, with improvements evident in newer consumer-based headsets such as the Oculus, HTC Vive, and Pico, as listed on VR Compare for hardware specifications [24]. The cost of headsets has also decreased, making them more widely available. As the content continues to grow exponentially, it is expected that the adoption of these devices will increase over time [19].

In 2022, VR technology had fewer content options compared to platforms like PCs or consoles. However, newer hardware innovations revealed in 2024, such as smaller headset sizes and optimized simulation rendering, have significantly advanced the field. This advancement has made it possible for content that was previously exclusive to consoles, PCs, and other platforms to be adapted for VR. Simplifying the system also lowers the learning curve for developers, enabling them to create content and packages that assist others. This, in turn, leads to increased VR usage and a greater variety of simulations in the market.

As the VR market grows, commercial uses are hindered by issues like cybersickness [6,13]. Cybersickness, a form of motion sickness caused by spending time in virtual reality environments [10], affects some individuals more than others [12,22]. Several theories explain why cybersickness might occur in VR, such as reduced immersion or spatial conflicts between the real and virtual worlds [3,5,13]. For example, changes in gravity and movement speed compared to the simulated environment and the accustomed real world can contribute to this issue. The sensory conflict theory [11] is widely accepted as a primary cause of cybersickness. According to this theory, conflicts between the sensory information provided by the headset and the body's sensory systems result in cybersickness. This can lead to symptoms including dizziness, mental fatigue, and, in severe cases, vomiting or prolonged discomfort [11]. Most studies on cybersickness use the sensory conflict theory as a foundation for their experiments and literature.

Other studies, such as those investigating prolonged postural instability [15], supplement the sensory conflict theory as a cause of motion sickness. This introduces hardware issues, such as uneven weight distribution, and external factors like ventilation [17]. These variables can be challenging to control since it is often influenced by user preferences and location. Instead, cybersickness can be prevented through a unified application package of mitigation techniques.

Mitigation techniques aim to reduce or prevent cybersickness through software. However, these techniques still require further study to understand their effectiveness and trade-offs, especially since some techniques may affect immersion or alter the game environment in the original content. In this paper, we present our design of a simulation tool that evaluates the effectiveness of these techniques.

The remainder of this paper is organized as follows: Sect. 2 presents the related work that motivates the development of the cybersickness mitigation evaluation tool. Section 3 discusses the assessment of data collection process. Section 4 details the Ball Hunting Game, including the experimental tool, game levels, and types of data collected. Section 5 presents the preliminary results of the pilot study and explores its potential applications. Section 6 concludes the paper.

2 Related Work

2.1 Human Posture and Hardware Variables

In the study conducted by Riccio and Stroffregen [18], many of their simulations describe postural instability and constraints as part of the factors that create motion sickness. They suggest that sensory conflict which is the interference with inductive inferences, occurs when the animal is unstable. Therefore this theory is a separate process and factor for motion sickness. In continuation of their theory, animals who have not learned how to regain stability or are currently prevented from stabilizing trigger motion sickness. Penumudi et al. [15] conducted a study of prolonged usage of VR equipment while users must maintain uncomfortable positions. It was found that users having muscle activities of the neck and shoulder, excessive vertical target locations (15° above and 30° below eye height) caused strains and possible injuries and fatigue. Clifton et al. [4] when studying cybersickness, found that symptoms occur more during standing up for both full eight degrees of motion and teleportation.

Matirosov et al. [14] tested the effects of cybersickness with different applications such as the Cave Automatic Virtual Environment (CAVE) system, Oculus, PC, and physical tests. In the experiment, they found that the CAVE system had a lower risk of cybersickness effects. However, the Oculus had higher reports of symptoms and discontinuation from the simulation. It is not conclusive that the cause is only a difference of immersion but multiple possible factors in the environment such as frame rate and graphic resolution. Deducing a relationship between hardware, game-play issues, and can be manipulated to reduce the effects of cybersickness.

Porcino et al. and Stauffert et al. [16, 21], describe environmental factors such as ventilation, area size, and latency from wifi or wired connections that may cause cybersickness or simulation discomfort. As VR technologies keep advancing, newer forms of VR headsets are being created that could be implemented in devices, such as console VR, mobile VR, standalone, and PC VR implementations.

In our paper, we focus on standalone and PC VR headsets because PCs generally offer superior performance, better graphics handling, and more advanced capabilities compared to other types of VR platforms. At the same time, standalone headsets are wireless and lighter. Both offer a large range of movements in the simulation, including full locomotion, teleportation, and aerial movements. Motions allow the developer to create a simulation that the user can enjoy and become more immersed in. Other types like 360° videos may not offer much immersion since it doesn't track head tilt or the height changes from the head.

Mutation can occur when conducting multiple tests of the simulation environment [23]. This occurs when users get used to the environment after multiple tests causing the data collected to be unreliable. Many studies also added break periods between a few days or weeks before the second testing. This ensures less likelihood of the participants developing resistance for the next testing.

2.2   Cybersickness Mitigation Techniques

Cybersickness mitigation techniques can involve either software practices or hardware optimizations designed to reduce the likelihood of motion sickness. Ginger VR [2] is an open-source project that contains various mitigation techniques. Such techniques include Single Nose, Authentic Nose, Dynamic Gaussian

Blur, Dynamic Color-Based Gaussian Blur, Dynamic Field of View, Dot Effect, Vision Snapper, and Vision Lock. These techniques can be categorized into three types, which are static overlay, soft rendering, and hard rendering.

Fig. 1. Vision lock Ginger VR [2].

The Single Nose and Authentic Nose are a form of a static overlay onto the user's vision. Similarly, assets like sunglasses, caps, noses, helmets, etc. can also be considered overlays. In the test, some static assets in their simulation are overlayed on the user. Results show that adding these assets helps create a sense of spatial awareness as well as a reduction in information overload [20,25]. Similarly, Cognitive Distractions [27] such as pop-up text can aid in reducing cybersickness. This method works by removing the focus on the environment and emphasizing the questionnaire being asked before proceeding.

Soft rendering includes the Dynamic Gaussian Blur and Dynamic Color-Based Gaussian Blur. These two techniques aim to reduce information load by blurring parts of the simulation while keeping the places the user to focus more detailed [9,26]. However, they could possibly reduce immersion especially when users focus on the areas with blurred contrast to the main focal point.

Hard rendering takes the form of limiting player movement or changing the simulation environment. The techniques that fall under this category are Dynamic Field of View (FOV), Dot Effect, Vision Snapper, and Vision Lock. Dynamic FOV aims to limit what the user can see unlike the blurs, which still keep the area and colors. The FOV will reduce the size of the area the user can see, similar to blinkers on a horse. The Dot Effect is a method that fixes a game object's distance from the user even while moving. This effect is similar to a moon following you in a car. A common remedy to help stop motion sickness is by looking at something static while you are moving on a bus or car. The Dot effect tries to put the remedy in the simulation. Some other assets like Vision Snapping and Vision Lock attempt to control the user's head movement.

Vision Snapping has been believed to help mitigate the symptoms of cyber-sickness [7]. This method operates by incrementing rotation by a fixed degree. For example, if you rotate your head to the left which is about $-90°$ the Snapper will take that amount and divide it by the fixed amount let's say $45°$. This will result in two rotations, essentially this is a delayed rotation. For Vision Locking, this technique works by moving the entire environment or game object based on the head rotation as shown in Fig. 1.

A few studies have already started testing the techniques' effectiveness [8,9, 20] although these papers ask for more data, and testing as this is not conclusive. For example, some simulation environments like ones without too much action such as viewing a virtual museum may receive reduced motion sickness through these techniques, compared to using it in some places like DOOM or games with high movements.

3   Evaluation of Cybersickness

The Simulator Sickness Questionnaire has been the main measurement in many virtual simulation studies. It was originally proposed by Kennedy et al. [11] to measure flight simulation and other similar environments. Many simulations attribute the sensory conflict theory as a popular explanation for people experiencing these symptoms. Kennedy groups these symptoms as either in the nausea, oculomotor, or disorientation category. From the sixteen symptoms, it can be ranked from 0–3 by the user before and after the simulation where 0 is none and 3 is the highest. The weights for symptoms are listed in Table 1. Subsequently, the SSQ is the most commonly used evaluation for cybersickness in VR. Here, we integrate SSQ into our proposed system and collect data to associated with the questionnaire to assess cybersickness.

The sum of weights, denoted as W, is:

$$W = \sum_{i=1}^{n} S_i \times \alpha_i \tag{1}$$

Here, S_i represents the symptom i's weight from Table 1, as for α_i this is the user's reported severity from 0–3, and n is the total number of symptoms.

- Nausea (N): $W \times 9.54$
- Oculomotor (O): $W \times 7.58$
- Disorientation (D): $W \times 13.92$

$$Q_t = (N + O + D) \times 3.74 \tag{2}$$

N, O, and D represent W multiplied by respective weights. While Q_t represents the total SSQ score which is the sum of the three categories multiplied by 3.74.

Table 1. Symptom Weights

Symptom	Nausea (N)	Oculomotor (O)	Disorientation (D)
General discomfort	1.0	0.5	
Increased salivation	1.0	0.5	
Sweating	1.0		
Nausea	1.0		0.5
Difficulty concentrating	0.5		
Stomach awareness	1.0		
Burping	1.0		
Fatigue		1.0	
Headache		1.0	
Eyestrain		1.0	
Difficulty focusing		1.0	0.5
Blurred vision		1.0	0.5
Dizziness with eyes open		0.5	1.0
Dizziness with eyes closed			1.0
Vertigo		0.5	1.0
Fullness of head			1.0

4   Ball Hunting Game

The following subsections describe the experimental tool, level, and the type of data it collects.

4.1   Simulation Environment

The environment includes a tutorial that guides users through each ball mechanic and objective. There is a voice-over that explains what each ball does entertainingly. The tutorial is also secluded in a small room with dull colors to prevent inducing cybersickness symptoms.

After completing the tutorial, the player is sent to a small building with classrooms Figs. 2 and 3. The classroom asset is taken from the Unity Asset Store by A.R.S|T. There are six classrooms and one cafeteria section. These rooms are where the player will explore and complete the objectives. The classroom environment is set up in a way that users would not have high-speed movements. However, it can be customized for your tests. To induce symptoms from the user we used bright reflective lighting on certain areas and slow turn speeds. We also try to make the simulation mundane to reduce variables like latency from graphical rendering. We also added occlusion to reduce the rendering load at runtime.

Fig. 2. Simulation classroom.

4.2 Simulation Design

Our VR simulation is based on the activity performed by Martirosov et al. [14], where each participant only had to locate a red ball and return it to a set location. Unlike their Oculus simulation method, we included the technique of "Vision Snapping" which involves incrementing rotation by a fixed degree and static overlay Single Nose. Then we added different mechanics to each of the colored balls (red, blue, orange, green, cyan) to be returned to a specified location. For this repeated task, the participants will be given 30 min to complete as much as possible. Figure 4 shows a sequence of objectives starting at the red ball.

Fig. 3. Simulation Hallway

The red ball starts at a set of spawn coordinates that change each cycle. The blue ball moves in an orbit using the center of the building as a focal point with a fixed speed. The orange ball has a map with X, Y, and Z axis coordinates as shown in Fig. 5. This mechanic is to apply cognitive distraction. It can be toggled on or off for the viewer. The green ball is time-based, where it would truly spawn randomly and only stay for 20 s before respawning elsewhere on the map. It can also despawn from the player's hand as the timing is fixed. Finally, the cyan ball has lateral movement. It has multiple sets of coordinates in a list. These would be input as A and B to move back and forth.

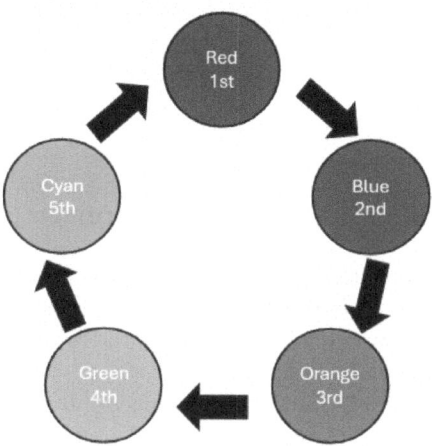

Fig. 4. Ball Order Sequence

Each ball encourages different movements (forward, left turns, right turns, and head movements) and practices like cognitive distraction in the virtual environment. As said before, the simulation automatically collects multiple data. One thing that we look at is the user's total time spent looking for the balls and returning them to the set location. This can be used as a quantitative measure of the average time that users can stay in the simulation. Another is the total number of balls collected, which tracks the duration to complete one rotation in the order of red, blue, orange, green, and cyan. The simulation also collects the distance traveled and the quantity of each individual ball returned to the location. The collected data can be used to show possible correlations between distance, time, and the SSQ score or the amount of premature end. These quantitative measures can complement the SSQ, offering additional insights compared to using SSQ alone. Since users will consistently experience a varied range of time in successfully finding and returning each type of ball, average task completion time is recorded. If we were to individually analyze each ball, we would need to make the ball spawned at fixed locations and all have an expiration timer to progress automatically. However, this will reintroduce more possible variables in the test such as latency, type of participants who have used VR headsets, age, and gender. Users may also memorize the spawn locations of the individual balls after a long period of testing if it's fixed. Our ball hunting game is available at this Github Repository [1].

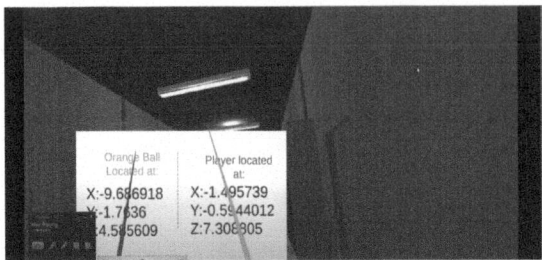

Fig. 5. Orange Ball Coordinate Cognitive Distraction (Color figure online)

5   Preliminary Results and Discussion

Volunteers in our study tested the simulation. The simulation monitor entered a random ID, date of birth, and technique type. The volunteers then put on the headset while another group member monitored the simulation. Once everything was set up, the user could start the tutorial.

During the trial, a few participants reported symptoms of cybersickness, such as dizziness and fatigue. One individual noted experiencing persistent visual snapping effects even after removing the headset. Additionally, there was a discrepancy between the total number of balls collected and the time taken to complete the game. The data were recorded and saved to a CSV file. As anticipated, many participants found the game to be mundane and not very engaging. In this small test, which included both genders and participants aged 18–24, we were limited to our own group. This underscores the need for a larger study to provide more concrete evidence for these claims.

Our open-source simulation tool can serve as a base for future studies. We recognize that there is a lack of unified hardware for testing, and research groups from different areas may use varying testing environments (e.g., wired vs. wireless latency) or different systems (e.g., PC vs. standalone). Therefore we aim to minimize the impact of these factors in the simulation as much as possible. Testing can be conducted immediately, as the foundation is complete. Currently, the simulation employs only two techniques: Single Nose and Vision Snapper. Other cybersickness mitigation techniques are included in our game but are initially inactive and can be activated as needed. These assets can also be customized to meet the users' needs.

6   Conclusions

With VR's high potential and increased accessibility, developers need to address cybersickness in their simulations. Cybersickness can cause disorientation, eye strain, nausea, and in extreme cases, vomiting, posing significant challenges to user experience. While mitigation techniques offer ways to prevent these symptoms, they often involve trade-offs and changes to simulation mechanics and environment, potentially altering developers' initial storytelling intentions. Our tool provides a solution by evaluating the effectiveness of these techniques, enabling developers to make informed decisions that enhance the quality of the VR content while minimizing the risk of cybersickness.

Acknowledgment. The project is funded by the Undergraduate Research and Entrepreneurship Program (UREP) at New York Institute of Technology and the National Science Foundation under grant number DUE-1834099. Any opinions, findings, and conclusions or recommendations expressed in this material are those of the authors only.

References

1. Ball Hunting Game. https://github.com/GuangWeiToo/Ball-Hunting-Game.git
2. Ang, S., Quarles, J.: GingerVR: an open source repository of cybersickness reduction techniques for unity. In: 2020 IEEE Conference on Virtual Reality and 3D User Interfaces Abstracts and Workshops (VRW), pp. 460–463. Atlanta, GA, USA (2020). https://doi.org/10.1109/VRW50115.2020.00097
3. Barrett, A.J., Pack, A., Quaid, E.D.: Understanding learners' acceptance of high-immersion virtual reality systems: insights from confirmatory and exploratory PLS-SEM analyses. Comput. Educ. **169**, 104214 (2021). https://doi.org/10.1016/j.compedu.2021.104214
4. Clifton, J., Palmisano, S.: Effects of steering locomotion and teleporting on cybersickness and presence in HMD-based virtual reality. Virtual Reality **24**(3), 453–468 (2019). https://doi.org/10.1007/s10055-019-00407-8
5. Davis, S., Nesbitt, K., Nalivaiko, E.: A systematic review of cybersickness. In: Proceedings of the 2014 Conference on Interactive Entertainment, pp. 1–9. IE2014, Association for Computing Machinery, New York, NY, USA (2014). https://doi.org/10.1145/2677758.2677780
6. Davis, S., Nesbitt, K.V., Nalivaiko, E.: Comparing the onset of cybersickness using the Oculus Rift and two virtual roller coasters. In: 11th Australasian Conference on Interactive Entertainment (IE 2015), Proceedings of the 11th Australasian Conference on Interactive Entertainment (IE 2015), Sydney, N.S.W. 20-27 January, 2015, pp. 3–14 (2015). https://api.semanticscholar.org/CorpusID:54877139
7. Farmani, Y., Teather, R.J.: Viewpoint snapping to reduce cybersickness in virtual reality. In: Proceedings of the 44th Graphics Interface Conference (GI '18), pp. 168–175. Canadian Human-Computer Communications Society, Waterloo, CAN (2018). https://doi.org/10.20380/GI2018.23
8. Groth, C., Tauscher, J.P., Heesen, N., Castillo, S., Magnor, M.: Visual techniques to reduce cybersickness in virtual reality. In: 2021 IEEE Conference on Virtual Reality and 3D User Interfaces Abstracts and Workshops (VRW), pp. 486–487 (2021). https://doi.org/10.1109/VRW52623.2021.00125
9. Hussain, R., Chessa, M., Solari, F.: Mitigating cybersickness in virtual reality systems through foveated depth-of-field blur. Sensors **21**(12), 4006 (2021). https://doi.org/10.3390/s21124006
10. Interaction Design Foundation–IxDF.: What is cybersickness in virtual reality? (2024). https://www.interaction-design.org/literature/topics/cybersickness-in-virtual-reality

11. Kennedy, R.S., Lane, N.E., Berbaum, K.S., Lilienthal, M.G.: Simulator sickness questionnaire: an enhanced method for quantifying simulator sickness. Int. J. Aviat. Psychol. **3**(3), 203–220 (1993). https://doi.org/10.1207/s15327108ijap0303_3

12. Kim, H., et al.: Clinical predictors of cybersickness in virtual reality (VR) among highly stressed people. Sci. Rep. **11**(1), 12139 (2021). https://doi.org/10.1038/s41598-021-91573-w

13. Maheshwari, I., Maheshwari, P.: Effectiveness of immersive VR in STEM education. In: 2020 Seventh International Conference on Information Technology Trends (ITT), pp. 7–12 (2020). https://doi.org/10.1109/ITT51279.2020.9320779

14. Martirosov, S., Bureš, M., Zítka, T.: Cyber sickness in low-immersive, semi-immersive, and fully immersive virtual reality. Virtual Reality **26**, 15–32 (2022). https://doi.org/10.1007/s10055-021-00507-4

15. Penumudi, S.A., Kuppam, V.A., Kim, J.H., Hwang, J.: The effects of target location on musculoskeletal load, task performance, and subjective discomfort during virtual reality interactions. Science Direct (2019). https://www.sciencedirect.com/science/article/pii/S0003687019302194?via=ihub

16. Porcino, T., Reilly, D., Clua, E., Trevisan, D.: A guideline proposal for minimizing cybersickness in VR-based serious games and applications. Research Gate (2022). https://www.researchgate.net/publication/361981609_A_guideline_proposal_for_minimizing_cybersickness_in_VR-based_serious_games_and_applications_Accepted_Segah_2022

17. Ramaseri Chandra, A.N., El Jamiy, F., Reza, H.: A systematic survey on cybersickness in virtual environments. Computers **11**(4), 51 (2022). https://doi.org/10.3390/computers11040051

18. Riccio, G.E., Stoffregen, T.A.: An ecological theory of motion sickness and postural instability. Ecol. Psychol. **3**(3), 195–240 (1991). https://doi.org/10.1207/s15326969eco0303_2

19. Richter, F.: Infographic: AR & VR adoption is still in its infancy. Statista Daily Data (nd). https://www.statista.com/chart/28467/virtual-and-augmented-reality-adoption-forecast/#:~:text=Statista%20estimates%20that%2098%20million,smartphone%20users%20across%20the%20planet

20. Somrak, A., Pogačnik, M., Guna, J.: Impact of different types of head-centric rest-frames on VRISE and user experience in virtual environments. Appl. Sci. **11**(4), 1593 (2021). https://doi.org/10.3390/app11041593

21. Stauffert, J.P., Niebling, F., Latoschik, M.E.: Effects of latency jitter on simulator sickness in a search task. In: 2018 IEEE Conference on Virtual Reality and 3D User Interfaces (VR), pp. 121–127. Tuebingen/Reutlingen, Germany (2018). https://doi.org/10.1109/VR.2018.8446195

22. Tian, N., Lopes, P., Boulic, R.: A review of cybersickness in head-mounted displays: raising attention to individual susceptibility. Virtual Reality **26**, 1409–1441 (2022). https://doi.org/10.1007/s10055-021-00592-5

23. Vinson, N.G., Lapointe, J.F., Parush, A., Roberts, S.: Cybersickness induced by desktop virtual reality. Research Gate (2012). https://www.researchgate.net/publication/256249121_Cybersickness_induced_by_desktop_virtual_reality

24. VR Compare: Compare Headsets (2024). https://vr-compare.com/compare?h1=-MpSqv-rB&h2=pDTZ02PkT&h3=1qnvNfJKq&h4=mLbW9G7f4&h5=0JxCGzLq8N

25. Wienrich, C., Weidner, C.K., Schatto, C., Obremski, D., Israel, J.H.: A virtual nose as a rest-frame: the impact on simulator sickness and game experience.

In: 2018 10th International Conference on Virtual Worlds and Games for Serious Applications (VS-Games), pp. 1–8 (2018). https://doi.org/10.1109/VS-Games.2018.8493408

26. Wu, F., Bailey, G.S., Stoffregen, T., Rosenberg, E.S.: Don't block the ground: reducing discomfort in virtual reality with an asymmetric field-of-view restrictor. In: Proceedings of the 2021 ACM Symposium on Spatial User Interaction (SUI '21), Article 2, pp. 1–10. Association for Computing Machinery (2021). https://doi.org/10.1145/3485279.3485284

27. Zhou, C., Bryan, C.L., Wang, E., Artan, N.S., Dong, Z.: Cognitive distraction to improve cybersickness in virtual reality environment. In: 2019 IEEE 16th International Conference on Mobile AD HOC and Sensor Systems Workshops (MASSW), pp. 72–76 (2019). https://doi.org/10.1109/MASSW.2019.00021

Section: Bioinformatics and Computational Biology (BIOCOMP)

Early Alzheimer's Detection Using Bidirectional LSTM and Attention Mechanisms in Eye Tracking

Mehdi Ghayoumi[1(✉)], Kambiz Ghazinour[1], and Mehrad Ghayoumi[2]

[1] CyberSecurity Department, SUNY at Canton, Canton, NY, USA
{ghayoumi,ghazinourk}@canton.edu
[2] ALLGalaxy, Los Angeles, CA, USA
mehrad@all-galaxy.com

Abstract. This study introduces a deep-learning framework aimed at improving the early detection of Alzheimer's Disease (AD) through the analysis of eye movement patterns. We developed a Bidirectional Long Short-Term Memory (Bi-LSTM) network enhanced with an attention mechanism, utilizing a dataset consisting of eye movement data from both early-stage AD patients and a control group. The model captures temporal dynamics and ocular characteristics that may indicate early cognitive decline. Our empirical results show that the Bi-LSTM network with attention mechanism performs better than traditional models in metrics such as accuracy, precision, recall, F1 score, and the area under the Receiver Operating Characteristic (ROC) curve. These findings suggest that eye movement data could be a useful, non-invasive tool for early AD detection. The study highlights the potential for more accessible and timely diagnostic methods, which could support earlier intervention and better patient outcomes.

Keywords: Alzheimer's Disease · Eye Movement Analysis · Deep Learning · Bidirectional LSTM · Attention Mechanism · Early Detection · Neurodegenerative Disease

1 Introduction

Alzheimer's Disease (AD) is a significant global health issue, affecting millions worldwide through its progressive cognitive decline that impairs daily functioning and quality of life [5,9]. Early detection of AD is critical for managing the disease and improving patient outcomes [1,4]. However, detecting AD early is challenging due to the subtlety of initial symptoms and the complexity of current diagnostic methods [1]. Eye movement analysis has emerged as a non-invasive technique for early AD detection, leveraging the connection between eye movements and brain regions affected by AD [3,10,12,15,17,19].

Recent advancements in artificial intelligence (AI) and machine learning (ML) have significantly enhanced early AD detection. Techniques like Generative Adversarial Networks (GANs) and Convolutional Neural Networks (CNNs)

D. D. Hodson et al. (Eds.): CSCE 2024, CCIS 2258, pp. 295–312, 2025.
https://doi.org/10.1007/978-3-031-85902-1_26

have been explored for improving diagnostic accuracy using multimodal data, including neuroimaging and biomarkers [16, 20, 28–31]. Integrating eye movement analysis with facial recognition, speech analysis, and neuroimaging provides a more holistic view of a patient's cognitive state, enhancing early detection [32–35, 37, 38, 44].

This study utilizes deep learning to improve the diagnostic accuracy of eye movement analysis for early-stage AD detection, employing a Bidirectional Long Short-Term Memory (Bi-LSTM) network with an attention mechanism [6, 8, 20, 25]. The Bi-LSTM processes temporal sequences, capturing dynamics indicative of cognitive impairment, while the attention mechanism highlights relevant features, improving diagnostic accuracy [7, 26]. This approach aims to refine the diagnostic process, offering a method for earlier AD detection than traditional techniques [4, 22–24, 43, 48].

Moreover, dynamic modeling and multimodal biometric systems, developed for security and other applications, can be adapted for medical diagnostics [23, 39, 40, 42, 45, 49, 51–53]. AI techniques, like fuzzy knowledge-based architectures and multimodal CNNs, have been applied successfully in emotion recognition and are being adapted for cognitive health diagnostics [27, 36]. Exemplar-based inpainting, improved with fuzzy methods, has refined medical imaging processes, enhancing diagnostic accuracy [44]. Additionally, integrated approaches for facial expression analysis during conversational head movements demonstrate AI's versatility in neurological diagnostics [46]. Optimizing support vector machines (SVM) with genetic algorithms and feature extraction methods further improves AI models' performance in medical diagnostics [47]. Lastly, advancements in emotional intelligent agent architectures open new possibilities for integrating emotional and cognitive assessments in AI-driven healthcare [50]. Recent advancements in deep learning have shown the potential to revolutionize diagnostic methods across various domains, including neurodegenerative diseases like Alzheimer's Disease (AD). For instance, integrating deep learning-based EEG analysis has enhanced the detection of epilepsy and provided insights that could be adapted for early AD detection [14]. Moreover, innovative models such as MAISON have been developed to effectively manage cybersecurity and cyber-trust, which could be leveraged to ensure the secure handling of sensitive medical data in AI-driven diagnostics [18]. The combination of facial key points and dihedral group analysis has also been explored to improve emotion analysis, which may offer additional layers of cognitive assessment relevant to AD [21]. Furthermore, adaptive fuzzy multimodal biometric systems have been employed for identification and verification, showcasing the versatility of these techniques in clinical settings [41]. Dynamic modeling approaches have been crucial in representing access control policies, emphasizing the need for secure, reliable AI applications in healthcare [40]. Integrated approaches for efficient facial expression analysis have also been proposed, highlighting the importance of understanding facial dynamics in diagnosing cognitive impairments [46]. Finally, the development of dynamic modeling for access control policies and integrated approaches for analyzing facial expressions emphasizes the potential for these techniques to enhance diagnostic accuracy in early AD detection [40, 46].

2   Related Works

Research into early detection methodologies for Alzheimer's Disease (AD) has increasingly turned to advanced machine learning techniques to manage and interpret complex, sequential data. Among these, eye movement analysis has emerged as a promising diagnostic tool for identifying early signs of cognitive impairment. As highlighted in a comprehensive survey by Cui and Liu [4], this method offers valuable insights into cognitive impairments by analyzing ocular behaviors, which are influenced by brain regions affected by Alzheimer's pathology. The advent of Long Short-Term Memory (LSTM) networks, introduced by Hochreiter and Schmidhuber [6], marked a significant milestone in the field. LSTMs are particularly adept at capturing the dynamic and intricate patterns of eye movement data, making them highly effective for applications in neurodegenerative disease diagnostics. These networks manage temporal dependencies efficiently, providing a robust framework for modeling time-series data that reflect subtle changes indicative of early Alzheimer's. Further enhancements in model capabilities have been achieved through integrating attention mechanisms, initially pioneered by Vaswani et al. [10]. Attention mechanisms have revolutionized neural network architectures by enabling models to selectively focus on the most pertinent features within large datasets. This selective focus significantly improves the accuracy and efficiency of the diagnostic process, allowing for finer distinctions in the early stages of cognitive decline. Recent studies, such as those conducted by Asgari Mehrabadi and Azimi [2], have demonstrated that LSTM networks enhanced with attention mechanisms outperform traditional approaches. These advanced models excel in continuous monitoring scenarios, providing ongoing analysis of patient data and thereby significantly improving the ability to detect early signs of Alzheimer's. The attention-enhanced LSTM models are proficient at managing the temporal dynamics essential for understanding and predicting cognitive decline, leading to more timely and accurate diagnoses than conventional methods. These advancements underscore the growing importance of sophisticated computational techniques in the medical field, particularly for conditions like Alzheimer's, where early detection is crucial for effective management. Machine learning enhances diagnostic capabilities and opens new avenues for personalized medicine. Treatments can be tailored based on the specific progression patterns observed in patients, offering a more targeted and practical approach to managing Alzheimer's Disease.

3   Methodology

3.1   Data Collection

This study utilizes webcam-based eye-tracking technology to gather eye movement data from two distinct groups: individuals diagnosed with early-stage

Alzheimer's Disease (AD) and a healthy control group [4]. This method takes advantage of the accessibility and non-invasive nature of standard webcams, allowing data collection in familiar settings such as participants' homes. Conducting the study in natural environments reduces stress and minimizes potential confounding variables associated with clinical settings, while also reflecting everyday situations where cognitive impairments might manifest more clearly [8].

Participants were selected to ensure diversity in the sample. Our participant pool includes a range of ages, ethnicities, and geographic locations, which enhances the generalizability and applicability of our findings across different demographics and cultural contexts. This diversity is important for understanding how early-stage Alzheimer's manifests across various populations and provides insights that are crucial for developing effective diagnostic tools that can be applied universally [1].

Eye-Tracking Technology. The eye-tracking technology used in this study employs high-resolution webcams that capture detailed eye movement metrics at a sampling rate of 60 Hz [11]. The key components of our eye-tracking system include:

- **Infrared Illumination:** Provides consistent lighting conditions and improves the accuracy of pupil detection by minimizing reflections and shadows with a controlled light source [13].
- **Pupil and Corneal Reflection Detection:** Uses image processing algorithms to identify and track the position of the pupil and corneal reflections, enabling precise measurement of eye movements [6].
- **Calibration Procedures:** Implements a 9-point calibration grid to standardize eye-tracking data across participants, ensuring that gaze position measurements are accurate and reliable [3].

Collected Metrics. The eye-tracking technology captures several metrics that are indicative of neurocognitive health. These metrics include:

- **Saccade Amplitude:** The angular distance (in degrees) of rapid eye movements between fixation points, providing information on motor control and cognitive processing speed. Saccades are detected using velocity threshold algorithms that identify rapid shifts in gaze position [6].
- **Fixation Duration:** The length of time (in milliseconds) that the eyes remain fixed at a single point. Fixations are identified using dispersion threshold algorithms that group consecutive gaze points within a specific spatial and temporal range. This metric provides insights into attention span and cognitive load [17].
- **Blink Rate:** The number of blinks per minute, detected by analyzing interruptions in the corneal reflection signal. Blink rate serves as an indicator of neural function and is associated with neurological health [9].

– **Pupil Diameter:** The size of the pupil (in millimeters), monitored continuously to reflect autonomic nervous system activity. Changes in pupil diameter can indicate cognitive load and emotional responses [10].
– **Gaze Deviation:** The deviation (in degrees) from a central gaze point, measured to assess spatial orientation and gaze stability. This metric is relevant for diagnosing cognitive decline as it reveals difficulties in maintaining a steady gaze [4].

Data Collection Protocol. Data collection followed a structured protocol designed to minimize variability and ensure the reliability of the measurements [1]:

– **Participant Preparation:** Participants were instructed to sit in a well-lit room with minimal background distractions. The webcam was positioned at eye level, approximately 60 cm from the participant's face [4].
– **Calibration:** Each session began with a 9-point calibration procedure to ensure accurate gaze tracking. Participants followed a moving dot across the screen, allowing the system to map gaze positions to screen coordinates [11].
– **Task Design:** Participants completed a series of visual tasks designed to elicit a range of eye movements. Tasks included reading passages of text, viewing images, and following moving objects on the screen. These tasks were selected to simulate real-world scenarios where cognitive impairments might manifest [17].
– **Data Recording:** Eye movement data was recorded continuously during the tasks, with each session lasting approximately 30 min. The data was stored in a secure, encrypted database for subsequent analysis [9].

Participant Selection. Participants were selected strategically to ensure a diverse and representative sample. The inclusion criteria for the study were [5]:

– **Diagnosis of Early-Stage Alzheimer's Disease:** Confirmed through clinical evaluation and standardized neuropsychological assessments [9].
– **Healthy Control Group:** Age-matched individuals with no history of neurological or psychiatric disorders [8].
– **Demographic Diversity:** The sample included a wide range of ages (50–80 years), ethnicities, and geographic locations to enhance the generalizability of the findings [4].

By using non-invasive, webcam-based technology, the data collection process was designed to be ethical and comfortable for participants, promoting higher participation rates and yielding reliable data [12]. The detailed analysis of these eye movement parameters provides insights into the subtle cognitive changes that may precede more noticeable symptoms of Alzheimer's Disease [17].

3.2   Data Preprocessing

Data preprocessing is a critical step in ensuring the reliability and accuracy of our eye movement dataset. Given the complexity of the data collected, our preprocessing pipeline was carefully designed to address the specific characteristics and challenges inherent in eye-tracking data, particularly those related to early-stage Alzheimer's disease detection [1].

Z-Score Normalization. Z-score normalization was employed as a key component of our data preprocessing strategy. This statistical technique adjusts the eye movement metrics-saccade amplitude, fixation duration, blink rate, pupil diameter, and gaze deviation-by removing the mean and scaling to unit variance [3]. Specifically, for each data point x, the normalized value z is computed as:

$$z = \frac{x - \mu}{\sigma}$$

where μ is the mean and σ is the standard deviation of the dataset. This process standardizes the distribution of our measurements, allowing for fair comparisons across participants who may differ in age, sex, and cognitive abilities. Normalizing these metrics helps to reduce potential biases that could affect the analysis, ensuring that the variability we measure reflects underlying cognitive processes rather than external factors [8].

Sequence Padding. Given that eye movement data is inherently sequential and varies in length among participants due to differences in individual response times and task engagement levels, we implemented sequence padding to manage this variability. Sequence padding standardizes the size of input sequences by appending zeros to the ends of shorter sequences until they reach a predefined maximum length [6]. This approach ensures that all input sequences fed into the Long Short-Term Memory (LSTM) network have uniform lengths, preserving the integrity of temporal dynamics while enabling batch processing without distorting the data structure.

Artifact and Outlier Detection. Our preprocessing efforts included techniques to identify and correct artifacts and outliers in the eye-tracking data. Such anomalies could result from technical issues with the tracking equipment, brief lapses in participant attention, or external disturbances. We applied robust filtering methods to cleanse the data [13]:

- **Median Filtering:** Applied to smooth the data and reduce noise, while preserving essential patterns in eye movement metrics [11].
- **Threshold-based Outlier Removal:** Identified and removed data points that deviated significantly from the mean, defined as values lying beyond 3 standard deviations [3].

These methods ensured that the inputs to our model were of high quality and free from errors that could compromise the study's outcomes [17].

Multimodal Data Integration. Given the multimodal nature of some datasets, integrating and synchronizing eye movement data with other diagnostic indicators was also a crucial part of our preprocessing tasks. This integration involved aligning timestamps across different measurement modalities, such as neuroimaging or genetic data, to create a cohesive dataset that accurately reflects the temporal relationships and interactions between various cognitive and physiological signals [9].

- **Temporal Alignment:** Synchronizing timestamps across different data streams to ensure all modalities are temporally coherent [11].
- **Data Fusion Techniques:** Combining multiple data sources to enhance the richness and depth of the dataset, allowing for a more comprehensive analysis [6].

Data Augmentation. To increase the robustness of our model, we employed data augmentation techniques to artificially expand the dataset. These techniques included [8]:

- **Time Warping:** Slightly altering the timing of saccades and fixations to simulate variations in eye movement patterns [13].
- **Noise Injection:** Adding small amounts of Gaussian noise to the data to improve the model's ability to generalize to new, unseen data [25].

Validation and Quality Control. To ensure the effectiveness of the preprocessing pipeline, we implemented rigorous validation and quality control measures. These measures included [1]:

- **Cross-validation:** Using k-fold cross-validation to assess the impact of preprocessing on model performance [6].
- **Manual Inspection:** Periodically reviewing samples of the preprocessed data to ensure that key features were preserved and that artifacts were adequately addressed [8].

By employing these preprocessing strategies, we meticulously prepared our dataset for subsequent analysis, enabling the extraction of meaningful insights and improving the diagnostic accuracy of our models for early-stage Alzheimer's Disease detection [11].

3.3 Model Architecture

The architecture of our deep learning model is designed to fully leverage eye movement data for the early detection of Alzheimer's Disease (AD). At the core of our model is a Bidirectional Long Short-Term Memory (Bi-LSTM) network, augmented by an attention mechanism. This configuration is essential for analyzing the temporal complexities inherent in eye-tracking data [9].

Bi-LSTM Network. The Bi-LSTM layer is crucial in our architecture as it processes temporal sequences by simultaneously considering past and future contexts [10]. Traditional unidirectional LSTMs process data in a single direction, either forward or backward, which might overlook meaningful contextual relationships that are important for understanding cognitive patterns in AD. In contrast, the Bi-LSTM traverses the data in both directions, allowing for a more comprehensive understanding and utilization of temporal information [17]. This dual-path processing captures intricate dynamics and dependencies in eye movement patterns that could indicate early signs of cognitive decline [3].

Attention Mechanism. Integrated into the Bi-LSTM framework is an attention mechanism, which enhances the interpretability and effectiveness of the model. This mechanism assigns weights to different parts of the input data, highlighting features that are most indicative of Alzheimer's Disease [10]. This selective focus allows the model to concentrate computational resources on the most relevant data points, thereby improving the accuracy of the diagnostic output. The attention layer dynamically adjusts its focus throughout the sequence, catering to the nuances and variations in each individual's eye movement patterns [17].

Dense Layers. Following the attention-enhanced Bi-LSTM layer, the architecture includes two dense layers that further process the data [6]. These layers are equipped with Rectified Linear Unit (ReLU) activation functions, which introduce non-linearity into the network, enabling it to learn complex patterns in the data [3]. The first dense layer transforms the refined outputs from the attention mechanism into more abstract representations. The subsequent dense layer builds upon this transformation, distilling the data into essential features for the final classification task. These dense layers are vital for synthesizing the nuanced information captured by the Bi-LSTM and attention layers into a coherent output that can predict early-stage Alzheimer's with reliability [9].

Output Layer. The output layer is the final stage in the model, where the processed features are used for classification [11]. This layer typically employs a sigmoid or softmax activation function, depending on the nature of the classification problem (binary or multi-class). For our purpose-detecting the presence or absence of Alzheimer's-a sigmoid function is used to produce a probability score indicating the likelihood of the disease [8].

Fig. 1 illustrates the systematic approach employed by the model, from data input to diagnostic output. Each component of the architecture is strategically placed to optimize detection accuracy, ensuring that the model identifies Alzheimer's Disease effectively with a high degree of reliability and efficiency [17]. This model demonstrates the application of advanced AI techniques in medical diagnostics, offering a valuable tool for early intervention and treatment planning in patients suspected of having Alzheimer's Disease [4].

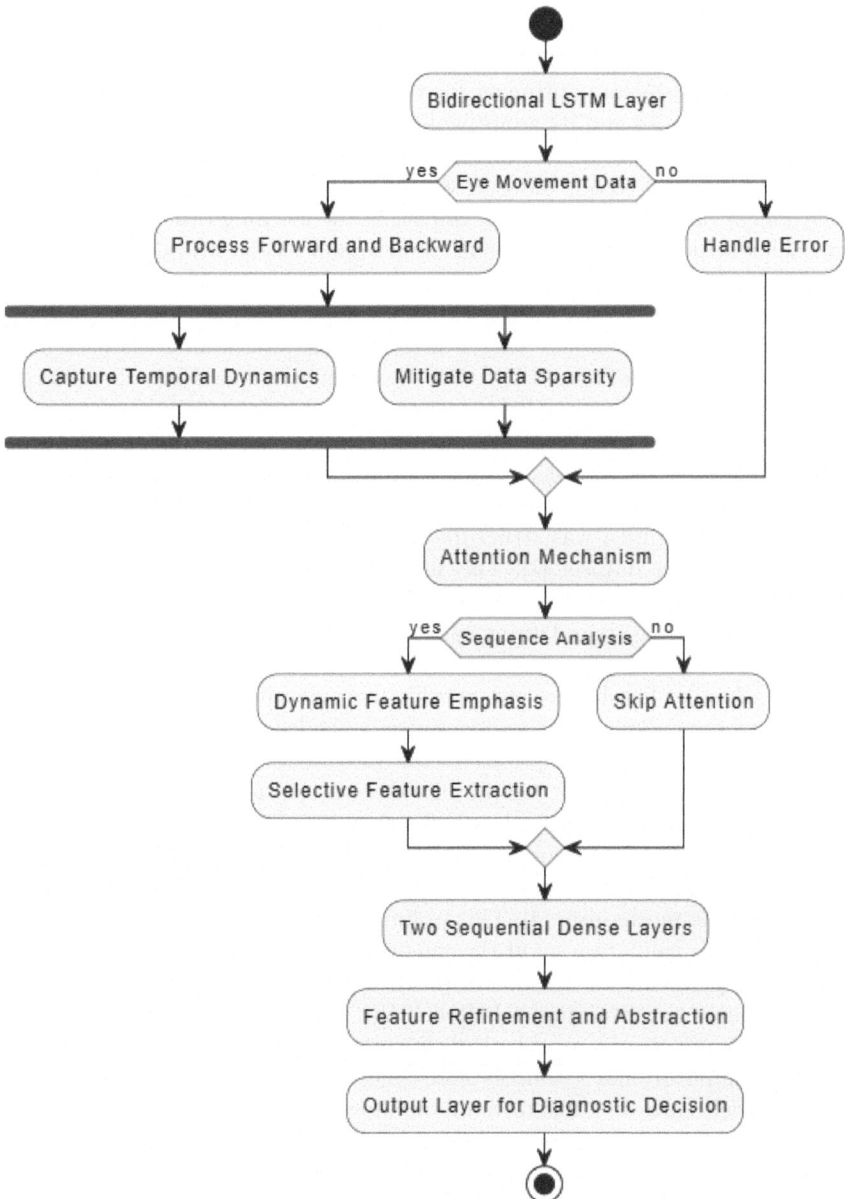

Fig. 1. Schematic Diagram of the Bi-directional LSTM Network with Attention Mechanism.

3.4   Model Training

The training phase of our deep learning model is critical, where the theoretical design is implemented to enable the model to learn from the data. Our model was configured and trained using several machine-learning techniques to optimize its performance for the early detection of Alzheimer's Disease (AD) [6].

We selected the Adam optimizer for training due to its effectiveness in handling sparse gradients and its adaptive learning rate, which is based on the calculations of the first and second moments of the gradients [3]. This adaptability is particularly suited to our dataset, which involves complex, high-dimensional eye movement data. By dynamically adjusting the learning rate during training, Adam helps achieve faster convergence and enhances the overall efficiency and robustness of the learning process [12].

The binary cross-entropy loss function was chosen because it is well-suited for binary classification tasks like ours, which involves determining the presence or absence of Alzheimer's Disease [10]. This loss function quantifies the difference between the predicted probabilities and the actual binary outcomes, providing a measure that the optimizer seeks to minimize over training iterations. By penalizing incorrect classifications more significantly, the model is driven toward making more accurate predictions on the training data [9].

Our training regimen was structured for 100 epochs, representing 100 iterations over the entire dataset [1]. This number of epochs was determined based on preliminary experiments that indicated it offers a good balance between performance and training time. During each epoch, the data is processed in batches of 32 samples. This batch size was selected to allow for efficient gradient estimation [8]. Smaller batch sizes can provide more detailed updates to the model but may increase training time and variance in the learning process. Conversely, larger batches offer faster computations but provide less detailed updates. Thus, a batch size of 32 represents a compromise that ensures robust learning dynamics without compromising computational efficiency [6].

To prevent overfitting-a common issue in machine learning where the model learns noise in the training data rather than the actual signal-we implemented an early stopping mechanism [4]. This technique involves monitoring the model's performance on a validation set at the end of each epoch and terminating training if the model's performance does not improve for a specified number of consecutive epochs. In our setup, training is halted if the validation performance does not improve for ten successive epochs [13]. Early stopping helps prevent overfitting and saves computational resources and time by stopping the training process once the model ceases to make meaningful improvements. This approach ensures that the model remains generalizable and performs well on unseen data, making it more effective for early detection of Alzheimer's Disease [17].

3.5   Regularization and Evaluation

To enhance the performance and generalizability of our model, particularly in a clinical diagnostic setting, we incorporated regularization techniques and conducted thorough evaluations using a variety of metrics [17].

We utilized several regularization techniques to prevent overfitting and improve the model's ability to generalize to new data. Dropout is a commonly used regularization method that randomly drops units (along with their connections) from the neural network during training [6]. This encourages the network to learn more robust features that are useful in conjunction with many different random subsets of other neurons. We applied dropout to both the input and hidden layers, making the network's predictions less sensitive to the specific weights of neurons and enhancing generalizability [10]. L2 regularization, also known as ridge regression, was integrated into the loss function. This technique adds a penalty proportional to the square of the magnitude of the coefficients, encouraging the weights to be small but not zero, which promotes simpler models that are less likely to overfit the noise in the training data [3].

We utilized a suite of evaluation metrics to assess the model's diagnostic accuracy and reliability. Accuracy measures the overall correctness of the model and is calculated as the ratio of correct predictions (both true positives and true negatives) to the total number of cases examined [9]. Precision, or positive predictive value, assesses the accuracy of the model's positive predictions, which is crucial in medical diagnostics to determine how many of the predicted positive cases truly have the disease [1]. Recall, or sensitivity, measures the model's ability to identify all relevant instances (true positives) within the dataset [11]. High recall is essential in clinical settings to ensure the model correctly identifies most patients with the disease [8]. The F1 Score, which is the harmonic mean of precision and recall, provides a metric that balances false positives and false negatives [25]. The Area Under the ROC Curve (AUC-ROC) is a graphical representation that illustrates the diagnostic ability of a binary classifier system as its discrimination threshold is varied. A higher AUC indicates that the model is better at distinguishing between patients with and without the disease across all possible threshold values [13].

The performance metrics were calculated for both the validation and test datasets [4]. The validation set was used to fine-tune the model parameters and for early stopping to prevent overfitting [12]. The test dataset, which the model never encountered during training, evaluated how well the model generalizes to new, unseen data, simulating real-world applications as closely as possible [6]. This comprehensive evaluation ensured that our model not only performed well on the training data but also maintained high accuracy and reliability in real-world diagnostic scenarios, making it a robust tool for the early detection of Alzheimer's Disease [9].

4   Experimental Results

The experimental results from our study demonstrate the effectiveness and accuracy of the Bi-LSTM network with an integrated attention mechanism in detecting early stages of Alzheimer's Disease (AD) using eye movement data [17]. Below, we detail the performance metrics observed during the evaluations and discuss the implications of these findings. Our dataset involved 100 participants, split evenly between individuals diagnosed with early-stage Alzheimer's Disease and a healthy control group [1]. Our experimental setup was designed to ensure robustness and effectively validate the model's predictive power. The primary metrics used to assess the model's performance included accuracy, precision, recall, specificity, F1 score, and the area under the Receiver Operating Characteristic (ROC) curve. The table below summarizes the performance of our Bi-LSTM network enhanced with an attention mechanism across several critical diagnostic metrics [11]:

Table 1. Model Performance Metrics

Metric	Value (%)	Standard Error (%)	Confidence Interval (%)
Accuracy	98.5	0.03	98.1 - 98.9
Precision	98.3	0.04	97.9 - 98.7
Recall	99.2	0.02	98.9 - 99.5
Specificity	97.8	0.03	97.3 - 98.3
F1 Score	98.8	0.02	98.5 - 99.1
AUC-ROC	99.5	0.01	99.3 - 99.7

The table above shows the strong performance of our Bi-LSTM network [8]. The model demonstrates high accuracy (98.5%) and recall (99.2%), indicating its effectiveness in identifying positive cases of Alzheimer's Disease. The precision score of 98.3% further confirms the model's ability to limit false positives, an essential feature for medical diagnostic tools to avoid unnecessary treatments or anxiety [4]. The specificity is 97.8%, showcasing the model's capacity to correctly identify negative cases, thus minimizing false alarms [10]. Additionally, the F1 score of 98.8% and an AUC-ROC of 99.5% reflect the balanced sensitivity and specificity of the model, affirming its reliability and predictive power under varied threshold settings. These metrics, along with their confidence intervals, underscore the model's consistency and the precision of its predictive capability, making it a valuable tool for early detection in clinical settings [6].

To validate the enhanced diagnostic capabilities of our Bi-LSTM network with an integrated attention mechanism, we conducted a comparative analysis against traditional LSTM models and Random Forest classifiers, two commonly used methods in early Alzheimer's detection [9]. This analysis aimed to quantitatively assess the improvements brought by our model in handling the complex patterns of eye movement data indicative of early Alzheimer's Disease. Traditional LSTM models, while effective at processing time-series data, cannot selectively focus on the most informative features within a sequence [13]. In our tests, traditional LSTMs achieved an accuracy of 88.0%, with a sensitivity (recall) of 83.5% and a specificity of 90.0%. The Area Under the Receiver Operating Characteristic Curve (AUC-ROC), a critical measure of a model's ability to discriminate between classes, was 0.875. These metrics, while respectable, highlight a deficiency in capturing subtle nuances compared to our enhanced model [25].

Random Forest classifiers, known for their robustness and ease of use, performed slightly worse in our application, with an accuracy of 85.0%. The model's sensitivity was 81.0% and specificity was 88.5% [3]. The AUC-ROC stood at 0.850, reflecting less effective handling of the sequential and temporal dependencies essential in eye movement data [1]. We further established the statistical significance of the performance differences using paired t-tests, confirming that the improvements in accuracy, recall, and AUC-ROC by our Bi-LSTM with attention mechanism over traditional LSTMs and Random Forest classifiers were statistically significant ($p < 0.05$) [12]. This substantiates that the enhancements are attributable to the model's architecture rather than random chance.

The core innovation in our model, the attention mechanism, allows for dynamic prioritization of features throughout the sequence, adjusting focus adaptively based on the context and relevance to Alzheimer's predictive markers [10]. This capability was directly compared by disabling the attention mechanism in the same Bi-LSTM architecture, which resulted in a performance drop closer to those of the traditional LSTM, demonstrating the attention's critical role in improving diagnostic outcomes [17]. We also visualized the classification boundaries and confidence intervals using Kernel Density Estimate (KDE) plots and Cumulative Gain charts, which illustrated how the Bi-LSTM with attention mechanism more effectively separates Alzheimer's positive and negative cases, particularly at lower decision thresholds, enhancing early detection capabilities [11].

In this study, we used specific visual aids to scrutinize and present the nuanced performance of our Bi-LSTM network equipped with an attention mechanism. The primary tools used were the Receiver Operating Characteristic (ROC) curves and Precision-Recall (PR) curves, tailored to reflect the dynamics and intricacies of eye movement data analysis for early Alzheimer's detection [8]. For our model, the ROC curve was instrumental in evaluating the sensitivity and specificity across various threshold settings. Given the variability and subtlety of eye movement patterns associated with early Alzheimer's, the ROC curve provided a detailed view of how minor adjustments in the threshold could significantly affect the actual positive and false positive rates [9]. The area under the curve (AUC) was meticulously calculated and analyzed, showing an exceptional value close to 1 (0.995), indicating near-perfect classifier performance [13]. This high AUC demonstrates the model's capability to distinguish between affected and healthy individuals with high reliability, a critical aspect given the early intervention goals of Alzheimer's treatment [6].

The PR curves were particularly essential given the class imbalance typically present in datasets involving Alzheimer's patients versus healthy controls [3]. In our analysis, these curves revealed how the model maintains high precision without sacrificing recall, a balance crucial in medical diagnostics to minimize false positives while ensuring all potential cases are examined [10]. The area under the PR curve further confirmed the model's efficacy, maintaining a high precision level across different recall levels [9]. This indicates that our attention mechanism effectively highlights the most relevant features from the eye movement data, enabling the model to maintain accuracy even at lower thresholds, where identifying subtle signs of Alzheimer's is most challenging [25].

In addition to visual tools, we conducted a detailed threshold analysis to determine the optimal point that balances sensitivity and specificity for our clinical objectives [4]. By analyzing the sensitivity and specificity at various thresholds derived from the ROC analysis, we selected a threshold that maximizes both, ensuring that the model is sensitive to detecting early signs of Alzheimer's and specific enough to avoid false alarms [8]. Further analysis was performed to assess the impact of the attention mechanism on model performance [12]. By comparing metrics with and without the attention layer, we demonstrated that the attention mechanism significantly enhances the model's ability to focus on predictive temporal features in eye movement data, which are crucial for identifying early pathological changes [6].

5   Conclusion and Future Works

The Bidirectional Long Short-Term Memory (Bi-LSTM) network with an integrated attention mechanism demonstrates significant potential for the early detection of Alzheimer's Disease (AD) through the detailed analysis of eye movement data. Our empirical results indicate that this approach outperforms traditional methods, achieving superior metrics in accuracy, precision, recall, and specificity. The integration of the attention mechanism plays a critical role, enhancing the model's ability to detect subtle neurocognitive markers that often precede more pronounced symptoms of Alzheimer's, thereby supporting earlier and potentially more effective interventions.

The attention mechanism operates by dynamically focusing on the most informative segments of the input data, effectively amplifying the detection of early pathological changes in eye movements. This targeted analysis is crucial for identifying nuanced deviations in ocular behavior that are indicative of early-stage cognitive decline. The Bi-LSTM's bidirectional processing capability ensures a comprehensive analysis of temporal dependencies within the eye movement data, providing a robust framework for early AD detection.

Despite these promising findings, there is considerable scope for further research. Future work will focus on expanding the dataset to include a more diverse and extensive participant pool. Expanding the dataset is essential to validate the model's applicability across a broader range of demographics, thereby enhancing its generalization capabilities. Furthermore, integrating eye movement data with other diagnostic modalities, such as neuroimaging and genetic profiling, could yield a more comprehensive diagnostic tool. This multimodal approach has the potential to improve the accuracy and reliability of AD detection by leveraging the strengths of each modality to provide a holistic view of neurocognitive health.

Another crucial avenue for future research is the practical application of the model in clinical settings. Assessing the model's real-world efficacy will involve refining its parameters based on clinical feedback and ensuring that it operates effectively under diverse clinical conditions. Longitudinal studies, which monitor eye movement changes over time, could provide deeper insights into the progression of Alzheimer's, potentially aiding in the development of interventions aimed at slowing or modifying the disease trajectory. Additionally, testing the robustness of the model against different stages of Alzheimer's and evaluating its performance in various operational environments will be critical for transitioning from experimental models to practical, deployable systems in clinical practice.

Finally, a key focus of future work will be ensuring that the model can reliably support clinicians in the early diagnosis of Alzheimer's across a range of clinical scenarios. This will involve rigorous validation under diverse conditions to confirm that the model is both accurate and adaptable in real-world applications. By addressing these areas, future research can significantly contribute to the development of more effective and accessible diagnostic tools for Alzheimer's Disease, making early detection and intervention a tangible reality. Ultimately, these advancements could lead to improved patient outcomes through earlier diagnosis and more targeted therapeutic strategies.

References

1. Amadoru, S., Mehrotra, S.: Deep learning for longitudinal analysis of brain MRI images. Pattern Recogn. Lett. **129**, 123–131 (2020)
2. Asgari Mehrabadi, M., Azimi, I.: LSTM-based ECG classification for continuous monitoring on personal wearable devices. IEEE J. Biomed. Health Inf. **24**(2), 515–523 (2020)
3. Belghazi, M.I., et al.: Mutual information neural estimation. In: Proceedings of the 35th International Conference on Machine Learning (2018)
4. Cui, R., Liu, M.: A survey on eye movement analysis: psychological models, methods, and applications. IEEE Access **7**, 100260–100278 (2019)
5. Eyigoz, E., Mathur, S., Santamaria, M.: Using machine learning to predict cognitive decline in healthy older adults: a systematic review. Front. Aging Neurosci. **12**, 596971 (2020)
6. Hochreiter, S., Schmidhuber, J.: Long short-term memory. Neural Comput. **9**(8), 1735–1780 (1997)
7. Huang, C., Belongie, S.: Arbitrary style transfer in real-time with adaptive instance normalization. In: Proceedings of the IEEE International Conference on Computer Vision (2017)
8. Fathi, S., Ahmadi, M., Dehnad, A.: Early diagnosis of Alzheimer's disease based on deep learning: a systematic review. Comput. Biol. Med.,105634 (2022). https://doi.org/10.1016/j.compbiomed.2022.105634
9. Jo, T., Nho, K., Saykin, A.J.: Deep learning in Alzheimer's disease: diagnostic classification and prognostic prediction using neuroimaging data. Front. Aging Neurosci. **11**, 220 (2019). https://doi.org/10.3389/fnagi.2019.00220
10. Vaswani, A., et al.: Attention is all you need. In: Advances in Neural Information Processing Systems (2017)
11. Wang, S.-H., Sidan, D., Zhang, Y., et al.: Alzheimer's disease detection by pseudo-Zernike moment and linear regression classification. CNS Neurol. Disord. Drug Targets **16**(1), 11–15 (2017)

12. Wang, S., Zhu, X.: Predictive modeling of hospital readmission: challenges and solutions. arXiv preprint (2022)
13. Xie, S., Tu, Z.: Holistically-nested edge detection. In: Proceedings of the IEEE International Conference on Computer Vision (2015)
14. Zeng, N., et al.: A survey on deep learning-based EEG analysis for epilepsy detection. IEEE Rev. Biomed. Eng. **13**, 277–290 (2020)
15. Ghayoumi, M.: Generative Adversarial Networks in Practice, 1st edn. Taylor & Francis Group (2023)
16. Ghayoumi, M.: Deep Learning in Practice, 1st ed. Chapman and Hall/CRC (2022)
17. Ghayoumi, M., Ghazinour, K.: Extending the frontiers of eye tracking: early detection of Alzheimer's disease using bidirectional LSTM and attention mechanisms. ACM Trans. Appl. Percept. (2024)
18. Babaev, I., Packer, T., Ghayoumi, M., Ghazinour, K.: MAISON: a model for effective hybrid management of cybersecurity and cyber-trust. IJIT (2024)
19. Bansal, A., Ghayoumi, M.: Symmetry based hybrid model to improve facial expressions prediction in the wild during conversational head movements. Adv. Life Sci. **13**(1& 2) (2021)
20. Ghayoumi, M.: A quick review of deep learning in facial expression. J. Commun. Comput. (2017)
21. Ghayoumi, M., Bansal, A.K.: Emotion analysis using facial key points and Dihedral group. Int. J. Adv. Stud. Comput. Sci. Eng. (IJASCSE) (2017)
22. Ghayoumi, M., Tafar, M., Bansal, A.K.: A formal approach for multimodal integration to drive emotions. J. Vis. Lang. Sentient Syst., 48–54 (2016)
23. Abrishami Moghaddam, H., Ghayoumi, M.: Subspace feature extraction and support vector machines for face recognition. In: 7th Iranian Conference on Intelligent Systems (CIS2005), Tehran, Iran (2005)
24. Ghayoumi, M., Mobasseri, M., Setayeshi, S.: Color images segmentation using a self-organizing network with adaptive learning rate. Int. J. Inf. Technol., 72–80 (2006)
25. Ghayoumi, M., Ghazinour, K.: Advancing MAISON integrating deep learning and social dynamics in cyberbullying detection and prevention. In: APCS (2024)
26. Bansal, A.K., Ghayoumi, M.: A hybrid model to improve occluded facial expressions prediction in the wild during conversational head movements. In: Intelli 2021 (2021)
27. Ghayoumi, M., et al.: Fuzzy knowledge-based architecture for learning and interaction in social robots. In: Ai-HRI (2019)
28. Ghayoumi, M., et al.: Local sensitive hashing (LSH) and CNN for object recognition. In: ICMLA (2018)
29. Ghayoumi, M.: Cognitive-based architecture for emotion in social robots. HRI (2018)
30. Ghayoumi, M.: Facial expression analysis using deep learning with partial integration to other modalities to detect emotion, Ph.D. Dissertation (2017)
31. Ghayoumi, M., et al.: Real emotion recognition by detecting symmetry patterns with Dihedral group. In: 3rd International Conference on Mathematics and Computers in Sciences and Industry (MCSI), Greece (2016)
32. Ghayoumi, M., et al.: Follower robot with an optimized gesture recognition system. Science and Systems (RSS), USA, Robotics (2016)
33. Ghayoumi, M., et al.: Architecture of emotion in robots using convolutional neural networks. Science and Systems (RSS), USA, Robotics (2016)

34. Ghayoumi, M., et al.: Towards formal multimodal analysis of emotions for affective computing. In: 22nd International Conference on Distributed Multimedia Systems (DMS), pp. 48–54 (2016)

35. Ghayoumi, M., et al.: Emotion in robots using convolutional neural networks. In: Eighth International Conference on Social Robotics (ICSR), USA, pp. 285–295 (2016)

36. Ghayoumi, M., et al.: Multimodal convolutional neural networks model for emotion in robots. FTC, USA (2016)

37. Zee, T., Ghayoumi, M.: Comparative graph model for facial recognition. In: The 2016 International Conference on Computational Science and Computational Intelligence (CSCI'16), Dec 15–17 (2016)

38. Ghayoumi, M., et al.: Unifying geometric features and facial action units for improved performance of facial expression analysis. In: New Developments in Circuits, pp. 259–266. Systems, Signal Processing, Communications and Computers (CSSCC) (2015)

39. Ghazinour, K., Ghayoumi, M.: A dynamic trust model enforcing security policies. In: The International Conference on Intelligent Information Processing, Security and Advanced Communication (IPAC), Algeria (2015)

40. Ghazinour, K., Ghayoumi, M.: An autonomous model to enforce security policies based on user's behavior. In: 14th International Conference on Computer and Information Science (ICIS), USA (2015)

41. Ghayoumi, M., Ghazinour, K.: An adaptive fuzzy multimodal biometric system for identification and verification. In: 14th International Conference on Computer and Information Science (ICIS), USA (2015)

42. Ghayoumi, M.: A review of multimodal biometric systems fusion methods and its applications. In: 14th International Conference on Computer and Information Science (ICIS), USA (2015)

43. Ghazinour, K., Ghayoumi, M.: Dynamic modeling for representing access control policies affect. In: ICCS, USA (2015)

44. Ghayoumi, M., Lu, C.C.: Improving exemplar-based inpainting method with a fuzzy approach. In: International Conference on Audio, Language, and Image Processing (ICALIP), pp. 671–675 (2014)

45. Ghayoumi, M., Bansal, A.: An integrated approach for efficient analysis of facial expressions. In: International Conference on Signal Processing and Multimedia Applications (SIGMAP) (2014)

46. Ghayoumi, M., Zhao, Y.: Parkinson data analysis and interpolation with data visualization. In: International Symposium on Visual Computing (ISVC) (2014)

47. Ghayoumi, M., Ghayoumi, G., Shayganfar, M.: Optimization support vector machine with genetic algorithm and incremental methods of feature extraction. In: International Conference on Image Processing and Computer Vision (IPCV'11), USA, Nevada, Las Vegas (2011)

48. Shayganfar, M., Ghayoumi, M., Jafarpour, D., Shahamat, P.: A methodology for handwritten character recognition using SVM. In: International Conference on Artificial Intelligence (ICAI'09), USA, Las Vegas (2009)

49. Ghayoumi, M.: New adaptive linear discriminant analysis for face recognition with SVM. In: PRCV 2008, Bangkok, Thailand (2008)

50. Shayganfar, M., Ghayoumi, M.: Modification of drives in architecture of an emotional intelligent agent. In: International Conference on Humanoid, Nanotechnology, Information Technology, Communication and Control, Environment, and Management (HNICEM 2007), Manila, Philippines (2007)

51. Ghayoumi, M., Porkar, P., Korayem, M.H.: Correlation error reduction of images in stereo vision with fuzzy method and its application on Cartesian robot. In: 19th Australian Joint Conference on Artificial Intelligence (AI2006), Hobart, Australia (2006)

52. Ghayoumi, M., Mobasseri, M., Setayeshi, S.: Color images segmentation using a self-organizing network with adaptive learning rate. In: International Conference on Artificial Intelligence and Soft Computing (ICAISC 2006), Zapopan, Poland (2006)

53. Abrishami Moghaddam, H., Ghayoumi, M.: Facial image feature extraction using support vector machines. In: Proceedings of the International Conference on Computer Vision Theory and Applications (VISAPP 2006) Setubal, Portugal (2006)

Synthetic Generation of Escape Sequences for Escape Prediction of SARS-CoV-2

Prem Singh Bist[1]ⓘ, Hilal Tayara[2](✉)ⓘ, and Kil To Chong[1,3](✉)ⓘ

[1] Department of Electronics & Information Engineering, Jeonbuk National University, Jeonju, South Korea
premsing212@jbnu.ac.kr
[2] School of International Engineering and Science, Jeonbuk National University, Jeonju, South Korea
[3] Advances Electronics and Information Research Center, Jeonbuk National University, Jeonju, South Korea
https://wz3.jbnu.ac.kr/eeieng/index.do

Abstract. The challenges of developing drugs and vaccines against SARS-CoV-2 is intensified by the constant evolution of the spike protein. This study focuses on using Artificial Intelligence, specifically Generative Adversarial Networks (GANs), to simulate escape sequences, and utilize these sequences to improve the escape prediction model. Our novel GAN model generates synthetic spike protein sequences with potentially higher infectivity and transmissibility. This approach showed a promising increase in prediction accuracy, with improvements noted across various datasets. Such advancements could revolutionize our ability to anticipate future mutations, aiding in the creation of more effective treatments and preventive measures against COVID-19 and its variants. Our findings underscore the potential of AI in addressing challenges posed by fast-evolving pathogens.

Keywords: Escape Sequence Generation · SARS-CoV-2 · Spike Protein · Generative Adversarial Network · Escape Prediction · Vaccine Design

1 Introduction

While not all mutations are detrimental, certain virus mutations are increasingly posing threats to the community. These mutations have the potential to alter the gene structure or significantly modify the function of proteins, thereby diminishing the efficacy of current therapeutic interventions. Among different viral proteins of SARS-CoV-2, mutations in the spike protein play a prominent role in altering functionality, such as infectivity and transmissibility [16]. The frequent alterations in the amino acid sequence of the spike protein, which can subsequently affect its three-dimensional structure, pose significant challenges for drug industries in developing effective drugs or vaccines that can serve as

D. D. Hodson et al. (Eds.): CSCE 2024, CCIS 2258, pp. 313–324, 2025.
https://doi.org/10.1007/978-3-031-85902-1_27

stable remedies for viral infections [18]. Identifying the evolutionary patterns of these frequent spike mutations, which pose significant threats, is an important yet highly challenging task [17].

Accurately identifying the nature of these spike protein sequences could provide valuable insights into the potential functional consequences of the virus on humans [7]. An efficient escape prediction tool can provide advanced warning to the community regarding the potential consequences of newly mutated viruses. This enables the timely implementation of effective measures to address corresponding issues, helping to prevent the devastating effects witnessed during the initial surge of the COVID-19 pandemic. Furthermore, it could also provide indications for the development of effective vaccines or drugs, offering valuable insights into susceptible mutation positions and residues. This knowledge can assist researchers in pinpointing specific regions of the virus and devising interventions that are more capable of effectively countering the mutated strains.

The study titled "NLP Predicts Viral Escape Model" [13], which investigates viral evolution and evasion, showcases the potential to predict escape mutations. These mutations are characterized by higher infectivity and transmissibility, allowing them to evade antibody neutralization. Importantly, this prediction is achieved using sequence data alone through the application of artificial intelligence. Prior to this study, we also developed an escape prediction model called the "Sars-escape network for escape prediction of SARS-CoV-2" [4,24], however, the prediction performance of the escape model was constrained due to the limited availability of escape datasets.

With the rapid advancement in Artificial Intelligence tools and techniques, there is a vast scope to understand, analyze, and identify useful patterns among various categories of mutations. These categories encompass a range of mutations, including those that occur more frequently, those that are rare, escape mutations, non-escape mutations, and others. Furthermore, the advancement of large language models enables the analysis and comprehension of protein sequences in a manner analogous to human languages [23,25]. Generative models possess remarkable capabilities in generating synthetic sequences that closely resemble the observed characteristics found in natural spike protein sequences [5,20]. Furthermore, they offer the potential to generate previously unseen and distinct mutated sequences while still exhibiting characteristics associated with higher transmissibility and infectivity.

By employing a generative architecture based on GAN, we developed a model that generates probable escape sequences. In order to ascertain the presence of escape characteristics within these generated sequences, we proceeded to retrain our previously developed escape model [24]. This retraining process involved the integration of 8000 synthetically generated samples as escape sequences, in conjunction with the original training dataset. Using three diverse datasets: a wet-lab-based Greany dataset, a Baum dataset, and an in-silico Validation dataset, we replicated the experimental setup of our previous work. Next, we evaluated the performance of the model for predicting escape sequences. The augmentation of these synthetically generated sequences resulted in a statistically significant 4% increase in AUC score, from the original 71% to 75%, in the gold standard Greany dataset. Similarly, the Baum and Validation datasets exhibited significant improvements in the AUC score (from 0.74 to 0.81 and 0.90 to 0.92, respectively). These findings suggest that our model can effectively identify escape sequences with potentially higher infectivity and transmissibility.

Viral escape protein prediction holds great potential to significantly benefit future drug discovery, given its prospective applications in various areas including drug target identification, anti-viral drug design, drug resistance mitigation, and vaccine development. Predicting escape aids in gaining a deeper understanding of the identification of critical regions and the position of residues where the virus evades the human immune system - these regions hold potential as drug targets. Enhanced anti-viral drugs can be developed by identifying protein regions that are less prone to mutation and escape. Escape mutants may prompt a reassessment of drug resistance issues and the development of combinations of therapies accordingly. Comprehending viral escape mechanisms could also prove equally advantageous in the development of vaccines targeting multiple variants. Furthermore, it can aid in monitoring potential future variants that can be anticipated. In this context, escape protein prediction tools can become valuable assets in drug discovery and design.

2 Methodology

2.1 Dataset Preparation

We utilized the escape sequence dataset referred to under the subsection titled "Significant Training Window Generation" to train the generative model that was constructed in our previous work [14, 22, 24]. We curated this training dataset by employing computational filters on SARS-CoV-2 sequences retrieved from GISAID. Capitalizing on our access to escape residue information [22] in contrast to the wild sequence [26], we screened sequences for specific mutational changes at defined positions. Only sequences meeting these criteria were included in our significant training dataset. Furthermore, to enhance the dataset's quality, we implemented a filter excluding sequences with spike lengths below 1000, ensuring its robustness and reliability.

The dataset consists of 32,000 spike protein sequence segments with a length of 20, exhibiting characteristics highly probable for escape. The escape nature of spike proteins was assessed using position-based escape information obtained from the escape datasource [22], which provides comprehensive details about escape positions along with mutated residues. A sequence was categorized as an escape spike if it featured a mutated residue at a specific position. Each sequence is encoded using One-hot encoding and converted to TensorFlow's Tfrecord file format to train the network [11]. Two separate Tfrecord files were created to segregate the training and validation records in a ratio of 0.7–0.3.

2.2   Construction of Blast Database

We constructed a Blast database using the escape sequences to compare the similarity of the generated sequence against the reference BlastDB [1]. Alignment with the training and validation datasets using BLAST was automatically performed every 1,200 steps without interrupting the network training process. During the execution of 2.5 million training steps, the alignment of generated sequences was performed approximately 2084 times to assess the quality of generated sequences in comparison to natural ones. The sequence identity scores were calculated by comparing the generated sequences with the natural ones using the BLAST algorithm and the BLOSUM45 matrix. BLAST played a key role in model optimization by repeatedly comparing generated spike sequences to known escape variants during training. This ongoing assessment ensured the generated sequences resembled natural variants, ultimately strengthening the model's generative capability.

2.3   Model Architecture

Our escape-sequence generation model is built upon the architecture of GAN [10], which incorporates a residual network that enables the network to learn long-term dependencies (Fig. 1). Additionally, the integration of a self-attention module allows the model to assign varying degree of significance to different residues while understanding global sequence features, inspired by the architecture [21]. The Generator network generates an escape sequence using a random input vector, while the Discriminator network assesses its authenticity by comparing it to natural escape sequences. The objective of the generator is to progressively deceive the discriminator by generating sequences that closely resemble real ones. The residual block of the generator network is comprised of a transposed convolution layer [9] for upsampling. During the training process, we assess the similarity of the generated sequence to the natural ones using BLAST. In addition to this, BLOSUM45 identity scores [19] and standard deviation of the discriminator layer were computed and observed. The model is optimized using the non-saturating loss [8] with R1 regularization that produces a smooth, nonlinear output, allowing the model to capture more complex relationships and handle the issue of mode collapse.

2.4   Network Training

The input spike protein sub-sequence, consisting of 20 residues, was one-hot encoded. The input dimension for the discriminator was defined as 58×20, with each residue represented by 58 features and a sequence length of 20. The selected loss type for training was non-saturating, which is a commonly employed method in generative models. Additionally, a dilation rate of 2 was applied to control the spacing between the receptive field elements. A learning rate of 0.0001, with a step value of 1, was chosen to regulate the step size during optimization, determining how the generator learns from the data. The generator utilizes a random

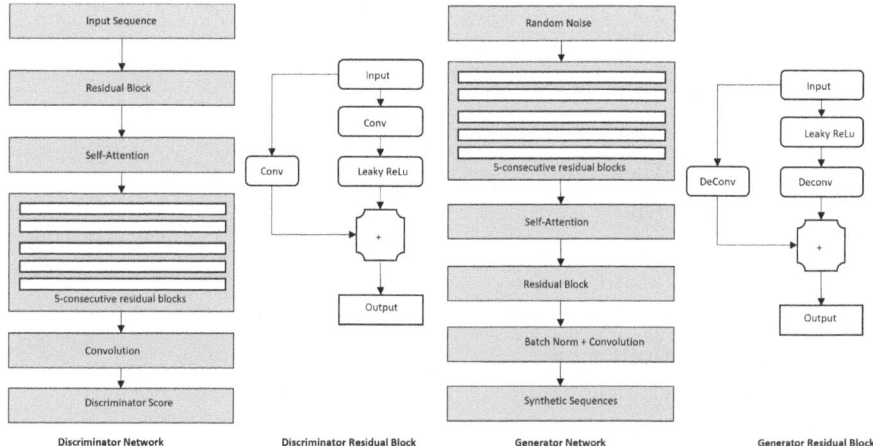

Fig. 1. High-level architecture of discriminator and generator network; When provided with a random input noise vector, the Generator network generates a synthetic Sars-CoV-2 spike protein. This generated protein is then evaluated by the Discriminator network, which compares it with the natural spike protein. The goal of the generator is to deceive the discriminator by creating sequences that closely resemble genuine ones.

noise vector, sampled from a truncated normal distribution with 128 dimensions, as an input to generate diverse synthetic samples. The model consists of a total of 714,639 parameters, out of which 237,702 parameters are trainable. The discriminator network has 45,662 trainable parameters, while the generator network has 192,040 trainable parameters (Table 1). The discriminator outputs a score representing the probability of each sequence being either natural or synthetic. The generator outputs sequences of length 20. We concentrated on a specific 20-amino-acid segment within the spike protein for both training and sequence generation. This targeted strategy helped circumvent unnecessary duplication, emphasizing regions critical for escape learning. By strategically focusing on this pivotal spike protein segment, we not only significantly reduced the computational complexity of training but also adeptly captured essential mutational patterns.

3   Results

3.1   Escape Generative Model Generates Escape Sequences

Our escape generative model, built upon GAN architecture, successfully learned patterns from existing biological escape sequences. As a result, it was capable of generating entirely new and plausible escape sequences. To verify the escape potential of the generated sequences, we leveraged the capabilities of the SARS-Escape Network(SEN) [6,24]. This network, trained on a large corpus of SARS-CoV-2 spike sequences, assigns potential escape scores to input spike proteins. We hypothesized that retraining the SEN model on an augmented

Table 1. General Parameters: Generative Adversarial Network parameters used for training discriminator and generator network.

Parameter	Value
Batch Size	32
Beta 1	0.0
Beta 2	0.9
Input Dimension	58*20
Pooling	Average
Dilation rate	2
Learning rate	0.0001
Discriminator trainable parameters	45,662
Generator trainable parameters	192,040
Total trainable parameters	237,702
Total parameters	714639
Total train steps	2500000

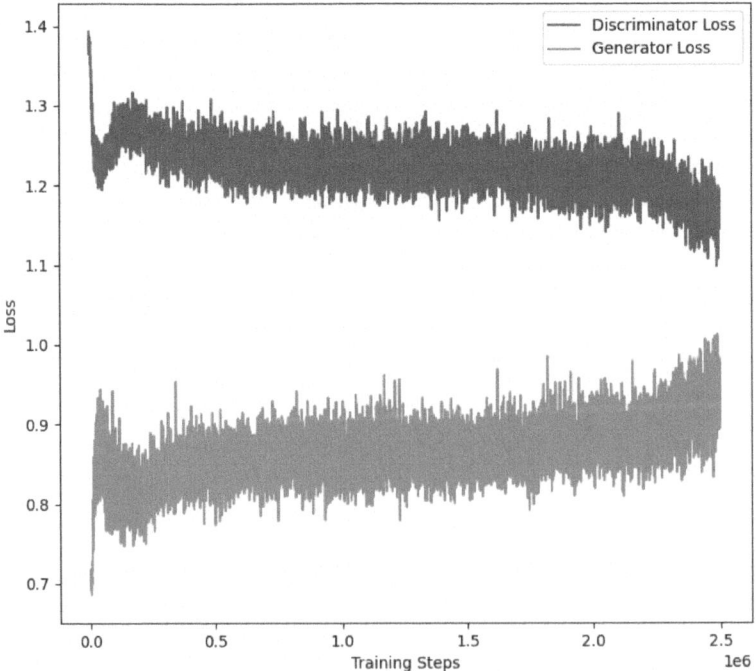

Fig. 2. Discriminator and Generator training loss of escape sequence generation model.

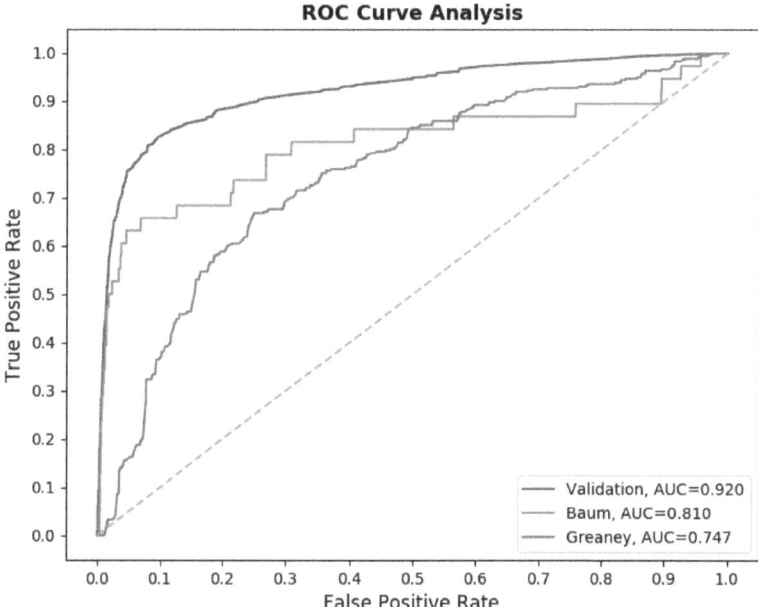

Fig. 3. AUC Scores (Greaney, Baum and Validation Dataset): Evaluating the model's performance using AUC scores after training with both natural and GAN-generated spike protein sequences.

dataset, inclusive of our newly generated sequences, would enhance its escape detection performance, provided those generated sequences indeed possess escape potential.

To validate the hypothesis, we generated 8000 raw spike sequences through our generative model to test their escape potential. We utilized these generated sequences as an augmented training dataset in SEN model [6,24]. Subsequently, We evaluated the escape detection performance of the model using three diverse datasets. The Greaney dataset [12] provides a detailed mapping of mutations in the SARS-CoV-2 Spike Receptor-Binding Domain that enable the virus to escape antibody recognition. This mapping is achieved through a deep mutational scanning method. The inclusion of data augmentation resulted in an increase in the escape prediction capability of the network on the Greaney dataset, with the AUC score improving from 71% to 74% (Fig. 3). The AUC score on the validation dataset improved from 0.90 to 0.92, the Baum dataset [2] improved from 0.74 to 0.81 (Fig. 6). The Baum dataset [2] incorporated wetlab-validated escape mutants along with computationally generated non-escape mutations derived from the Wuhan reference sequence [26]. In contrast, the Greaney dataset, the gold standard, consisted of an in vitro-verified set of both escape and non-escape mutant sequences. Figure 6 explores how augmenting SEN model with synthetically generated sequences affects its AUC scores.

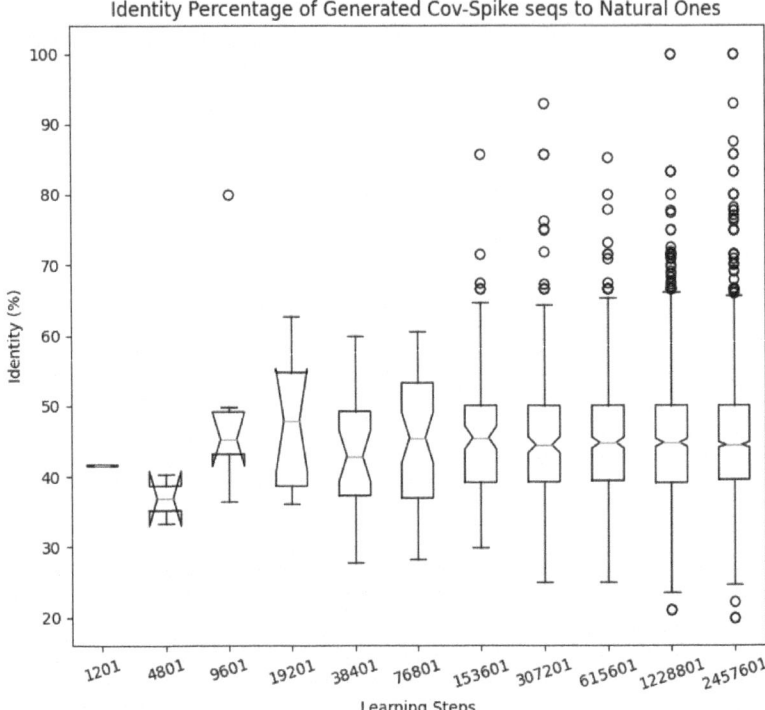

Fig. 4. Sequence Identity Scores (Box and whisker plot): Network optimization was achieved by comparing the identity of generated sequences to natural ones during the training process. The Identity of generated sequences was compared after every 1200 training steps up to 25 million steps.

The ability of our model to produce natural-like escape mutants underscores its significance to viral escape detection and mutant identification. While the discriminator loss in Fig. 2 fluctuated between 1.1 and 1.3, the generator loss remained relatively stable between 0.8 and 1.0. Notably, the generated sequences exhibited a wide range of pairwise identity (30%-95%) with respect to natural escape sequences, with a median of 45%(Fig. 4,5). This indicates the model's ability to generate diverse escape mutations while staying within naturally observed sequence boundaries.

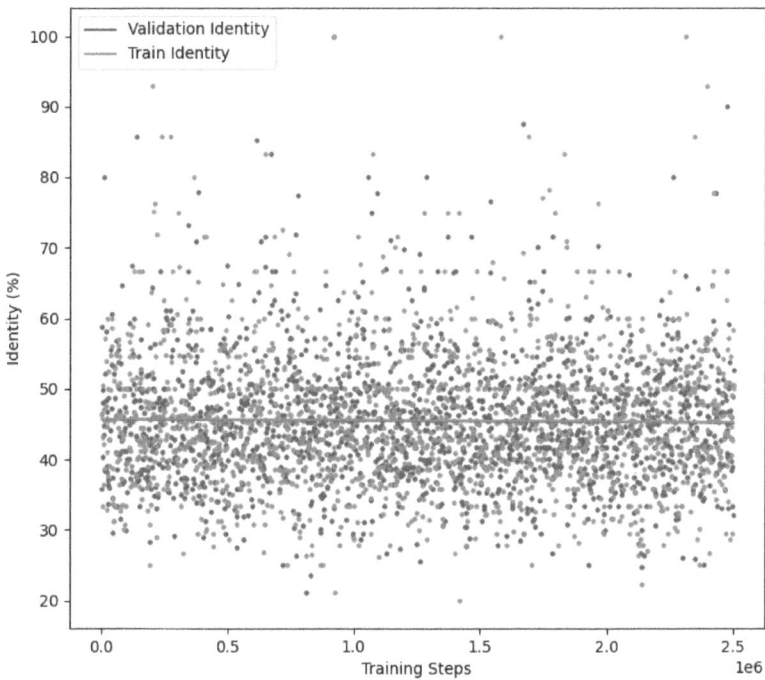

Fig. 5. Comparison of Generated sequences to Natural sequences: During network training, average identity scores of generated sequences were compared to both natural training sequences and validation sequences after every 1200 training steps.

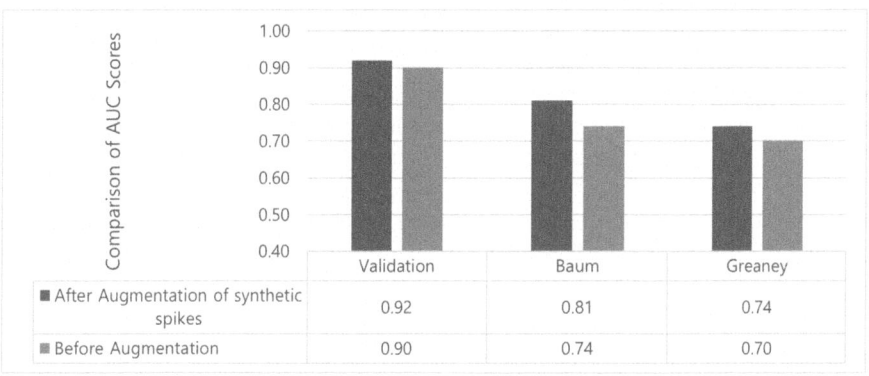

	Validation	Baum	Greaney
■ After Augmentation of synthetic spikes	0.92	0.81	0.74
■ Before Augmentation	0.90	0.74	0.70

Fig. 6. AUC scores of Sars-escape model before and after data augmentation.

4   Discussions

We leveraged our study to generate SARS-CoV-2 escape sequences and computationally verified that AI-based generative models such as GAN could be utilized for this purpose. However, it is essential to note that wet lab experiments are still required to confirm the escape nature of these generated sequences. Although the synthetic sequences generated using our model improved the AUC scores of the escape-prediction model [24] on the wet-lab-based escape datasets, the limited improvements indicate that there is still a considerable gap to be addressed in optimizing the model to generate more natural-like sequences. Computational complexity escalates rapidly when generating longer sequences, leading to a notable decline in the reliability and accuracy of producing natural-like sequences. Consequently, we restricted the spike protein generation task to a window length of 20. Although there isn't a specific rationale for choosing this size, we hypothesize that this segment's length adequately captures antigenic escape relationships.

The generated spikes could be aligned with existing natural spike protein sequences. This may provide significant clues about suspected escape positions and residual mutations. These insightful statistics could guide wet-lab experiments, shedding light on the true nature and escape strength of synthetically generated spike sequences. Furthermore, it holds the potential to become a valuable tool for viral escape analysis and experimentation. Thus, this approach opens avenues for further studies, exploring the efficacy of therapeutic antibodies and their potential connections with escape mechanisms.

The model's ability to generate complete protein sequences and analyze them to understand the global context might reveal hidden information about the impact of residues located at distant positions relative to the current one. This could serve as a potential area for further studies.A similar approach could be applied in case studies, such as generating anti-corona peptides [3,15]. Generative models aim to capture generalized representations of underlying data distributions, enabling the creation of synthetic samples that closely resemble natural ones. Our study showcased the capability to generate diverse escape sequences that were absent in the training data. These novel sequences proved invaluable in improving escape prediction scores when incorporated into the training of the escape prediction model, particularly in enhancing prediction scores for wet-lab-recognized escape sequences.

Acknowledgments. We would like to express our sincere appreciation to the authors from the Originating Laboratories who collected the specimens and the submission laboratories where genetic sequence data were produced and shared through the GISAID Initiative, which served as the foundation for this research.

Disclosure of Interests. This work was supported in part by the National Research Foundation of Korea (NRF) grant funded by the Korean government (MSIT) (No. 2020R1A2C2005612) and (No. 2022R1G1A1004613) and in part by the Korea Big Data Station (K-BDS) with computing resources including technical support.

References

1. Altschul, S.F., Gish, W., Miller, W., Myers, E.W., Lipman, D.J.: Basic local alignment search tool. J. Mol. Biol. **215**(3), 403–410 (1990). https://doi.org/10.1016/S0022-2836(05)80360-2

2. Baum, A., et al.: Antibody cocktail to Sars-CoV-2 spike protein prevents rapid mutational escape seen with individual antibodies. Science **369**(6506), 1014–1018 (2020)

3. Bist, P.S., Bhattarai, S., Tayara, H., Chong, K.T.: AntiCPs-CompML: a comprehensive fast track ml method to predict anti-corona peptides. bioRxiv (2024)

4. Bist, P.S., Tavara, H., Chong, K.T.: Identification of Sars-CoV-2 viral escape sequences using Escapetrans network. In: IEEE Proceedings, pp. 664–667 (2022)

5. Bist, P.S., Tayara, H., Chong, K.T.: Generative ai in the advancement of viral therapeutics for predicting and targeting immune-evasive Sars-CoV-2 mutations. IEEE J. Biomed. Health Inf. (2024)

6. Singh, B.P.: Sars-CoV-2-Escape-Model. GitHub repository (2023). https://github.com/PremSinghBist/Sars-CoV-2-Escape-Model

7. Chakraborty, C., Sharma, A.R., Bhattacharya, M., Lee, S.S.: A detailed overview of immune escape, antibody escape, partial vaccine escape of Sars-CoV-2 and their emerging variants with escape mutations. Front. Immunol. **13**, 801522 (2022)

8. Ciuparu, A., Nagy-Dăbâcan, A., Mureşan, R.C.: Soft++, a multi-parametric non-saturating non-linearity that improves convergence in deep neural architectures. Neurocomputing **384**, 376–388 (2020)

9. Gao, H., Yuan, H., Wang, Z., Ji, S.: Pixel transposed convolutional networks. IEEE Trans. Pattern Anal. Mach. Intell. **42**(5), 1218–1227 (2019)

10. Goodfellow, I., et al.: Generative adversarial networks. Commun. ACM **63**(11), 139–144 (2020)

11. Google LLC: Tensorflow. Tensorflow (2021). https://www.tensorflow.org/

12. Greaney, A.J., et al.: Complete mapping of mutations to the Sars-CoV-2 spike receptor-binding domain that escape antibody recognition. Cell Host Microbe **29**(1), 44–57 (2021)

13. Hie, B., Zhong, E.D., Berger, B., Bryson, B.: Learning the language of viral evolution and escape. Science **371**(6526), 284–288 (2021). https://doi.org/10.1126/science.abd7331

14. Khare, S., et al.: Gisaid's role in pandemic response. China CDC Weekly **3**(49), 1049 (2021)

15. Kumar, A., Singh, D.: Generative adversarial network-based augmentation with noval 2-step authentication for anti-coronavirus peptide prediction. IEEE/ACM Trans. Comput. Biol. Bioinf. (2024)

16. Li, F.: Structure, function, and evolution of coronavirus spike proteins. An. Rev. Virol. **3**, 237–261 (2016)

17. Markov, P.V., et al.: The evolution of Sars-CoV-2. Nat. Rev. Microbiol. **21**(6), 361–379 (2023)

18. Mehra, R., Kepp, K.P.: Structure and mutations of Sars-CoV-2 spike protein: a focused overview. ACS Infect. Dis. **8**(1), 29–58 (2021)

19. Pearson, W.R.: Selecting the right similarity-scoring matrix. Curr. Protoc. Bioinf. **43**(1), 3–5 (2013)

20. Ramachandran, A., Lumetta, S.S., Chen, D.: PandoGen: generating complete instances of future Sars-CoV-2 sequences using deep learning. PLoS Comput. Biol. **20**(1), e1011790 (2024)

21. Repecka, D., et al.: Expanding functional protein sequence spaces using generative adversarial networks. Nat. Mach. Intell. **3**(4), 324–333 (2021)

22. Rophina, M., Pandhare, K., Shamnath, A., Imran, M., Jolly, B., Scaria, V.: ESC: a comprehensive resource for Sars-CoV-2 immune escape variants. Nucleic Acids Res. **50**(D1), D771–D776 (2022)

23. Shrestha, P., Kandel, J., Tayara, H., Chong, K.T.: Post-translational modification prediction via prompt-based fine-tuning of a GPT-2 model. Nat. Commun. **15**(1), 6699 (2024)
24. Singh Bist, P., Tayara, H., To Chong, K.: Sars-escape network for escape prediction of SARS-COV-2. Brief. Bioinf. **24**(3), bbad140 (2023). https://doi.org/10.1093/bib/bbad140
25. Vu, M.H., et al.: Linguistically inspired roadmap for building biologically reliable protein language models. Nat. Mach. Intell. **5**(5), 485–496 (2023)
26. Wu, F., et al.: A new coronavirus associated with human respiratory disease in China. Nature **579**(7798), 265–269 (2020)

Dihedral Angle Adherence: Evaluating Protein Structure Predictions in the Absence of Experimental Data

Musa Azeem$^{(\boxtimes)}$ and Homayoun Valafar

University of South Carolina, Columbia, SC 29208, USA
mmazeem@email.sc.edu, homayoun@cse.sc.edu

Abstract. Determining the 3D structures of proteins is essential in understanding their behavior in the cellular environment. Computational methods of predicting protein structures have advanced, but assessing prediction accuracy remains a challenge. The traditional method, RMSD, relies on experimentally determined structures and lacks insight into improvement areas of predictions. We propose an alternative: analyzing dihedral angles, bypassing the need for the reference structure of an evaluated protein. Our method segments proteins into amino acid subsequences and searches for matches, comparing dihedral angles across numerous proteins to compute a metric using Mahalanobis distance. Evaluated on many predictions, our approach correlates with RMSD and identifies areas for prediction enhancement. This method offers a promising route for accurate protein structure prediction assessment and improvement.

Keywords: Computational Biology · Bioinformatics · Molecular Structural Biology · Applied Computing · AlphaFold

1 Background

1.1 Significance

From enabling movement in your body to catalyzing biochemical reactions within your cells, proteins are the building block of life and the backbone behind all biological processes [16]. Proteins are present in every facet of biology, and understanding the complex functionality of proteins is essential to the advancement of modern medicine. This, however, is not always so simple.

One of the key characteristics of proteins is their three-dimensional shape. Proteins are made up of molecular units known as amino acid residues (residues, for short). All proteins consist of sequences of the 20 amino acid residues present in biology and are identified by their own unique sequence. This sequence determines the protein's three-dimensional structure, which in turn plays a major role in determining the protein's function. In practice, however, the complex interactions between these compounds create intricate structures that are difficult to determine using the protein's amino acid sequence alone.

D. D. Hodson et al. (Eds.): CSCE 2024, CCIS 2258, pp. 325–336, 2025.
https://doi.org/10.1007/978-3-031-85902-1_28

1.2   Determining Protein Structures

Discovering protein structures is an essential step in determining their function in the cellular environment. Naturally, a significant portion of biological research has been dedicated to the discovery of protein structures through experimentation [13]. In practice, X-ray Crystallography and NMR Spectroscopy are the two primary methods of experimentally determining protein structures [1]. These methods, albeit slow and expensive, have given way to the ~200,000 protein structures known today [17].

Given the high cost and time requirements associated with determining protein structures experimentally, modern, computational methods have emerged to bypass this process. In particular, with the advancements of artificial intelligence in recent years, experimentally predetermined structures have been utilized in the training and developing of technologies to predict protein structures using the amino acid sequence alone, circumventing the slow, expensive, and otherwise necessary experimentation [2]. AlphaFold, developed by Deepmind at Google, is a landmark instance of these tools, leading the way toward the next stage of protein structure discovery [9,15].

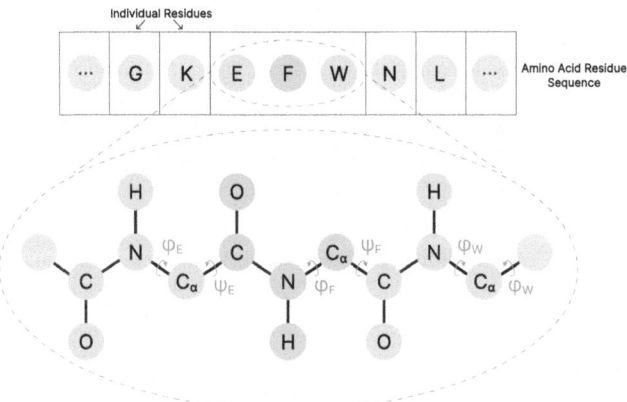

Fig. 1. Visualization of the location of dihedral angles, ϕ and ψ. Example shows the amino acid subsequence of residues E, F, and W. Here, a window size of 3 is illustrated for conciseness.

1.3   Representing Protein Structures

Discovered protein structures are stored in numerous online databases, with the globally maintained RCSB Protein Data Bank (PDB) being the most representative [16,17]. Protein structures, whether determined through experimentation or prediction, are typically represented in databases via one of two key attributes. The data most frequently stored in databases such as PDB are the coordinates in 3D space of all heavy atoms of the protein's molecular structure.

An alternative property capable of representing a protein's structure is its set of dihedral angles [6]. Illustrated in Fig. 1, between every residue in a protein's sequence are a pair of bond angles: phi (ϕ) and psi (ψ). Rotations in these angles between residues are the only degrees of freedom allowed for a protein during its formation and are established based on the molecular interactions between residues. As such, these bond angles can be calculated if the 3D coordinates of the protein's molecules are known. Together, the values of these angles at every residue are sufficient to represent the entire protein structure.

2   Objective

A key limitation of the current state of protein structure prediction is the process of evaluating and improving predictions. The current industry standard for evaluating prediction accuracy is Root Mean Square Deviation (RMSD) [3]. This method involves calculating the distance between the corresponding atoms of a prediction and the true structure of a protein, which must be predetermined experimentally. In practice, however, the fundamental goal of predicting protein structures is to circumvent the need for experimentation altogether. To effectively evaluate the performance of protein structure predictions in the absence of the experimentally determined–"ground truth"–structures, an alternative method of evaluation is necessary.

Another limitation of RMSD we address is its lack of insight into which residues in the amino acid sequence of a protein are impacting the overall score most significantly. RMSD produces a single metric for a prediction, representing the adherence of the predicted structure as a whole to the true structure. An alternative metric that provides not just a score, but insight into where a prediction has gone wrong will enable future development in improving protein structure predictions through focus on these locations.

In subsequent sections, we discuss our approach and methods for the development of a metric to resolve these issues. Namely, we suggest a method of evaluating protein structures capable of:

1. Effectively evaluating protein structure predictions in the absence of their experimentally determined structures.
2. Pinpointing where predictions could be improved to facilitate the improvement of these points of prediction.

To achieve these goals, we propose examining the dihedral angles of a protein structure rather than its three-dimensional coordinates, as done by methods such as RMSD. We hypothesize that, in general, the dihedral angles of residues appearing in certain amino acid subsequences follow similar patterns across proteins. Consequently, we propose that a predicted structure's dihedral angles adhere to the distribution of angles found across other proteins. Following this approach, we define the following items as a path to achieve the high-level goals for this project:

1. Generate a distribution of dihedral angles given amino acid subsequences of a prediction to serve as a baseline for comparison.
2. Develop a metric to evaluate the performance of a protein structure prediction, comparing its dihedral angles to the baseline distributions.
3. Extend the tool to determine which points within a prediction perform the worst based on our metric and mark such areas as those that necessitate improvement.

3   Methodology

Here we discuss our methods of collecting data and computing our proposed metric. An overview of our methodology is shown in Fig. 2.

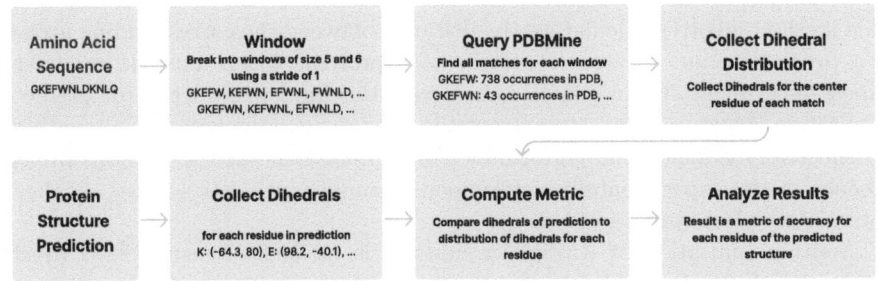

Fig. 2. Overview of our methodology. Amino acid sequences and numeric figures are shown as examples

3.1   Data Collection

As will be explored, a key requirement of our method is the collection of dihedral angles across experimentally determined structures housed in the Protein Data Bank [17]. To facilitate efficient querying and collection of dihedral angles, we utilize PDBMine [5], an application built on top of PDB to provide an alternative view of its data.

We initiate the data collection process by windowing the amino acid sequence of a protein with a stride of 1, such that each residue r_i forms a window W_i of size 5 with its neighboring residues. Each window is sent to query PDBMine, which searches the amino acid sequences of all proteins in PDB (other than the protein being evaluated) and returns all occurrences of the window. The dihedral angles of the center residue of every match are extracted, resulting in distributions $f_5^{(i)}(\phi, \psi)$ for every window W_i and corresponding center residue r_i at position i in the amino acid sequence. This collection process is illustrated in Fig. 1, where the pictured ϕ_F and ψ_F are extracted from each match for the example window. In essence, each $f_5^{(i)}$ captures the distribution of dihedral angles

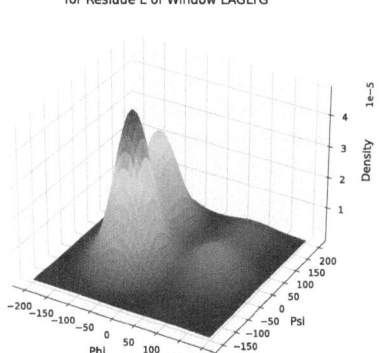

Fig. 3. KDE plot of the (ϕ, ψ) distribution queried from PDBMine for the subsequence LAGLTG. It is clear that certain values of ϕ and ψ are highly probable given this subsequence, while others are near zero.

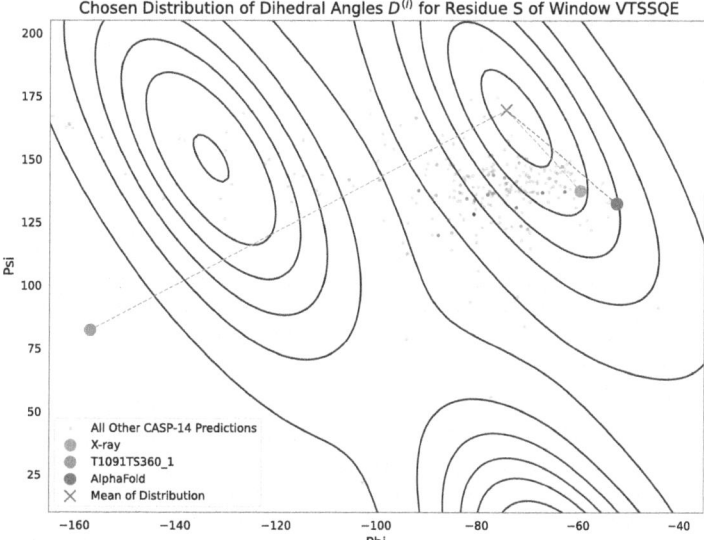

Fig. 4. The dihedral distribution chosen as most probable, $D^{(397)}$, for residue S in the protein 7W6B is shown in the KDE plot. Overlaid are (ϕ, ψ) data points of interest. The dihedral angles for the X-ray-determined structure at this residue are shown in orange. The same for the AlphaFold prediction, the prediction T1091TS360_1, and all other predictions submitted to CASP-14 are shown in purple, green, and black, respectively. The mean value of the distribution is shown in red. Dashed lines from each point of interest illustrate the process of calculating the Mahalanobis distance metric. We can see the X-ray-determined structure and AlphaFold's predictions have relatively small distances, while T1091TS360_1 and some other predictions are very far. (Color figure online)

for some amino acid (e.g. residue E at position i) given its window of context (e.g. $W_i = \text{GKEFW}$). Figure 3 demonstrates how certain values of ϕ and ψ occur with especially high probability, indicating that predicted values should follow a similar pattern. Finally, this collection process is repeated with a window size of 6, resulting in less populated, but more context-specific, distributions.

A similar process is conducted for the protein structure prediction being evaluated. For each amino acid residue r_i in the sequence, the predicted (ϕ_i, ψ_i) is extracted, resulting in one dihedral pair per residue, corresponding to the set of distributions found in the previous step. Figure 4 shows one such dihedral pair for a prediction by AlphaFold and the experimentally determined structure overlaid on a KDE plot of the distribution from the previous step. Note that the dihedral angles for the experimentally determined structure serve only as a point of comparison, but are not incorporated into computing our metric.

3.2 Computing the Metric

The data collection process outlined in Sect. 3.1 produces:

a. A predicted angle pair (ϕ_i, ψ_i) for each residue r_i.
b. A pair of distributions $f_5^{(i)}(\phi, \psi)$ and $f_6^{(i)}(\phi, \psi)$ of dihedral angles for each residue r_i.

Now, the following procedure is conducted on each residue r_i in the protein's sequence to produce a per-residue distance metric:

1. **Kernel Density Estimation** [4] produces the estimated combined distribution $\hat{f}^{(i)}(\phi, \psi)$ of $f_5^{(i)}$ and $f_6^{(i)}$ with weights 1 and 128, respectively.
2. **K-Means clustering** [8] on $\{f_5^{(i)}(\phi, \psi), f_6^{(i)}(\phi, \psi)\}$ from PDBMine produces n clusters. n is chosen dynamically to maximize the clustering silhouette score [14].
3. The **most probable** dihedral cluster $D^{(i)}(\phi, \psi)$ is chosen as the cluster that maximizes $\sum \hat{f}^{(i)}(\phi_j, \psi_j)$ for all points j in the cluster. Following this method, the cluster with the overall most likely dihedral angles is always chosen as the point of comparison.
4. **Mahalanobis Distance** [7] M_i is computed from the predicted (ϕ_i, ψ_i) to $D^{(i)}$ using the estimated covariance matrix of $D^{(i)}$.

The outcome is a distance metric M_i for every residue r_i in the protein's amino acid sequence. We refer to this metric as the *dihedral adherence* of each residue. An illustration of this process for a single window is shown in Fig. 4.

4 Experiment

To test our hypothesis and achievement of goals outlined in Sect. 2, we formulate an experiment involving 4 target proteins of the 14th Critical Assessment of Structure Prediction competition (CASP-14) [12]. We look at the following structures:

1. **Experimentally determined structures**: These protein structures were found through experimentation by X-ray crystallography, and were retrieved from the RCSB Protein DataBank [17]. These structures were used in the evaluation of Goal 2.
2. **AI-predicted structures**: For each protein, we collected all predicted protein structures submitted to CASP-14, for a total of ∼1300 predictions. Of particular interest from this cohort are the predictions of the AlphaFold model [9, 15].

For each predicted structure, we follow the procedures outlined in Sect. 3 to compute the dihedral adherence M_i for each residue.

5   Analysis and Results

With a quantified metric of evaluation for each of these predictions, we study two approaches to analyzing our method's achievement of our goals.

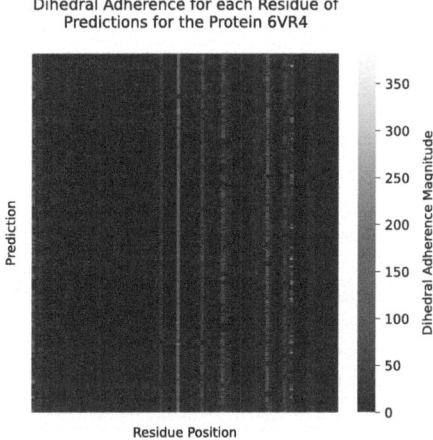

Fig. 5. Our calculated dihedral adherence for each residue of each prediction for the protein 6VR4. Variations in certain columns indicate key residues where many predictions disagree.

5.1   Goal 1: Our Metric as a Viable Method of Evaluating Predictions

We first examine the viability of our metric in evaluating protein structure predictions. Illustrated in Fig. 5, we see a variation in dihedral adherence over a multitude of protein structure predictions for the protein 6POO (PDB accession code). We see that there are certain "key" residues in this protein for which there is much variation between predictions in the adherence of the dihedrals to the distribution. Based on our hypothesis, predictions with a stronger adherence to the dihedral distribution for these residues are more accurate overall.

To test our hypothesis, we compare our metric to the industry-standard RMSD score of each structure prediction. A correlation between the two indicates that our metric provides insight into the accuracy of a prediction similar to that of the industry standard. To effectively compare the two metrics, we fit a linear regression model [11] for each prediction from M, the set of the 400 dihedral adherences with the greatest magnitudes, to the structure's RMSD. This regression model combines the scores of numerous predictions for 4 proteins submitted to CASP-14, and demonstrates a significant correlation, as presented in Fig. 6. We see an R^2 correlation score of 0.755 with an F-test p-value < 0.01.

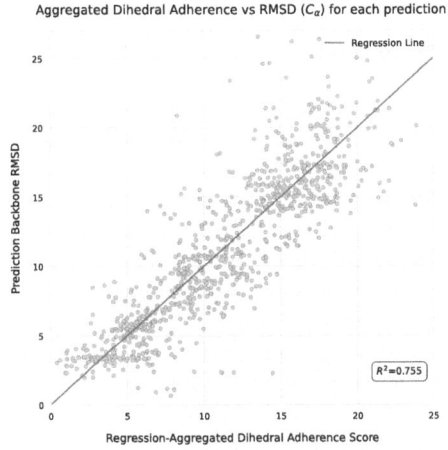

Fig. 6. $RMSD_j$ vs M_j for every prediction j submitted to CASP-14 for 4 proteins. Each M is found through the fitted linear regression model. Plotted in red is the line of best fit, with an R^2 score of 0.755. (Color figure online)

We see from these results that there is a significant correlation between our metric and the industry standard of RMSD, demonstrating the viability of our metric in providing similar insight as RMSD without the use of an experimentally determined structure. Although the development of a generalized method of translating our per-residue metric into a single value remains a challenge, the current state of the metric still provides valuable insight into the performance of a protein prediction. In particular, when predicting protein structures that have not yet been discovered experimentally, our metric serves as a viable method of measuring progress to determine which predictions are most optimal. Utilizing this metric in such a way opens the door for future advancements in protein structure predictions.

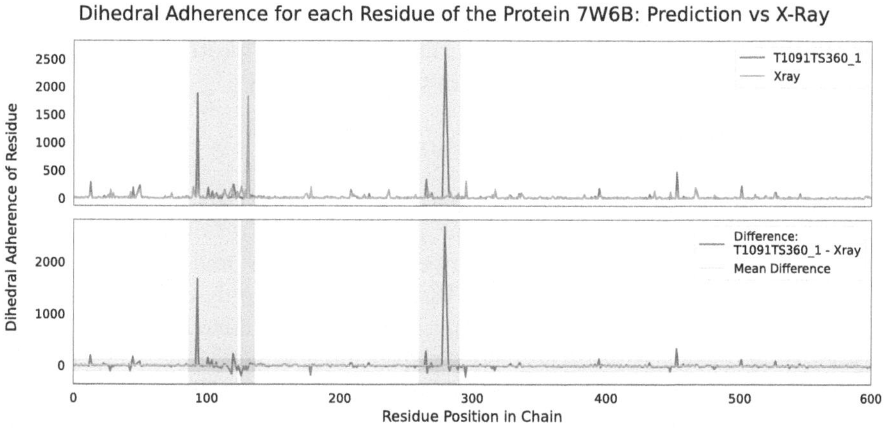

Dihedral Adherence for each Residue of the Protein 7W6B: Prediction vs X-Ray

Fig. 7. The upper plot pictures the dihedral adherence, M_i, for each residue r_i of the protein 7W6B. Our metric is shown in blue for a prediction submitted to CASP-14 (labeled T1091TS360_1) and in orange for the X-ray-determined structure. The lower plot pictures the per-residue difference ($M_{\text{pred}} - M_{\text{xray}}$) of our metric. The mean difference is shown in tan. On both plots, the regions in red highlight where our metric determines a much greater error in the prediction's performance compared to that of the X-ray structure. On the other hand, the area highlighted in green represents where both the predicted structure and the experimentally determined structure receive a high magnitude of error based on our metric, indicating an area of weakness in our metric rather than a faulty prediction. (Color figure online)

5.2   Goal 2: Pinpointing Areas of a Prediction in Need of Improvement

Our method produces a metric of accuracy for every residue within a protein structure prediction. From Fig. 5, we see there exists particular residues in which some predictions perform much better or worse based on our metric. Here, we demonstrate the viability of utilizing these values to pinpoint which residues, in particular, require the most attention to improve a prediction. Ideally, a high magnitude of error computed for a residue would indicate a faulty prediction at this point. For robustness and to account for inaccuracies in our metric itself, however, we compare $M_{\text{prediction}}$ to M_{true} to see which residues in a prediction produce the highest error *relative* to the error of the X-ray-determined structure. The residues with the greatest discrepancies are highlighted as potential points of interest.

Figure 7 illustrates our results when comparing a prediction to the X-ray-determined structure for the protein 7W6B. Regions of high discrepancies between the two structures can clearly be identified. These points represent locations where the dihedral angles of a certain residue in a prediction do not closely adhere to the distribution of angles found across other proteins, indicating that something may be off at this location. By comparing the dihedral adherence to that of the experimentally determined structure, we confirm that the predicted angle should ideally be shifted to a more optimal location in the distribution. Following this approach, we identify prime locations in protein structures for investigation in improving predictions in the future.

6   Future Work and Conclusions

In this paper, we have demonstrated our method's ability to achieve the goals outlined in Sect. 2. The analysis of our per-residue metric of dihedral adherence has high potential in evaluating a protein structure prediction's accuracy. This metric provides similar insight as RMSD, but relies only on predetermined structures in PDB, rather than the experimentally determined structure of the protein being evaluated. Furthermore, by providing a metric for every protein residue, we can identify where in the protein structure a prediction is scoring worse than the experimentally determined structure. These locations serve as prime targets for future improvement of protein structure predictions. Here, we summarize future work that will build upon the foundational methods presented to improve and expand this tool.

6.1   Goal 1: Effectively Evaluating Protein Structure Predictions

As it is, our metric provides insight into the performance of a protein with a significant correlation to industry-standard methods. However, translating our per-residue metric into a single value comparable to RMSD remains a challenge. In the future, methods of producing a single metric sufficient for evaluating the accuracy of a prediction as a whole will be developed to generalize the linear regression approach outlined in Sect. 5.

6.2   Goal 2: Pinpointing Prediction Errors

Future work will be directed toward protein structure prediction improvement, utilizing the tools presented here to increase the accuracy of existing predictions. We define the following high-level objectives:

1. Effectively identify residues in a prediction with the worst score without, ideally, comparing them to the ground truth structure.
2. For such residues, shift the prediction's dihedral angles to a more probable location in the distribution.
3. After performing energy optimization [10], determine if the new structure is more optimal.

Acknowledgments. Research reported in this publication was supported by the National Institute of General Medical Sciences of the National Institutes of Health under Award Number P20GM103499. The content is solely the responsibility of the authors and does not necessarily represent the official views of the National Institutes of Health. This project was supported by the NASA South Carolina Space Grant Consortium under the STEM Outreach Award.

Disclosure of Interests. The authors have no competing interests to declare that are relevant to the content of this article.

References

1. Alberts, B., Johnson, A., Lewis, J., Raff, M., Roberts, K., Walter, P.: Molecular Biology of the Cell, 4th edn. Garland Science, New York (2002)

2. Baker, D., Sali, A.: Protein structure prediction and structural genomics. Science **294**(5540), 93–96 (2001). https://doi.org/10.1126/science.1065659. https://www.science.org/doi/abs/10.1126/science.1065659

3. Carugo, O., Pongor, S.: A normalized root-mean-square distance for comparing protein three-dimensional structures. Protein Sci. **10**(7), 1470–1473 (2001). https://doi.org/10.1110/ps.690101. https://onlinelibrary.wiley.com/doi/abs/10.1110/ps.690101

4. Chen, Y.C.: A tutorial on kernel density estimation and recent advances. Biostatistics Epidemiol. **1**(1), 161–187 (2017). https://doi.org/10.1080/24709360.2017.1396742

5. Cole, C., Ott, C., Valdes, D., Valafar, H.: Pdbmine: a reformulation of the protein data bank to facilitate structural data mining. In: 2019 International Conference on Computational Science and Computational Intelligence (CSCI), pp. 1458–1463 (2019). https://doi.org/10.1109/CSCI49370.2019.00272

6. Dayalan, S., Dilshan, N., Bevinakoppa, S., Schroeder, H.: Dihedral angle and secondary structure database of short amino acid fragments. Bioinformation **1**, 78–80 (2006). https://doi.org/10.6026/97320630001078

7. De Maesschalck, R., Jouan-Rimbaud, D., Massart, D.: The mahalanobis distance. Chemom. Intell. Lab. Syst. **50**(1), 1–18 (2000). https://doi.org/10.1016/S0169-7439(99)00047-7. https://www.sciencedirect.com/science/article/pii/S0169743999000477

8. Jain, A.K., Dubes, R.C.: Algorithms for clustering data. Prentice-Hall Inc., USA (1988)

9. Jumper, J., et al.: Highly accurate protein structure prediction with alphafold. Nature **596**(7873), 583—589 (2021). https://doi.org/10.1038/s41586-021-03819-2

10. Koretke, K.K., Luthey-Schulten, Z., Wolynes, P.G.: Self-consistently optimized energy functions for protein structure prediction by molecular dynamics. Proc. Natl. Acad. Sci. **95**(6), 2932–2937 (1998). https://doi.org/10.1073/pnas.95.6.2932. https://www.pnas.org/doi/abs/10.1073/pnas.95.6.2932

11. Montgomery, D.C., Peck, E.A., Vining, G.G.: Introduction to linear regression analysis. Wiley (2021)

12. Pereira, J., Simpkin, A.J., Hartmann, M.D., Rigden, D.J., Keegan, R.M., Lupas, A.N.: High-accuracy protein structure prediction in CASP14. Proteins **89**(12), 1687–1699 (2021)

13. Research, Markets: Global 3D protein structure analysis market analysis report 2022: a $2.67 billion market by 2032 - surging collaborations between major key players to enhance their market presence (2022). https://finance.yahoo.com/news/global-3d-protein-structure-analysis-123300167.html

14. Rousseeuw, P.J.: Silhouettes: a graphical aid to the interpretation and validation of cluster analysis. J. Comput. Appl. Math. **20**, 53–65 (1987). https://doi.org/10.1016/0377-0427(87)90125-7. https://www.sciencedirect.com/science/article/pii/0377042787901257

15. Varadi, M., et al.: AlphaFold protein structure database: massively expanding the structural coverage of protein-sequence space with high-accuracy models. Nucleic Acids Res. **50**(D1), D439–D444 (2021). https://doi.org/10.1093/nar/gkab1061

16. Whitford, D.: Proteins: structure and function. Wiley (2013)
17. Zardecki, C., Dutta, S., Goodsell, D.S., Lowe, R., Voigt, M., Burley, S.K.: PDB-101: educational resources supporting molecular explorations through biology and medicine. Protein Sci. **31**(1), 129–140 (2022). https://doi.org/10.1002/pro.4200. https://onlinelibrary.wiley.com/doi/abs/10.1002/pro.4200

Enhancing Diabetes Prediction with Advanced Machine Learning Techniques

Yuan Tian[2], Chuan Wang[1], Wen Shi[3], Ying Zhou[2], and Yi Zhou[3(✉)]

[1] Vanderbilt University, Nashville, TN 37232, USA
chuan.wang@vanderbilt.edu
[2] Department of Chemical Engineering, Department of Biosystems Engineering,
Auburn University, Auburn, AL 36849, USA
{yzt0028,yzz0121}@auburn.edu
[3] Department of Economics, TSYS School of Computer Science,
Columbus State University, Columbus, GA 31907, USA
{shi_wen,zhou_yi}@columbusstate.edu

Abstract. Diabetes stands as one of the foremost causes of mortality in the United States. The imperative to predict diabetes in the country arises from its widespread prevalence, substantial healthcare expenses, potential severe complications, and the prospect of proactive prevention and early intervention. This study leverages data from the Framingham study to investigate the utilization of machine learning models in the realm of diabetes prediction. Consequently, the implementation of predictive models to combat diabetes holds the promise of yielding substantial positive outcomes for public health, optimizing healthcare resource allocation, and enhancing the overall health and welfare of individuals and communities.

Keywords: Diabetes · Machine Learning · Disease Prediction

1 Introduction

Diabetes is a pervasive global health challenge, that not only affects millions of people's lives [23] but also brings heavy economic burdens [4]. Thus, early detection is critical in effective management of diabetes. Diabetes progresses through three stages: prediabetes, type 1 diabetes, and type 2 diabetes. Early detection can help reduce complications and improve outcomes. Prediabetic patients may benefit from lifestyle modifications or pharmacological interventions. Additionally, early intervention can lower the risk of mortality in prediabetic individuals without a history of cardiovascular disease [12]. Early detection of exercise patterns in individuals with type 1 diabetes may enable therapeutic adjustments to prevent hypoglycemia [5]. Type 2 diabetes is a complex condition that can affect multiple major organs, including the heart, blood vessels, nerves, eyes, and kidneys [1,11,14]. The appearing advancements in machine learning(ML) provide

© The Author(s), under exclusive license to Springer Nature Switzerland AG 2025
D. D. Hodson et al. (Eds.): CSCE 2024, CCIS 2258, pp. 337–348, 2025.
https://doi.org/10.1007/978-3-031-85902-1_29

transformative potential in predictive diagnostics [3]. Therefore, early detection is crucial to reduce the risk of complications in these areas. In this study, we apply the application of various ML models for diabetes prediction, this is an endeavor that stands the intersection of technology and healthcare.

The primary aim of this study is to assess the performance of multiple machine learning algorithms, specifically XGBoost, AdaBoost, Random Forest, and LightGBM, in accurately predicting diabetes. These models are selected for their proven capabilities in handling complex datasets and providing accurate predictions in various domains [6,10,22,24]. Through the utilization of these models on health-related datasets, our objective is to identify the algorithm that excels in crucial diagnostic metrics such as accuracy, sensitivity, specificity, and the Matthews Correlation Coefficient (MCC), thereby determining the most effective model for medical diagnostic purposes. This research is driven by the urgent need to enhance early diabetes detection methods [9]. Traditional diagnostic methods, while effective, often come into play at later stages of the disease, limiting the opportunities for early intervention. This capability of machine learning models can significantly enhance the ability of healthcare providers to take preemptive measures, improving patient outcomes by offering timely and targeted interventions based on the predicted risks. In conducting this study, we also emphasize the importance of feature selection in model performance. Many noninvasive factors such as Body Mass Index (BMI), age, and blood pressure are crucial in understanding and predicting diabetes although glucose level is an indispensable invasive factor in diabetes prediction. A comprehensive analysis of these features could provide insights into the most significant indicators of the disease, thereby improving prediction accuracy.

The incorporation of machine learning into healthcare marks a substantial advancement towards a more individualized and preemptive approach to medical treatment. Leveraging ML algorithms, our study seeks to enrich the domain of medical data analytics, enhancing strategies for diabetes management and prevention. We expect our results to lay a groundwork for subsequent research and real-world applications in the realm of predictive healthcare.

2   Machine Learning Models for Diabetes Prediction

In this section, we outline a comprehensive framework for the development of machine learning models aimed at predicting diabetes (Fig. 1). The pipeline utilizes relational data from the Framingham study to predict the likelihood of diabetes in individuals not included in our original dataset. Our methodology is divided into four distinct phases, as illustrated in Fig. 1: preprocessing, model development, tuning, and testing, each representing a functional component of our pipeline.

Data Pre-processing: We split our dataset into two sets: training and testing sets. We randomly sample 80% of the dataset as the training set, with the rest of 20% of the dataset as the testing set. To better evaluate our prediction models, we perform 7-fold cross-validation. In particular, we further split the training

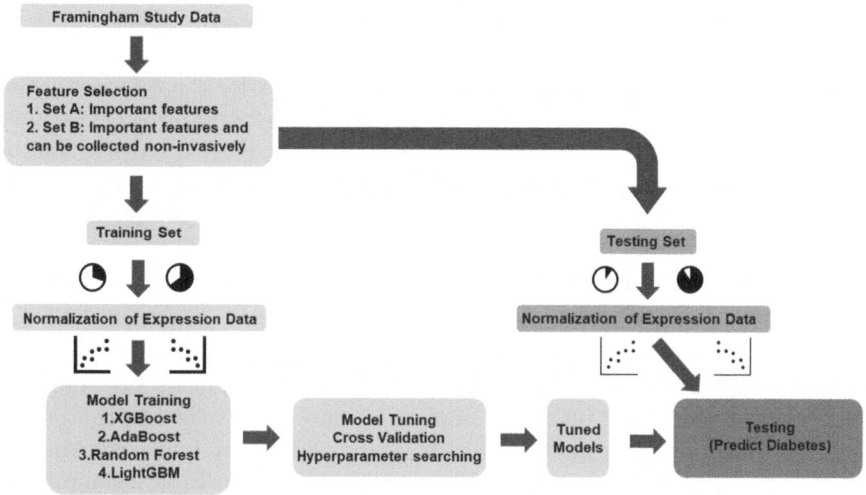

Fig. 1. Predication model development pipeline.

set randomly into seven distinct subsets (or folds). Then, we train and evaluate our prediction models seven times. We pick a fold for evaluation and train on the other six folds each time until all seven folds are used for evaluation.

Model Development: The FHS dataset we utilize in this study contains m (4,240) samples, each of which bears n (16) unique features and a binary label y. Let each sample be represented as a vector $x \in \mathbb{R}^n$ with its label denoted as $y \in \mathbb{Z}^2$. Then, we can represent the whole dataset and the labels as a matrix $X \in \mathbb{R}^{m*n}$ and a vector $Y \in \mathbb{Z}_2^m$, respectively. The diabetes prediction can be formalized as the approximating of a function, $f^* : \mathbb{R}^n \to \mathbb{Z}_2$, to determine if a patient has diabetes (i.e., sample x is associated with its label y). Thus, we can approximate f^* as $\hat{y} = f\{x\}$. To this end, we employ four machine-learning algorithms to address the diabetes prediction problem, which demonstrate excellent effects. The algorithms utilized in this study include XGBoost, AdaBoost, Random Forest, and LightGBM. Moreover, we also investigate feature importance with these four algorithms. Table 1 summarizes the properties of these four machine-learning models.

Table 1. A comparison of machine learning models applied in this study.

Model	Ensemble	Instance-based	Gradient-based	Feature Selector	Parameters
XGBoost	✓	✗	✓	✓	15
AdaBoost	✓	✗	✓	✓	15
Random Forest	✓	✓	✗	✓	15
LightGBM	✓	✗	✓	✓	15

Tuning: To efficiently probe the hyperparameter search space and control the computing budget allocated to the hyperparameter searching process, we harness the randomized search strategy to find out the best set for these four machine learning models. Specifically, we evaluate 100 different hyperparameter combinations to find the best-performing set. We utilize stratified k-fold cross-validation on the validation set to generate a scalar metric, allowing for comparison of different model configurations. Besides, to ensure consistent evaluation across different models, we maintain a constant k value of 7 throughout the study's k-fold cross-validation process.

Testing: Recall that each data sample $x^{(i)}$ in a set of data samples $\{x^{(1)}, \ldots, x^{(m)}\} \in \mathbb{R}^{m x n}$ has n features and its associated label $y^{(i)}$, we need to assess the prediction performance of our proposed machine learning models. The confusion matrix depicted in Fig. 2 offers a complete picture that facilitates the performance assessment of our models. In this study, we employ four scalar performance metrics (*accuracy, sensitivity, specificity,* and *MCC*). Table 2 summarizes the details of the four metrics we adopted in this study.

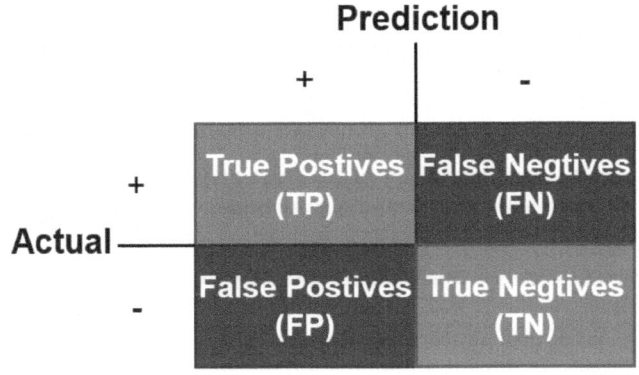

Fig. 2. The confusion matrix for assessing our models.

Table 2. The four performance metrics used to assess the performance of our models

Metric	Formula	Interpretation
Accuracy	$\frac{TP+TN}{TP+TN+FP+FN}$	Overall accuracy of a model
Sensitivity	$\frac{TP}{TP+FN}$	The proportion of actual positive cases that are correctly identified
Specificity	$\frac{TN}{TN+FP}$	The proportion of actual negative cases that are correctly identified
MCC	$\frac{TPxTN-FPxFN}{\sqrt{(TP+FP)(TP+FN)(TN+FP)(TN+FN)}}$	A balanced measure that takes into account true and false positives and negatives

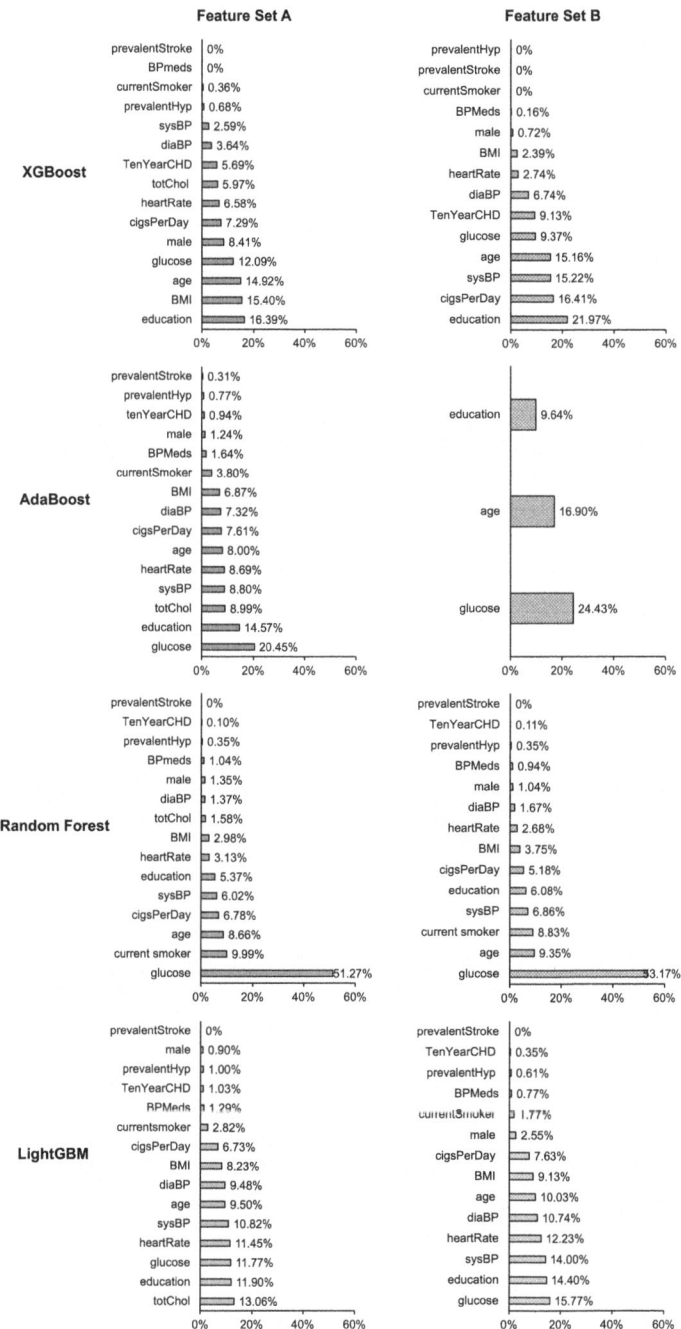

Fig. 3. Feature importance for each model with feature set A and B.

3   Results

3.1   Training Results

For diabetes prediction modeling, we chose four diverse machine-learning models, each employing a distinct approach to data fitting, to ensure a comprehensive analysis of their respective capabilities. We identified two distinct feature sets for diabetes prediction: Set A and Set B. Set A comprises features deemed crucial based on our analysis. Set B, while also encompassing these important features, is exclusively made up of those that can be collected non-invasively. To assess the effectiveness of each model, we gather key performance metrics: accuracy, sensitivity, specificity, and the Matthews Correlation Coefficient (MCC). In our study, accuracy quantifies the model's overall precision in predicting diabetes. Sensitivity evaluates the model's ability to correctly identify actual cases of diabetes, while specificity gauges its accuracy in recognizing individuals without diabetes. Given the imbalance in class labels within our testing data, we utilize the Matthews Correlation Coefficient (MCC) to furnish an impartial evaluation of the models' performance across both categories. To optimize the performance of each model, we employ a range of strategies for tuning their hyperparameters. Figure 2 shows the training metrics for each algorithm. Each algorithm we examined demonstrates the ability to effectively fit the training dataset concerning the metrics under study. The models consistently achieved impressive accuracy and specificity, surpassing 90% in both feature sets A and B (Fig. 4 and 5). In terms of sensitivity, the Random Forest model outperformed others in both sets, showcasing its proficiency in accurately detecting the actual diabetic cases in the dataset. Regarding the Matthews Correlation Coefficient (MCC), AdaBoost recorded the highest score in feature set A, whereas LightGBM topped in feature set B. XGBoost, however, consistently registered the lowest MCC percentage in both feature sets.

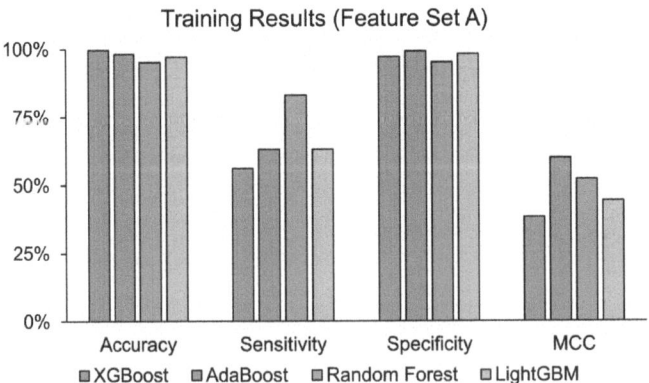

Fig. 4. Training results with feature set A.

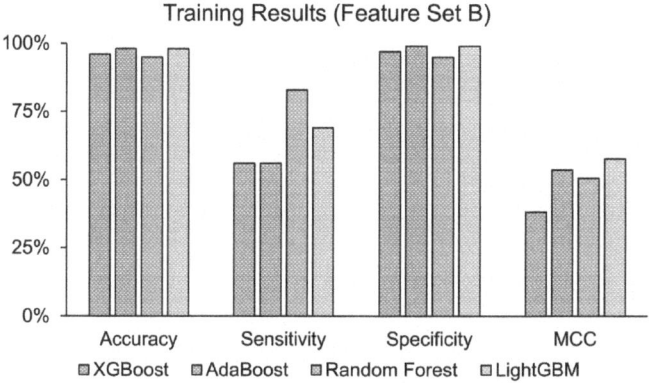

Fig. 5. Training results with feature set B.

3.2   Cross-Validation Results

To evaluate the robustness of our models against data variability and their ability to generalize to independent datasets, we conducted a 7-fold cross-validation for each model. Figure 6 and 7 display the training accuracy for each model across the 7 folds of the cross-validation process using feature set A and B, respectively. Notably, the accuracy remained high and stable across each fold for a given model, as evidenced by the low standard deviation in accuracy. This consistency in performance across various data subsets suggests that our models are well-suited for practical applications.

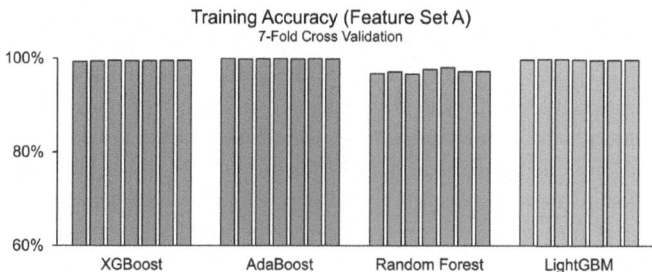

Fig. 6. Training accuracy of each of the 7-folds cross validation for feature set A.

3.3   Testing Results

Figures 8 and 9 present the outcomes of the testing phase. It was observed that, utilizing the features from both sets A and B, each model attained a minimum accuracy of 95%, indicative of a strong fit within the problem space. Moreover, the high specificity observed in the test results of each model underscores

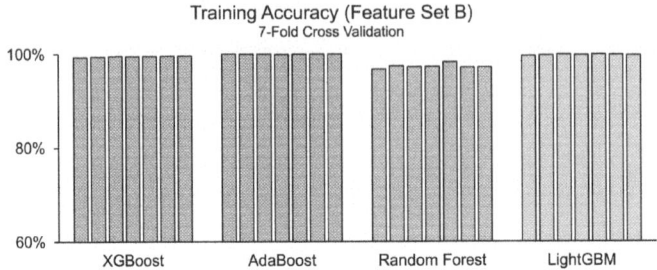

Fig. 7. Training accuracy of each of the 7-folds cross validation for feature set B.

their proficiency in accurately identifying individuals who do not have diabetes. However, it was noted that even minor fluctuations in accuracy and specificity appeared to correlate with substantial changes in sensitivity and the Matthews Correlation Coefficient (MCC). For example, in feature set A, while XGBoost exhibits only a 1% higher accuracy compared to the Random Forest model, it demonstrates a significantly lower sensitivity, being 27% less effective, and a 14% lower MCC. These findings are probably attributable to the imbalanced distribution of class labels (such as "diabetic" and "non-diabetic") in the validation and testing datasets. Given that the quantity of non-diabetic significantly surpasses that of diabetic, models which predominantly predict the more frequent label ('non-diabetic') can easily attain high accuracy and perfect specificity. On the contrary, models inclined to predict the less frequent label ('diabetic') would exhibit lower accuracy but achieve perfect sensitivity. This imbalance affects the models' performance metrics, underscoring the impact of label distribution in model evaluation.

In contrast to accuracy, sensitivity, and specificity, the Matthews Correlation Coefficient (MCC) offers a more balanced and uniform measure of each model's performance, particularly in the context of imbalanced data. When evaluated against this metric, the AdaBoost and the LightGB model stand out as the most consistent and reliable models across feature set A and set B. This highlights the MCC's effectiveness in providing a comprehensive assessment of model performance, taking into account the true positives, true negatives, false positives, and false negatives, especially in datasets where class distribution is skewed.

3.4 Feature Importance

For each feature, we calculated its importance in every model (Fig. 3). Within feature set A, key features were identified for each model. As anticipated, BMI, glucose, age, and total cholesterol emerged as the most critical features across various models. Specifically in the Random Forest model, the importance of glucose was predominant, accounting for 51.27%. Surprisingly, contrary to our initial assumptions, the factor of education also held a significant role in each model.

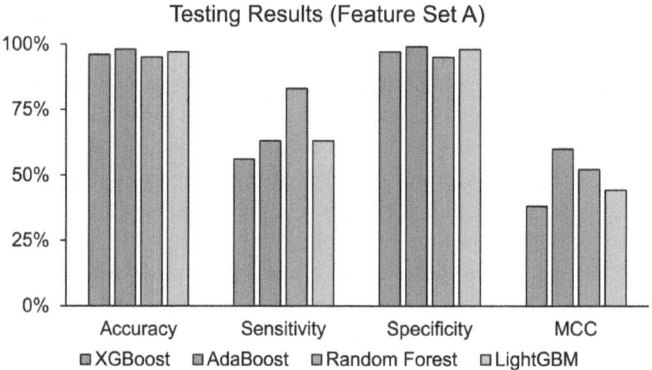

Fig. 8. Testing results with feature set A.

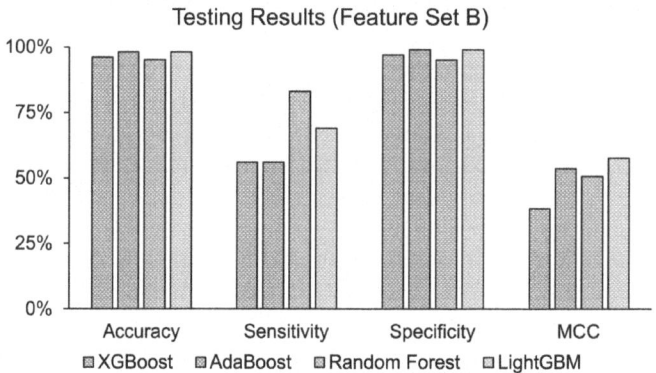

Fig. 9. Testing results with feature set B.

Moving to feature set B, our goal is to pinpoint vital features that can be gathered non-invasively, enabling individuals to assess their diabetes risk harmlessly. However, it became evident that glucose level remains an essential feature, indispensable in all models. By combining glucose with other non-invasive features, the models maintained comparable performance levels to those utilizing feature set A. This finding underscores the crucial role of glucose in diabetes prediction, even when integrated with less invasive data points.

4   Discussion

Diabetes is a chronic disease. Having diabetes may not cause immediate death, but can lead to various serious complications if not properly managed [20]. These complications include cardiovascular disease [15,18], which is the primary cause of death among diabetics, due to increased risk of heart attack and stroke. Kidney damage (nephropathy) can also occur, potentially leading to kidney failure or irreversible end-stage kidney disease [2,21]. Diabetic retinopathy, a leading cause of blindness, results from damage to the blood vessels of the retina [8,19]. Additionally, diabetes can cause nerve damage (neuropathy) [16] and poor blood flow to the limbs, increasing the risk of infections and sores that can lead to limb amputation [17]. Thus, predicting diabetes at the very early stage and managing it effectively is crucial in reducing the risk of these severe complications.

In this study, we used the data from a Framingham study [13]. We aim to address the research question concerning the application of machine learning methodologies for predicting diabetes and facilitating early management. Thus, a suite of machine-learning models was developed and rigorously evaluated to identify the algorithm delivering the most superior performance, assessed through four key metrics (Accuracy, Sensitivity, Specificity, MCC). Accuracy measures the proportion of correctly classified instances (both positive and negative) out of the total instances, which is best used when classes are balanced. Sensitivity measures the proportion of actual positive instances that are correctly identified by the model and is critical in applications where it is more important to catch positives, even at the risk of higher false positives. Specificity measures the proportion of actual negative instances that are correctly identified by the model, which is vital in applications where it is crucial to correctly identify negatives. MCC is a metric that takes into account all four quadrants of the confusion matrix and provides a balanced measure even if the classes are of very different sizes and is useful for a more balanced evaluation in imbalanced datasets, providing a single score that takes into account the complete confusion matrix. All four models performed well on accuracy and specificity (over 95%). Given that the dataset we used is imbalanced, with significantly more non-diabetic cases than diabetic cases, the Matthews Correlation Coefficient (MCC) will be the most useful metric for evaluating the binary classifier for diabetes prediction. Upon reviewing the results, we acknowledge the significant impact these findings could have on healthcare systems. AdaBoost and LightGBM emerged as the most effective (highest MCC), achieving 59.85% and 57.71% effectiveness, respectively. It's important to highlight that while the Random Forest model didn't rank as the top performer quantitatively, it achieved the highest sensitivity in both feature sets A and B, and also maintained a strong MCC score. A high sensitivity is notably beneficial in accurately identifying true positive cases of diabetes. While this may result in a few false positives, the trade-off is generally acceptable. True positive detections enable individuals to seek early treatment for diabetes, which is crucial for effective management. On the other hand, the cost associated with false positives typically involves additional hospital visits for reconfirmation, a minor inconvenience compared to the benefits of early detection.

The American Heart Association (AHA) has identified several risk factors for Type 2 diabetes including family history, race, age, gestational diabetes, weight, physical activity, blood pressure, and smoking [7]. In our analysis, we determined the importance of each feature within the models. Consistent with what AHA disclosed, critical factors like glucose levels, age, and BMI were identified as primary contributors to diabetes prediction. Counterintuitively, the factor of education emerged as a key feature in predicting diabetes, a finding that was unexpected and highlights the multifaceted nature of diabetes risk factors. Furthermore, we attempted to solely utilize non-invasive features (Set B) for diabetes prediction, given their ease of collection and lower associated costs. However, it became apparent that relying exclusively on non-invasive features significantly diminished the models' predictive accuracy. This highlighted the indispensable role of glucose measurement in diabetes prediction. When we combined glucose measurement with the selected non-invasive features (Set B), our machine-learning models achieved performance levels that were comparable to those using the features in Set A. This underscores the necessity of glucose data in effective diabetes prediction, even when supplemented with less invasive parameters. Given that glucose levels can be conveniently measured with just a few drops of blood using a home blood glucose meter, our models are highly applicable for effective diabetes prediction. This accessibility to glucose testing allows for easy integration of crucial data into our predictive models, thereby enhancing their usability and reliability in everyday settings for timely diabetes detection.

There are some limitations in this study. Key non-invasive risk factors such as race, family history, and gestational diabetes were not included in our dataset. For maximum convenience to people, it is essential to achieve high accuracy in diabetes prediction using only non-invasive features. Currently, relying solely on non-invasive features does not yield accurate predictions for diabetes. Collecting key features, such as race, family history, and gestational diabetes, could significantly improve the prediction accuracy of our machine learning models. This improvement would greatly benefit individuals concerned about diabetes.

5 Conclusion

Utilizing extensive operational data from the Framingham study, our research focused on evaluating various machine-learning models for predicting diabetes. We found that models like AdaBoost, Random Forest, and LightGBM demonstrated strong performance in this context. The effective deployment of these machine learning models in diabetes prediction showcases the harmonious integration of technology with healthcare. This success paves the way for a more proactive, tailored, and efficient approach to healthcare delivery, highlighting the significant impact of data-centric methods in the medical field.

References

1. Afkarian, M., et al.: Kidney disease and increased mortality risk in type 2 diabetes. J. Am. Soc. Nephrol. 24(2), 302–308 (2013)
2. Alicic, R.Z., Rooney, M.T., Tuttle, K.R.: Diabetic kidney disease: challenges, progress, and possibilities. Clin. J. Am. Soc. Nephrol. CJASN 12(12), 2032 (2017)

3. Aliramezani, M., Koch, C.R., Shahbakhti, M.: Modeling, diagnostics, optimization, and control of internal combustion engines via modern machine learning techniques: a review and future directions. Prog. Energy Combust. Sci. **88**, 100967 (2022)

4. American Diabetes Association: Economic costs of diabetes in the us in 2017. Diabetes Care **41**(5), 917–928 (2018)

5. Dasanayake, I.S., et al.: Early detection of physical activity for people with type 1 diabetes mellitus. J. Diab. Sci. Technol. **9**(6), 1236–1245 (2015)

6. Dong, W., Huang, Y., Lehane, B., Ma, G.: Xgboost algorithm-based prediction of concrete electrical resistivity for structural health monitoring. Autom. Constr. **114**, 103155 (2020)

7. American Heart Association editorial staff. Diabetes risk factors (2024). https://www.heart.org/en/health-topics/diabetes/understand-your-risk-for-diabetes

8. Fong, D.S., et al.: Retinopathy in diabetes. Diab. Care **27**(suppl_1), s84–s87 (2004)

9. George, C., Echouffo-Tcheugui, J.B., Jaar, B.G., Okpechi, I.G., Kengne, A.P.: The need for screening, early diagnosis, and prediction of chronic kidney disease in people with diabetes in low-and middle-income countries-a review of the current literature. BMC Med. **20**(1), 1–12 (2022)

10. Gupta, V.K., Gupta, A., Kumar, D., Sardana, A.: Prediction of covid-19 confirmed, death, and cured cases in India using random forest model. Big Data Mining Anal. **4**(2), 116–123 (2021)

11. Henning, R.J.: Type-2 diabetes mellitus and cardiovascular disease. Future Cardiol. **14**(6), 491–509 (2018)

12. Hsueh, W.A., Orloski, L., Wyne, K.: Prediabetes: the importance of early identification and intervention. Postgrad. Med. **122**(4), 129–143 (2010)

13. Kannel, W.B., McGee, D.L.: Diabetes and cardiovascular disease: the framingham study. JAMA **241**(19), 2035–2038 (1979)

14. Klein, R., Klein, B.: Diabetic eye disease. The Lancet **350**(9072), 197–204 (1997)

15. de Mattos Matheus, A.S., et al.: Impact of diabetes on cardiovascular disease: an update. Int. J. Hypertens. **2013** (2013)

16. Obrosova, I.G.: Diabetes and the peripheral nerve. Biochimica et Biophysica Acta (BBA)-Molecular Basis Disease **1792**(10), 931–940 (2009)

17. Pecoraro, R.E., Reiber, G.E., Burgess, E.M.: Pathways to diabetic limb amputation: basis for prevention. Diab. Care **13**(5), 513–521 (1990)

18. Sowers, J.R., Lester, M.A.: Diabetes and cardiovascular disease. Diab. Care **22**, C14 (1999)

19. Stitt, A.W., et al.: The progress in understanding and treatment of diabetic retinopathy. Prog. Retinal Eye Res. **51**, 156–186 (2016)

20. Susan van, D., Beulens, J.W., Yvonne T. van der, S., Grobbee, D.E., Nealb, B.: The global burden of diabetes and its complications: an emerging pandemic. Eur. J. Cardiovasc. Prev. Rehabil. **17**(1_suppl), s3–s8 (2010)

21. Thomas, M.C., et al.: Diabetic kidney disease. Nat. Rev. Dis. Primers. **1**(1), 1–20 (2015)

22. Wang, C., Shuzhan, X., Yang, J.: Adaboost algorithm in artificial intelligence for optimizing the IRI prediction accuracy of asphalt concrete pavement. Sensors **21**(17), 5682 (2021)

23. Wang, L., et al.: Trends in prevalence of diabetes and control of risk factors in diabetes among us adults, 1999–2018. JAMA **326**(8), 704–716 (2021)

24. Wang, Y., Wang, T.: Application of improved LightGBM model in blood glucose prediction. Appl. Sci. **10**(9), 3227 (2020)

Lung and Colon Cancer Classification Based on a Hybrid Deep Convolutional Neural Networks of Xception, VGG-16, and VGG-19 Using Histopathological Images

Amal O. Hasan and Zakariya A. Oraibi[(✉)]

Department of Computer Science, College of Education for Pure Sciences, Basrah, Iraq
{pgs.amal.oudah,zakaria_au}@uobasrah.edu.iq

Abstract. Lung and colon cancer are considered as two of the leading causes of fatalities in human beings. The ability to detect this cancer is very necessary to determine the subsequent actions. In this paper, we introduce to perform lung and colon cancer detection using a framework of multiple state-of-the-art deep learning architectures. The feature maps of three models: Xception, VGG-16, and VGG-19 are combined which will result in a bigger feature map. Then, we train this hybrid model from scratch on a large dataset of Lung and Colon images called LC25000 which consists of five classes with 5000 images per class. Finally, softmax layer of the combined model is used to classify images. Classification results show that our hybrid model achieves a high classification accuracy of 99.34% using four-fold cross-validation. Comparison has also been carried out on previous work experiments performed on the same dataset and results showed that our hybrid model outperforms state-of-the-art methods. Thus, our model has the potential to become a valuable tool in clinics, helping doctors in cancer diagnosis.

Keywords: Deep Learning · Colon Cancer · Lung Cancer · Hybrid Models · Xception · VGG

1 Introduction

One of the leading causes of deaths worldwide is attributed to lung and colon cancer accounting for 25% of all cancer-related deaths [1]. Despite the low incidence of synchronous lung and colon cancer, patients with lung and colon cancer must receive appropriate treatment [2]. The lack of early detection could lead to the risk of spreading cancer cells between the lung and colon organs. Medical doctors observed that patients that get lung cancer could easily get colon cancer

---

A. O. Hasan—Contributing author.

D. D. Hodson et al. (Eds.): CSCE 2024, CCIS 2258, pp. 349–358, 2025.
https://doi.org/10.1007/978-3-031-85902-1_30

next. This is because smoking is known to deteriorate lung and cause cancer in addition, patients with bad diets usually get colon cancers [3]. In other words, these two cancers are related and doctors investigate and diagnose both of them regularly at early stages.

It is crucial to achieve accurate diagnosis to allow provide detection and improve survival rates. Classical histopathology methods relied on analyzing tissue biopsies to diagnose cancer. However, these methods are slow and could lead to errors [4]. In addition, manual detection of these cancer cases by radiologists at early stages is very tough due to the difficulty of locating them precisely thus being unable to diagnose them [5]. The emergence of machine learning, more specifically Deep Learning (DL), has facilitated the process of diagnosing cancer by providing accurate and efficient cancer classification technology assisting medical doctors in diagnosing large number of patients [6].

The success of DL algorithms in detecting histopathology images at high accuracy led researchers to focus on using these models and improve them. However, the thrive of DL models relies mostly on the availability of datasets with large number of images. For the task of lung and colon cancer detection, it was not until 2019 where a large dataset of 25000 images has been made available online for research purposes [7]. Due to the large number of samples in this dataset, most researchers used only a subset of images in the experiments given the limited availability of GPU ram and disk space to handle such big data.

In [8]; authors proposed an integration technique between deep features and ensemble learning to build a lung and colon cancer classification system achieving a high accuracy of 99.30%. Authors in [9]; employed multiple state-of-the-art deep learning architectures and were successful in achieving a perfect prediction accuracy of 100% on LC25000 dataset. However, they reported results on two classes only meaning they were working on 10000 images. The work in [10] focused on employing multiple deep learning models, including: ResNet18, ResNet30, and ResNet50 to perform classification on colon image classes. They achived a 93.13% accuracy using ResNet50. In [11]; a prediction framework based on InceptionV3, Daisy features, and Histogram of Gradients (HoG) was developed and used in classifying lung tissues into two classes: benign and malignant using 15000 images of LC25000 and achieving an accuracy of 99.6%. In [12]; a CNN model with two paths was proposed to predict colon CT images only using 256 feature maps. They reported a sensitivity of 99.6%. In [13]; authors applied three DL models to classify colon cancer images. In their work, two models were trained from scratch while the third one was a pretrained model (MobileNetV2). The pretrained model of MbileNetV2 outperformed the performance of the other models by achieving 99.67% accuracy using 20% of data in testing while the rest of data were using for training.

A framework to improve the prediction accuracy of lung and colon cancer is introduced in this paper by exploiting the feature maps of three robust convolutional neural networks. Hence, the feature maps of Xception, VGG-16, and VGG-19 are concatenated and used as a single input layer. In addition, the concatenated model is followed by three dense layers. Finally, the new model is trained from scratch and the resultant weights are used during testing.

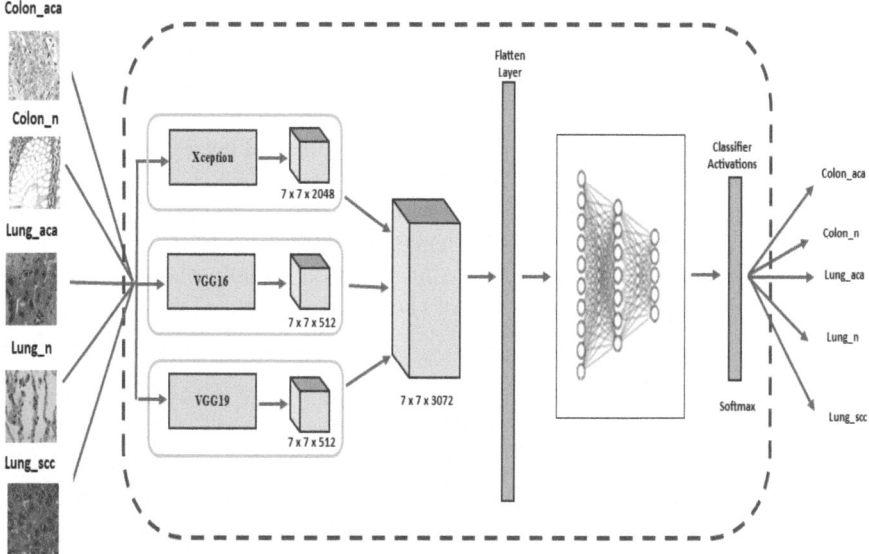

Fig. 1. The concatenation scheme of the three models used in our work.

This paper is organized into sections as: Sect. 2 illustrates in depth the proposed hybrid approach and the challenging database. Section 3 lists the results of the proposed approach and gives a comparison with the best methods in literature. Conclusions and future work are presented in Sect. 4.

2 Methodology

2.1 CNN Feature Maps

Big advances have been made using deep CNNs in many computer vision fields including image segmentation, classification, and detection. This success comes from using deep models that have the ability to extract meaningful features after being trained on large datasets [14,15]. In addition these models can be trained from scratch or fine-tuned to be applied on other datasets and generate high prediction accuracy [16]. These models include: Inception, Xception, VGG-16, VGG-19, and MobileNet.

Xception CNN model was developed by Google for image classification purposes [17]. The model is based on Inception but with several modifications to improve the prediction performance. The distinguish feature of Xception is that it employs depthwise separable convolutions which leads to the use of fewer parameters in comparison with other models. In addition, skip connections where introduced between network layers to improve the training process. The model showed impressive performance on standard datasets related to real world applications. Another powerful CNN architectures are VGG-16 and VGG-19 which were introduced in 2014 by Visual Geometry Group (VGG) [18]. They are favourable for image classification tasks due to their simple design and their effective performance. Both models depend on stacking convolutional layers using small receptive fields. Pooling layers are added in between these convolutional layers allowing for local features to be preserved. The difference between VGG-16 and VGG-19 is that the latter has three more convlutional layers which produces better performance.

In this paper, we propose to use a technique that concatenates the feature maps of multiple CNN architectures. Hence, a comprehensive representation of the input image is created using this concatenation to help the new model to better learn the features and patterns of the training data.

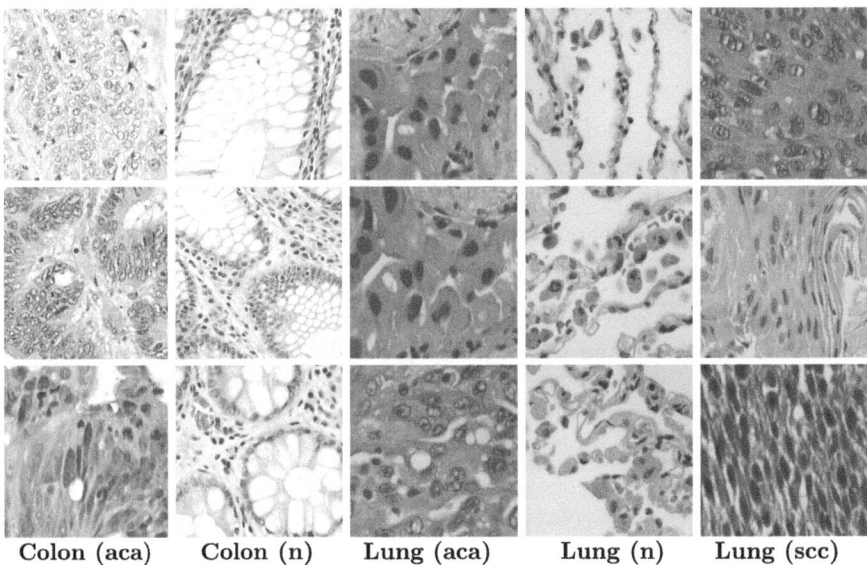

Fig. 2. Sample images from LC25000 dataset. Three samples are shown for each class.

The input images of the dataset used in the experiments have a dimension of 224×224. Xception model generates $7 \times 7 \times 2048$ feature maps on its last feature extractor layer given the input image. Both VGG-16 and VGG-19 generate $7 \times 7 \times 512$ features maps. When we concatenate the three models, we get a final feature map of $7 \times 7 \times 3072$. After that, a flatten layer is added followed by three dense layers. The final concatenated model is to be trained from scratch and will contain (210399147) parameters with (154798595) trainable parameters and (55600552) non-trainable parameters. The benefit of combining the feature maps of these robust architectures is to generate a reliable hybrid model that can classify biomedical images efficiently. Figure 1 shows the steps of merging the three models applied on five-class Lung and Colon dataset.

2.2   Dataset

The proposed methodology in this paper was applied on a large set of tissue images called lung and colon cancer dataset [7]. The dataset is separated into two folders: Lung and Colon. The lung folder consists of three classes which are Lung Benign (Lung_n), Lung Adenocarcinoma (Lung_aca), Lung squamous cell carcinoma (Lung_scc). On the other hand, the colon folder consists of two classes which are Colon Adenocarcinoma (Colon_aca) and Colon Benign (Colon_n). In total we have five classes with 5000 images allocated in each class. This brings the total number of images in the dataset to 25000. Images of the dataset has a resolution of 768 × 768. The unique criteria of this dataset is its diversity and volume which makes it suitable for research purposes. Figure 2 shows sample images from each class of the dataset.

In the experiments, some researchers used only two or three classes and report the classification performance. In our work, we applied our technique on the full dataset. The protocol used to split data is four-fold cross-validation. That is, we used 75% of data from each class in the training stage while the remaining 25% of images were used for testing. Hence, 18750 images in total were used for training and 6250 images were used for testing. The dataset is available for public and can be used for research purposes.

Table 1. Values of hyperparameters utilized during experiments.

Hyperparameter	Value
Epochs	15
Learning Rate	0.0001
Optimizer	Adam
Batch-Size	64
Loss-Function	Categorical Crossentropy

Table 2. Results of applying our approach on LC25000 dataset. The average of four-fold results are reported in this table.

Method	Accuracy	Precision	F1-Score	Recall
Xception	98.55	98.65	98.60	98.55
VGG-16	98.98	98.85	98.75	98.80
VGG-19	98.79	98.90	98.80	98.85
Xception + VGG-16	99.19	99.20	99.25	99.30
Xception + VGG-16 + VGG-19	**99.34**	**99.40**	**99.50**	**99.50**

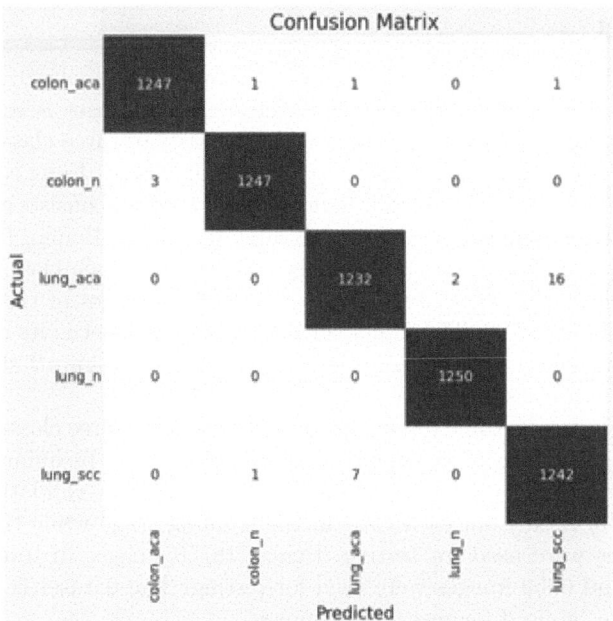

Fig. 3. Fold-2 confusion matrix of the proposed hybrid method.

3 Experiments and Analysis

3.1 Classification Results

Performance evaluation of our proposed hybrid CNN model is done by carrying out experiments using each model alone on the five-class lung and colon dataset. Xception, VGG-16, and VGG-19 models are first trained from scratch and the weights are used to evaluate the model performance on the test subset of images. We should emphasize that no transfer learning has been used as networks are trained on the raw samples of the dataset. We used four-fold cross-validation setup on the dataset. As a result, the final accuracy reported in the paper is the average of the four folds results for each model. After that, we carry out experiments on the hybrid feature maps of both Xception and VGG-16. Finally, experiments are done after the merge of the three models. Before training, images are first re-sized to $224 \times 224 \times 3$ to meet the requirements of the CNN architectures.

Table 1 shows the hyberparameter values used during training of each model. The number of epochs was fixed to 15 across all experiments. In addition, learning rate was set to 0.0001 and the optimizer used was Adam. Furthermore, since we have huge number of images, we used a bigger batch size of 64. Finally, the loss function applied was categorical crossentropy with a pooling size of 2×2.

Table 2 shows the results of applying our methodology on the 25000 images dataset using the training setup mentioned earlier. All figures in the table are

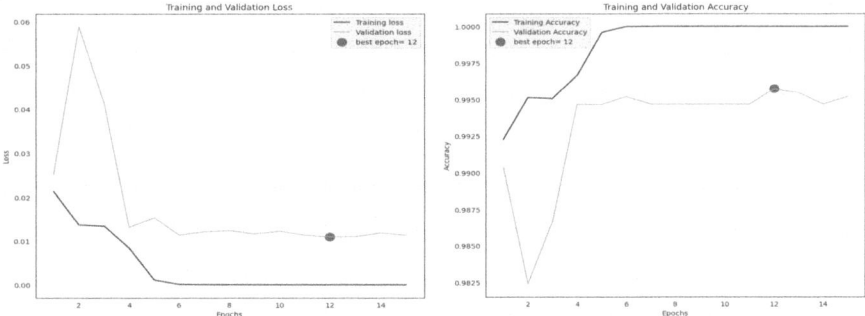

Fig. 4. Results of training applied on fold-2 Stage with training accuracy vs validation accuracy represented in the graph on right while training loss and validation loss represented in the graph on left.

Table 3. Comparison between our hybrid approach and state-of-the-art methods on the LC25000 dataset.

Reference	Methodology	Dataset	Year	Acc. (%)
Hadiyoso et al. [19]	CNN-CLAHE-VGG-16	LC-25000	2023	98.96
Hasan et al. [20]	LW-MS-CCN	LC-25000	2024	99.20
Anjum et al. [21]	EfficientNet-B2	LC-25000	2023	97.24
Wadekar et al. [22]	Modified VGG-19	L-15000	2023	97.73
Mohamed et al. [23]	SqueezeNet and GOA	C-10000	2023	99.12
Proposed	**Hybrid CNN**	**LC25000**	-	**99.34**

the average of four-fold results. As we can observe, the standalone models of Xception, VGG-16, and VGG-19 generate a high accuracy of 98.55%, 98.98%, and 98.79% respectively. The concatenation of features maps of both Xception and VGG-16 generates 99.19% accuracy which is higher than any standalone model. Furthermore, the accuracy is improved by over 0.2% when the feature maps of the three models are concatenated generating 99.34%. Results of the other three evaluation metrics are also shown in Table 2. These metrics are: Precision, F1-Score, and Recall which are all improved by concatenating the standalone models. The equations used to compute the four metrics are as follow:

$$Accuracy = \frac{TP + TN}{TP + FP + FN + TN} \tag{1}$$

$$Precision = \frac{TP}{TP + FP} \tag{2}$$

$$Recall = \frac{TP}{TP + FN} \tag{3}$$

$$F1 - Score = 2 * \frac{precision * recall}{precision + recall} \tag{4}$$

where TP (True Positive), TN (True Negative), FP (False Positive), and FN (False Negative). Figure 3 shows the confusion matrix of fold-2 using the proposed method. From this matrix, only 32 images were misclassified out of the 5000 images used in testing. It is worthy to mention that fold-2 generated the best results. Figure 4 illustrates the performance of training the hybrid model (Xception, Vgg-16, and VGG-19) in terms of loss and accuracy. The graph on the left shows the training and validation loss while the graph on the right shows the training and validation accuracy. From these graphs, we can observe that 15 epochs were enough for the model to converge during training and avoid overfitting.

3.2   Comparison with the Best Approaches in Literature

To show the robustness of our hybrid approach, a comparison has been carried out with the best approaches in literature applied on the same dataset. It is crucial to highlight that there are many approaches that were applied to only two or three classes only of the LC25000 dataset. Other methods considered using different number of cross-validation folds thereby reducing the total number of testing images resulting in a better classification performance. Table 3 lists the figures of the previous methods in comparison with our approach.

Hadiyoso et al. [19] proposed a hybrid CNN method of VGG-16 architecture and Contrast Limited Adaptive Histogram Equalization (CLAHE) and achieved a maximum classification accuracy of 98.96%. Hasan et al. [20] proposed a new LightWeight Multi-Scale (LW-MS) end-to-end CNN model to classify Lung and Colon images. Their model generated a high accuracy of 99.20%. Anjum et al. [21] suggested to use a multiresolution EfficientNets achieving a high accuracy of 97.24% on the five classes LC25000 dataset using EffcientNet-B0 model. Wadekar et al. [22] proposed to use a modified VGG-19 architecture to classify the three classes of Lung cancer images. They achieved 97.73% accuracy. Talukder et al. [8] introduced a method that uses deep features with ensemble learning and achieved a classification accuracy of 99.30% on LC25000 dataset using 10-fold cross-validation. Mohamed et al. [23] proposed a method that uses both CNN and Grasshopper Optimization Algorithm (GOA) and applied their method on two classes of Colon cancer images acquiring 99.12% accuracy. Our proposed methodology of combining the feature maps of three powerful CNN architectures generated a high accuracy of 99.34% which outperforms all the other methods.

4   Conclusions

In this paper, we proposed a powerful technique of merging multiple CNN architectures to detect Lung and Colon cancer. Our method combines the feature maps of Xception, VGG-16, and VGG-19 networks to create a bigger feature maps that will be used during training. Hence, the new model has the ability to exploit cancer image features better than using each standalone model. Experiments carried out using this new approach on a challenging dataset of 25000 where 18750 images were used for training and the rest of images (6250) were used for testing.

Experiments demonstrated that our method achieved state-of-the-art accuracy in comparison with other methods with 99.34% accuracy. We showed that using the hybrid model of multiple CNN architectures can improve the classification accuracy of any standalone model. In the future, we intend to expand the technique to extract features from the models and combine them and use machine learning classifiers to further enhance the prediction accuracy.

References

1. Sung, H., et al.: Global cancer statistics 2020: Globocan estimates of incidence and mortality worldwide for 36 cancers in 185 countries. CA Cancer J. Clin. **71**(3), 209–249 (2021). https://doi.org/10.3322/caac.21660

2. Kurishima, K., et al.: Lung cancer patients with synchronous colon cancer. Mol. Clin. Oncol. **8**(1), 137–140 (2018). https://doi.org/10.3892/mco.2017.1471

3. Kumar, N., Sharma, M., Singh, V.P., Madan, C., Mehandia, S.: An empirical study of handcrafted and dense feature extraction techniques for lung and colon cancer classification from histopathological images. Biomed. Signal Process. Control **75**, 103596 (2022). https://doi.org/10.1016/j.bspc.2022.103596

4. Paulsen, F.P., Eichhorn, M., Bräuer, L.: Virtual microscopy-the future of teaching histology in the medical curriculum? Ann. Anatomy-Anatomischer Anzeiger **192**(6), 378–382 (2010). https://doi.org/10.1016/j.aanat.2010.09.008

5. Masud, M., Sikder, N., Nahid, A.-A., Bairagi, A.K., AlZain, M.A.: A machine learning approach to diagnosing lung and colon cancer using a deep learning based classification framework. Sensors **21**(3), 748 (2021). https://doi.org/10.3390/s21030748

6. Lowe, M., Qin, R., Mao, X.: A review on machine learning, artificial intelligence, and smart technology in water treatment and monitoring. Water **14**(9), 1384 (2022). https://doi.org/10.3390/w14091384

7. Borkowski, A.A., Bui, M.M., Thomas, L.B., Wilson, C.P., DeLand, L.A., Mastorides, S.M.: LC25000 lung and colon histopathological image dataset (2019)

8. Talukder, M.A., Islam, M.M., Uddin, M.A., Akhter, A., Hasan, K.F., Moni, M.A.: Machine learning-based lung and colon cancer detection using deep feature extraction and ensemble learning. Expert Syst. Appl. **205**, 117695 (2022). https://doi.org/10.1016/j.eswa.2022.117695

9. Garg, S., Garg, S.: Prediction of lung and colon cancer through analysis of histopathological images by utilizing pre-trained CNN models with visualization of class activation and saliency maps. In: Proceedings of the 2020 3rd Artificial Intelligence and Cloud Computing Conference, pp. 38–45 (2020)

10. Bukhari, S.U.K., Syed, A., Bokhari, S.K.A., Hussain, S.S., Armaghan, S.U., Shah, S.S.H.: The histological diagnosis of colonic adenocarcinoma by applying partial self supervised learning. MedRxiv, 2020-08 (2020). https://doi.org/10.1101/2020.08.15.20175760

11. Chen, M., Huang, S., Huang, Z., Zhang, Z.: Detection of lung cancer from pathological images using CNN model. In: IEEE International Conference on Computer Science, Electronic Information Engineering and Intelligent Control Technology (CEI), pp. 352–358. IEEE (2021). https://doi.org/10.1109/CEI52496.2021.9574590

12. Qasim, Y., Al-Sameai, H., Ali, O., Hassan, A.: Convolutional neural networks for automatic detection of colon adenocarcinoma based on histopathological images. In: Saeed, F., Mohammed, F., Al-Nahari, A. (eds.) IRICT 2020. LNDECT, vol. 72, pp. 19–28. Springer, Cham (2021). https://doi.org/10.1007/978-3-030-70713-2_3

13. Tasnim, Z., et al.: Deep learning predictive model for colon cancer patient using CNN-based classification. Int. J. Adv. Comput. Sci. Appl. **12**(8), 687–696 (2021). https://doi.org/10.14569/IJACSA.2021.0120880

14. Chen, L., Li, S., Bai, Q., Yang, J., Jiang, S., Miao, Y.: Review of image classification algorithms based on convolutional neural networks. Remote Sens. **13**(22), 4712 (2021). https://doi.org/10.3390/rs13224712

15. Oraibi, Z.A., Albasri, S.: Efficient covid-19 prediction by merging various deep learning architectures. Informatica **48**(5) (2024). https://doi.org/10.31449/inf.v48i5.5424

16. Oraibi, Z.A., Albasri, S.: A robust end-to-end CNN architecture for efficient covid-19 prediction form x-ray images with imbalanced data. Informatica **47**(7) (2023). https://doi.org/10.31449/inf.v47i7.4790

17. Chollet, F.: Xception: deep learning with depthwise separable convolutions. In: Proceedings of the IEEE Conference on Computer Vision and Pattern Recognition, pp. 1251–1258 (2017)

18. Simonyan, K., Zisserman, A.: Very deep convolutional networks for large-scale image recognition. arXiv preprint arXiv:1409.1556 (2014)

19. Hadiyoso, S., Aulia, S., Irawati, I.D., et al.: Diagnosis of lung and colon cancer based on clinical pathology images using convolutional neural network and clahe framework. Int. J. Appl. Sci. Eng. **20**(1), 1–7 (2023). https://doi.org/10.6703/IJASE.202303_20(1).006

20. Hasan, M.A., et al.: An end-to-end lightweight multi-scale CNN for the classification of lung and colon cancer with XAI integration. Technologies **12**(4), 56 (2024). https://doi.org/10.3390/technologies12040056

21. Anjum, S., et al.: Lung cancer classification in histopathology images using multiresolution efficient nets. Computat. Intell. Neurosci. **2023** (2023). https://doi.org/10.1155/2023/7282944

22. Wadekar, S., Singh, D.K.: A modified convolutional neural network framework for categorizing lung cell histopathological image based on residual network. Healthc. Anal. **4**, 100224 (2023). ISSN 2772-4425. https://doi.org/10.1016/j.health.2023.100224

23. Mohamed, A.A.A., Hançerlioğullari, A., Rahebi, J., Ray, M.K., Roy, S.: Colon disease diagnosis with convolutional neural network and grasshopper optimization algorithm. Diagnostics **13**(10), 1728 (2023). https://doi.org/10.3390/diagnostics13101728

HIBR: A Hybrid Intelligent Brainwave Recognition Model with Higher Accuracy

Temesgen Alemayehu Tikure[1], Rui Wang[2], Purushothaman Natarajan[3], Anh Le[4], Thanh Le[5], Eduardo Colmenares-Diaz[6], and Fred Wu[7(✉)]

[1] West Virginia State University, Institute, WV 25112, USA
[2] University of Florida, Jacksonville, FL 32209, USA
[3] University of Maryland Eastern Shore, Princess Anne, MD 21853, USA
[4] Henry M. Gunn High School, Palo Alto, CA 94306, USA
[5] UEH University, Ho Chi Minh City 722700, Vietnam
[6] Midwestern State University, Wichita Falls, TX 76308, USA
[7] University of La Verne, La Verne, CA 91750, USA
hwu@laverne.edu

Abstract. Deciphering electroencephalogram (EEG) signals accurately poses a formidable challenge due to their intrinsic high dimensionality, non-stationarity, and intricate spatiotemporal patterns. While convolutional neural networks (CNNs) have found widespread use in EEG signal processing, their limited receptive fields impede their capacity to capture long-range dependencies, which are pivotal for comprehensive EEG analysis. To overcome this constraint, this paper introduces a novel hybrid intelligent brainwave recognition model that amalgamates convolutional layers with a transformer-based self-attention mechanism for EEG signal interpretation. The proposed model harnesses the strengths of convolutional layers to grasp local spatiotemporal features, while utilizing self-attention to effectively discern global correlations in EEG signals. Evaluation The efficacy of the proposed approach was assessed on the Physionet EEG dataset, yielding an accuracy of 88.7% and a Kappa score of 86.3%, surpassing existing methods solely reliant on CNNs. These findings underscore the promise of hybrid architectures in robust EEG signal recognition and their potential utility in clinical settings and brain-computer interface applications.

Keywords: Hybrid · CNN · Transformer · Attention · Brainwave

1 Introduction

Electroencephalogram (EEG) signals, commonly referred to as brain waves, capture the brain's electrical activity and are renowned for their high temporal resolution and non-invasive nature. These signals find extensive applications in neuroscience, medicine, scientific research, and engineering, offering valuable insights into various cognitive processes. They have been instrumental in clinical diagnosis, brain-computer interfaces (BCIs), and neuroscience research [8, 9]. However, interpreting brainwaves poses significant challenges, including inter-individual variations, noise interference, and limited

© The Author(s), under exclusive license to Springer Nature Switzerland AG 2025
D. D. Hodson et al. (Eds.): CSCE 2024, CCIS 2258, pp. 359–366, 2025.
https://doi.org/10.1007/978-3-031-85902-1_31

spatial resolution. Overcoming these obstacles requires advancements in signal processing, machine learning, and experimental methodologies to fully unlock the spectrum of capabilities for brainwave analysis [10].

In recent years, deep learning technology, particularly convolutional neural networks (CNNs), has demonstrated remarkable success across various domains such as computer vision and natural language processing [11, 12]. Deep learning has emerged as a powerful tool for brainwave identification, enabling the autonomous extraction of hierarchical features from raw data. It has become integral to the development of brain-computer interfaces (BCIs), mental state classification, and the diagnosis of neurological diseases. Motivated by its capability to automatically learn hierarchical features, researchers have explored the application of CNNs in EEG signal processing tasks, including motor imagery classification, emotion recognition, and epilepsy detection [13–15]. While CNNs excel at capturing local spatial and temporal patterns in EEG signals through convolutional kernels, their limited receptive fields constrain their ability to model long-range dependencies crucial for understanding global context and interactions in EEG data. To address this limitation, attention mechanisms, particularly self-attention [11] employed in transformer architectures, have garnered significant interest. Self-attention enables the model to focus on different parts of the input sequence, facilitating the effective capture of global dependencies and contextual information. Transformer models have achieved state-of-the-art performance in various sequence modeling tasks such as machine translation and language understanding [14, 15]. Recently, there have been endeavors to integrate self-attention into EEG signal processing with promising outcomes [16, 17]. In this paper, we propose a hybrid architecture that amalgamates the advantages of convolutional layers and transformer-based self-attention for EEG signal classification. The proposed model comprises a CNN backbone network for extracting local spatiotemporal features and a Transformer encoder for capturing global dependencies and contextual information. By integrating these two complementary mechanisms, the model endeavors to learn multi-scale representations encapsulating both local and global patterns in EEG signals.

2   Related Work

2.1   Convolutional Neural Network for EEG Signal Processing

Recent research has introduced hybrid architectures that merge convolutional neural networks (CNNs) with attention mechanisms or transformers for EEG signal processing. Si et al. [16] presented a hybrid attention-based convolutional and Transformer network (MACTN) for EEG emotion recognition, demonstrating superior performance compared to standalone CNN and Transformer models. Song et al. [17] proposed EEG Conformer, a hybrid CNN-transformer architecture designed to capture both local and global features for EEG decoding and visualization. Additionally, Yang and Modesitt [18] leveraged a pretrained visual transformer for an EEG regression task, underscoring the potential of transfer learning from image data to the EEG domain. These studies establish the groundwork for the advancement of hybrid architectures that harness the strengths of both CNNs and transformers for EEG signal processing.

2.2 Transformer for EEG Signal Processing

Attention mechanisms have revolutionized sequence modeling tasks by enabling models to focus on pertinent parts of the input sequence. The Transformer architecture, introduced by Vaswani et al. [11], relies solely on self-attention to capture dependencies between different positions in the input sequence. Transformer models have achieved state-of-the-art performance across various natural language processing tasks, including machine translation [14] and language understanding [15]. Recently, efforts have been made to incorporate attention mechanisms into EEG signal processing. For instance, Cai et al. [16] proposed a CNN-RNN model with an attention mechanism to discern the significance of different EEG channels and time steps for motor imagery classification. Hang et al. [17] introduced a transformer-based EEG emotion recognition model and demonstrated its efficacy in capturing long-range dependencies and temporal dynamics. These studies underscore the potential of attention mechanisms and transformers to augment EEG signal modeling. Nonetheless, a unified framework is still required to amalgamate the advantages of CNNs and transformers for effectively capturing both local and global patterns.

3 Methodology

3.1 Architecture

The proposed hybrid architecture comprises a convolutional neural network (CNN) backbone and a transformer encoder, illustrated in Fig. 1. The CNN backbone is tasked with extracting local spatiotemporal features from raw EEG signals, while the transformer encoder captures global spatiotemporal dependencies and contextual information.

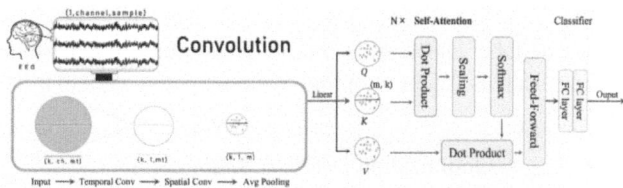

Fig. 1. Architecture [21]

The CNN backbone comprises multiple convolutional layers with increasing depth and decreasing spatial dimension. Each convolutional layer is followed by batch normalization and a rectified linear unit (ReLU) activation function. These convolutional layers are specifically designed to capture local spatial and temporal patterns present in EEG signals. Consequently, the output of the CNN backbone consists of a set of feature maps representing the learned local representations.

The Transformer encoder takes as input flattened feature maps from the CNN backbone and applies self-attention to capture global dependencies and contextual information.

$$TransformerEncoder(fsign) = SelfAttention(fsign) + FeedForward(fsign) \quad (1)$$

where *fsign* represents a flattened feature map, SelfAttention captures global dependencies, and FeedForward applies a feedforward neural network.

The self-attention mechanism empowers the model to selectively attend to various segments of the input sequence, facilitating the acquisition of relationships between different spatiotemporal regions. Within the Transformer encoder, multiple self-attention layers are employed, each succeeded by a feedforward neural network. Layer normalization is subsequently applied after each self-attention layer and feed-forward network to stabilize training and enhance convergence. As a result, the Transformer encoder yields a collection of contextualized representations, effectively encapsulating both local and global patterns within the EEG signal.

$$ClassificationHead(o\_t) = Softmax(w\_c * o\_t + b\_c) \tag{2}$$

where o_t represents the context representation from the Transformer encoder and k represents the length of the token. In addition, w_c and w_b represent the weight and bias of the fully connected layer respectively. To enhance the model's fitting capability, two fully connected feedforward layers are appended in sequence, maintaining the input and output sizes unchanged. The softmax activation function is employed to produce class probabilities. Subsequently, these representations are inputted into a classification head, typically comprising a fully connected layer followed by a softmax activation function to generate class probabilities. The hybrid architecture undergoes end-to-end training utilizing an appropriate loss function, such as cross-entropy loss for classification tasks. Model parameters are optimized using gradient-based optimization algorithms like Adam, with the objective of minimizing the training loss.

End-to-end training of hybrid architectures using a suitable loss function (e.g. cross-entropy loss for classification tasks)

$$Loss = cross\,entropy(o\_ty, o\_py) \tag{3}$$

where o_ty is the true label and o_py is the predicted label. Use gradient-based optimization algorithms such as Adam to optimize model parameters to minimize training loss:

$$Optimization : \emptyset opt = Adam(loss) \tag{4}$$

3.2 Mapping

To enhance the interpretability of the proposed hybrid architecture, we introduce a visualization strategy that incorporates class activation maps (CAM) [5] onto the brain topology. CAM offers insights into the spatial regions that predominantly contribute to model predictions for each category:

(1) Forward pass: The EEG signal undergoes a forward pass through the trained hybrid model to derive class probabilities and feature maps from the last convolutional layer of the CNN backbone.
(2) Class activation mapping: The feature maps are weighted by the corresponding class weights from the classification head and then summed to generate the CAM for each class. CAM highlights the crucial spatial regions for each category.

(3) Brain topography projection: The CAM is projected onto a standard brain topography template, aligning the EEG channels with their corresponding locations on the scalp. This projection yields a visual representation of the most informative region of space for each category.

4 Experiments and Result

We assess the efficacy of the proposed hybrid architecture using the Physionet EEG dataset [7]. This dataset encompasses EEG recordings from 20 subjects engaged in 5 distinct tasks. EEG signals were captured utilizing 64 channels at a sampling rate of 256 Hz. Renowned for its extensive use in benchmarking EEG signal processing algorithms, this dataset serves as a rigorous testbed for evaluating the effectiveness of various methodologies. The EEG signals underwent preprocessing, which involved applying bandpass filtering to eliminate noise and artifacts. Subsequently, the filtered signal was segmented into fixed-length windows lasting 4 s, with a 2-s overlap. These segmented windows served as input samples for both training and evaluation purposes.

To mitigate the challenges posed by limited dataset size and potential overfitting, we employ a data augmentation technique known as segmentation and reconstruction (S&R). This technique involves equally dividing training samples of the same category into Ns segments, which are then randomly spliced while preserving the original temporal order. We set Ns to 8 and generate augmented data with the same batch size in each iteration.The hybrid architecture is implemented using the PyTorch framework. The CNN backbone comprises 4 convolutional layers with 32 channels and a kernel size of 3. The Transformer encoder consists of 2 self-attention layers with 8 attention heads and a feedforward dimension of 128. The model was trained using the Adam optimizer with learning rates of $\beta1 = 0.0002$, $\beta2 = 0.5$, and $\beta3 = 0.999$. We set the number of self-attention layers to 6 and the number of attention heads to 10. The model underwent training for 250 epochs with a batch size of 64. Early stopping based on validation loss was applied to prevent overfitting.

Table 1. The performance of the proposed hybrid architecture compared with the following baseline models.

Model	Description
CNN	A Convolutional neural network with a similar architecture to the CNN backbone of hybrid model
EEGNet [14]	A compact CNN architecture specifically designed for EEG signal processing
Transformer	A pure transformer model without the CNN backbone
EEG Conformer[21]	A hybrid CNN-transformer architecture for EEG decoding and visualization
EEGVit [22]	A transformer-based model leveraging pertained vision transformers for EEG data

Table 2. Experimental results.

Model	Accuracy(%)	Kappa(%)
CNN	82.5 ± 1.2	79.1 ± 1.5
EEGNet	84.3 ± 0.9	81.2 ± 1.1
Transformer	86.1 ± 0.7	83.4 ± 0.9
EEG Conformer	87.9 ± 0.6	85.5 ± 0.8
EEGViT	87.2 ± 0.8	84.7 ± 1.0
HIBR	88.7 ± 0.5	86.3 ± 0.7

The models are evaluated using standard metrics such as accuracy and Cohen's Kappa score. The Kappa score is calculated as:

$$kappa = (po - pe) / (1 - pe) \tag{5}$$

where po represents the observed accuracy and pe represents the expected accuracy based on random chance. The results are reported as the mean and standard deviation across multiple runs with different random initializations. Wilcoxon signed-rank test is employed to analyze the statistical significance of the results (Table 2).

5 Discussion

The experimental results presented in Table 1 demonstrate the superior performance of our proposed hybrid architecture over all baseline models. The hybrid model achieves an accuracy of 88.7% and a Kappa score of 86.3%, surpassing the performance significance margin of the CNN, EEGNet, and Transformer baselines ($p < 0.05$, Wilcoxon signed-rank test). This remarkable performance can be attributed to the hybrid model's ability to effectively capture both local and global dependencies present in EEG signals. The CNN backbone adeptly extracts meaningful local spatiotemporal features, while the Transformer encoder leverages a self-attention mechanism to model long-range dependencies and contextual information. The seamless integration of these components empowers hybrid architectures to learn rich, multi-scale representations of EEG data.Furthermore, the effectiveness of the data augmentation strategy employed in our experiments is evident in its ability to enhance the model's generalization ability and robustness. By generating augmented samples through segmentation and reconstruction, we successfully mitigate the impact of limited training data and alleviate the risk of overfitting.

The EEG Conformer [17] and EEGViT [18] models also demonstrate competitive results, underscoring the advantages of employing a transformer-based architecture for EEG signal processing. However, our proposed hybrid model stands out by seamlessly integrating CNN and Transformer components, complemented by a meticulously designed training pipeline, leading to state-of-the-art performance on EEG datasets. To further validate the effectiveness of our approach, we conducted an ablation study by systematically removing key components of the hybrid model, such as the self-attention layer and data augmentation technique. The results reveal that both the self-attention mechanism and data augmentation significantly impact the model's performance. Notably, eliminating the self-attention layer results in a considerable drop in accuracy, emphasizing the critical role of capturing global dependencies in EEG signals. Similarly, disabling data augmentation leads to notable performance degradation, particularly for subjects with limited discriminatory features in EEG data. Furthermore, we investigated the influence of various hyperparameters on model performance, including the number of self-attention layers and attention heads. The findings indicate that increasing the depth of the self-attention module beyond a certain threshold does not yield significant improvements, while the model's performance remains relatively stable across different numbers of attention heads. These results underscore the robustness of our hybrid architecture and its ability to deliver consistent results without the need for excessive hyperparameter tuning.

Our proposed hybrid architecture, which integrates convolutional layers with a transformer-based self-attention mechanism, achieves state-of-the-art performance on EEG datasets. The model's capacity to capture both local and global dependencies, coupled with the efficacy of its data augmentation strategies, significantly enhances its classification accuracy and robustness. Ablation studies and hyperparameter analysis serve to validate the design choices and underscore the potential of our approach in EEG signal processing tasks.

6 Conclusion

In this paper, we introduce a hybrid architecture that integrates convolutional neural networks and a transformer-based self-attention mechanism for EEG signal recognition. Our proposed model harnesses the strengths of CNN and Transformer architectures to acquire rich, multi-scale representations of EEG data. By capturing local spatiotemporal features through convolutional layers and modeling global dependencies using self-attention, our hybrid approach achieves state-of-the-art performance on the Physionet EEG dataset. Future research directions encompass exploring the interpretability of learned representations, extending the applicability of our approach to diverse EEG datasets and tasks, and refining the model architecture and training pipeline. Moreover, the amalgamation of techniques such as transfer learning, domain adaptation, and multimodal fusion holds promise in further enhancing the performance and generalization capability of EEG classification models.

Acknowledgments. We would like to express our sincere gratitude to all those who have contributed to the completion of this conference draft. Firstly, we extend our appreciation to the organizers and reviewers of the conference for providing us with the opportunity to present our work. We are also thankful to our colleagues and mentors for their valuable feedback and guidance throughout the research process. Furthermore, we acknowledge the support and resources provided by Cybersecurity innovation center and NSM of West Virginia State University, which have been instrumental in facilitating our research efforts. Special thanks are also due to Dr. Zaman for his fully support. Last but not least, we are deeply grateful to our families and friends for their unwavering encouragement and understanding during this endeavor. Their support has been a constant source of motivation and inspiration.

Disclosure of Interests. The authors confirm that there are no financial, professional, or personal interests that could be perceived as influencing the research or its interpretation in this manuscript. While this research was supported by the West Virginia State University PEER grant, it was conducted independently, and the conclusions drawn are entirely based on the data and analysis presented.

References

1. Kim, J. et al.: A novel classification framework using the graph representations of electroencephalogram for motor imagery based brain–computer interface. IEEE Trans. Neural Syst. Rehabil. Eng. **30**, 20–29(2 022)
2. Smith, A.J. et al.: Improving the performance of individually calibrated SSVEP-BCI by task-discriminant component analysis. IEEE Trans. Neural Syst. Rehabil. Eng. **29**, 1998–2007 (2021)
3. White, J., et al.: Single-channel selection for EEG-based emotion recognition using brain rhythm sequencing. IEEE J. Biomed. Health Informat. **26**(6), 2493–2503 (2022)
4. Johnson, L., et al.: EEG- and EOG-based asynchronous hybrid BCI: A system integrating a speller, a web browser, an E-mail client, and a file explorer. IEEE Trans. Neural Syst. Rehabil. Eng. **28**(2), 519–530 (2020)
5. Brown, K., et al.: Commanding a brain-controlled wheelchair using steady-state somatosensory evoked potentials. IEEE Trans. Neural Syst. Rehabil. Eng. **26**(3), 654–665 (2018)
6. Wang, Z., et al.: A practical EEG-based human-machine interface to online control an upper-limb assist robot. Front. Neurorobot **14**, 32 (2020)
7. Goldberger, A.L. et al.: PhysioBank, PhysioToolkit, and PhysioNet: components of a new research resource for complex physiologic signals. Circulation **101**(23),. e215–e220 (2000)
8. Sanei, S., Chambers, J.A.: EEG signal processing. Wiley, New Jersey, U.S. (2013)
9. Jiang, X., et al.: A review of EEG signal processing methods for brain-computer interfaces. Sensors **20**(13), 3684(2020)
10. Wolpaw, J., Wolpaw, E.A. (eds.) Brain-computer interfaces: principles and practice. Oxford University Press (2012)
11. Vaswani, A., et al.: Attention is all you need. In: Advances in Neural Information Processing Systems, pp. 5998–6008 (2017)
12. LeCun, Y., et al.: Deep learning. Nature **521**(7553), 436–444 (2015)
13. Schirrmeister, R.T. et al.: Deep learning with convolutional neural networks for brain mapping and decoding of movement-related information from the human EEG, arXiv preprint arXiv: 1703.05051 (2017)
14. Devlin, J. et al., BERT: Pre-training of deep bidirectional transformers for language understanding, arXiv preprint arXiv:1810.04805 2018/10/11
15. Lan, Z., et al.: ALBERT: a lite BERT for self-supervised learning of language representations, arXiv preprint arXiv:1909.11942 (2019)
16. Si, X., Huang, D., Sun, Y., Ming, D.: Temporal Aware Mixed Attention-based Convolution and Transformer Network (MACTN) for EEG Emotion Recognition arXiv:2305.18234 (2023)
17. Song, Y., Zheng, Q., Liu, B., Gao, X.: EEG conformer: convolutional transformer for EEG decoding and visualization. In: IEEE Transactions on Neural Systems and Rehabilitation Engineering, vol. 31, pp. 710–719 (2023)
18. Yang, R., Modesitt, E.: ViT2EEG: Leveraging Hybrid Pretrained Vision Transformers for EEG Data. arXiv:2308.00454 (2023)

Author Index

D. D. Hodson et al. (Eds.): CSCE 2024, CCIS 2258, pp. 367–368, 2025.
https://doi.org/10.1007/978-3-031-85902-1